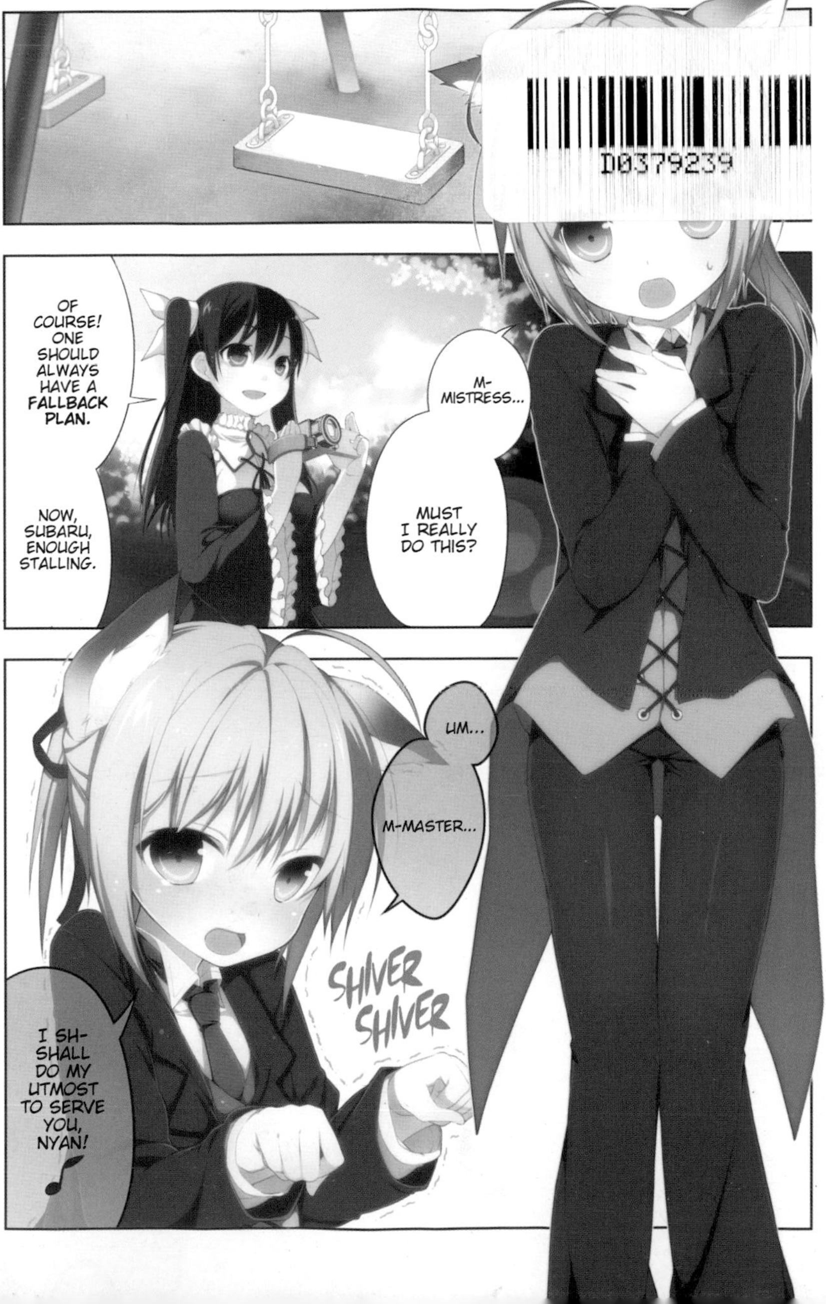
M-MISTRESS...
MUST I REALLY DO THIS?
OF COURSE! ONE SHOULD ALWAYS HAVE A **FALLBACK PLAN.**
NOW, SUBARU, ENOUGH STALLING.
UM...
M-MASTER...
SHIVER SHIVER
I SH-SHALL DO MY UTMOST TO SERVE YOU, NYAN!

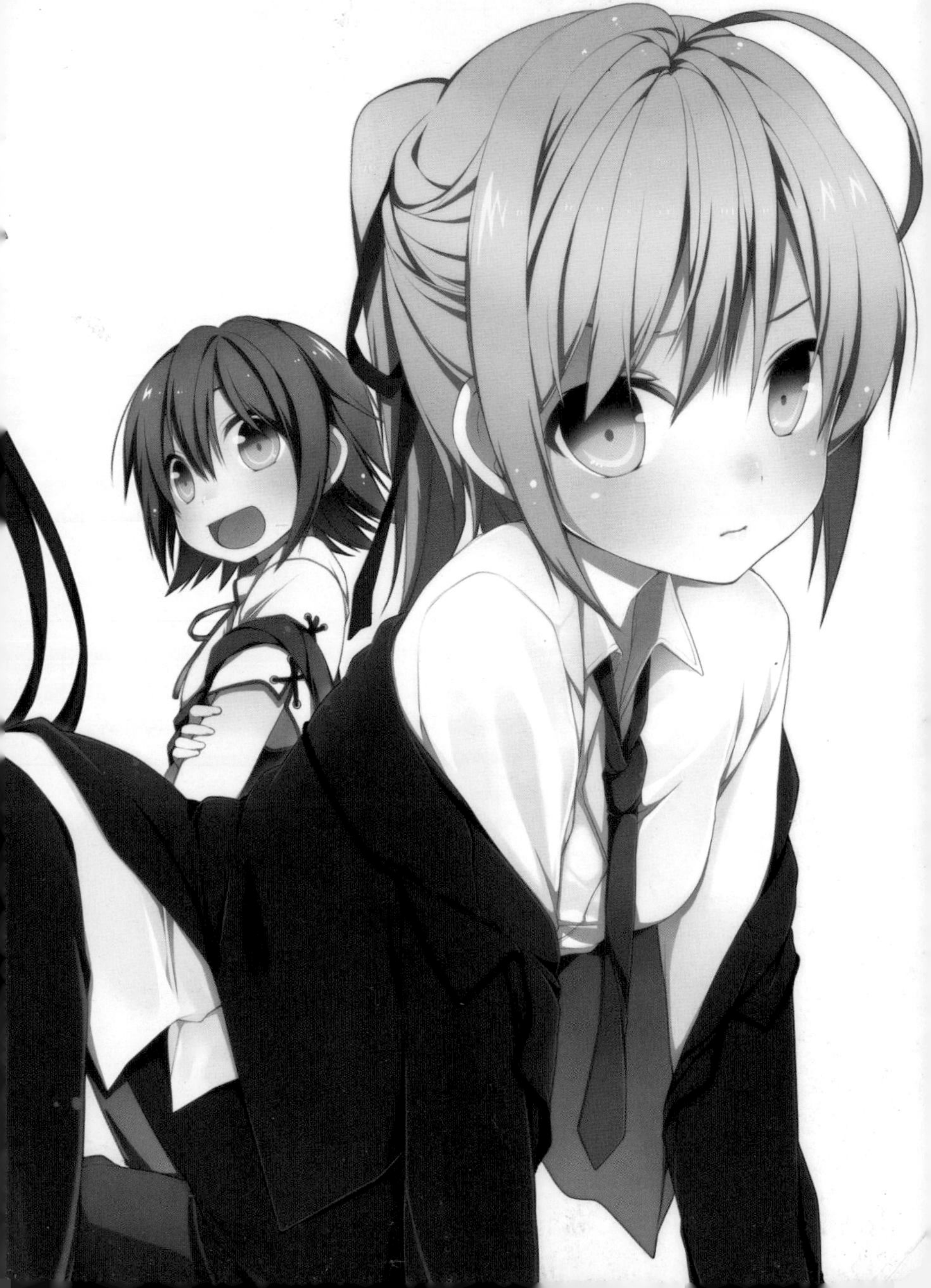

chapter 6

the butler's homecoming

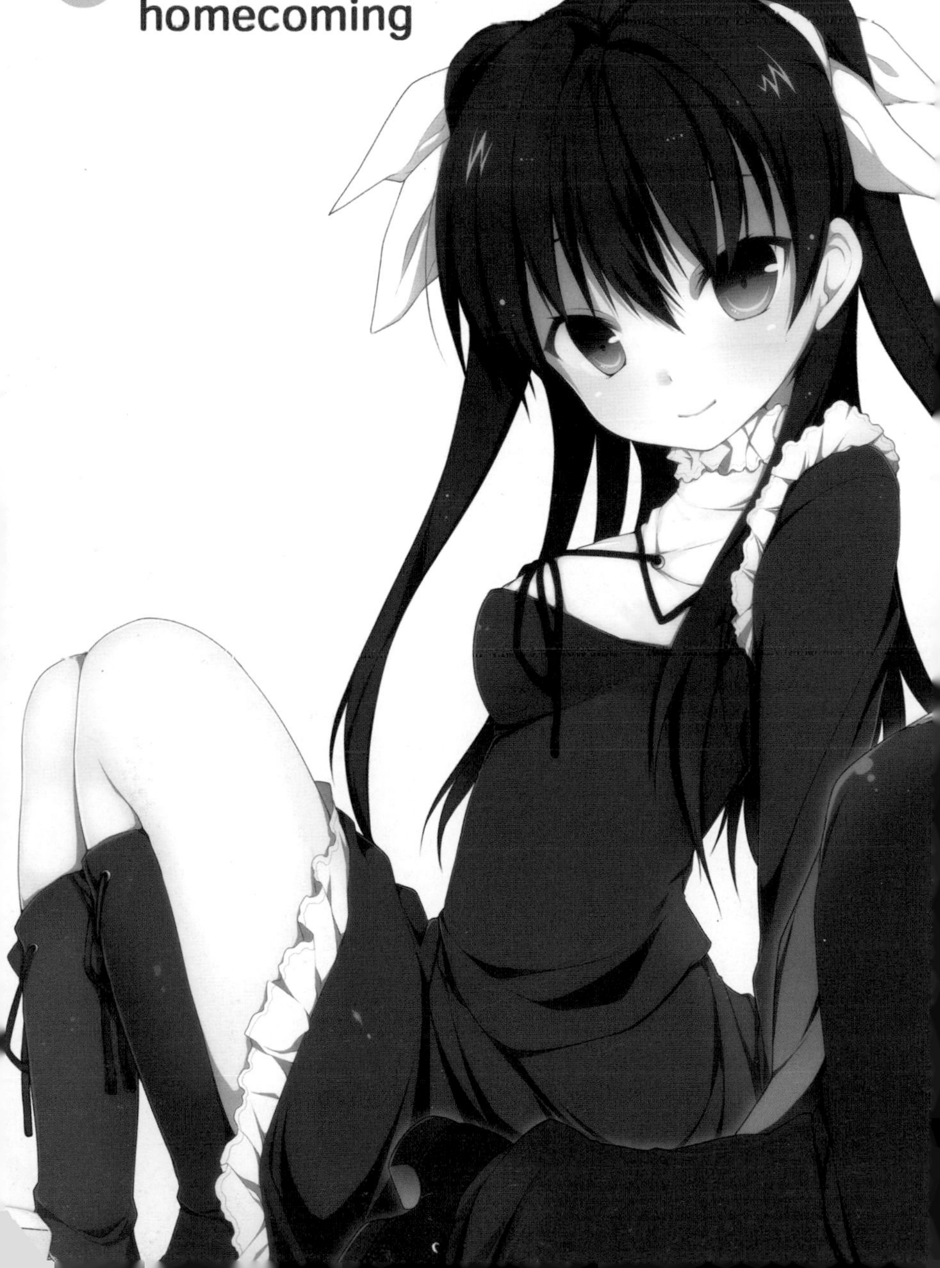

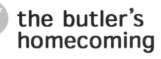

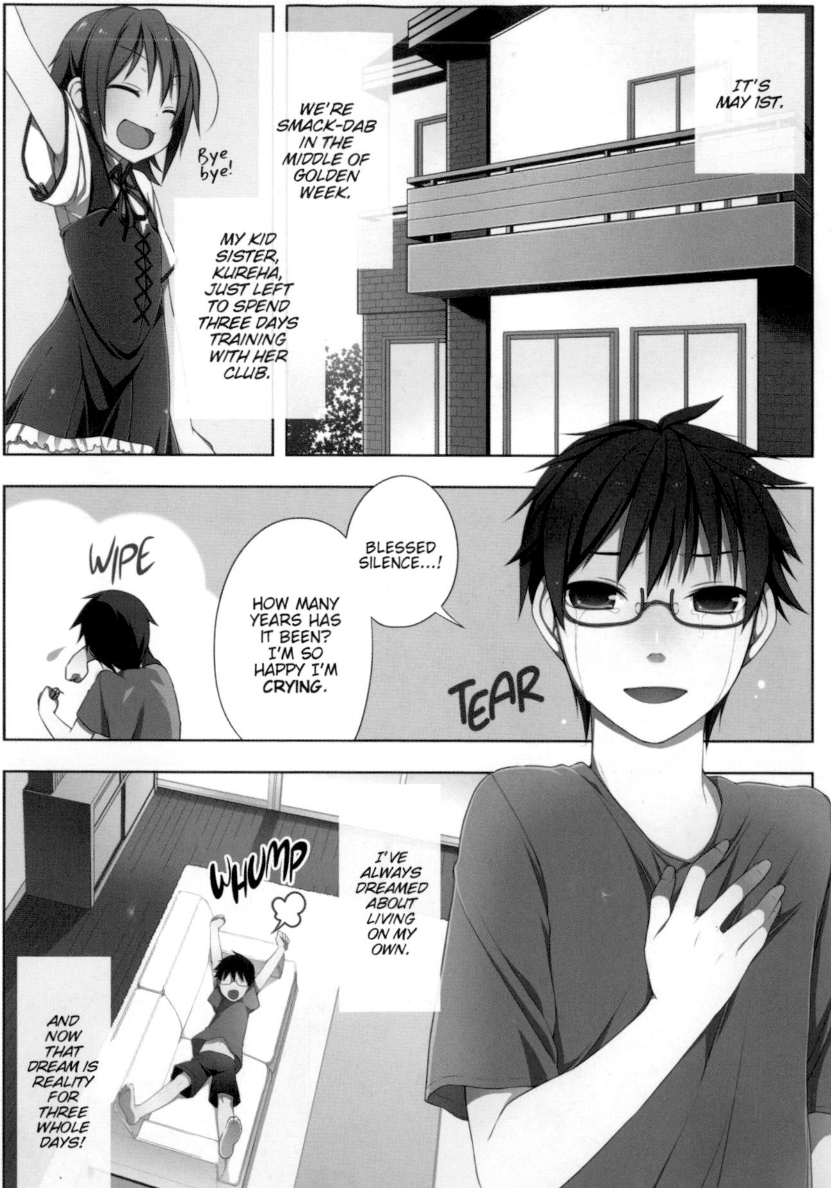
IT'S MAY 1ST.
WE'RE SMACK-DAB IN THE MIDDLE OF GOLDEN WEEK.
Bye bye!
MY KID SISTER, KUREHA, JUST LEFT TO SPEND THREE DAYS TRAINING WITH HER CLUB.
TEAR
BLESSED SILENCE...!
HOW MANY YEARS HAS IT BEEN? I'M SO HAPPY I'M CRYING.
WIPE
I'VE ALWAYS DREAMED ABOUT LIVING ON MY OWN.
WHUMP
AND NOW THAT DREAM IS REALITY FOR THREE WHOLE DAYS!

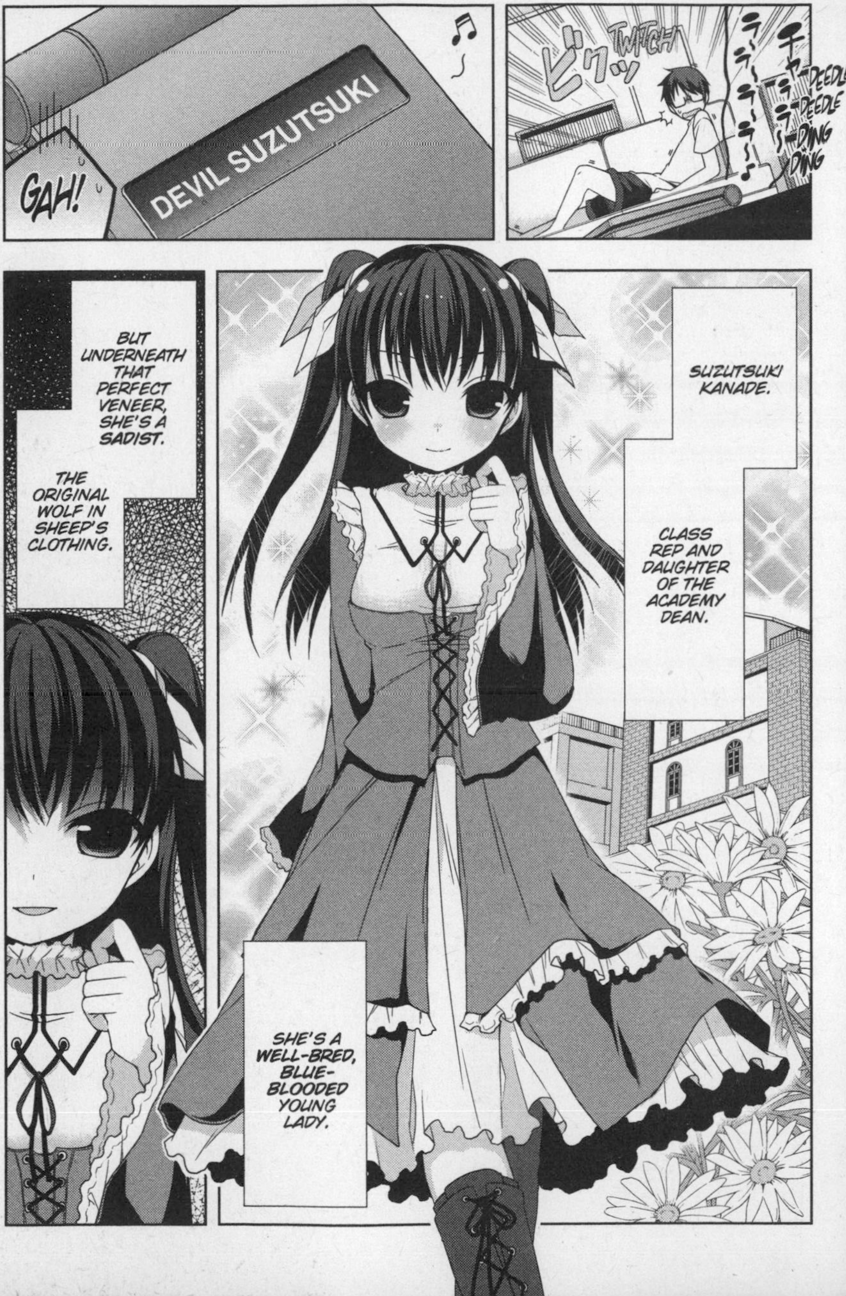
チャ〜ラ〜ラ〜ラ〜
ラ〜ラ〜ラ〜ラ〜♪
DEEDLE DEEDLE DING DING
ビクッ
TWITCH!
♪
DEVIL SUZUTSUKI
GAH!
SUZUTSUKI KANADE.
CLASS REP AND DAUGHTER OF THE ACADEMY DEAN.
SHE'S A WELL-BRED, BLUE-BLOODED YOUNG LADY.
BUT UNDERNEATH THAT PERFECT VENEER, SHE'S A SADIST.
THE ORIGINAL WOLF IN SHEEP'S CLOTHING.

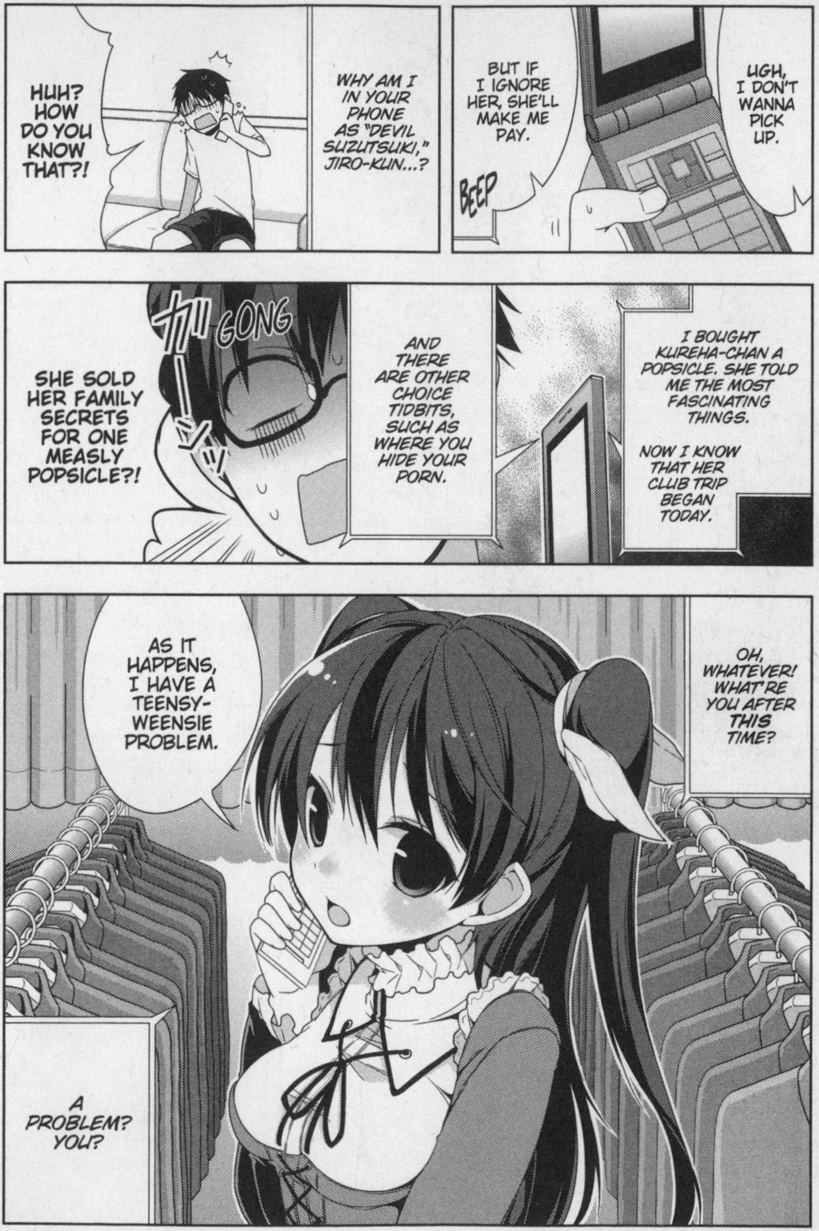
UGH, I DON'T WANNA PICK UP.
BUT IF I IGNORE HER, SHE'LL MAKE ME PAY.
BEEP
WHY AM I IN YOUR PHONE AS "DEVIL SUZUTSUKI," JIRO-KUN...?
HUH? HOW DO YOU KNOW THAT?!
I BOUGHT KUREHA-CHAN A POPSICLE. SHE TOLD ME THE MOST FASCINATING THINGS.
NOW I KNOW THAT HER CLUB TRIP BEGAN TODAY.
AND THERE ARE OTHER CHOICE TIDBITS, SUCH AS WHERE YOU HIDE YOUR PORN.
GONG
SHE SOLD HER FAMILY SECRETS FOR ONE MEASLY POPSICLE?!
OH, WHATEVER! WHAT'RE YOU AFTER THIS TIME?
AS IT HAPPENS, I HAVE A TEENSY-WEENSIE PROBLEM.
A PROBLEM? YOU?

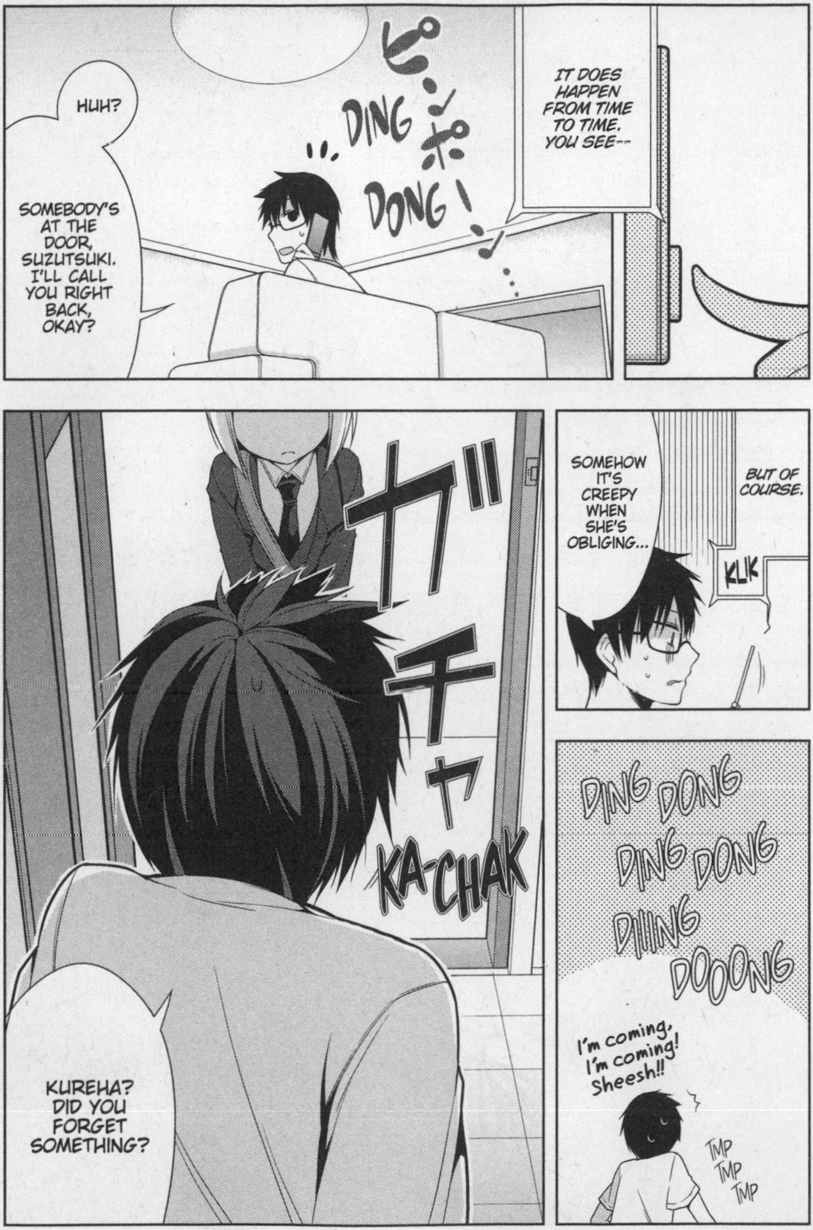
IT DOES HAPPEN FROM TIME TO TIME. YOU SEE--
ピンポン
DING DONG
HUH?
SOMEBODY'S AT THE DOOR, SUZUTSUKI. I'LL CALL YOU RIGHT BACK, OKAY?
BUT OF COURSE.
SOMEHOW IT'S CREEPY WHEN SHE'S OBLIGING...
KLIK
DING DONG DING DONG DIIING DOOONG
I'm coming, I'm coming! Sheesh!!
TMP TMP TMP
ガチャ
KA-CHAK
KUREHA? DID YOU FORGET SOMETHING?

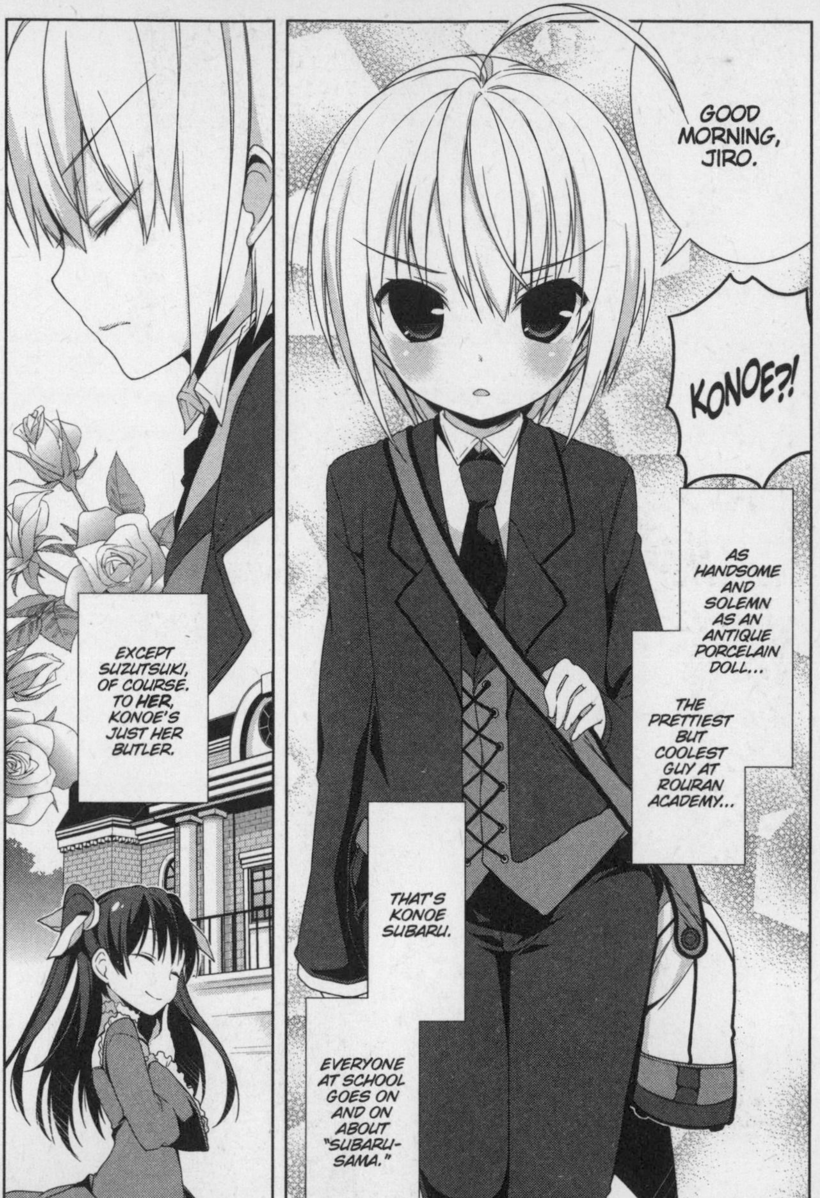
GOOD MORNING, JIRO.
KONOE?!
AS HANDSOME AND SOLEMN AS AN ANTIQUE PORCELAIN DOLL...
THE PRETTIEST BUT COOLEST GUY AT ROURAN ACADEMY...
THAT'S KONOE SUBARU.
EVERYONE AT SCHOOL GOES ON AND ON ABOUT "SUBARU-SAMA."
EXCEPT SUZUTSUKI, OF COURSE. TO HER, KONOE'S JUST HER BUTLER.

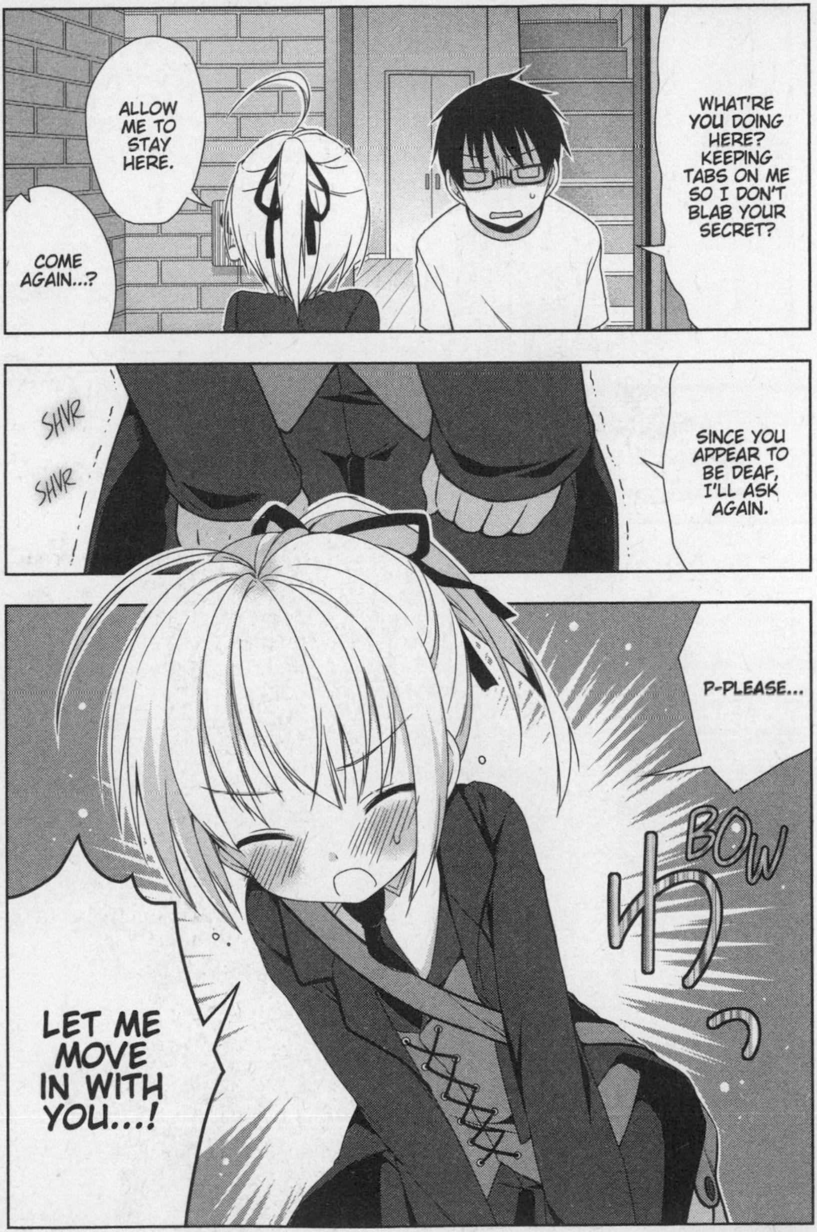
WHAT'RE YOU DOING HERE? KEEPING TABS ON ME SO I DON'T BLAB YOUR SECRET?
ALLOW ME TO STAY HERE.
COME AGAIN...?
SINCE YOU APPEAR TO BE DEAF, I'LL ASK AGAIN.
SHVR
SHVR
P-PLEASE...
BOW
LET ME MOVE IN WITH YOU...!

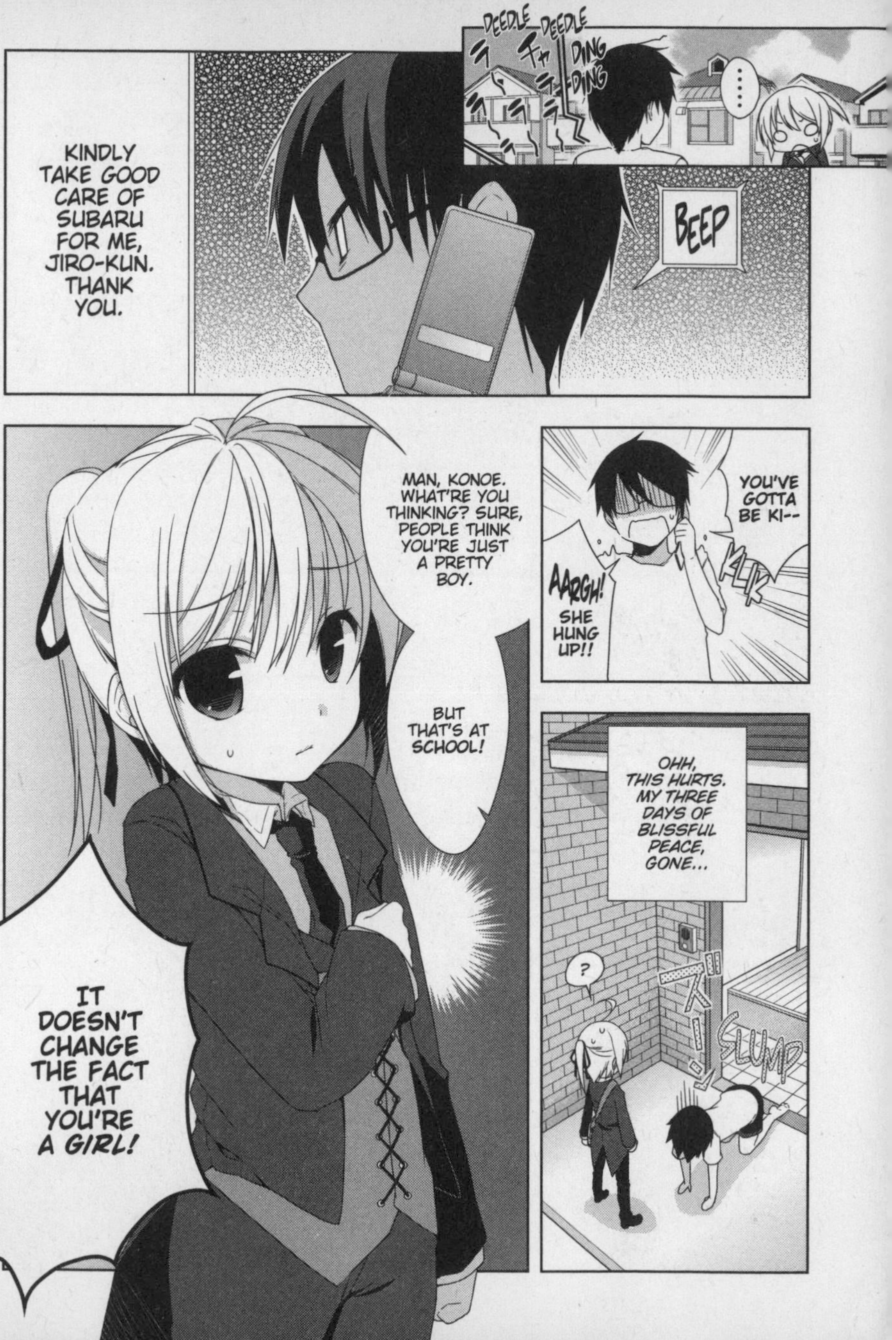
DEEDLE DEEDLE
DING DING
...
BEEP
KINDLY TAKE GOOD CARE OF SUBARU FOR ME, JIRO-KUN. THANK YOU.
YOU'VE GOTTA BE KI--
KLIK
AARGH! SHE HUNG UP!!
OHH, THIS HURTS. MY THREE DAYS OF BLISSFUL PEACE, GONE...
?
SLUMP
MAN, KONOE. WHAT'RE YOU THINKING? SURE, PEOPLE THINK YOU'RE JUST A PRETTY BOY.
BUT THAT'S AT SCHOOL!
IT DOESN'T CHANGE THE FACT THAT YOU'RE A *GIRL*!

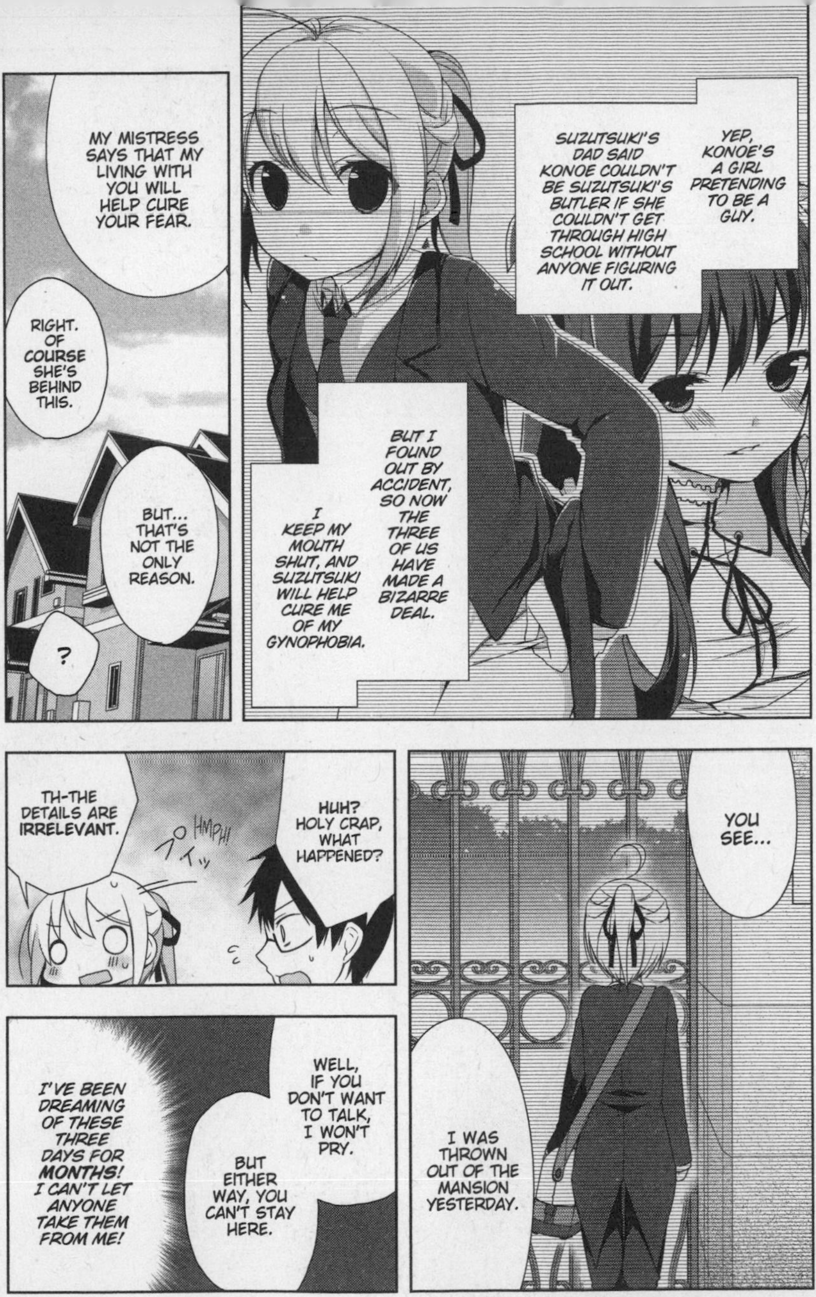
YEP, KONOE'S A GIRL PRETENDING TO BE A GUY.
SUZUTSUKI'S DAD SAID KONOE COULDN'T BE SUZUTSUKI'S BUTLER IF SHE COULDN'T GET THROUGH HIGH SCHOOL WITHOUT ANYONE FIGURING IT OUT.
BUT I FOUND OUT BY ACCIDENT, SO NOW THE THREE OF US HAVE MADE A BIZARRE DEAL.
I KEEP MY MOUTH SHUT, AND SUZUTSUKI WILL HELP CURE ME OF MY GYNOPHOBIA.
MY MISTRESS SAYS THAT MY LIVING WITH YOU WILL HELP CURE YOUR FEAR.
RIGHT. OF COURSE SHE'S BEHIND THIS.
BUT... THAT'S NOT THE ONLY REASON.
?
YOU SEE...
I WAS THROWN OUT OF THE MANSION YESTERDAY.
HUH? HOLY CRAP, WHAT HAPPENED?
TH-THE DETAILS ARE IRRELEVANT.
HMPH!
フイッ
WELL, IF YOU DON'T WANT TO TALK, I WON'T PRY.
BUT EITHER WAY, YOU CAN'T STAY HERE.
I'VE BEEN DREAMING OF THESE THREE DAYS FOR **MONTHS**! I CAN'T LET ANYONE TAKE THEM FROM ME!

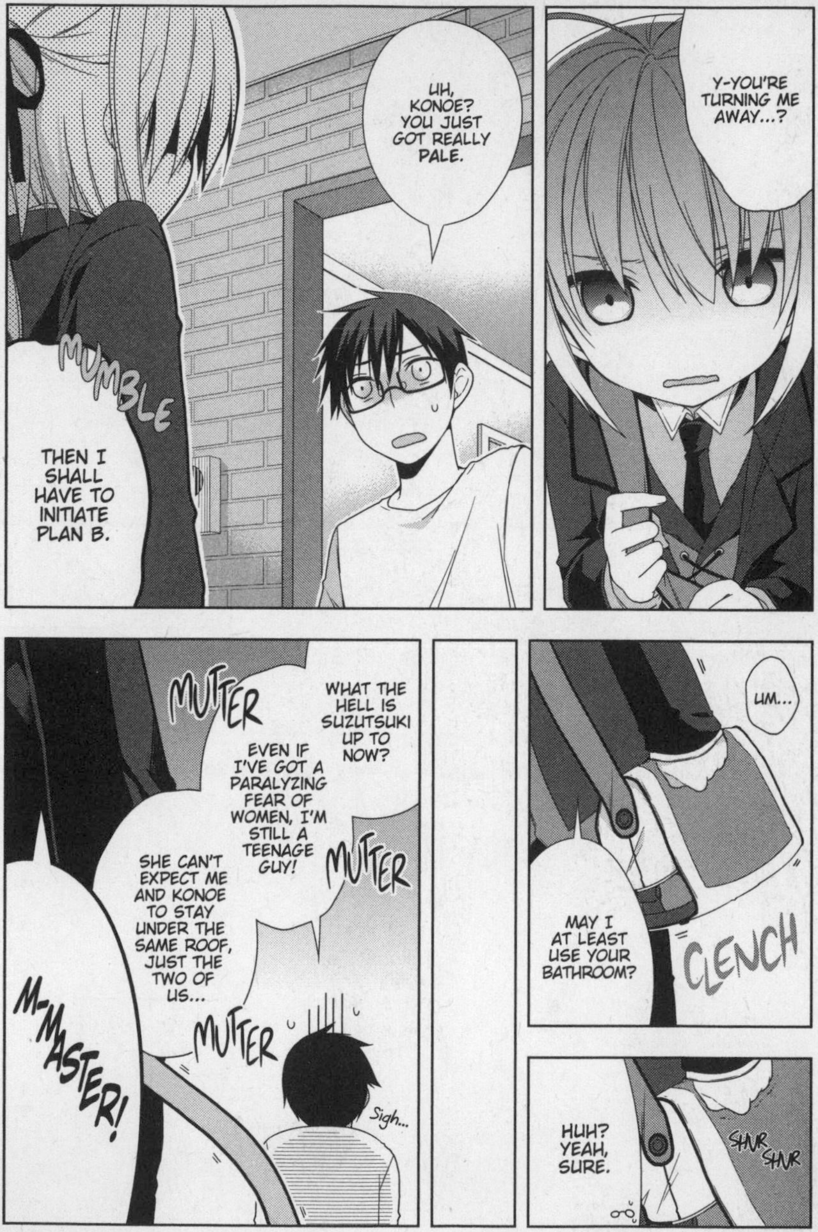
Y-YOU'RE TURNING ME AWAY...?
UH, KONOE? YOU JUST GOT REALLY PALE.
MUMBLE
THEN I SHALL HAVE TO INITIATE PLAN B.
UM...
MAY I AT LEAST USE YOUR BATHROOM?
CLENCH
HUH? YEAH, SURE.
WHAT THE HELL IS SUZUTSUKI UP TO NOW?
MUTTER
EVEN IF I'VE GOT A PARALYZING FEAR OF WOMEN, I'M STILL A TEENAGE GUY!
MUTTER
SHE CAN'T EXPECT ME AND KONOE TO STAY UNDER THE SAME ROOF, JUST THE TWO OF US...
MUTTER
Sigh...
M-MASTER!

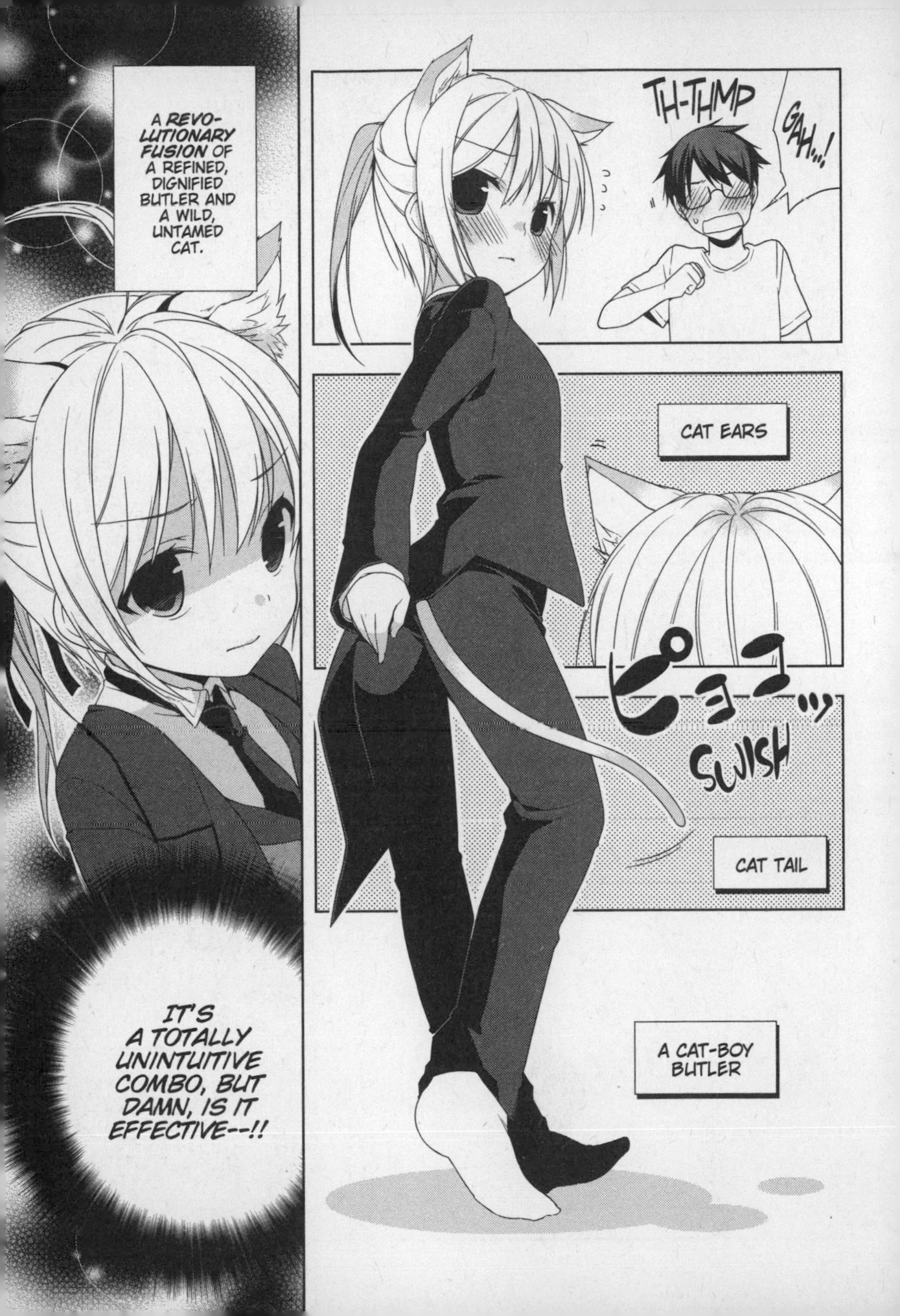
TH-THMP
GAH...!
CAT EARS
ピョコッ
SWISH
CAT TAIL
A CAT-BOY BUTLER
A REVOLUTIONARY FUSION OF A REFINED, DIGNIFIED BUTLER AND A WILD, UNTAMED CAT.
IT'S A TOTALLY UNINTUITIVE COMBO, BUT DAMN, IS IT EFFECTIVE--!!

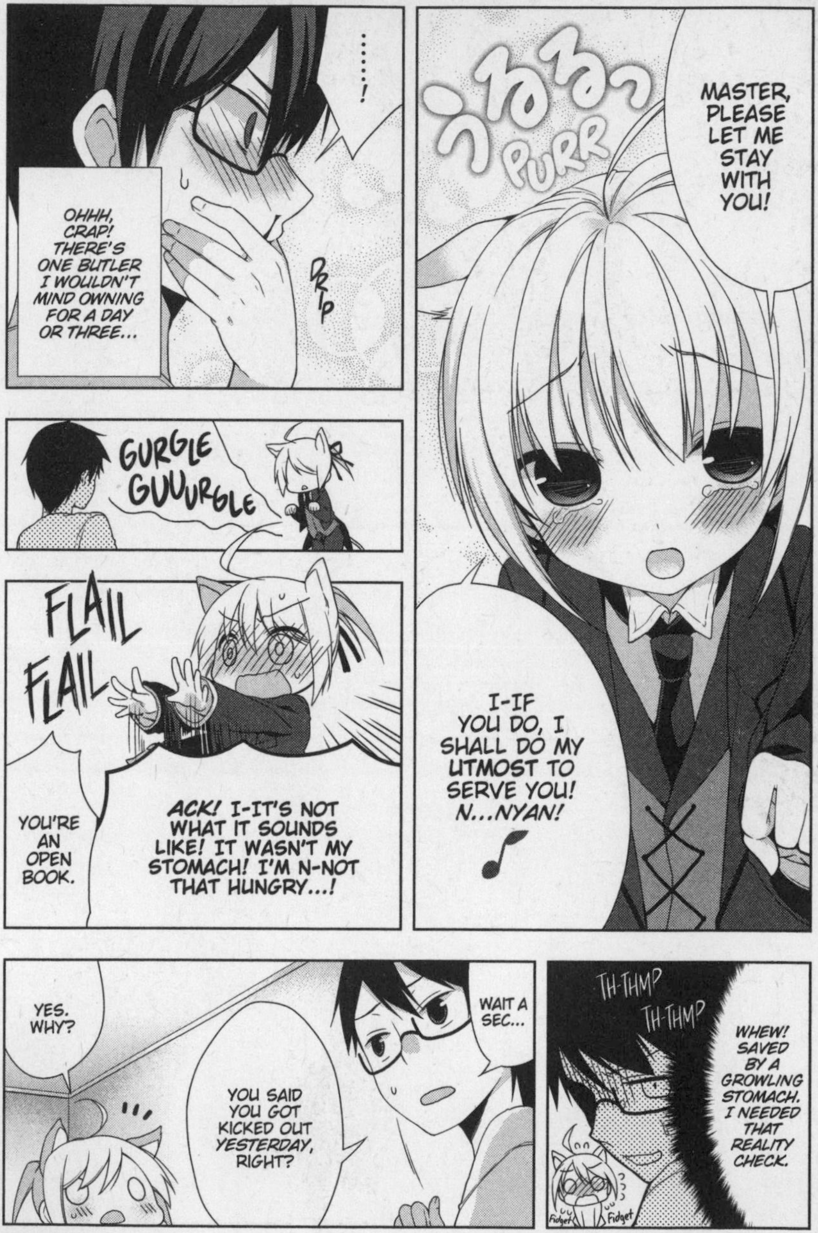
うるるっ
PURR
MASTER, PLEASE LET ME STAY WITH YOU!
I-IF YOU DO, I SHALL DO MY UTMOST TO SERVE YOU! N...NYAN! ♪
......!
OHHH, CRAP! THERE'S ONE BUTLER I WOULDN'T MIND OWNING FOR A DAY OR THREE...
DRIP
GURGLE GUUURGLE
FLAIL FLAIL
ACK! I-IT'S NOT WHAT IT SOUNDS LIKE! IT WASN'T MY STOMACH! I'M N-NOT THAT HUNGRY...!
YOU'RE AN OPEN BOOK.
TH-THMP TH-THMP
WHEW! SAVED BY A GROWLING STOMACH. I NEEDED THAT REALITY CHECK.
Fidget Fidget
WAIT A SEC...
YOU SAID YOU GOT KICKED OUT YESTERDAY, RIGHT?
YES. WHY?

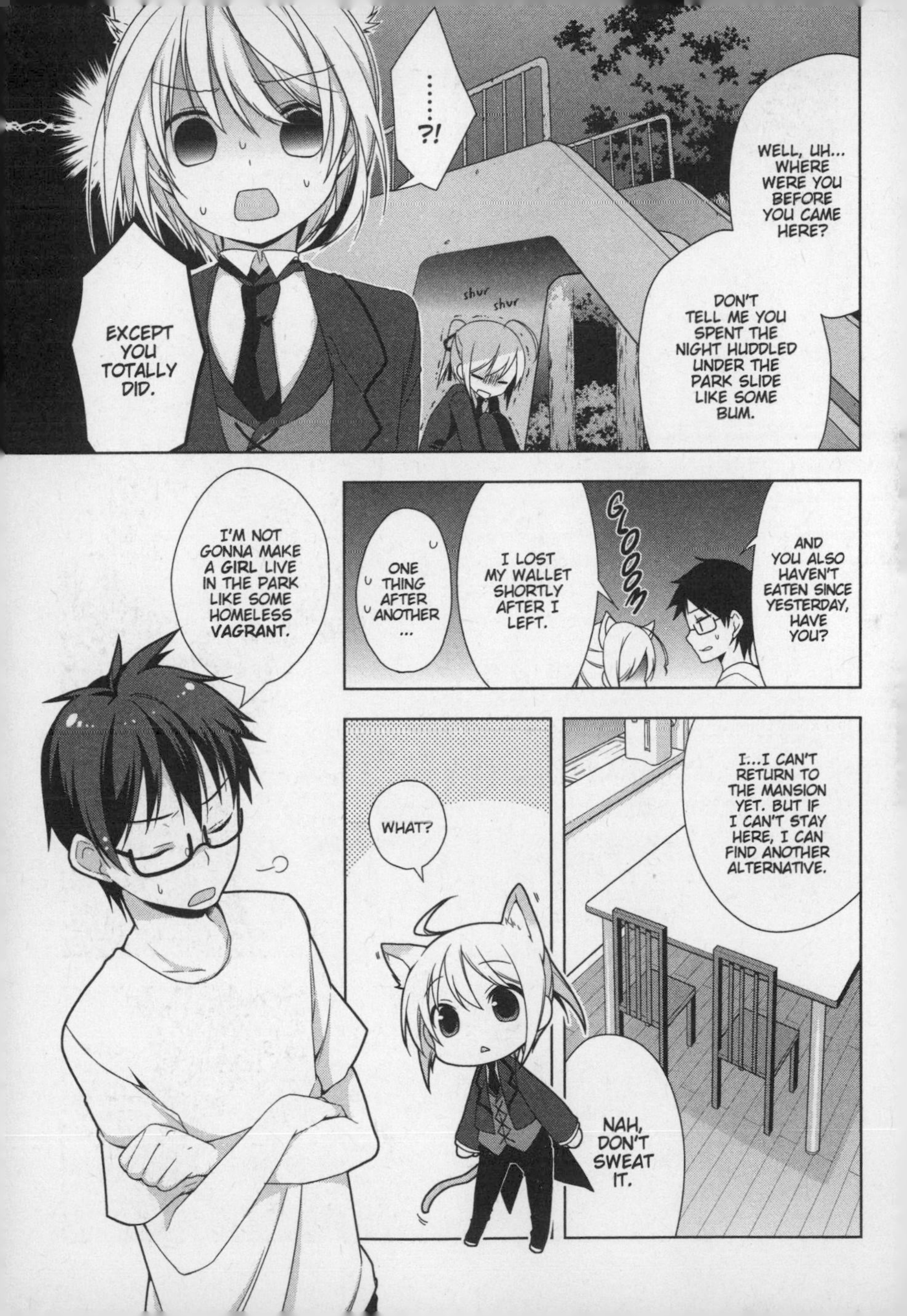
WELL, UH... WHERE WERE YOU BEFORE YOU CAME HERE?
......?!
DON'T TELL ME YOU SPENT THE NIGHT HUDDLED UNDER THE PARK SLIDE LIKE SOME BUM.
shur shur
EXCEPT YOU TOTALLY DID.
AND YOU ALSO HAVEN'T EATEN SINCE YESTERDAY, HAVE YOU?
GLOOOM
I LOST MY WALLET SHORTLY AFTER I LEFT.
ONE THING AFTER ANOTHER ...
I...I CAN'T RETURN TO THE MANSION YET. BUT IF I CAN'T STAY HERE, I CAN FIND ANOTHER ALTERNATIVE.
NAH, DON'T SWEAT IT.
WHAT?
I'M NOT GONNA MAKE A GIRL LIVE IN THE PARK LIKE SOME HOMELESS VAGRANT.

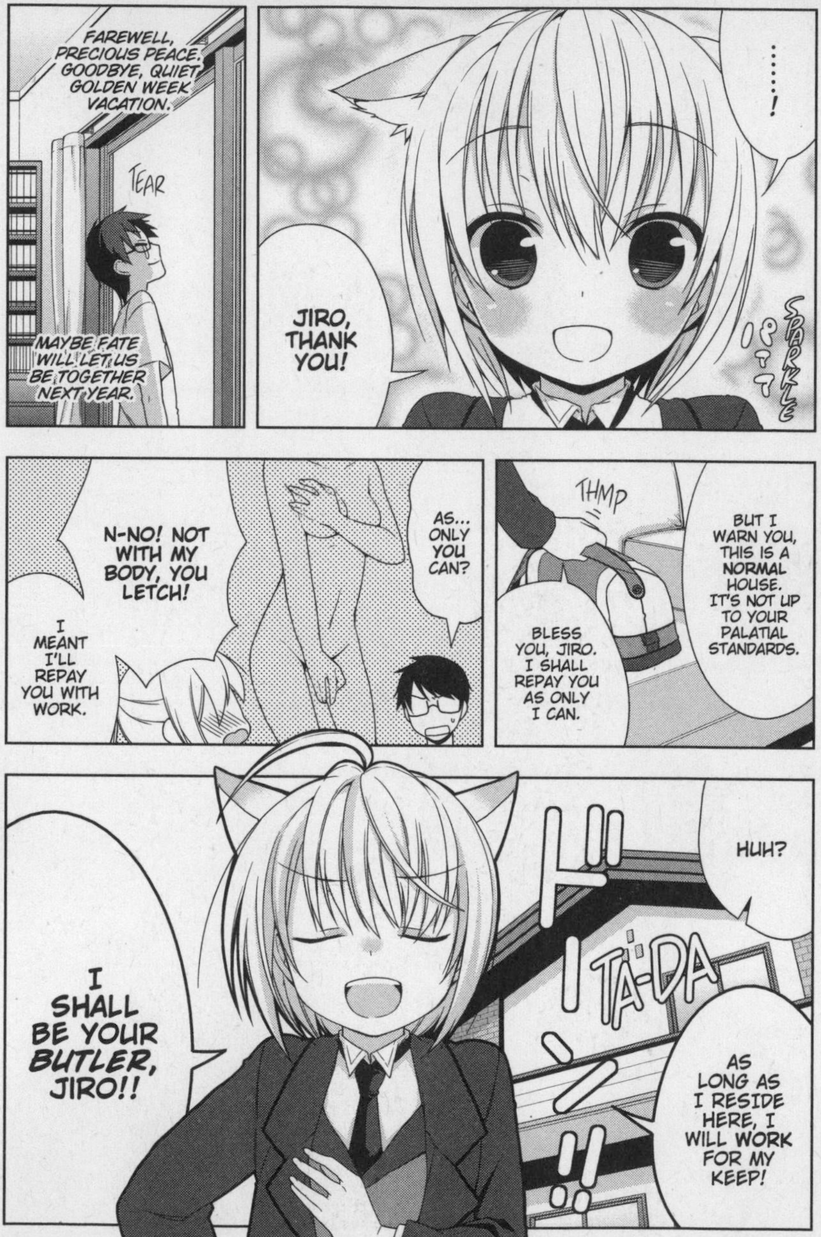
......!
JIRO, THANK YOU!
SPARKLE
FAREWELL, PRECIOUS PEACE. GOODBYE, QUIET GOLDEN WEEK VACATION.
TEAR
MAYBE FATE WILL LET US BE TOGETHER NEXT YEAR.
THMP
BUT I WARN YOU, THIS IS A NORMAL HOUSE. IT'S NOT UP TO YOUR PALATIAL STANDARDS.
BLESS YOU, JIRO. I SHALL REPAY YOU AS ONLY I CAN.
AS... ONLY YOU CAN?
N-NO! NOT WITH MY BODY, YOU LETCH!
I MEANT I'LL REPAY YOU WITH WORK.
HUH?
TA-DA
AS LONG AS I RESIDE HERE, I WILL WORK FOR MY KEEP!
I SHALL BE YOUR BUTLER, JIRO!!

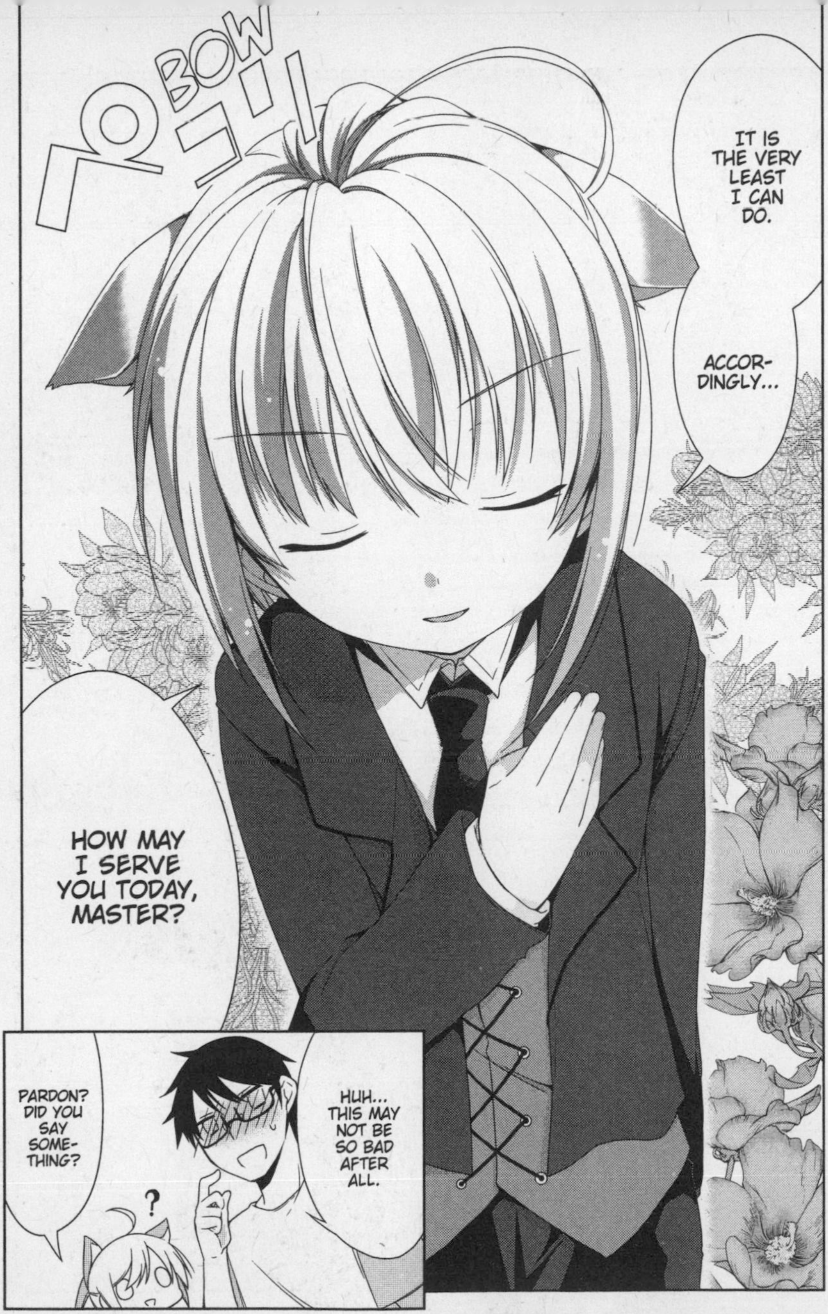
IT IS THE VERY LEAST I CAN DO.
ACCORDINGLY...
BOW
HOW MAY I SERVE YOU TODAY, MASTER?
HUH... THIS MAY NOT BE SO BAD AFTER ALL.
PARDON? DID YOU SAY SOME-THING?
?

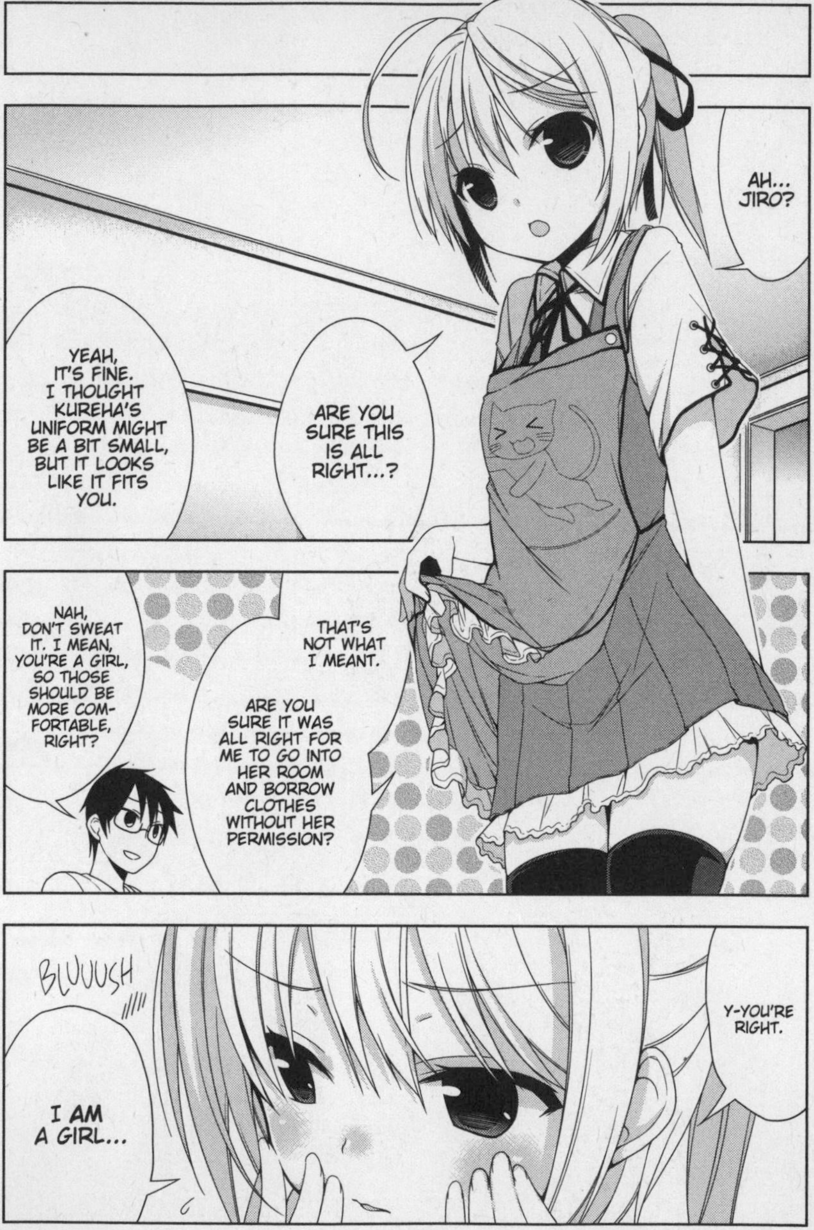
AH... JIRO?
ARE YOU SURE THIS IS ALL RIGHT...?
YEAH, IT'S FINE. I THOUGHT KUREHA'S UNIFORM MIGHT BE A BIT SMALL, BUT IT LOOKS LIKE IT FITS YOU.
THAT'S NOT WHAT I MEANT.
ARE YOU SURE IT WAS ALL RIGHT FOR ME TO GO INTO HER ROOM AND BORROW CLOTHES WITHOUT HER PERMISSION?
NAH, DON'T SWEAT IT. I MEAN, YOU'RE A GIRL, SO THOSE SHOULD BE MORE COM-FORTABLE, RIGHT?
Y-YOU'RE RIGHT.
BLUUUSH
I AM A GIRL...

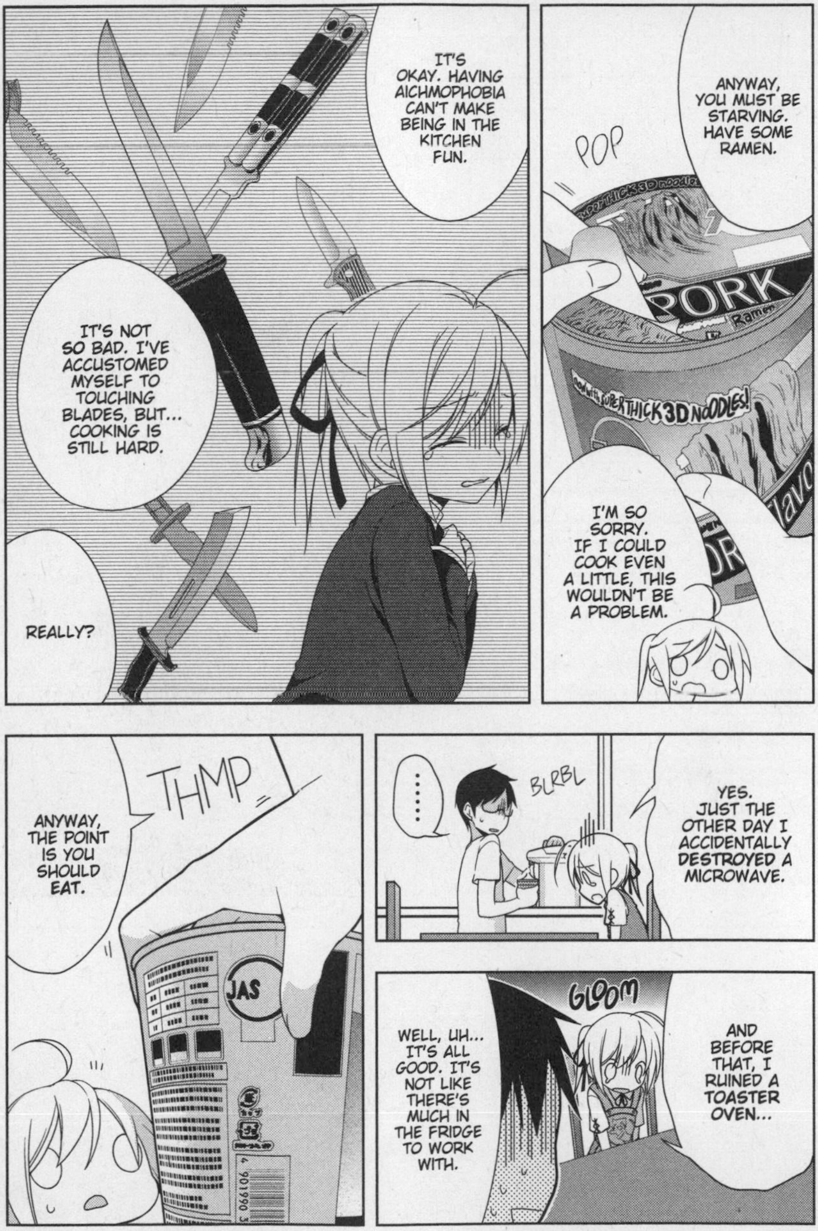
ANYWAY, YOU MUST BE STARVING. HAVE SOME RAMEN.
POP
SUPER THICK 3D noodles
PORK
Ramen
now with SUPER THICK 3D NOODLES!
I'M SO SORRY. IF I COULD COOK EVEN A LITTLE, THIS WOULDN'T BE A PROBLEM.
IT'S OKAY. HAVING AICHMOPHOBIA CAN'T MAKE BEING IN THE KITCHEN FUN.
IT'S NOT SO BAD. I'VE ACCUSTOMED MYSELF TO TOUCHING BLADES, BUT... COOKING IS STILL HARD.
REALLY?
YES. JUST THE OTHER DAY I ACCIDENTALLY DESTROYED A MICROWAVE.
BLRBL
......
AND BEFORE THAT, I RUINED A TOASTER OVEN...
GLOOM
WELL, UH... IT'S ALL GOOD. IT'S NOT LIKE THERE'S MUCH IN THE FRIDGE TO WORK WITH.
THMP
ANYWAY, THE POINT IS YOU SHOULD EAT.
JAS

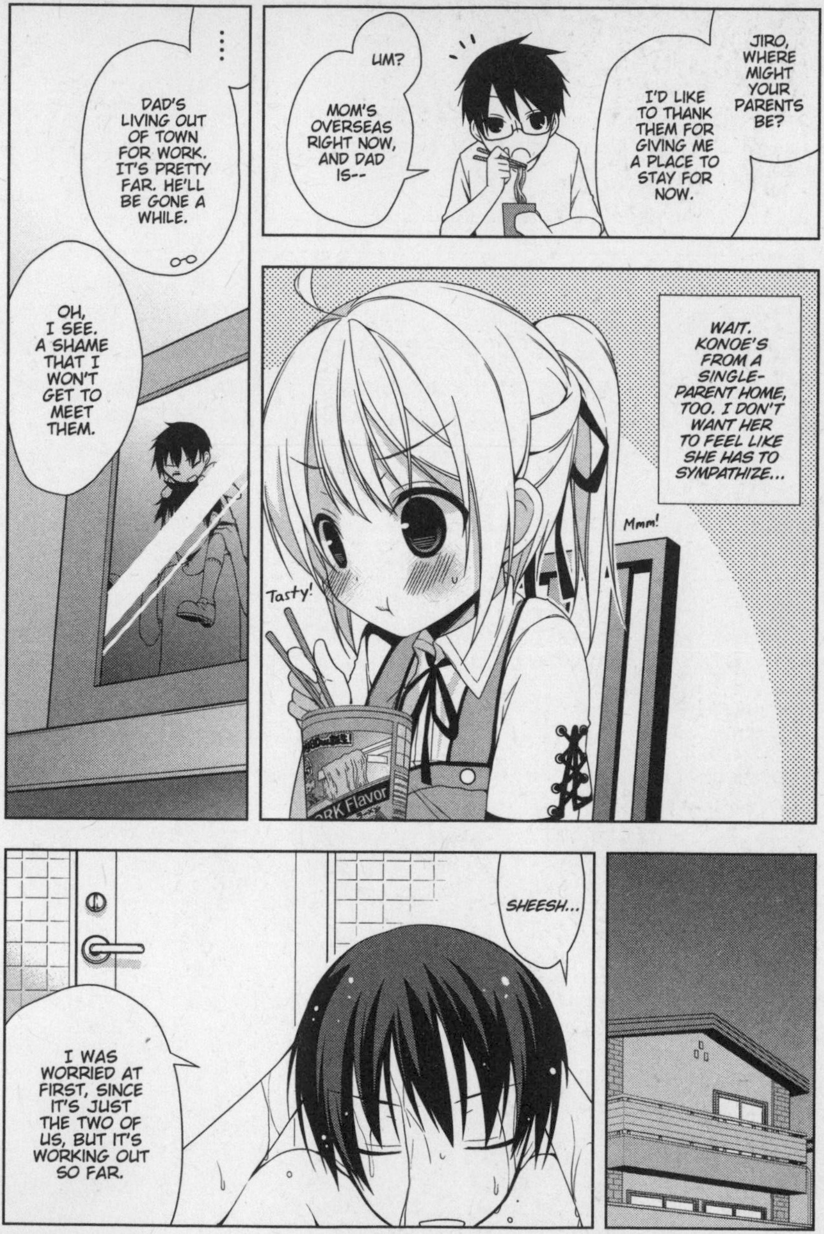
JIRO, WHERE MIGHT YOUR PARENTS BE?
I'D LIKE TO THANK THEM FOR GIVING ME A PLACE TO STAY FOR NOW.
UM?
MOM'S OVERSEAS RIGHT NOW, AND DAD IS--
WAIT. KONOE'S FROM A SINGLE-PARENT HOME, TOO. I DON'T WANT HER TO FEEL LIKE SHE HAS TO SYMPATHIZE...
Mmm!
Tasty!
....
DAD'S LIVING OUT OF TOWN FOR WORK. IT'S PRETTY FAR. HE'LL BE GONE A WHILE.
OH, I SEE. A SHAME THAT I WON'T GET TO MEET THEM.
SHEESH...
I WAS WORRIED AT FIRST, SINCE IT'S JUST THE TWO OF US, BUT IT'S WORKING OUT SO FAR.

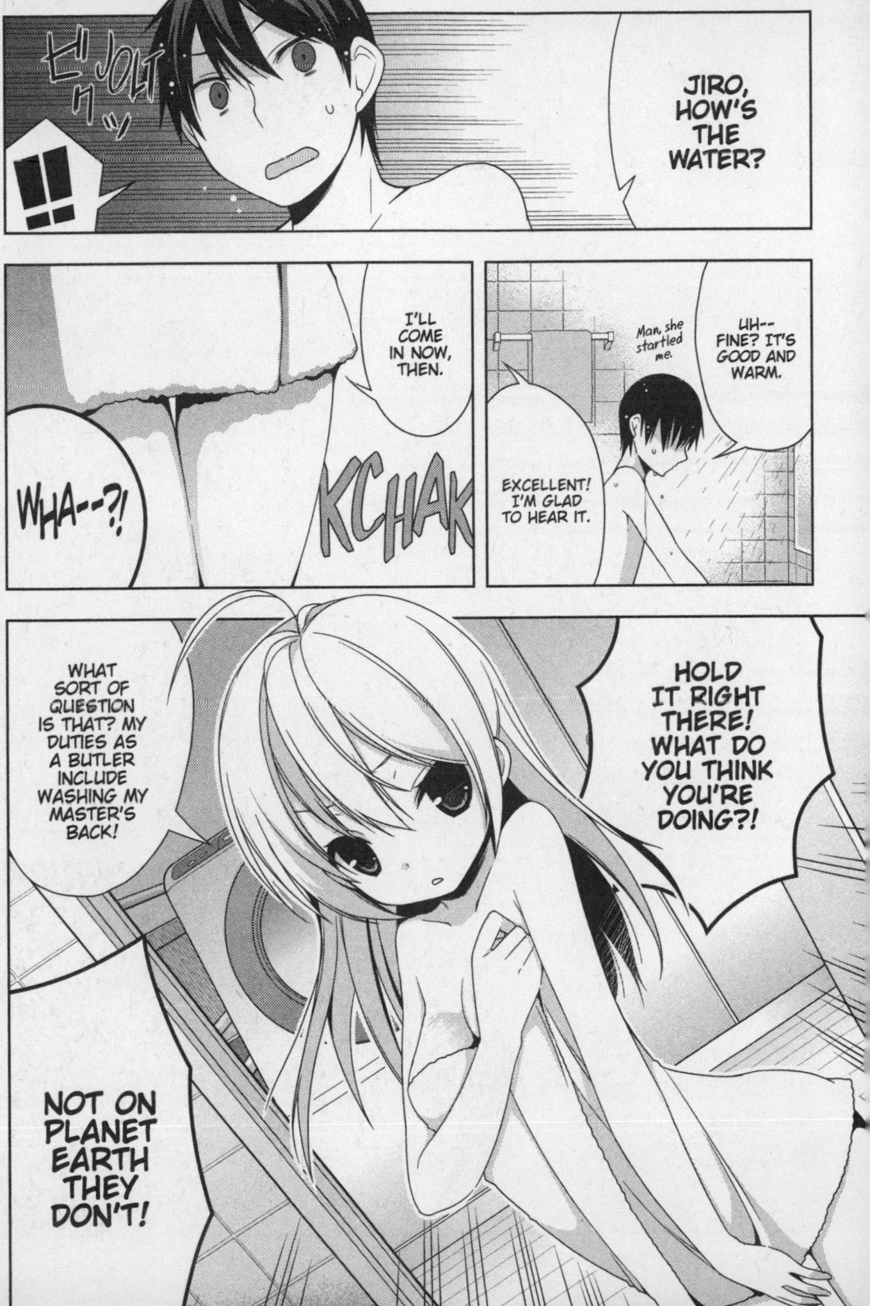
JIRO, HOW'S THE WATER?
ビクッ
JOLT
!!
UH-- FINE? IT'S GOOD AND WARM.
Man, she startled me.
EXCELLENT! I'M GLAD TO HEAR IT.
I'LL COME IN NOW, THEN.
KCHAK
WHA--?!
HOLD IT RIGHT THERE! WHAT DO YOU THINK YOU'RE DOING?!
WHAT SORT OF QUESTION IS THAT? MY DUTIES AS A BUTLER INCLUDE WASHING MY MASTER'S BACK!
NOT ON PLANET EARTH THEY DON'T!

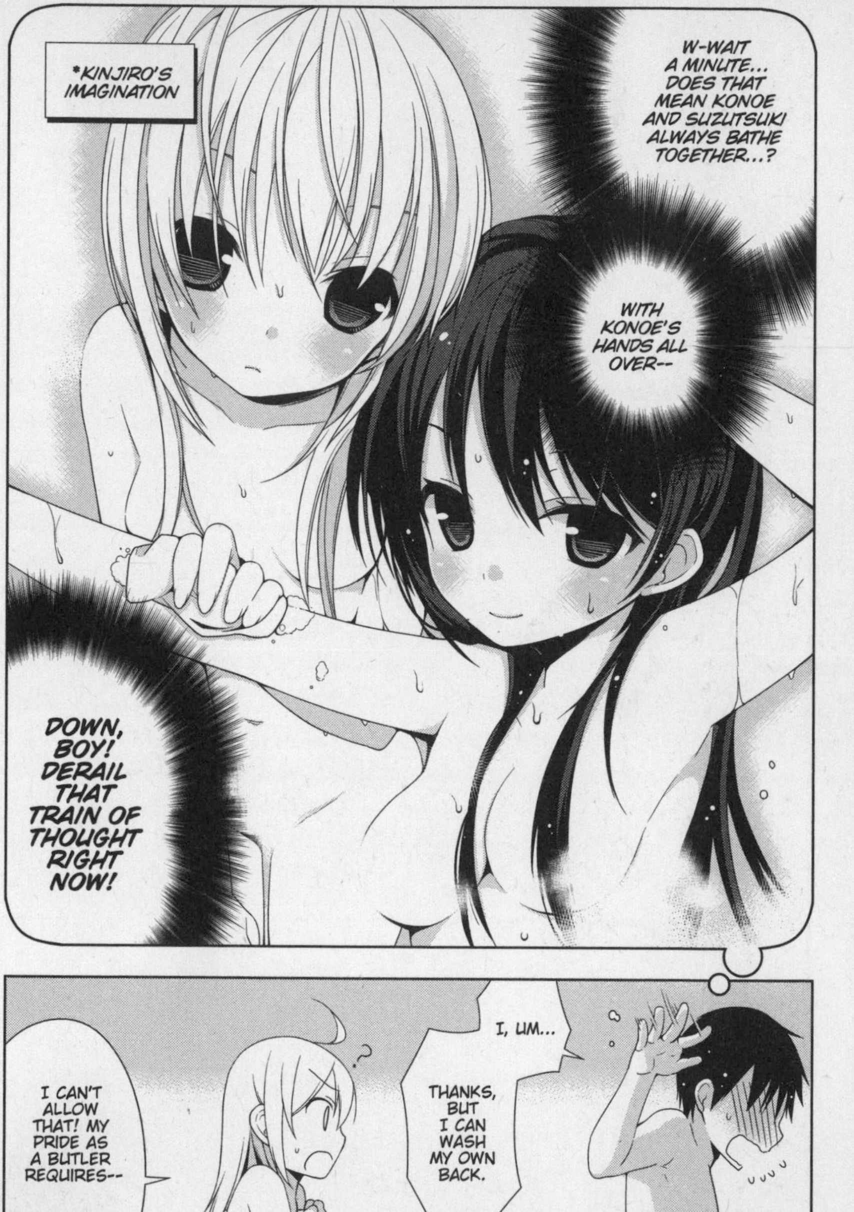
W-WAIT A MINUTE... DOES THAT MEAN KONOE AND SUZUTSUKI ALWAYS BATHE TOGETHER...?
*KINJIRO'S IMAGINATION
WITH KONOE'S HANDS ALL OVER--
DOWN, BOY! DERAIL THAT TRAIN OF THOUGHT RIGHT NOW!
I, UM...
THANKS, BUT I CAN WASH MY OWN BACK.
I CAN'T ALLOW THAT! MY PRIDE AS A BUTLER REQUIRES--

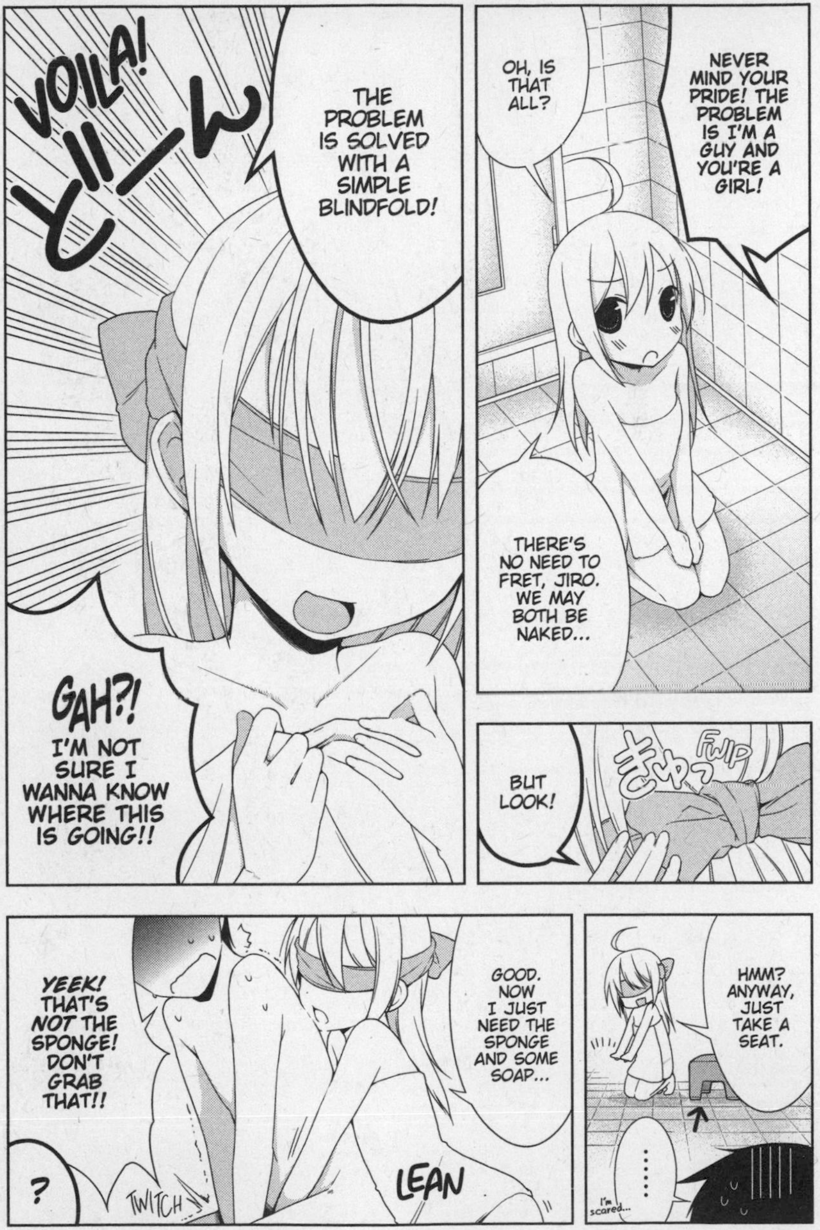
NEVER MIND YOUR PRIDE! THE PROBLEM IS I'M A GUY AND YOU'RE A GIRL!
OH, IS THAT ALL?
THERE'S NO NEED TO FRET, JIRO. WE MAY BOTH BE NAKED...
FWIP
きゅっ
BUT LOOK!
THE PROBLEM IS SOLVED WITH A SIMPLE BLINDFOLD!
VOILA!
どーん
GAH?!
I'M NOT SURE I WANNA KNOW WHERE THIS IS GOING!!
HMM? ANYWAY, JUST TAKE A SEAT.
......
I'm scared...
GOOD. NOW I JUST NEED THE SPONGE AND SOME SOAP...
LEAN
YEEK! THAT'S NOT THE SPONGE! DON'T GRAB THAT!!
?
TWITCH

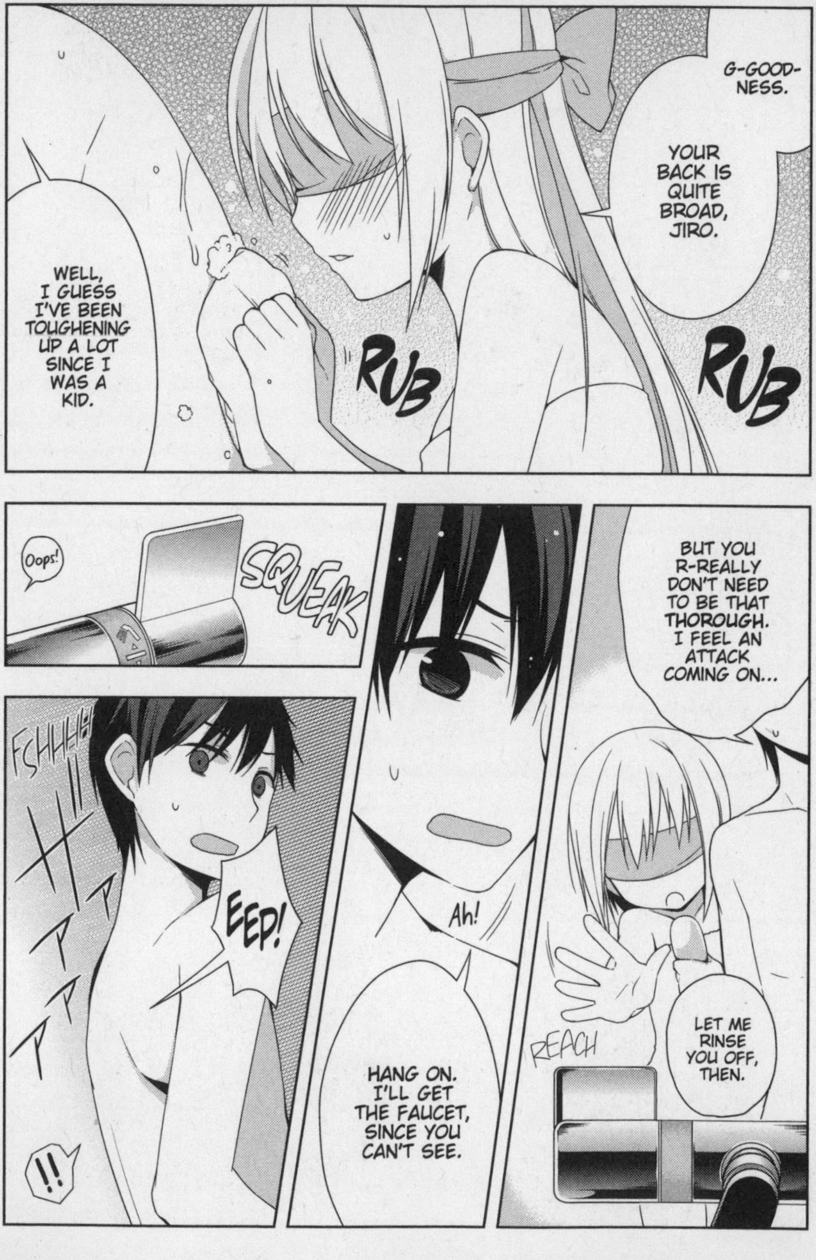
G-GOODNESS.
YOUR BACK IS QUITE BROAD, JIRO.
RUB
RUB
WELL, I GUESS I'VE BEEN TOUGHENING UP A LOT SINCE I WAS A KID.
BUT YOU R-REALLY DON'T NEED TO BE THAT THOROUGH. I FEEL AN ATTACK COMING ON...
LET ME RINSE YOU OFF, THEN.
REACH
Ah!
HANG ON. I'LL GET THE FAUCET, SINCE YOU CAN'T SEE.
Oops!
SQUEAK
FSHHH!!
EEP!
!!

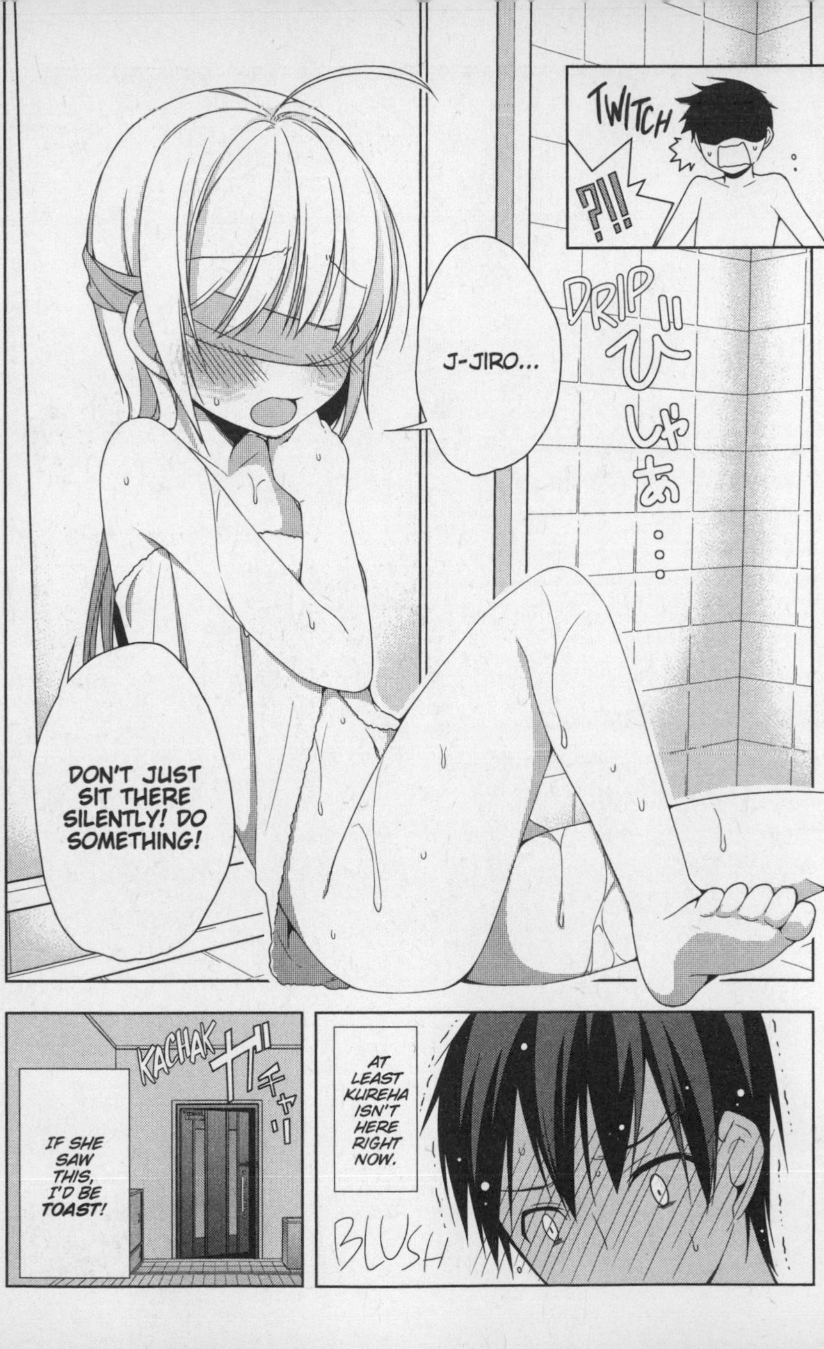
TWITCH
?!!
J-JIRO...
DRIP
びしゃあ...
DON'T JUST SIT THERE SILENTLY! DO SOMETHING!
AT LEAST KUREHA ISN'T HERE RIGHT NOW.
BLUSH
KACHAK
ガチャリ
IF SHE SAW THIS, I'D BE TOAST!

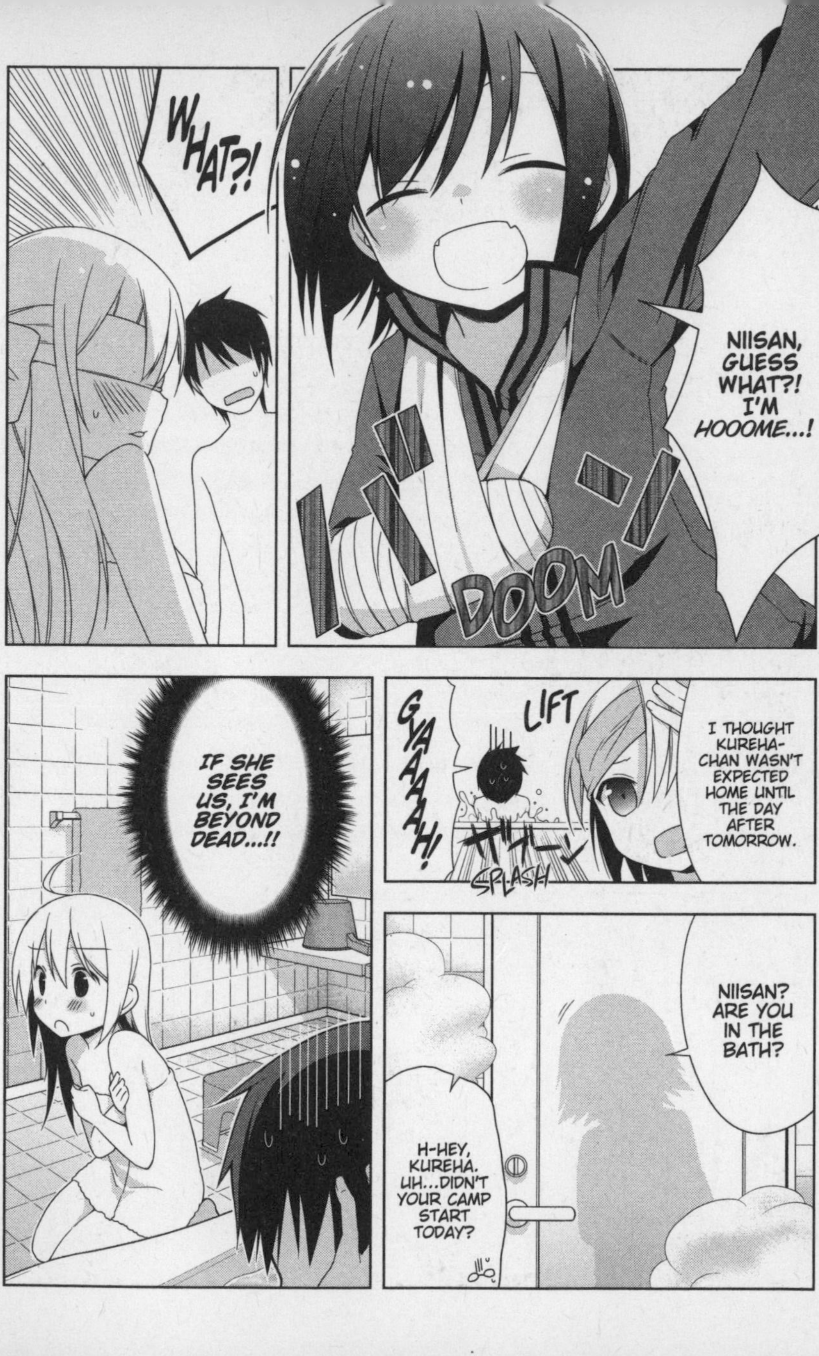
NIISAN, GUESS WHAT?! I'M HOOOME...!
DOOM
WHAT?!
I THOUGHT KUREHA-CHAN WASN'T EXPECTED HOME UNTIL THE DAY AFTER TOMORROW.
LIFT
GYAAAAH!
SPLASH
NIISAN? ARE YOU IN THE BATH?
H-HEY, KUREHA. UH...DIDN'T YOUR CAMP START TODAY?
IF SHE SEES US, I'M BEYOND DEAD...!!

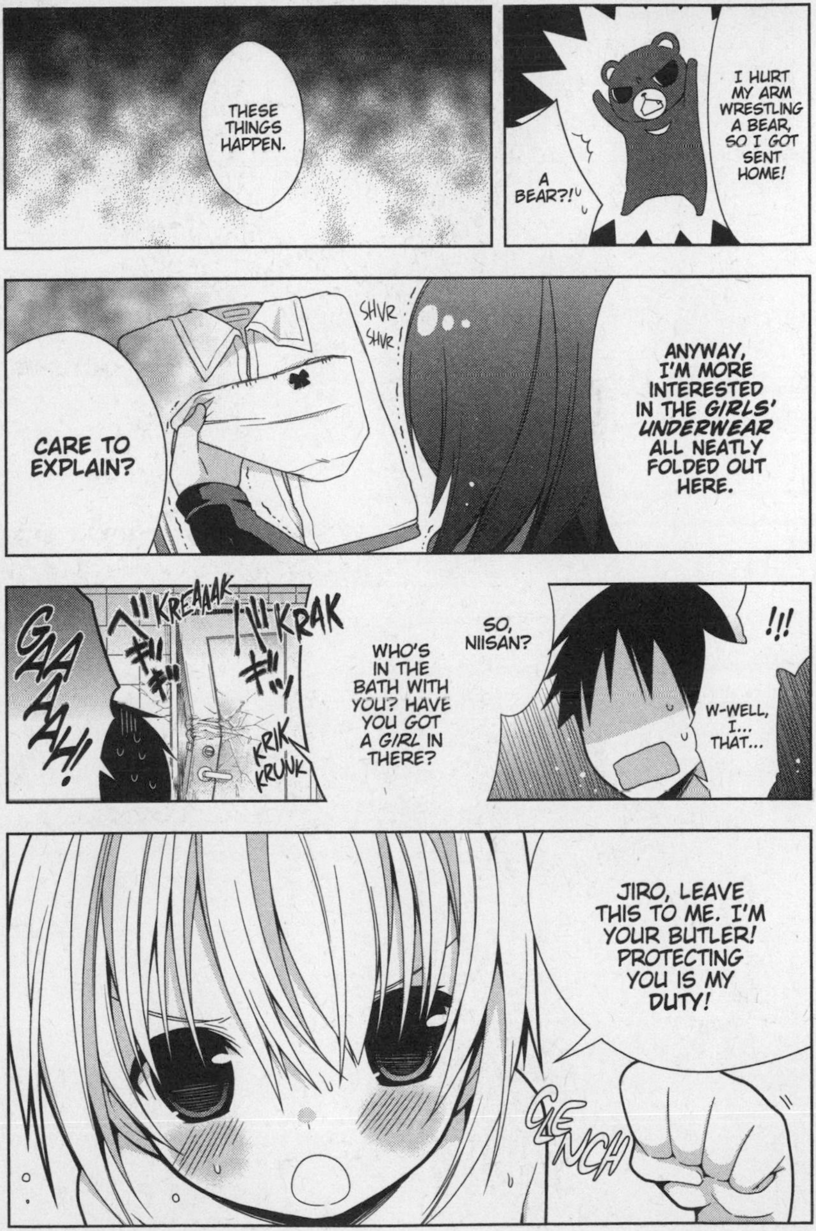
I HURT MY ARM WRESTLING A BEAR, SO I GOT SENT HOME!
A BEAR?!
THESE THINGS HAPPEN.
ANYWAY, I'M MORE INTERESTED IN THE *GIRLS' UNDERWEAR* ALL NEATLY FOLDED OUT HERE.
SHVR SHVR
CARE TO EXPLAIN?
!!!
SO, NIISAN?
W-WELL, I... THAT...
WHO'S IN THE BATH WITH YOU? HAVE YOU GOT A *GIRL* IN THERE?
KRAK
KREAAAK
KRIK KRUNK
GAAAAAH!!
JIRO, LEAVE THIS TO ME. I'M YOUR BUTLER! PROTECTING YOU IS MY DUTY!
CLENCH

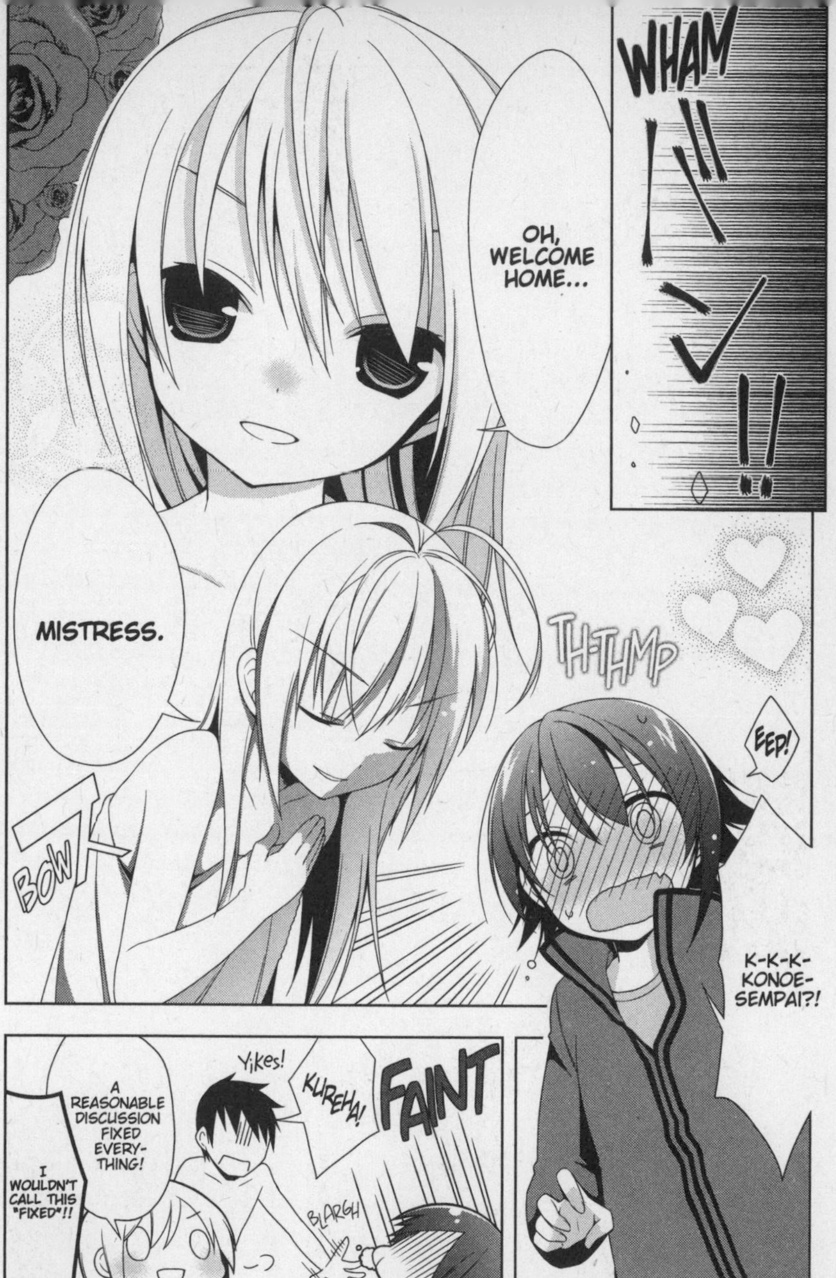
WHAM
OH, WELCOME HOME...
MISTRESS.
TH-THMP
BOW
EEP!
K-K-K-KONOE-SEMPAI?!
FAINT
KUREHA!
Yikes!
A REASONABLE DISCUSSION FIXED EVERYTHING!
I WOULDN'T CALL THIS "FIXED"!!
BLARGH

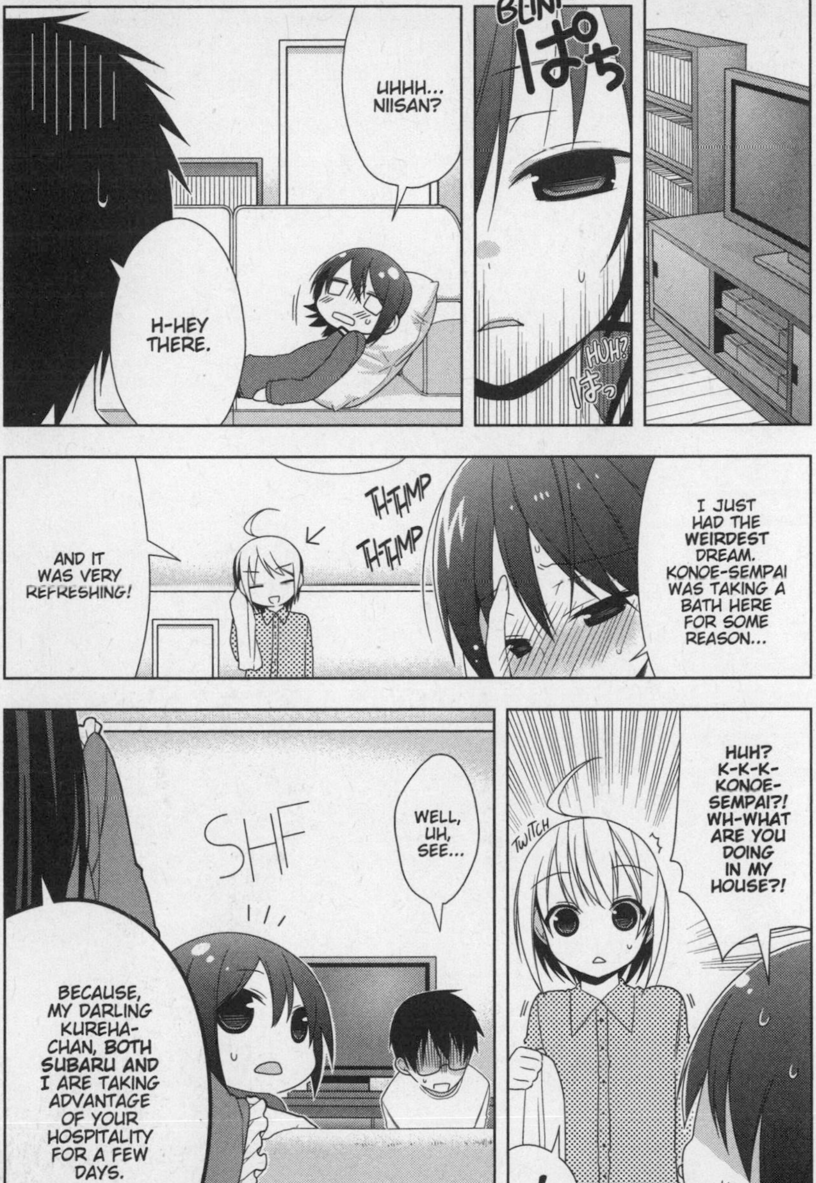
BLINK
ぱち
HUH?
はっ
UHHH... NIISAN?
H-HEY THERE.
I JUST HAD THE WEIRDEST DREAM. KONOE-SEMPAI WAS TAKING A BATH HERE FOR SOME REASON...
TH-THMP
TH-THMP
AND IT WAS VERY REFRESHING!
HUH? K-K-K-KONOE-SEMPAI?! WH-WHAT ARE YOU DOING IN MY HOUSE?!
TWITCH
!
WELL, UH, SEE...
SHF
BECAUSE, MY DARLING KUREHA-CHAN, BOTH SUBARU AND I ARE TAKING ADVANTAGE OF YOUR HOSPITALITY FOR A FEW DAYS.

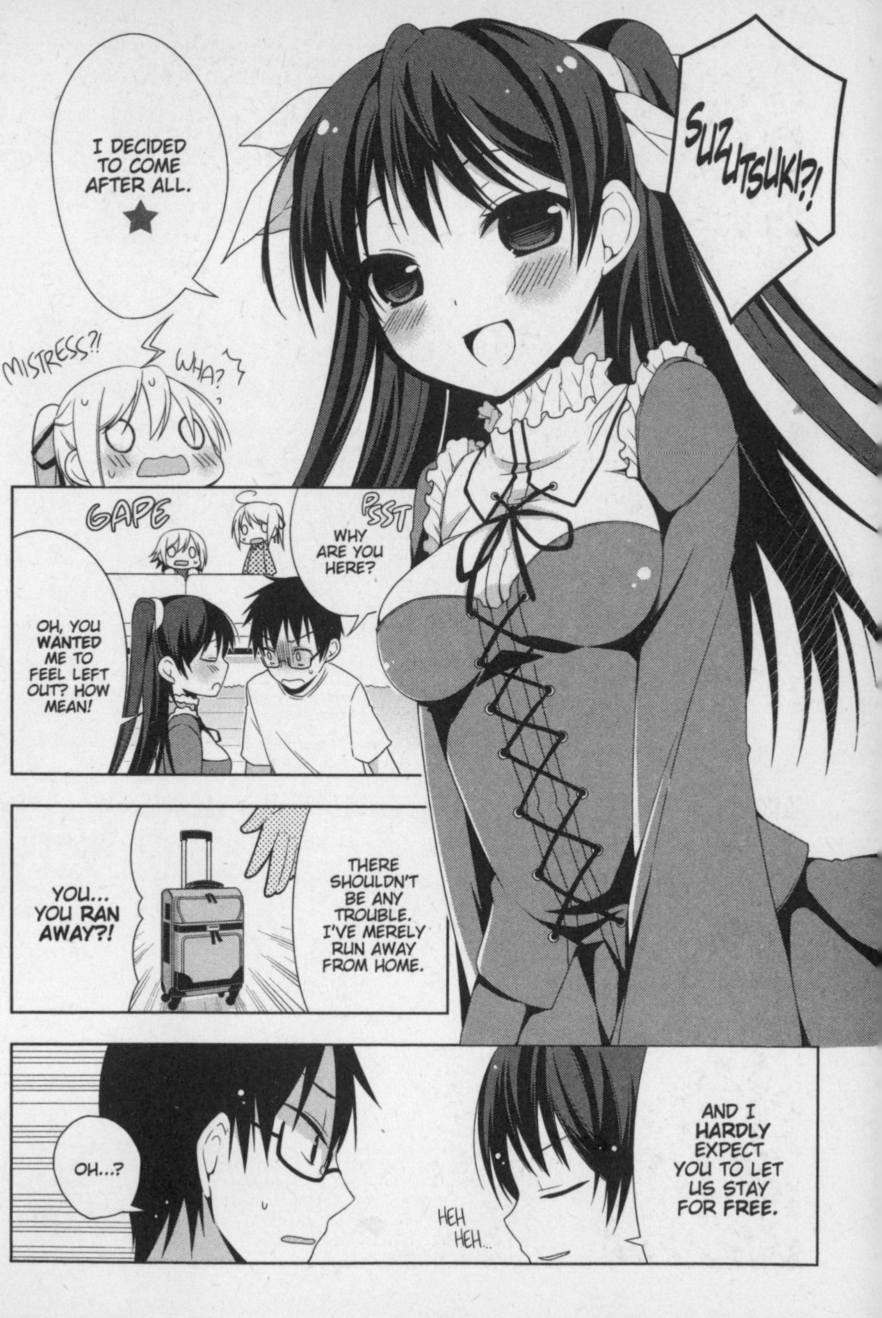
SUZUTSUKI?!
I DECIDED TO COME AFTER ALL. ★
WHA?
MISTRESS?!
PSST
WHY ARE YOU HERE?
GAPE
OH, YOU WANTED ME TO FEEL LEFT OUT? HOW MEAN!
THERE SHOULDN'T BE ANY TROUBLE. I'VE MERELY RUN AWAY FROM HOME.
YOU... YOU RAN AWAY?!
AND I HARDLY EXPECT YOU TO LET US STAY FOR FREE.
HEH HEH...
OH...?

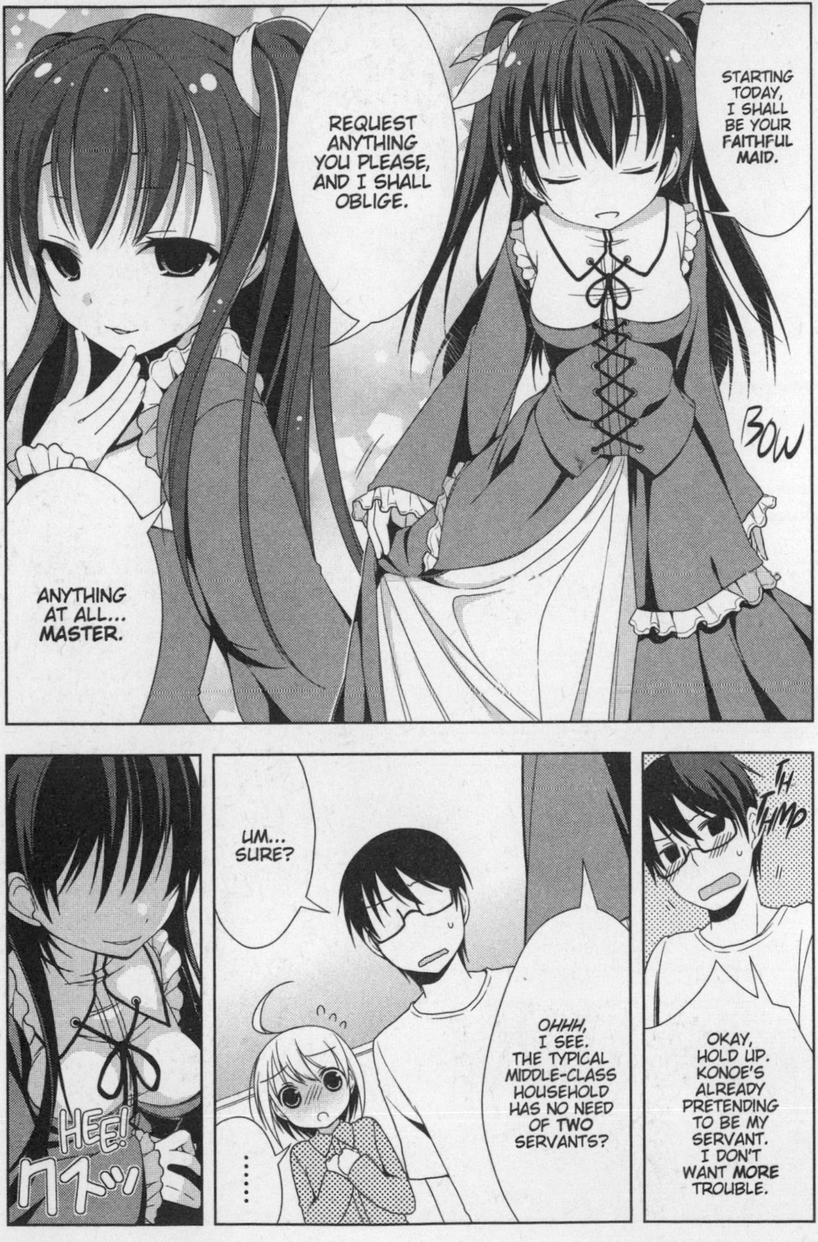
STARTING TODAY, I SHALL BE YOUR FAITHFUL MAID.
BOW
REQUEST ANYTHING YOU PLEASE, AND I SHALL OBLIGE.
ANYTHING AT ALL... MASTER.
TH THMP
OKAY, HOLD UP. KONOE'S ALREADY PRETENDING TO BE MY SERVANT. I DON'T WANT MORE TROUBLE.
OHHH, I SEE. THE TYPICAL MIDDLE-CLASS HOUSEHOLD HAS NO NEED OF TWO SERVANTS?
UM... SURE?
......
HEE!
クスッ

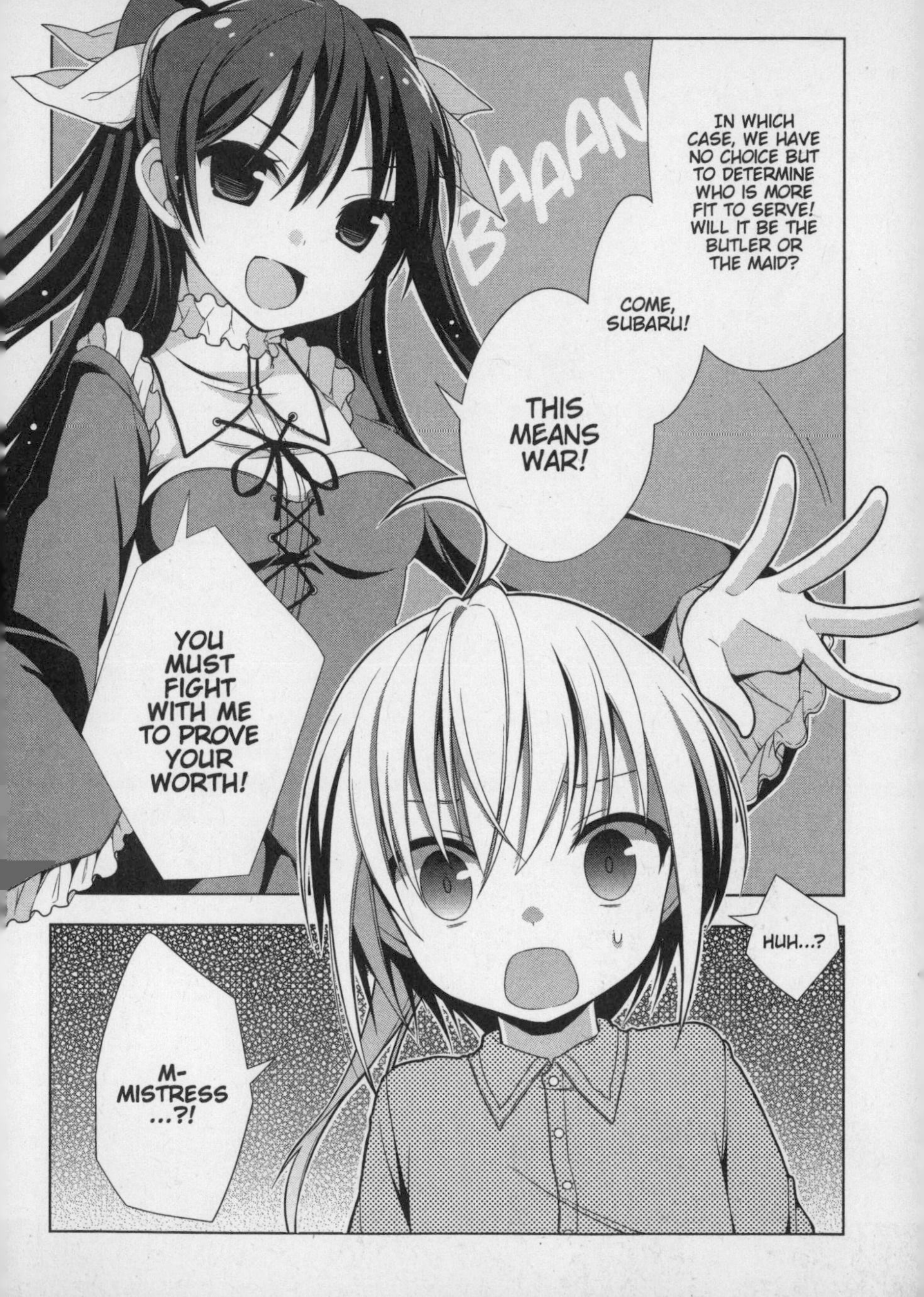
IN WHICH CASE, WE HAVE NO CHOICE BUT TO DETERMINE WHO IS MORE FIT TO SERVE! WILL IT BE THE BUTLER OR THE MAID?
BAAAN
COME, SUBARU!
THIS MEANS WAR!
YOU MUST FIGHT WITH ME TO PROVE YOUR WORTH!
HUH...?
M-MISTRESS ...?!

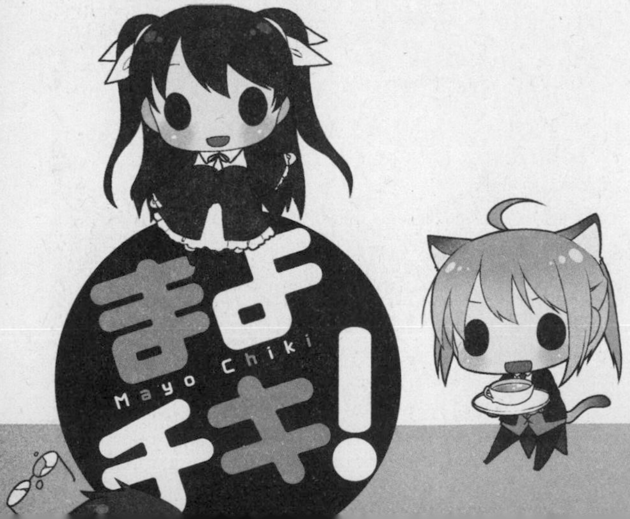
まよチキ!
Mayo Chiki

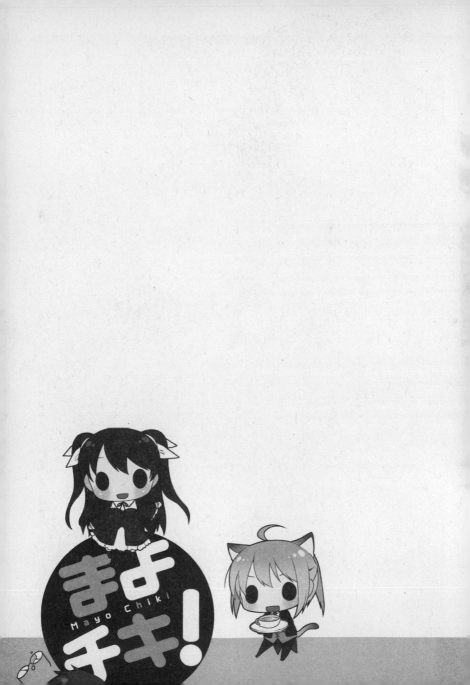

But as it's late evening already, the war will begin tomorrow. ♥

Wait, what?!

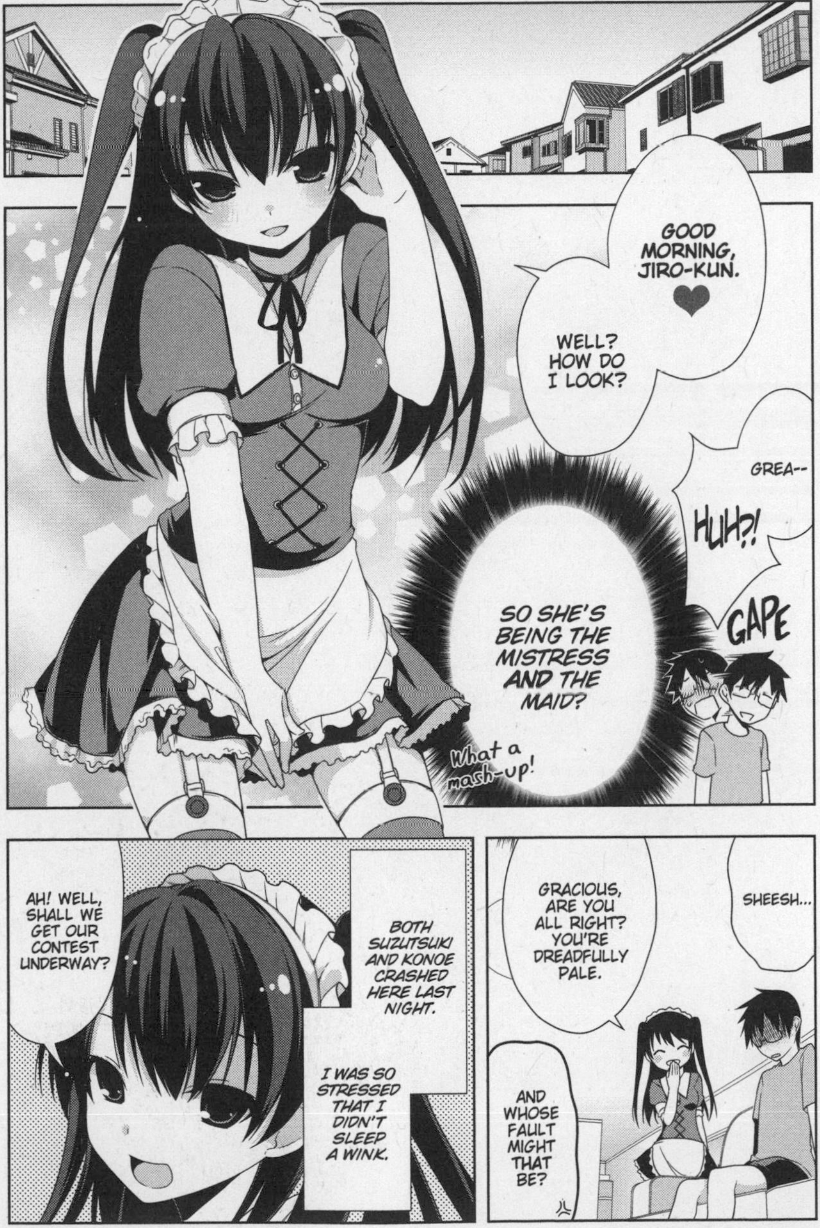
GOOD MORNING, JIRO-KUN. ❤
WELL? HOW DO I LOOK?
GREA--
HUH?!
GAPE
SO SHE'S BEING THE MISTRESS AND THE MAID?
What a mash-up!
SHEESH...
GRACIOUS, ARE YOU ALL RIGHT? YOU'RE DREADFULLY PALE.
AND WHOSE FAULT MIGHT THAT BE?
BOTH SUZUTSUKI AND KONOE CRASHED HERE LAST NIGHT.
AH! WELL, SHALL WE GET OUR CONTEST UNDERWAY?
I WAS SO STRESSED THAT I DIDN'T SLEEP A WINK.

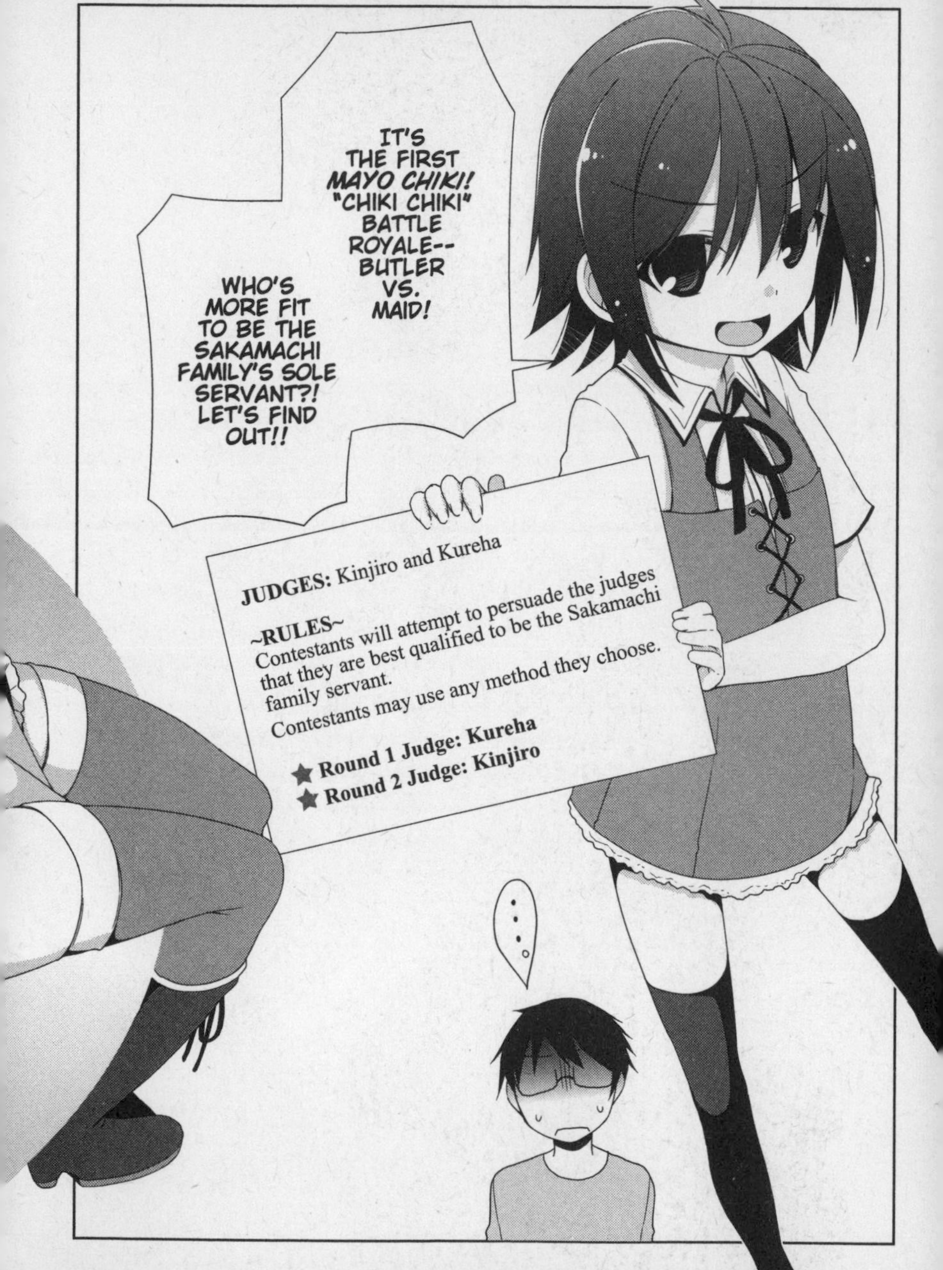
IT'S THE FIRST MAYO CHIKI! "CHIKI CHIKI" BATTLE ROYALE--BUTLER VS. MAID!
WHO'S MORE FIT TO BE THE SAKAMACHI FAMILY'S SOLE SERVANT?! LET'S FIND OUT!!
JUDGES: Kinjiro and Kureha
~RULES~
Contestants will attempt to persuade the judges that they are best qualified to be the Sakamachi family servant.
Contestants may use any method they choose.
★ Round 1 Judge: Kureha
★ Round 2 Judge: Kinjiro
...

chapter 7 butler vs. maid

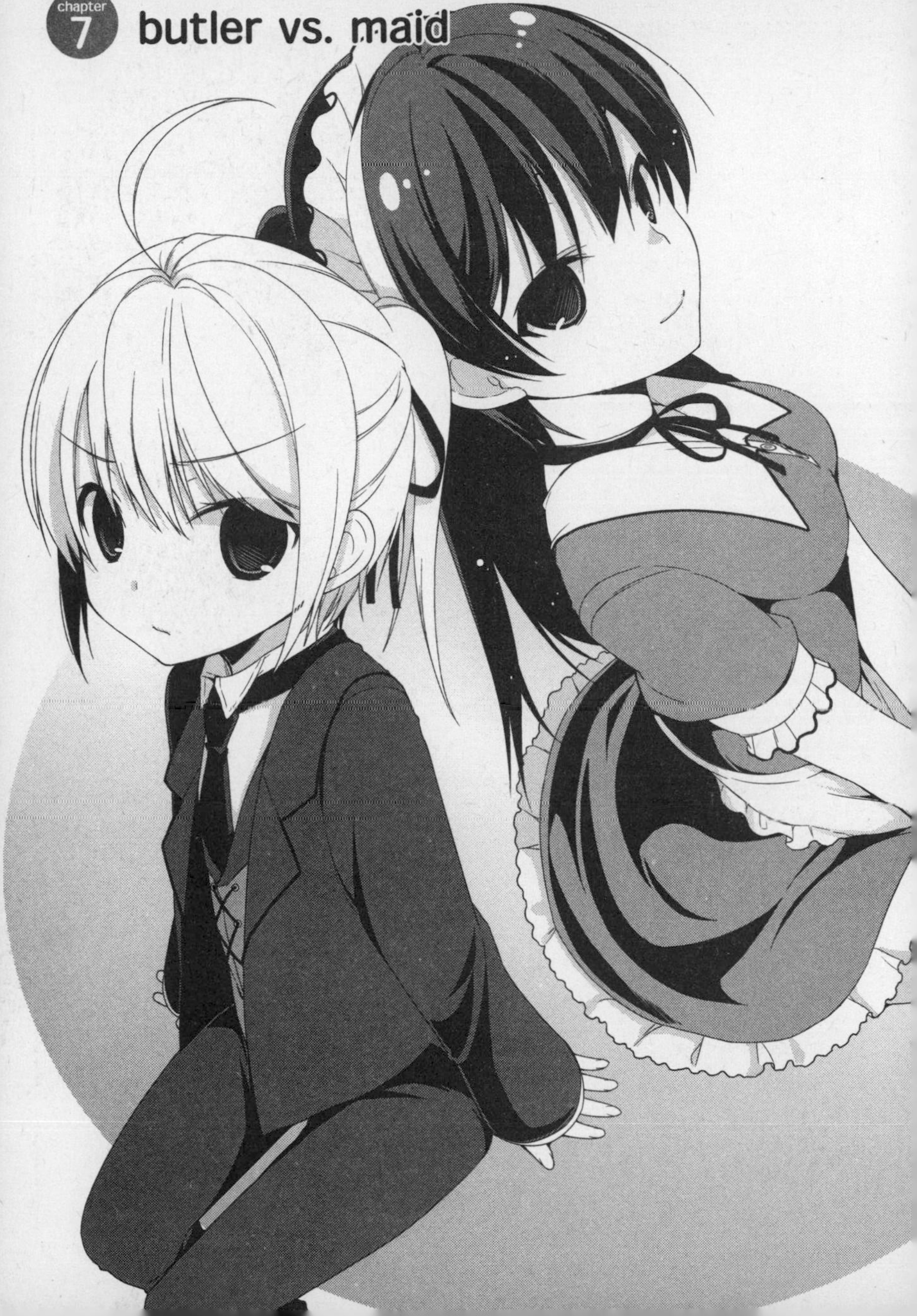

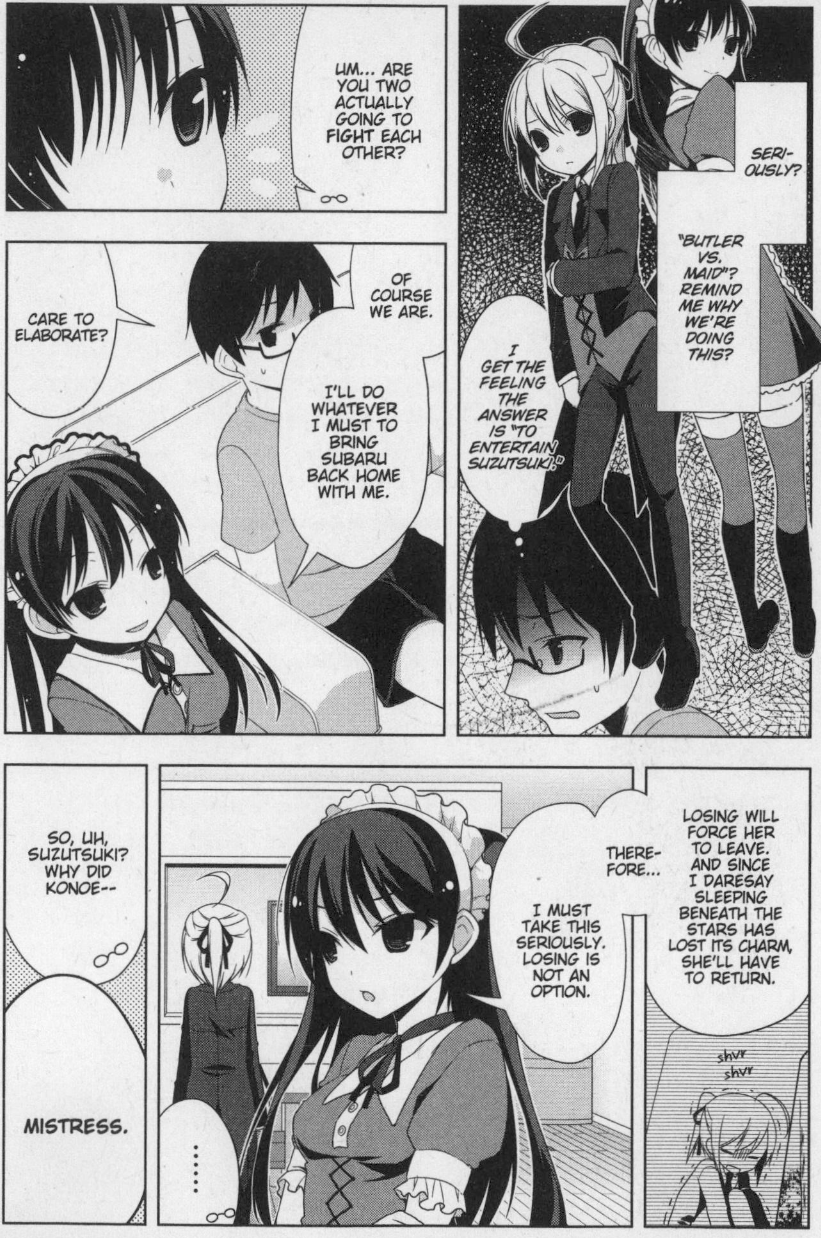
SERI-OUSLY?
"BUTLER VS. MAID"? REMIND ME WHY WE'RE DOING THIS?
I GET THE FEELING THE ANSWER IS "TO ENTERTAIN SUZUTSUKI."
UM... ARE YOU TWO ACTUALLY GOING TO FIGHT EACH OTHER?
OF COURSE WE ARE.
I'LL DO WHATEVER I MUST TO BRING SUBARU BACK HOME WITH ME.
CARE TO ELABORATE?
LOSING WILL FORCE HER TO LEAVE. AND SINCE I DARESAY SLEEPING BENEATH THE STARS HAS LOST ITS CHARM, SHE'LL HAVE TO RETURN.
shvr
shvr
THERE-FORE...
I MUST TAKE THIS SERIOUSLY. LOSING IS NOT AN OPTION.
......
SO, UH, SUZUTSUKI? WHY DID KONOE--
MISTRESS.

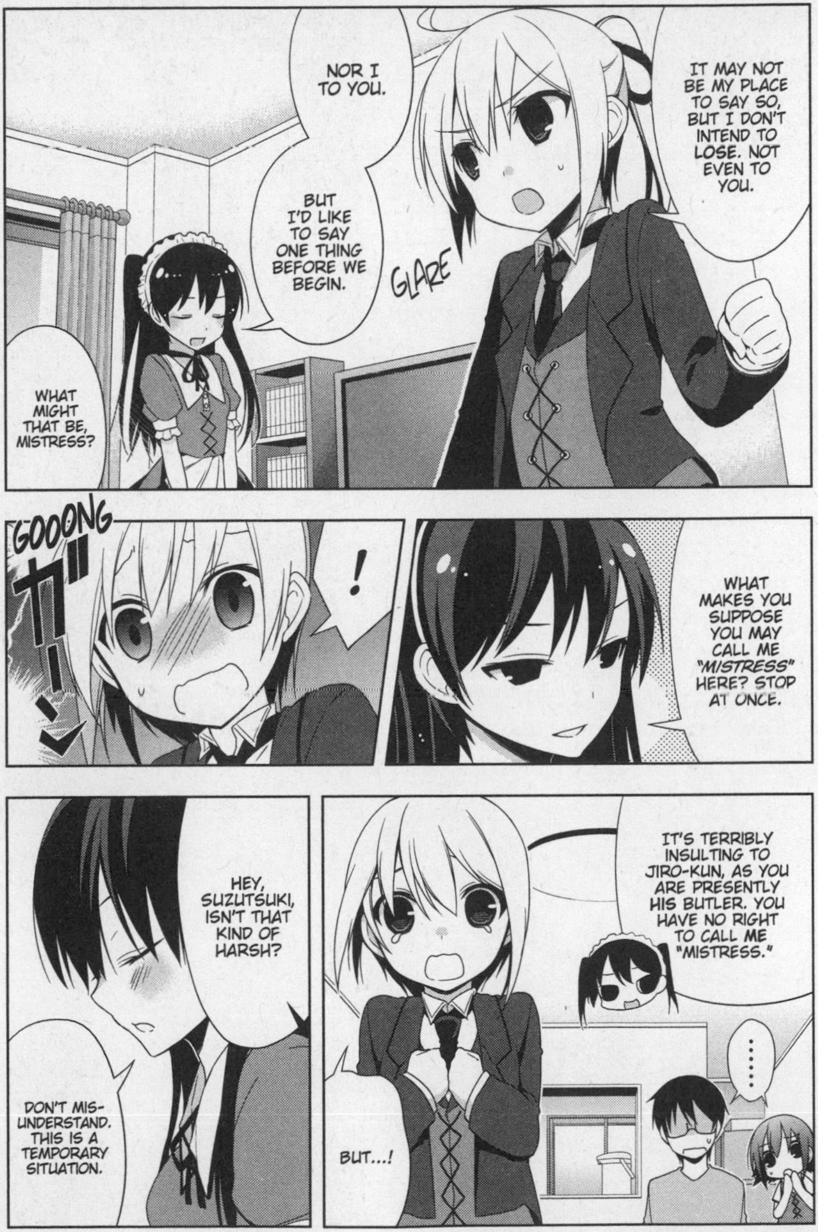
IT MAY NOT BE MY PLACE TO SAY SO, BUT I DON'T INTEND TO LOSE. NOT EVEN TO YOU.
NOR I TO YOU.
BUT I'D LIKE TO SAY ONE THING BEFORE WE BEGIN.
GLARE
WHAT MIGHT THAT BE, MISTRESS?
WHAT MAKES YOU SUPPOSE YOU MAY CALL ME "MISTRESS" HERE? STOP AT ONCE.
!
GOOONG
ガーン
IT'S TERRIBLY INSULTING TO JIRO-KUN, AS YOU ARE PRESENTLY HIS BUTLER. YOU HAVE NO RIGHT TO CALL ME "MISTRESS."
......
BUT...!
HEY, SUZUTSUKI, ISN'T THAT KIND OF HARSH?
DON'T MIS-UNDERSTAND. THIS IS A TEMPORARY SITUATION.

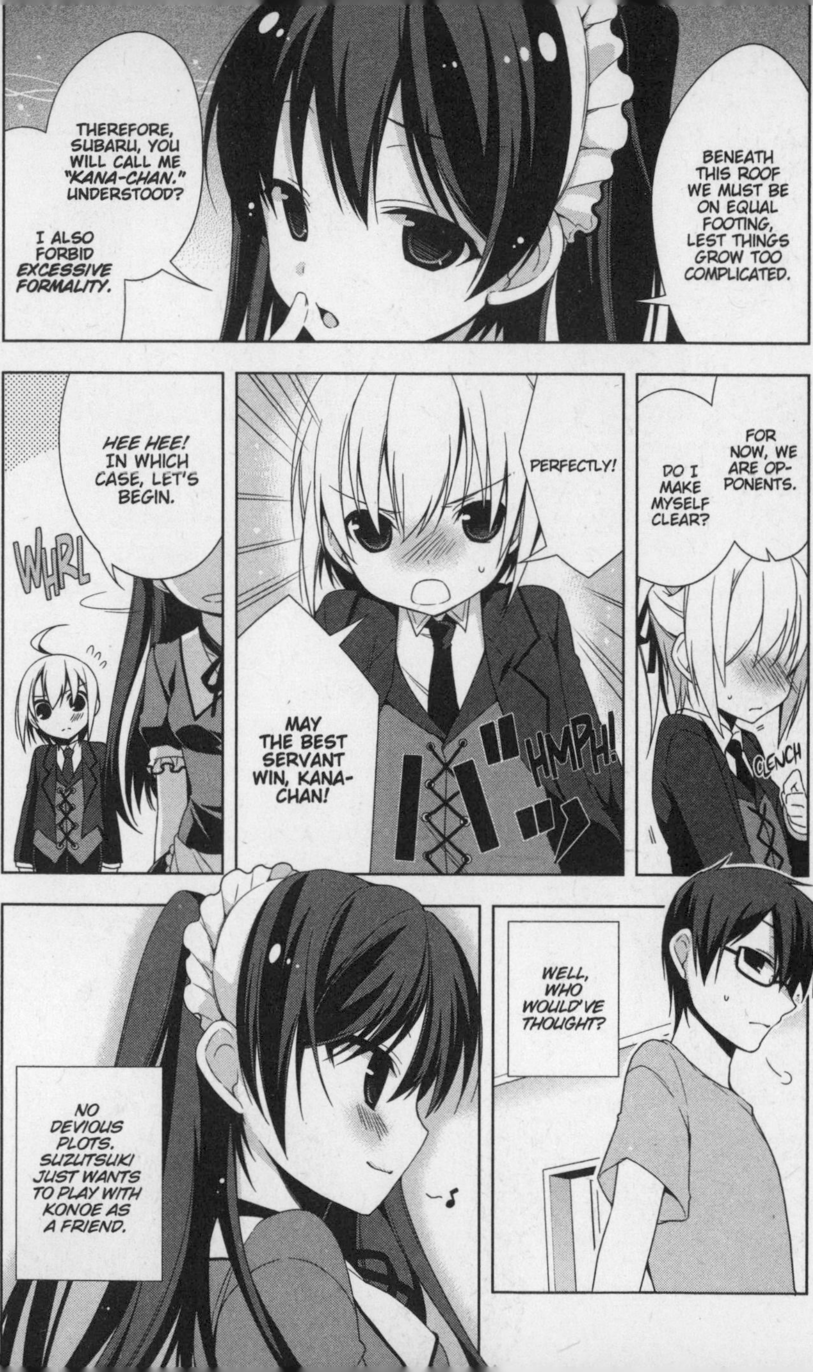
BENEATH THIS ROOF WE MUST BE ON EQUAL FOOTING, LEST THINGS GROW TOO COMPLICATED.
THEREFORE, SUBARU, YOU WILL CALL ME "KANA-CHAN." UNDERSTOOD?
I ALSO FORBID EXCESSIVE FORMALITY.
FOR NOW, WE ARE OP-PONENTS.
DO I MAKE MYSELF CLEAR?
CLENCH
PERFECTLY!
HMPH!
MAY THE BEST SERVANT WIN, KANA-CHAN!
HEE HEE! IN WHICH CASE, LET'S BEGIN.
WHRL
WELL, WHO WOULD'VE THOUGHT?
NO DEVIOUS PLOTS. SUZUTSUKI JUST WANTS TO PLAY WITH KONOE AS A FRIEND.

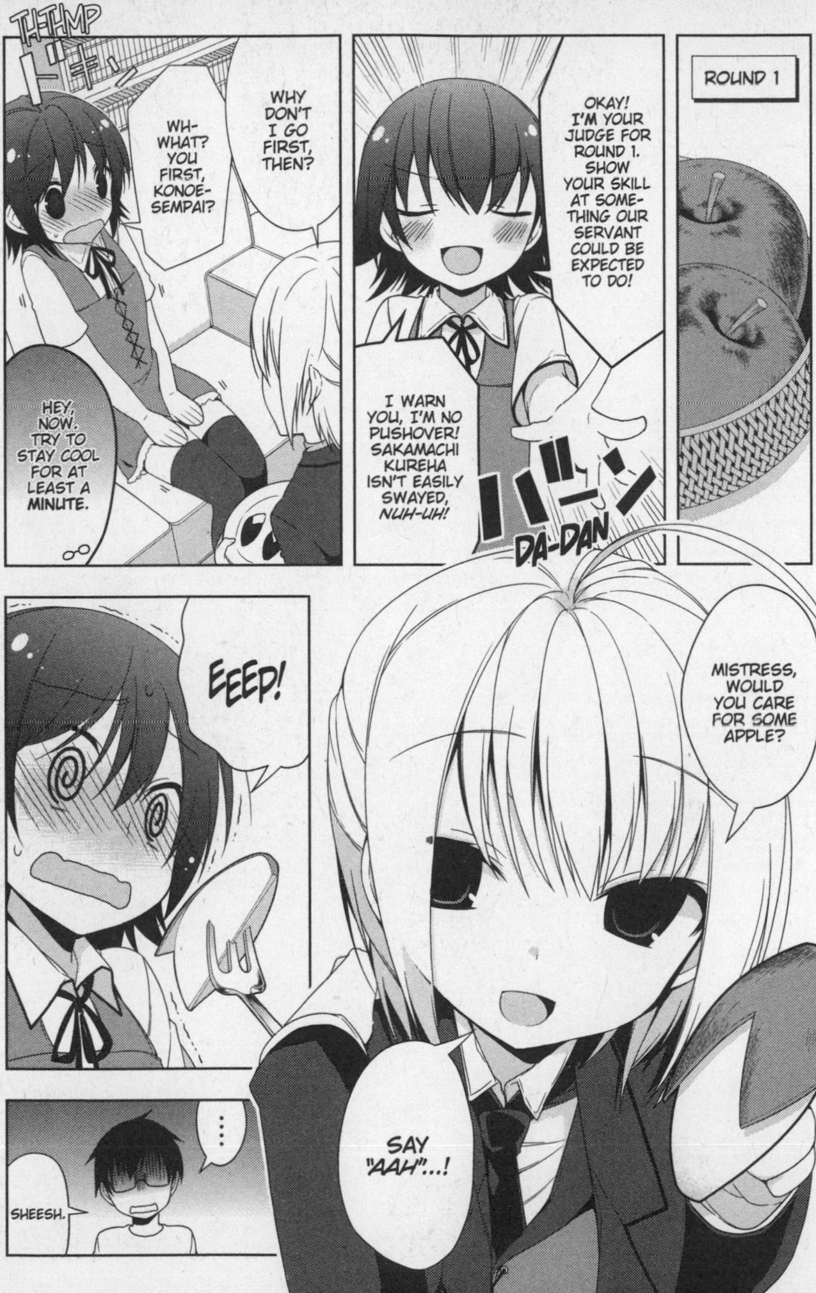
ROUND 1
OKAY! I'M YOUR JUDGE FOR ROUND 1. SHOW YOUR SKILL AT SOMETHING OUR SERVANT COULD BE EXPECTED TO DO!
I WARN YOU, I'M NO PUSHOVER! SAKAMACHI KUREHA ISN'T EASILY SWAYED, *NUH-UH!*
バーン
DA-DAN
TH-THMP
ドキッ
WHY DON'T I GO FIRST, THEN?
WH-WHAT? YOU FIRST, KONOE-SEMPAI?
HEY, NOW. TRY TO STAY COOL FOR AT LEAST A MINUTE.
MISTRESS, WOULD YOU CARE FOR SOME APPLE?
SAY "AAH"...!
EEEP!
....
SHEESH.

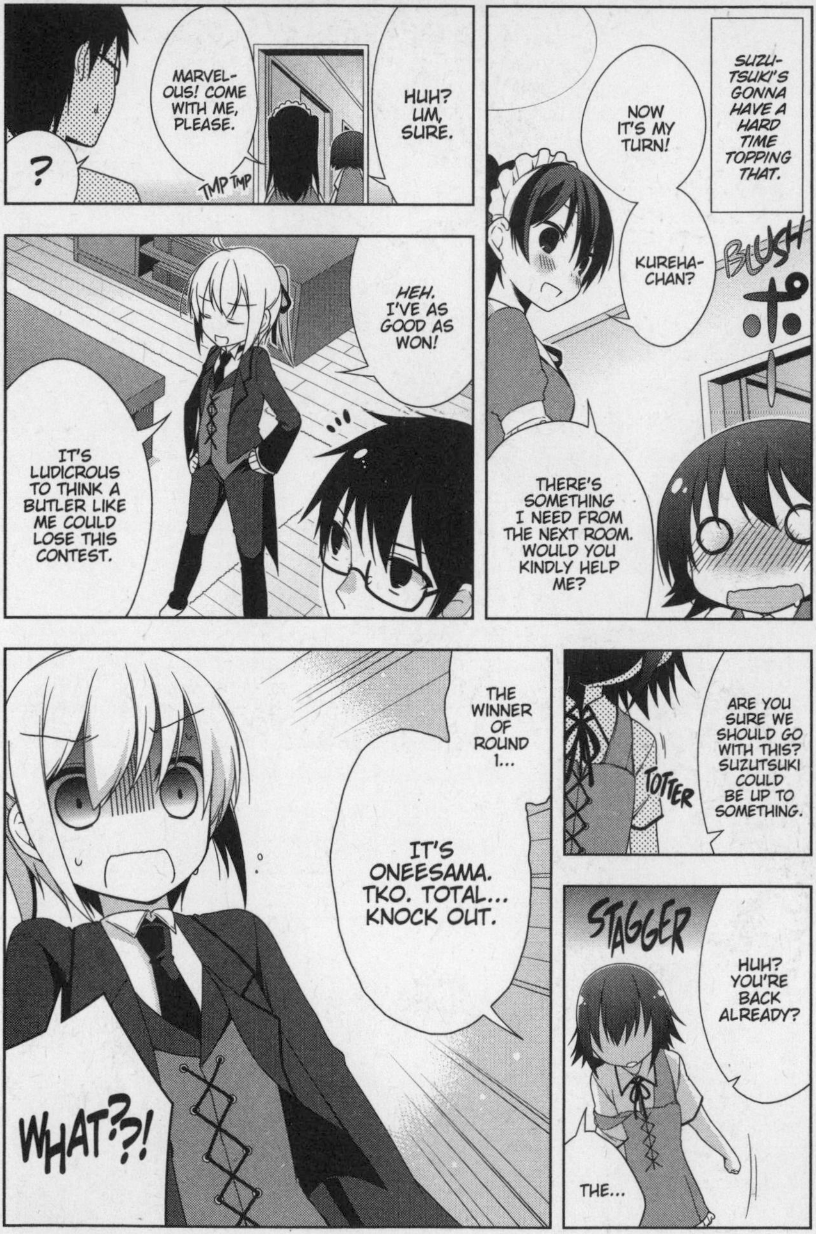
SUZU-TSUKI'S GONNA HAVE A HARD TIME TOPPING THAT.
NOW IT'S MY TURN!
BLUSH
KUREHA-CHAN?
THERE'S SOMETHING I NEED FROM THE NEXT ROOM. WOULD YOU KINDLY HELP ME?
HUH? UM, SURE.
MARVEL-OUS! COME WITH ME, PLEASE.
TMP TMP
?
HEH. I'VE AS GOOD AS WON!
IT'S LUDICROUS TO THINK A BUTLER LIKE ME COULD LOSE THIS CONTEST.
ARE YOU SURE WE SHOULD GO WITH THIS? SUZUTSUKI COULD BE UP TO SOMETHING.
TOTTER
STAGGER
HUH? YOU'RE BACK ALREADY?
THE...
THE WINNER OF ROUND 1...
IT'S ONEESAMA. TKO. TOTAL... KNOCK OUT.
WHAT?!?!

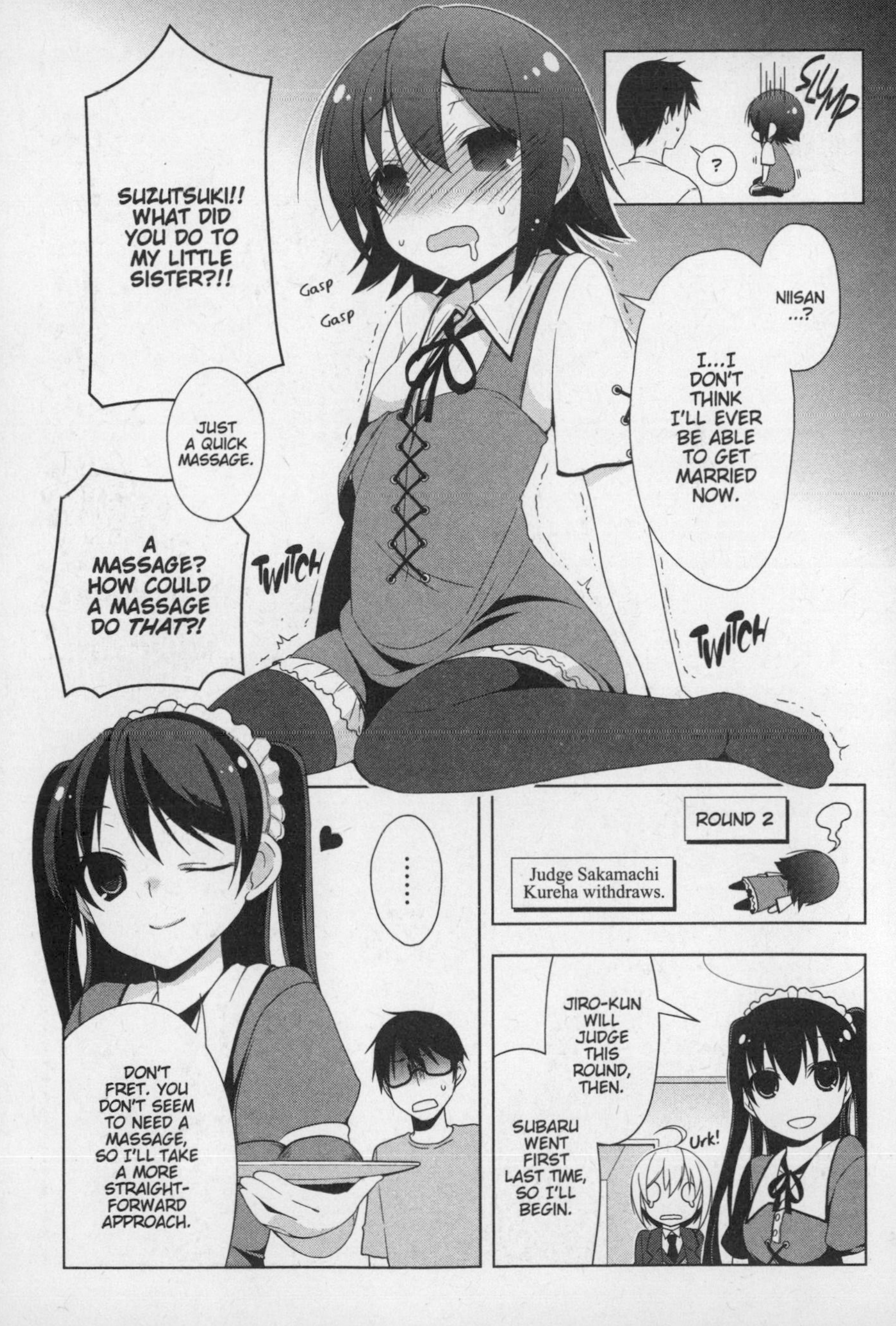
SLUMP
?
NIISAN ...?
I...I DON'T THINK I'LL EVER BE ABLE TO GET MARRIED NOW.
TWITCH
SUZUTSUKI!! WHAT DID YOU DO TO MY LITTLE SISTER?!!
Gasp
Gasp
JUST A QUICK MASSAGE.
A MASSAGE? HOW COULD A MASSAGE DO THAT?!
TWITCH
ROUND 2
Judge Sakamachi Kureha withdraws.
JIRO-KUN WILL JUDGE THIS ROUND, THEN.
SUBARU WENT FIRST LAST TIME, SO I'LL BEGIN.
Urk!
......
DON'T FRET. YOU DON'T SEEM TO NEED A MASSAGE, SO I'LL TAKE A MORE STRAIGHT-FORWARD APPROACH.

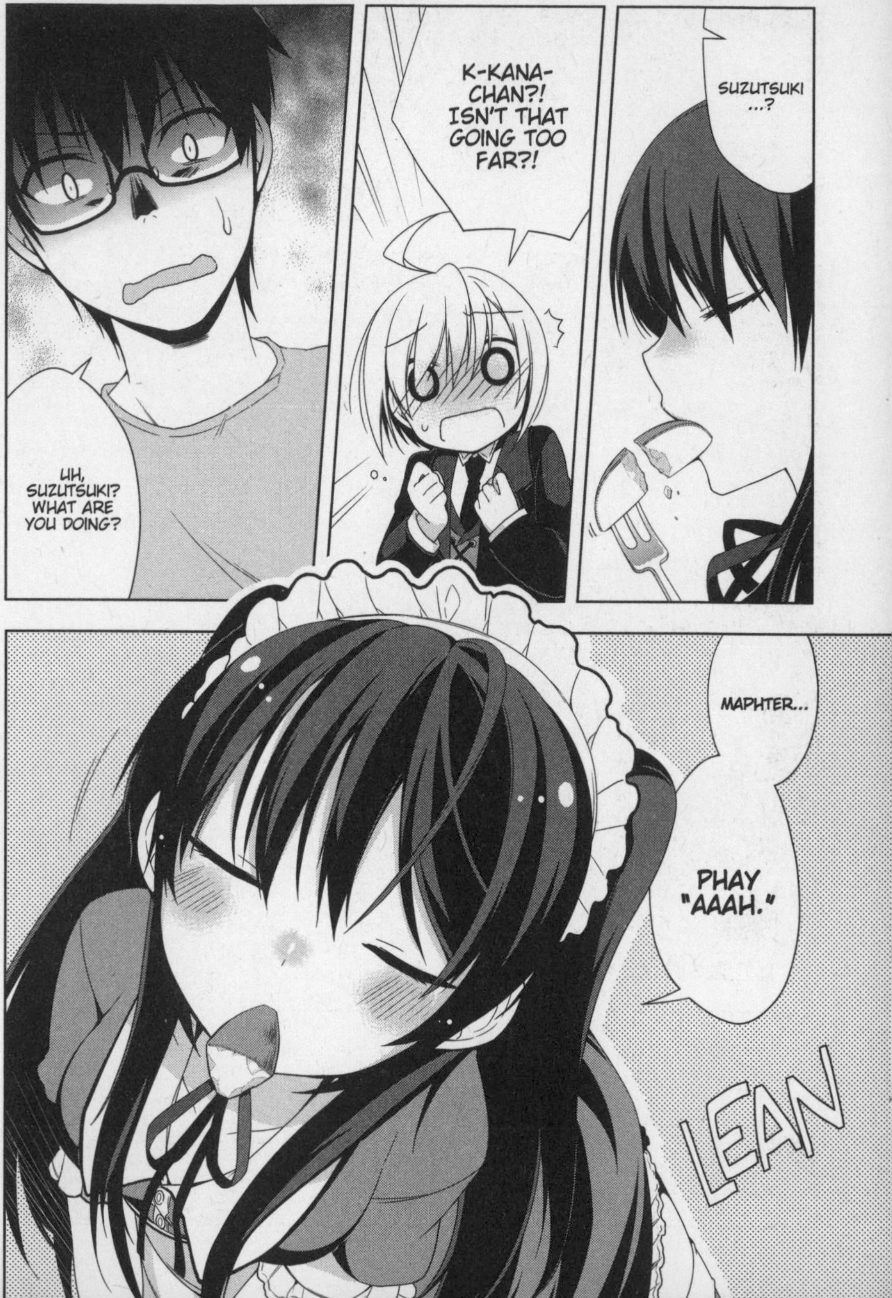
SUZUTSUKI ...?
K-KANA-CHAN?! ISN'T THAT GOING TOO FAR?!
UH, SUZUTSUKI? WHAT ARE YOU DOING?
MAPHTER...
PHAY "AAAH."
LEAN

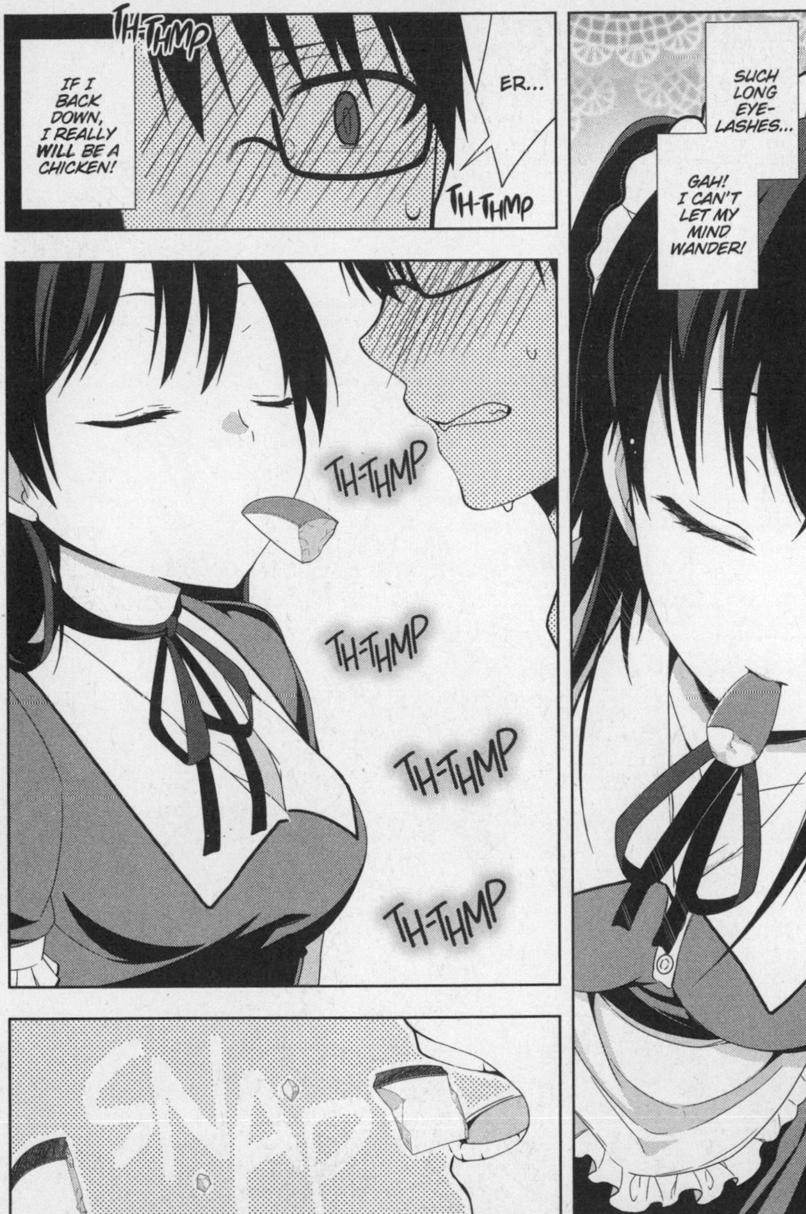
SUCH LONG EYE-LASHES...
GAH! I CAN'T LET MY MIND WANDER!
ER...
TH-THMP
TH-THMP
IF I BACK DOWN, I REALLY WILL BE A CHICKEN!
TH-THMP
TH-THMP
TH-THMP
TH-THMP
SNAP

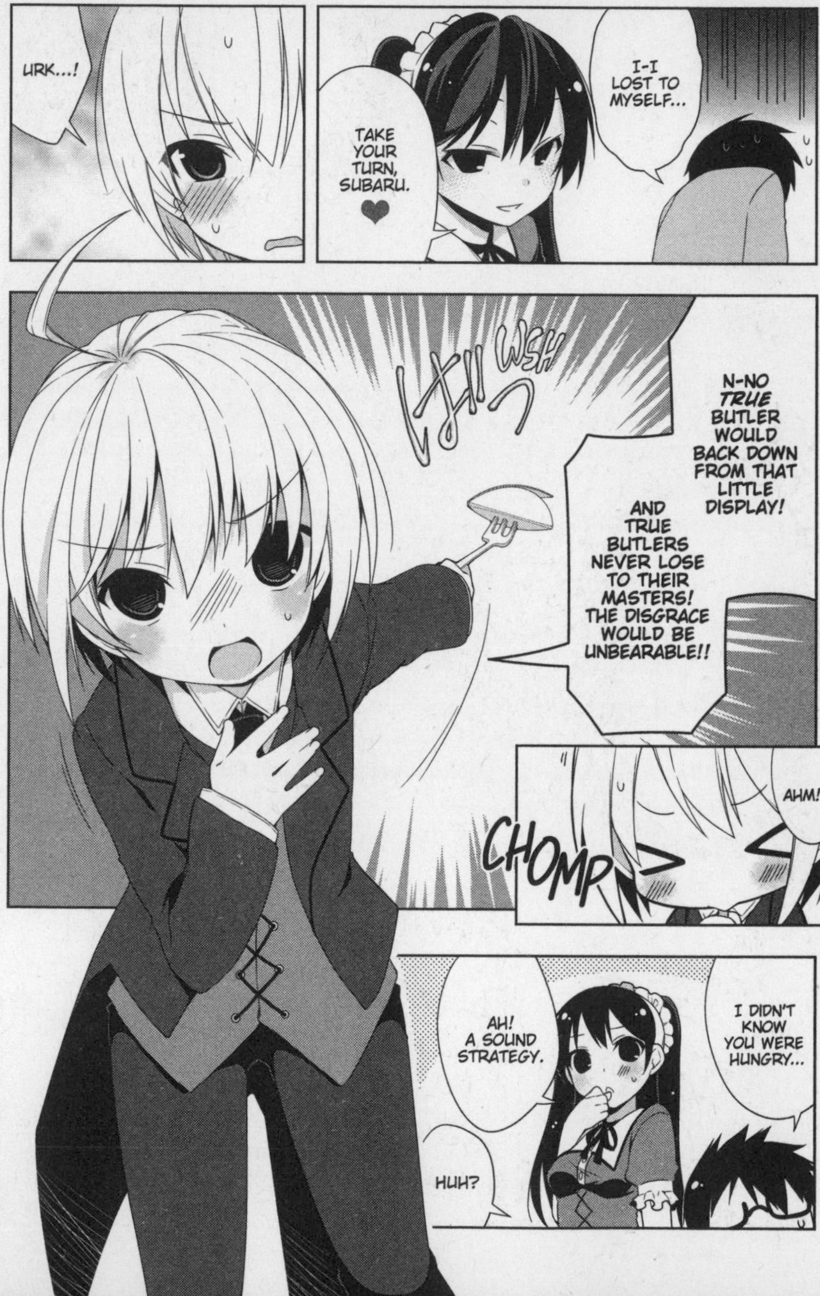
I-I LOST TO MYSELF...
TAKE YOUR TURN, SUBARU. ♥
URK...!
WSH
N-NO *TRUE* BUTLER WOULD BACK DOWN FROM THAT LITTLE DISPLAY!
AND TRUE BUTLERS NEVER LOSE TO THEIR MASTERS! THE DISGRACE WOULD BE UNBEARABLE!!
AHM!
CHOMP
I DIDN'T KNOW YOU WERE HUNGRY...
AH! A SOUND STRATEGY.
HUH?

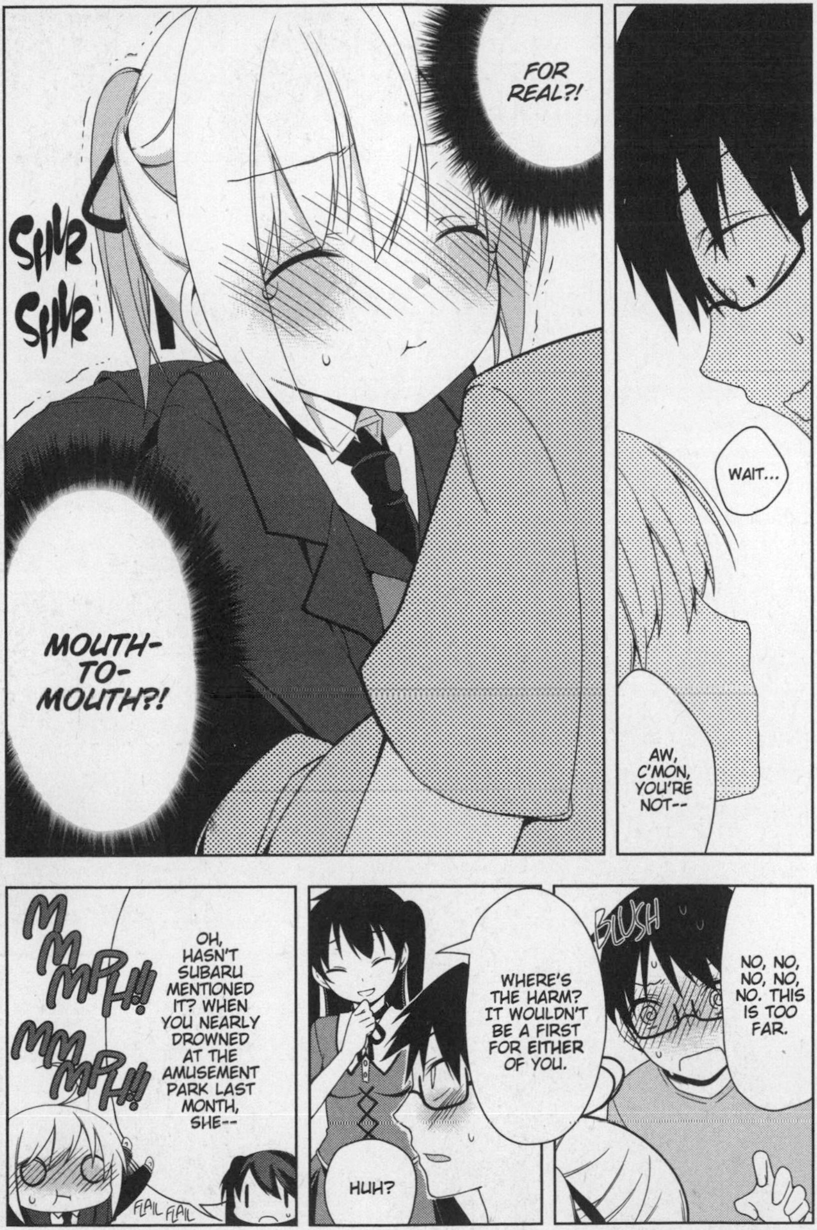
WAIT...
AW, C'MON, YOU'RE NOT--
FOR REAL?!
SHVR SHVR
MOUTH-TO-MOUTH?!
BLUSH
NO, NO, NO, NO, NO. THIS IS TOO FAR.
WHERE'S THE HARM? IT WOULDN'T BE A FIRST FOR EITHER OF YOU.
HUH?
OH, HASN'T SUBARU MENTIONED IT? WHEN YOU NEARLY DROWNED AT THE AMUSEMENT PARK LAST MONTH, SHE--
MMMPH!!
MMMPH!!
FLAIL FLAIL

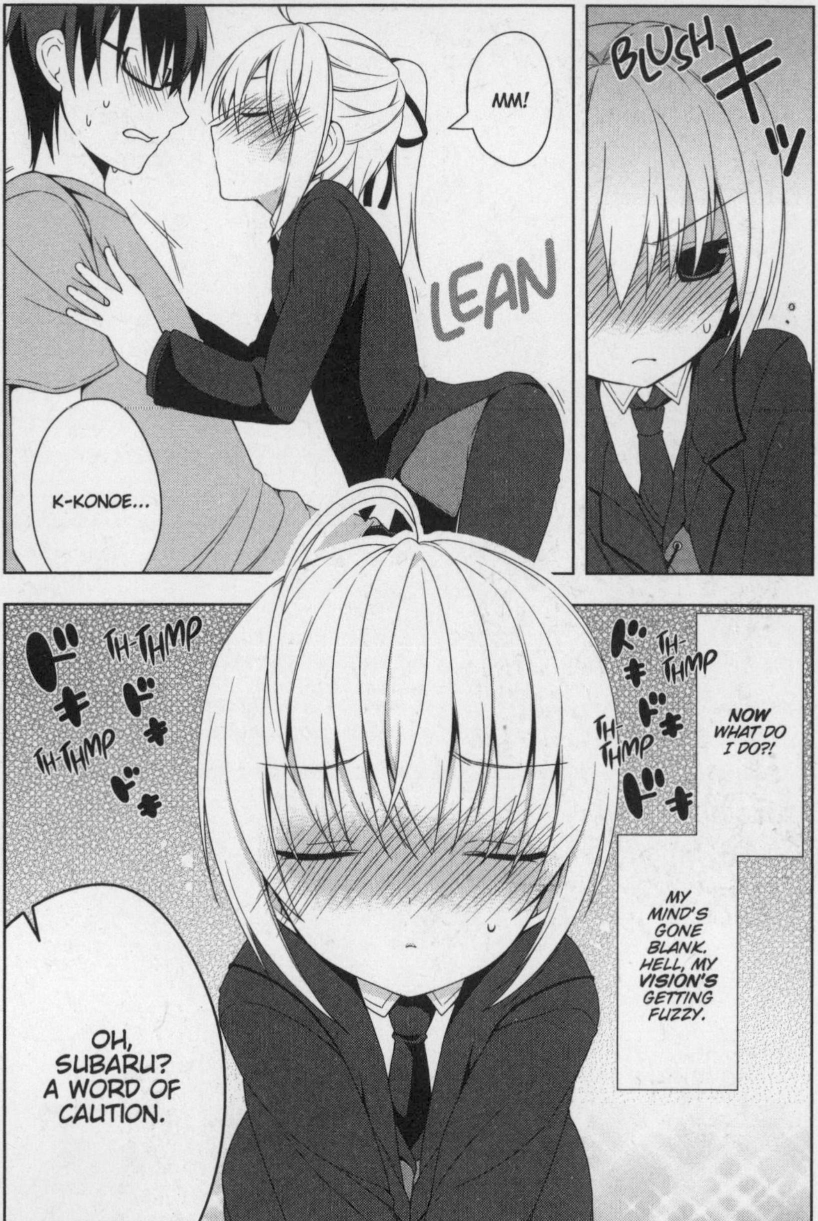
BLUSH
キッ
MM!
LEAN
K-KONOE...
TH-THMP
ドキ
TH-THMP
ドキ
ドキ
NOW WHAT DO I DO?!
MY MIND'S GONE BLANK. HELL, MY VISION'S GETTING FUZZY.
TH-THMP
ドキ
ドキ
TH-THMP
ドキ
OH, SUBARU? A WORD OF CAUTION.

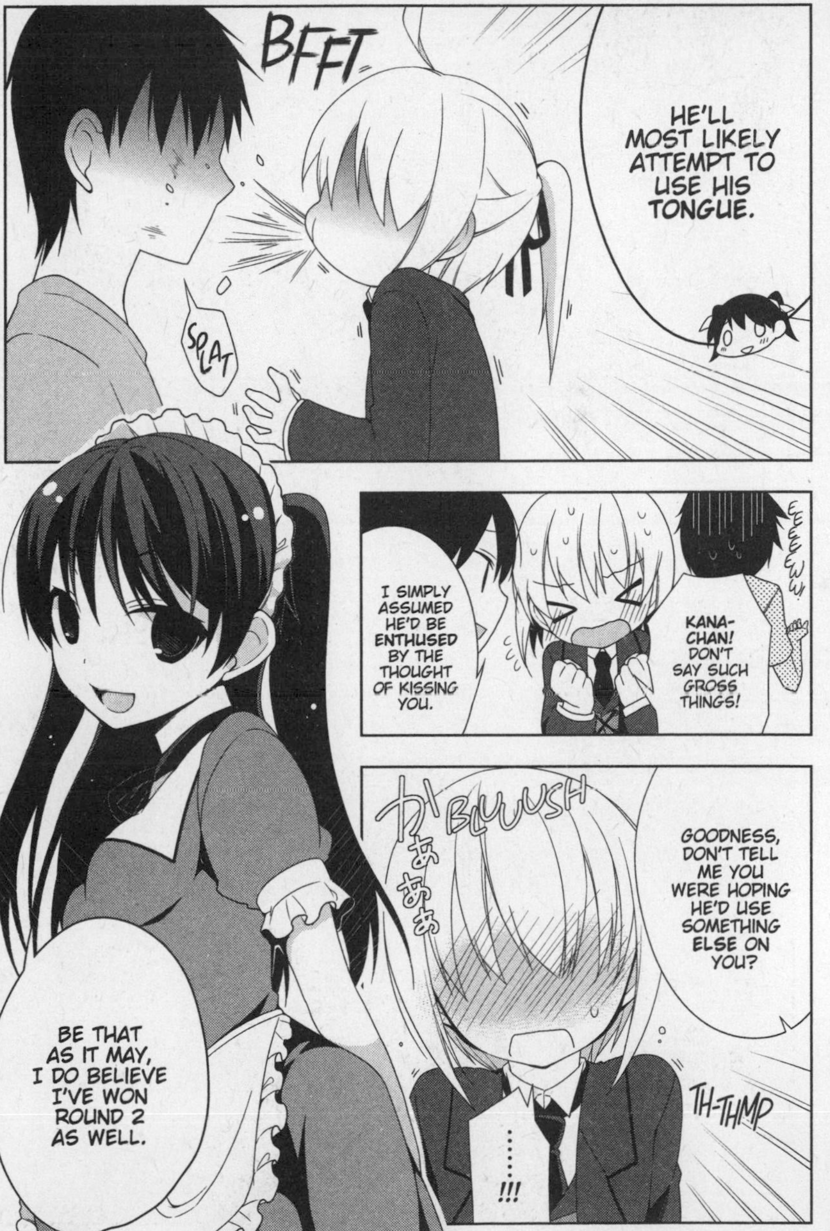
HE'LL MOST LIKELY ATTEMPT TO USE HIS TONGUE.
BFFT
SPLAT
EEEEWW!
KANA-CHAN! DON'T SAY SUCH GROSS THINGS!
I SIMPLY ASSUMED HE'D BE ENTHUSED BY THE THOUGHT OF KISSING YOU.
GOODNESS, DON'T TELL ME YOU WERE HOPING HE'D USE SOMETHING ELSE ON YOU?
BLUUUSH
わあああ
TH-THMP
......!!!
BE THAT AS IT MAY, I DO BELIEVE I'VE WON ROUND 2 AS WELL.

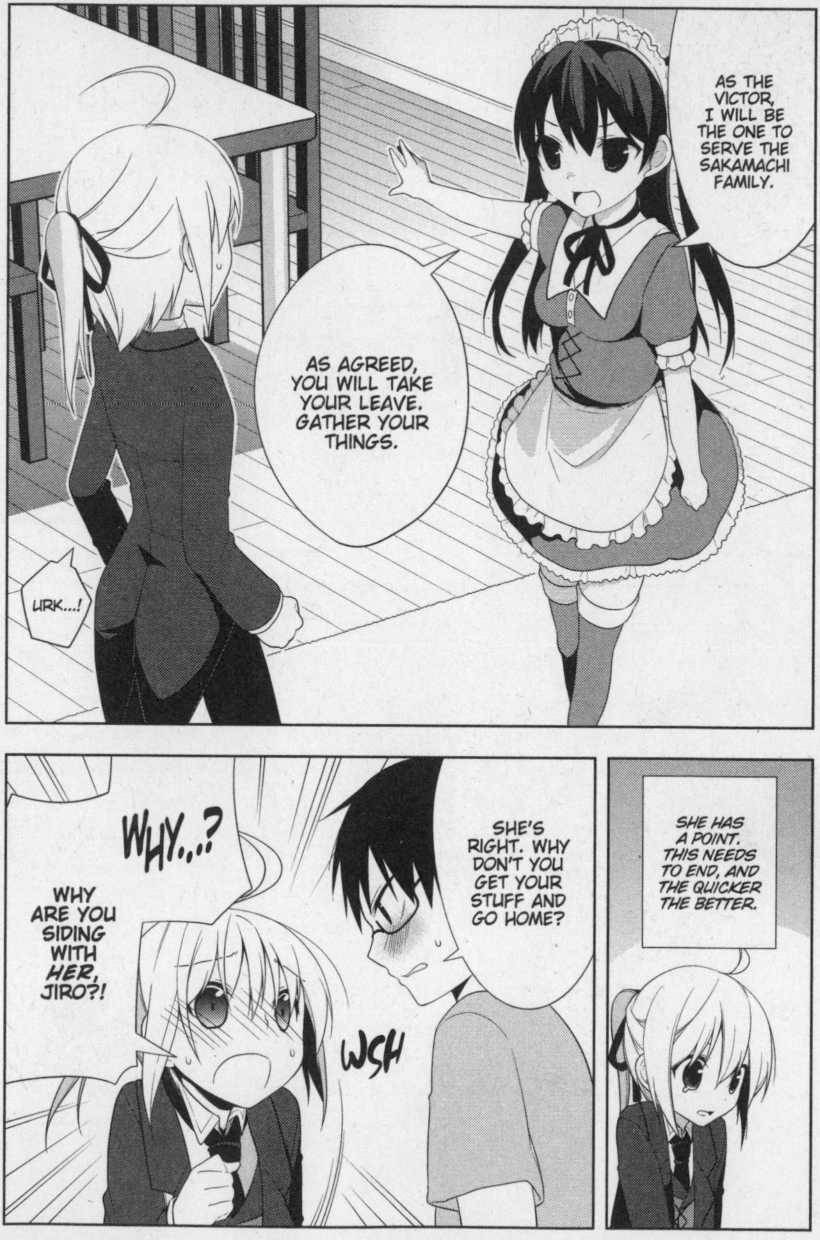
AS THE VICTOR, I WILL BE THE ONE TO SERVE THE SAKAMACHI FAMILY.
AS AGREED, YOU WILL TAKE YOUR LEAVE. GATHER YOUR THINGS.
URK...!
SHE HAS A POINT. THIS NEEDS TO END, AND THE QUICKER THE BETTER.
SHE'S RIGHT. WHY DON'T YOU GET YOUR STUFF AND GO HOME?
WHY...?
WHY ARE YOU SIDING WITH *HER*, JIRO?!
WSH

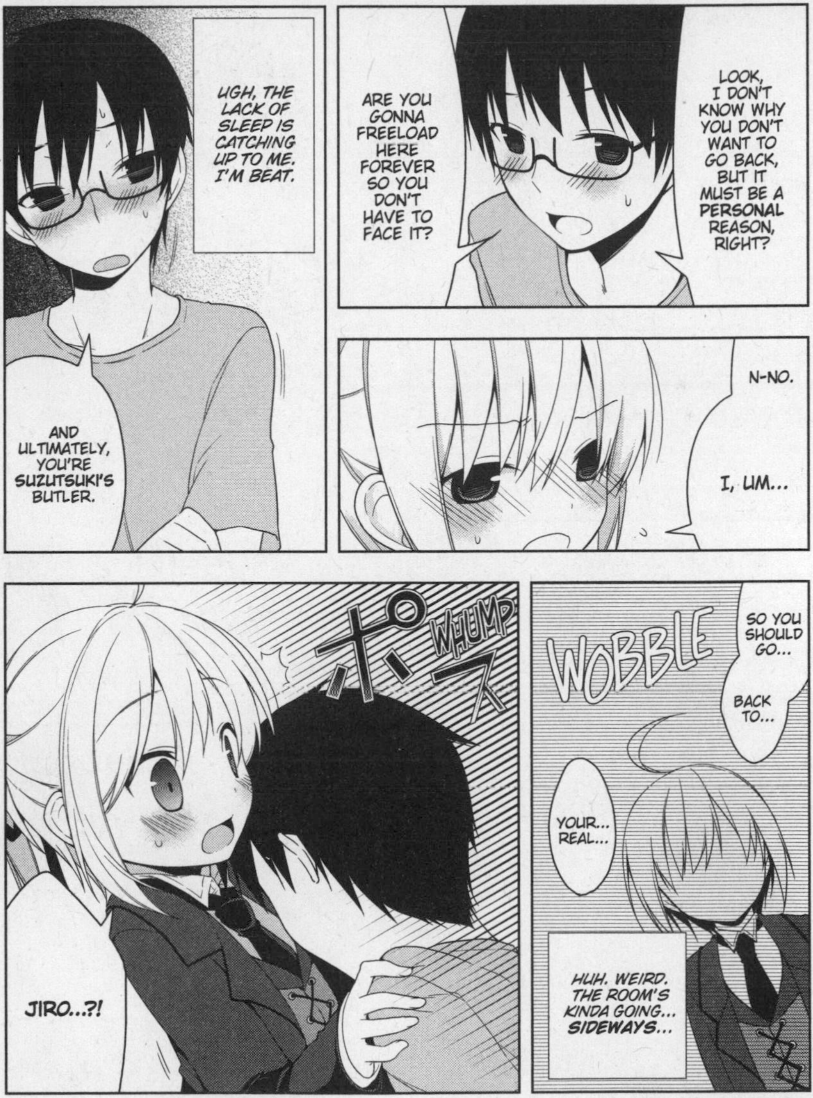
LOOK, I DON'T KNOW WHY YOU DON'T WANT TO GO BACK, BUT IT MUST BE A PERSONAL REASON, RIGHT?
ARE YOU GONNA FREELOAD HERE FOREVER SO YOU DON'T HAVE TO FACE IT?
N-NO.
I, UM...
UGH, THE LACK OF SLEEP IS CATCHING UP TO ME. I'M BEAT.
AND ULTIMATELY, YOU'RE SUZUTSUKI'S BUTLER.
SO YOU SHOULD GO...
BACK TO...
WOBBLE
YOUR... REAL...
HUH. WEIRD. THE ROOM'S KINDA GOING... SIDEWAYS...
WHUMP
JIRO...?!

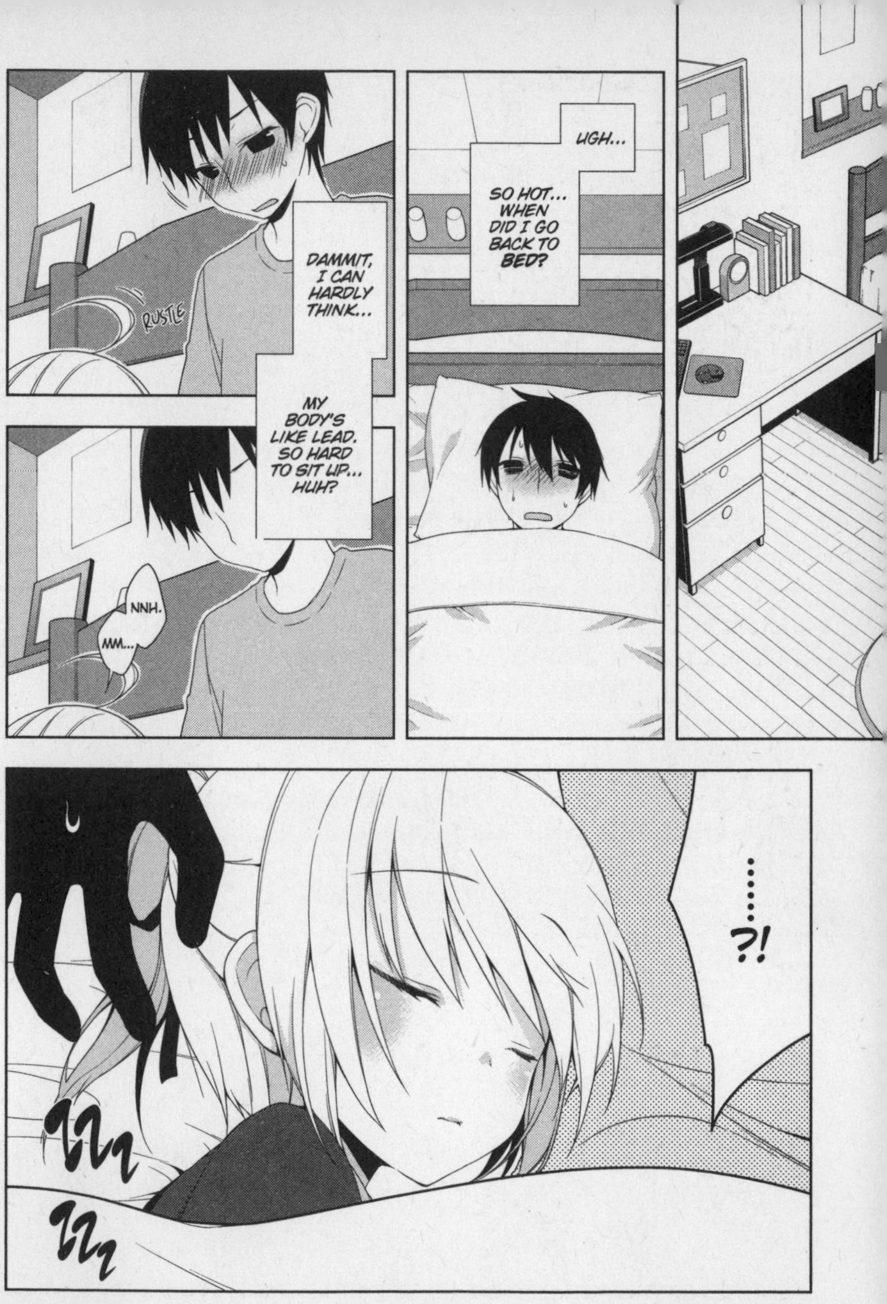
UGH...
SO HOT... WHEN DID I GO BACK TO BED?
DAMMIT, I CAN HARDLY THINK...
RUSTLE
MY BODY'S LIKE LEAD. SO HARD TO SIT UP... HUH?
NNH.
MM...
......?!
ZZZ
ZZZ

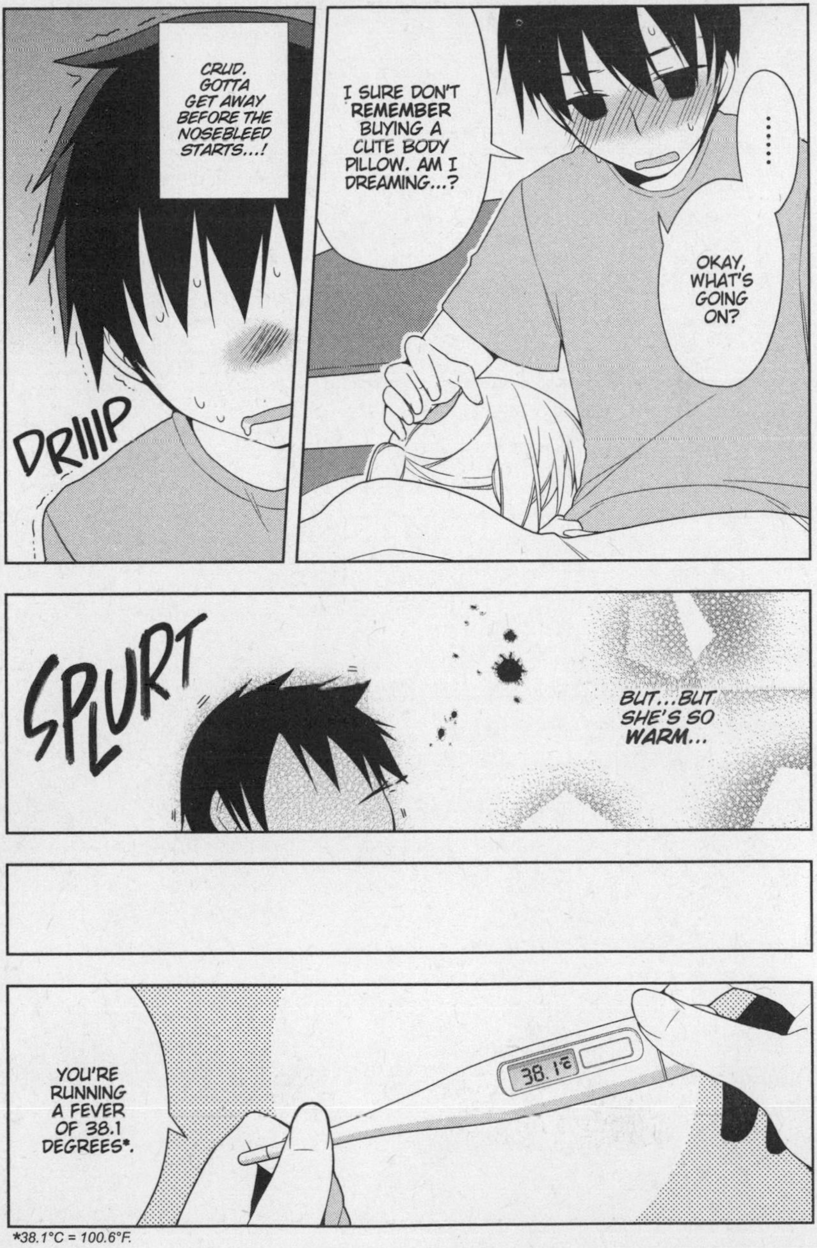
I SURE DON'T REMEMBER BUYING A CUTE BODY PILLOW. AM I DREAMING...?
......
OKAY, WHAT'S GOING ON?
CRUD. GOTTA GET AWAY BEFORE THE NOSEBLEED STARTS...!
DRIIIIP
SPLURT
BUT...BUT SHE'S SO WARM...
YOU'RE RUNNING A FEVER OF 38.1 DEGREES*.
38.1°C

*38.1°C = 100.6°F.

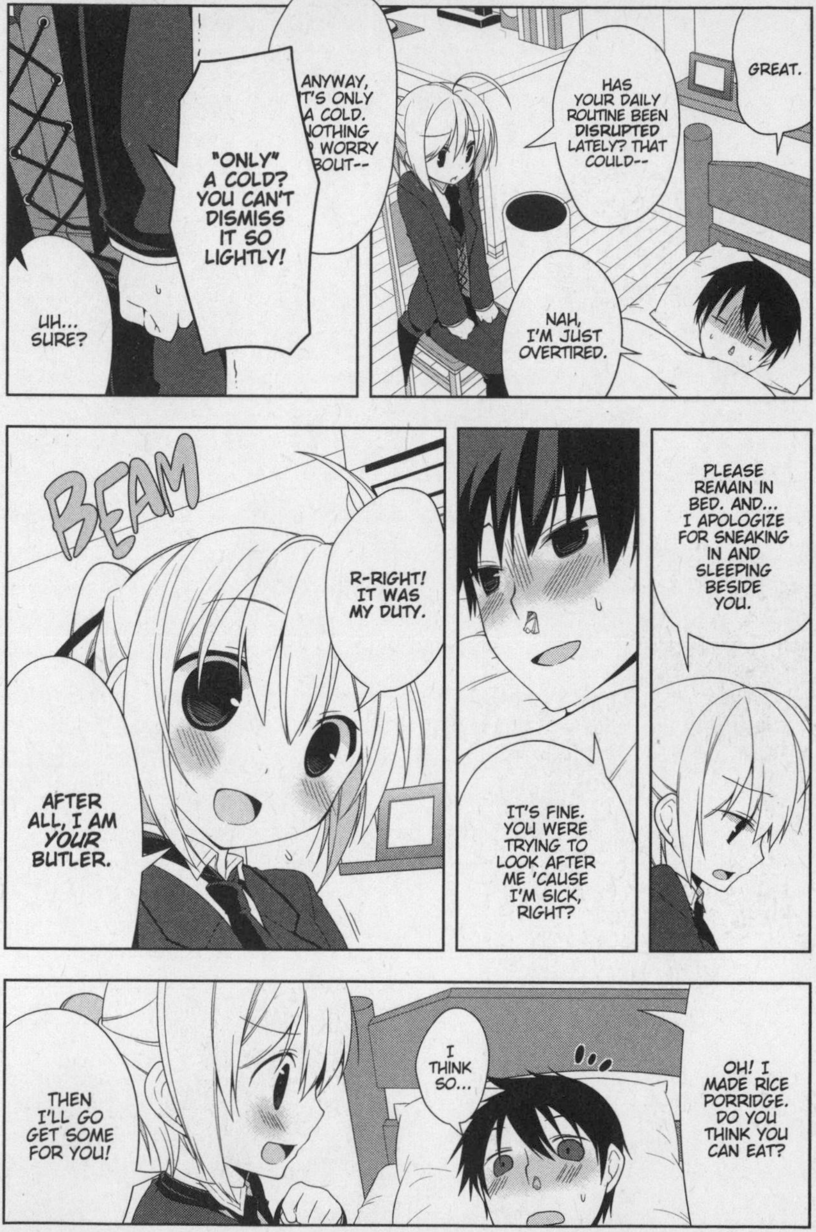
GREAT.
HAS YOUR DAILY ROUTINE BEEN DISRUPTED LATELY? THAT COULD--
NAH, I'M JUST OVERTIRED.
ANYWAY, 'T'S ONLY A COLD. OTHING O WORRY BOUT--
"ONLY" A COLD? YOU CAN'T DISMISS IT SO LIGHTLY!
UH... SURE?
PLEASE REMAIN IN BED. AND... I APOLOGIZE FOR SNEAKING IN AND SLEEPING BESIDE YOU.
IT'S FINE. YOU WERE TRYING TO LOOK AFTER ME 'CAUSE I'M SICK, RIGHT?
BEAM
R-RIGHT! IT WAS MY DUTY.
AFTER ALL, I AM *YOUR* BUTLER.
OH! I MADE RICE PORRIDGE. DO YOU THINK YOU CAN EAT?
...
I THINK SO...
THEN I'LL GO GET SOME FOR YOU!

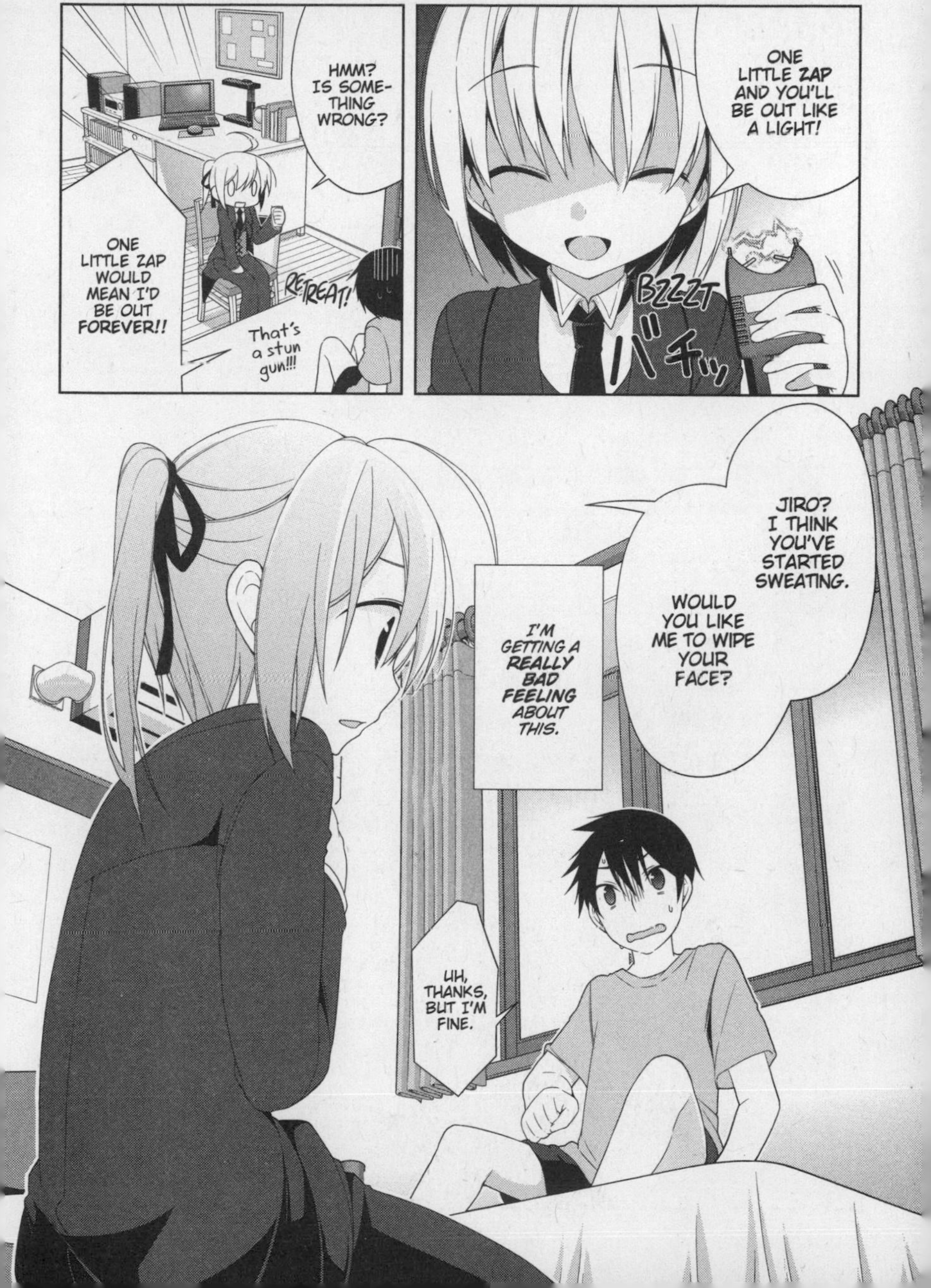
ONE LITTLE ZAP AND YOU'LL BE OUT LIKE A LIGHT!
BZZZT
バチッ
HMM? IS SOME-THING WRONG?
RETREAT!
ONE LITTLE ZAP WOULD MEAN I'D BE OUT FOREVER!!
That's a stun gun!!!
JIRO? I THINK YOU'VE STARTED SWEATING.
WOULD YOU LIKE ME TO WIPE YOUR FACE?
I'M GETTING A REALLY BAD FEELING ABOUT THIS.
UH, THANKS, BUT I'M FINE.

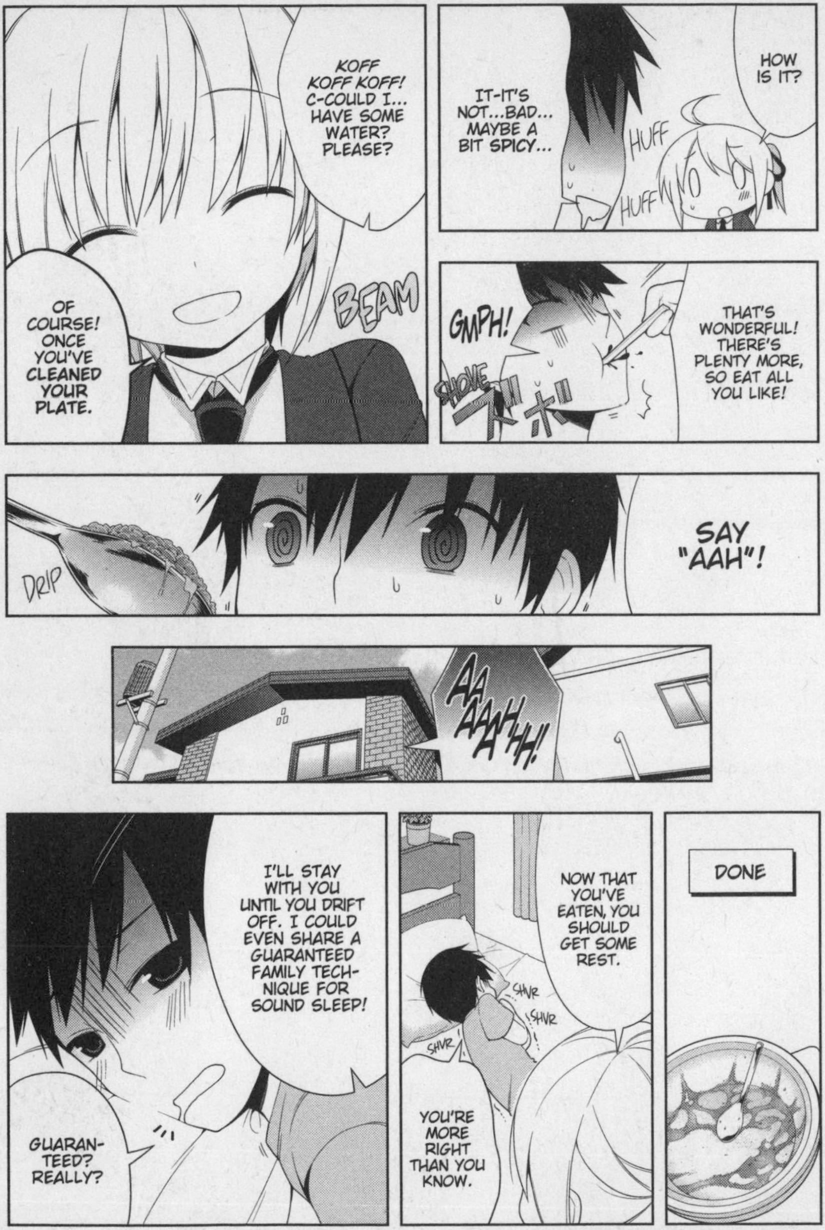
HOW IS IT?
IT-IT'S NOT...BAD... MAYBE A BIT SPICY...
HUFF
HUFF
THAT'S WONDERFUL! THERE'S PLENTY MORE, SO EAT ALL YOU LIKE!
GMPH!
SHOVE
KOFF KOFF KOFF! C-COULD I... HAVE SOME WATER? PLEASE?
BEAM
OF COURSE! ONCE YOU'VE CLEANED YOUR PLATE.
SAY "AAH"!
DRIP
AAAAAHHH!
DONE
NOW THAT YOU'VE EATEN, YOU SHOULD GET SOME REST.
SHVR
SHVR
SHVR
YOU'RE MORE RIGHT THAN YOU KNOW.
I'LL STAY WITH YOU UNTIL YOU DRIFT OFF. I COULD EVEN SHARE A GUARANTEED FAMILY TECHNIQUE FOR SOUND SLEEP!
GUARANTEED? REALLY?

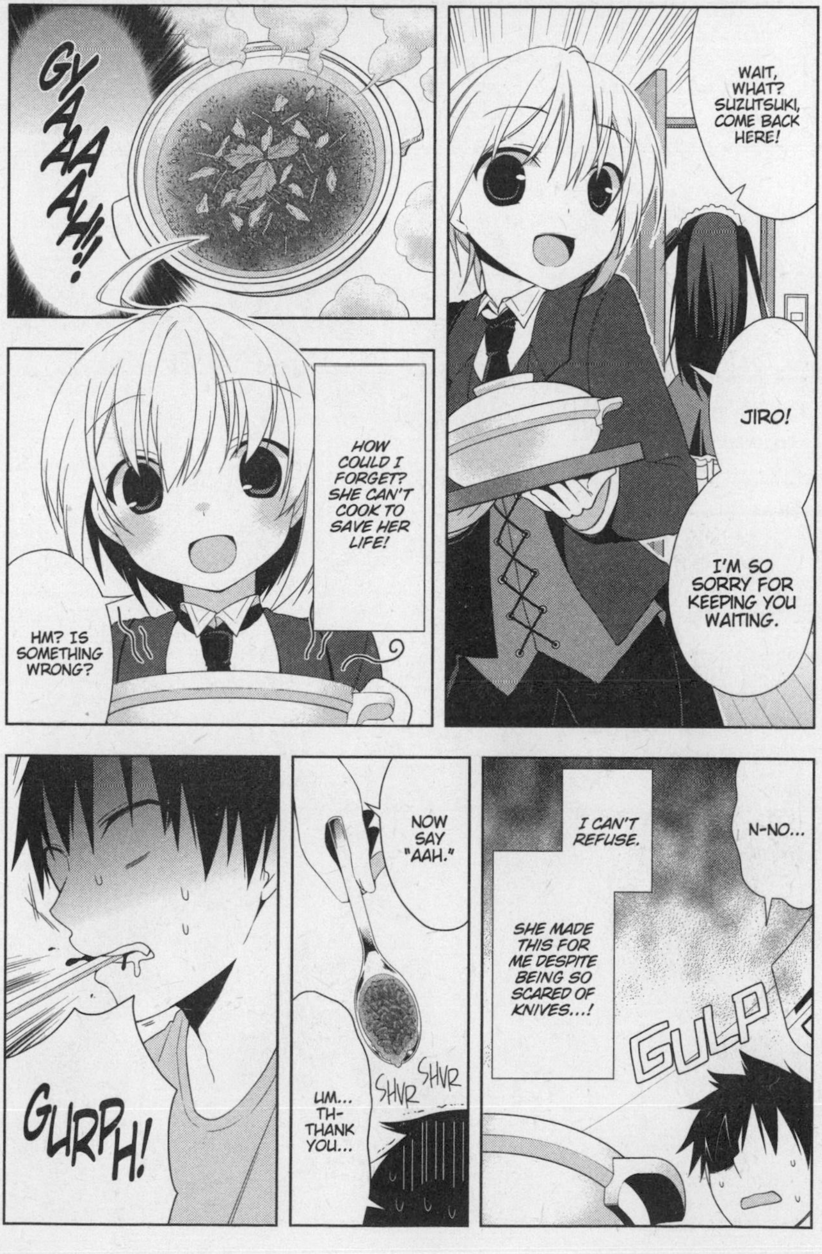
WAIT, WHAT? SUZUTSUKI, COME BACK HERE!
JIRO!
I'M SO SORRY FOR KEEPING YOU WAITING.
GYAAAAH!!
HOW COULD I FORGET? SHE CAN'T COOK TO SAVE HER LIFE!
HM? IS SOMETHING WRONG?
N-NO...
I CAN'T REFUSE.
SHE MADE THIS FOR ME DESPITE BEING SO SCARED OF KNIVES...!
GULP
NOW SAY "AAH."
SHVR
SHVR
UM... TH-THANK YOU...
GURPH!

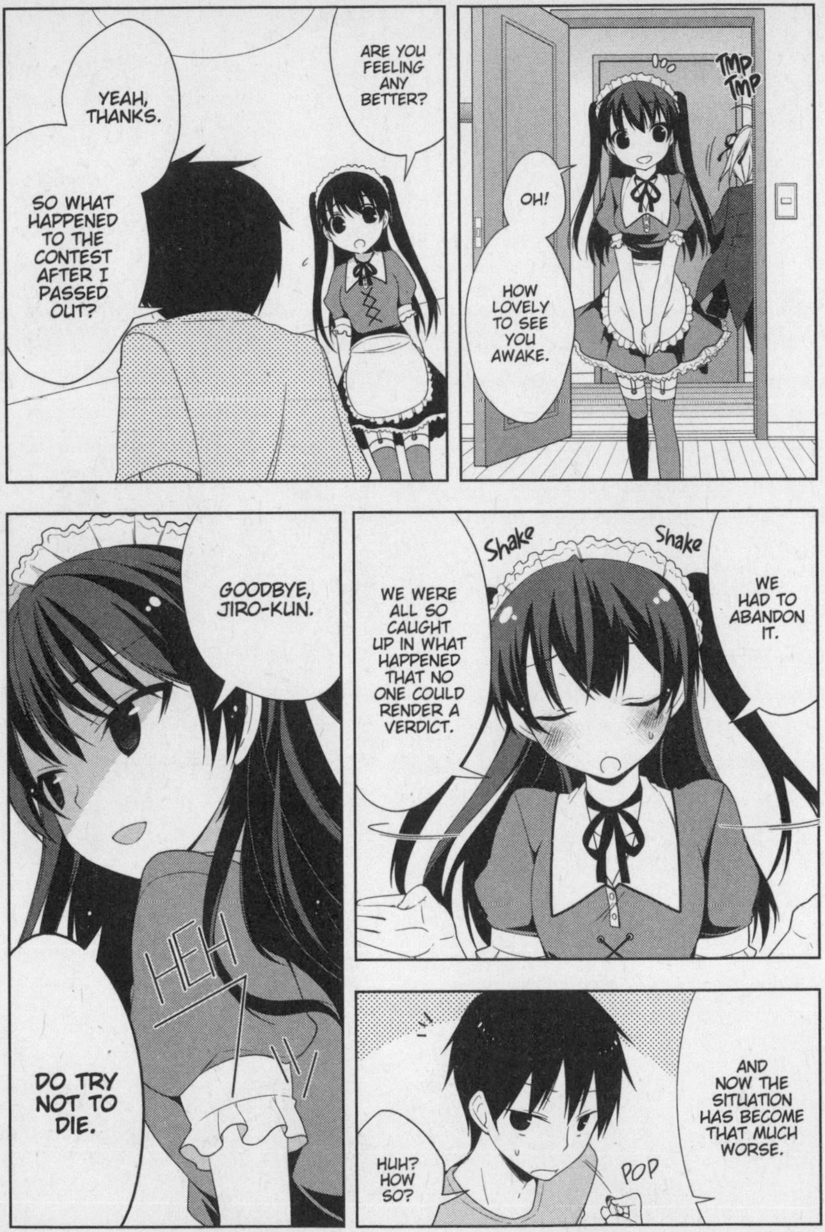

TMP TMP
OH!
HOW LOVELY TO SEE YOU AWAKE.
ARE YOU FEELING ANY BETTER?
YEAH, THANKS.
SO WHAT HAPPENED TO THE CONTEST AFTER I PASSED OUT?
Shake
Shake
WE HAD TO ABANDON IT.
WE WERE ALL SO CAUGHT UP IN WHAT HAPPENED THAT NO ONE COULD RENDER A VERDICT.
AND NOW THE SITUATION HAS BECOME THAT MUCH WORSE.
POP
HUH? HOW SO?
GOODBYE, JIRO-KUN.
HEH
DO TRY NOT TO DIE.

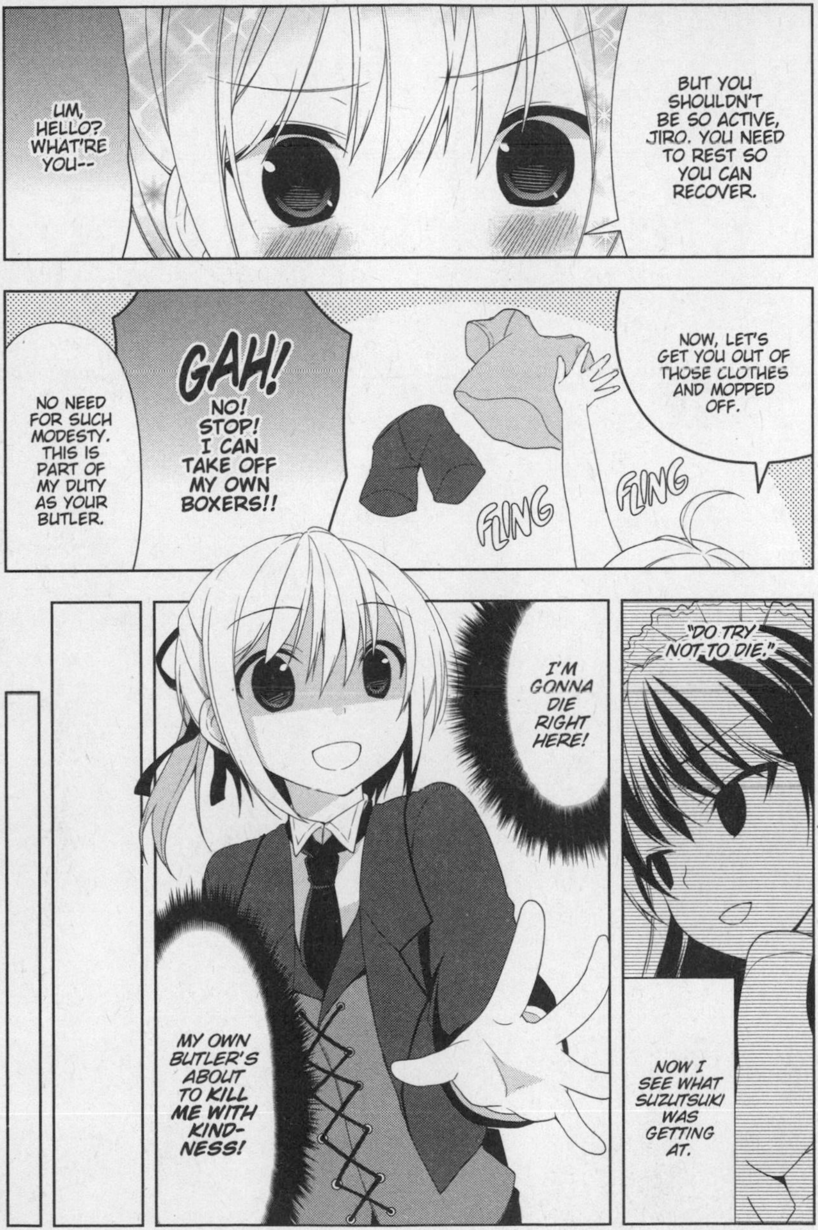
BUT YOU SHOULDN'T BE SO ACTIVE, JIRO. YOU NEED TO REST SO YOU CAN RECOVER.
UM, HELLO? WHAT'RE YOU--
NOW, LET'S GET YOU OUT OF THOSE CLOTHES AND MOPPED OFF.
FLING
FLING
GAH!
NO! STOP! I CAN TAKE OFF MY OWN BOXERS!!
NO NEED FOR SUCH MODESTY. THIS IS PART OF MY DUTY AS YOUR BUTLER.
"DO TRY NOT TO DIE."
NOW I SEE WHAT SUZUTSUKI WAS GETTING AT.
I'M GONNA DIE RIGHT HERE!
MY OWN BUTLER'S ABOUT TO KILL ME WITH KINDNESS!

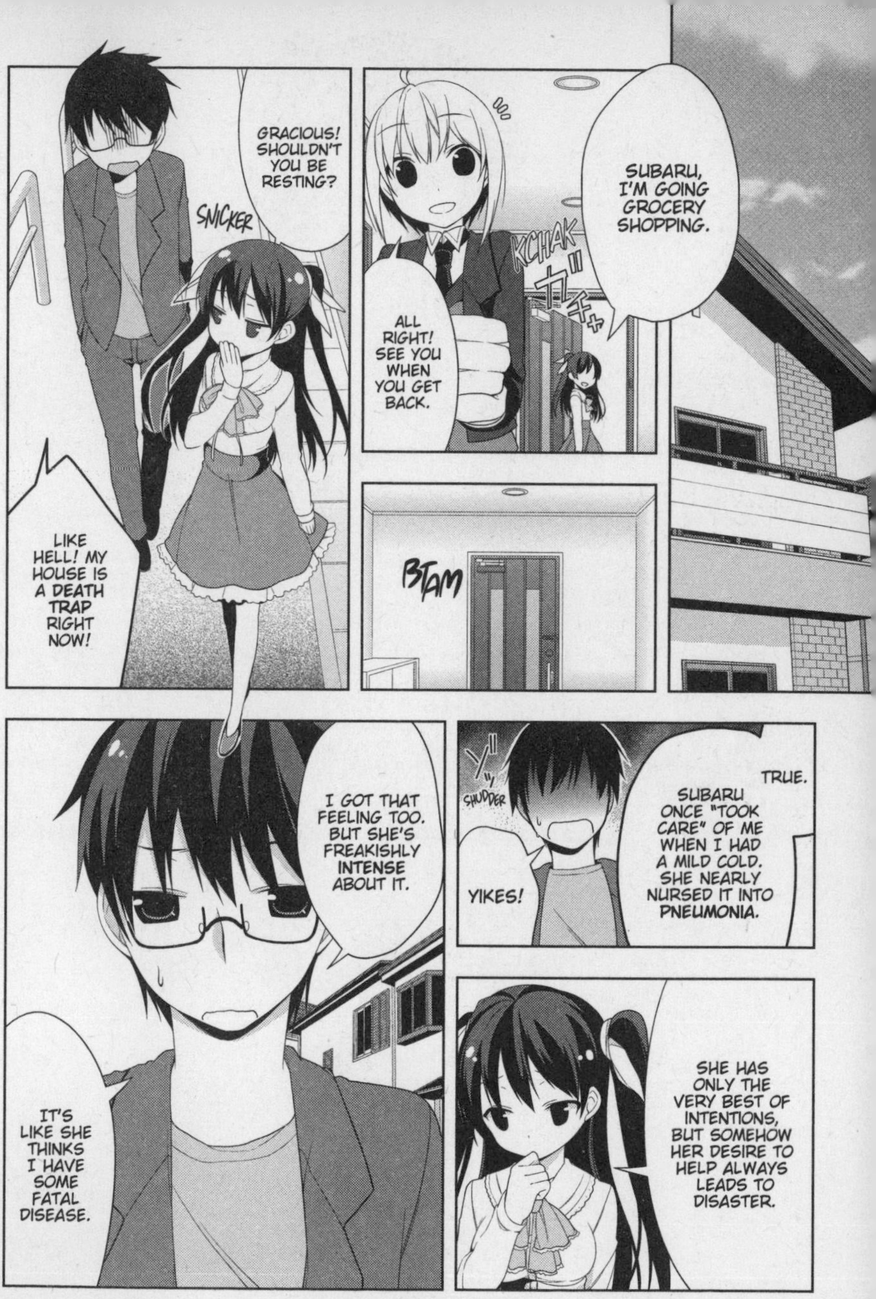
SUBARU, I'M GOING GROCERY SHOPPING.
KCHAK
ALL RIGHT! SEE YOU WHEN YOU GET BACK.
BTAM
GRACIOUS! SHOULDN'T YOU BE RESTING?
SNICKER
LIKE HELL! MY HOUSE IS A DEATH TRAP RIGHT NOW!
TRUE. SUBARU ONCE "TOOK CARE" OF ME WHEN I HAD A MILD COLD. SHE NEARLY NURSED IT INTO PNEUMONIA.
SHUDDER
YIKES!
SHE HAS ONLY THE VERY BEST OF INTENTIONS, BUT SOMEHOW HER DESIRE TO HELP ALWAYS LEADS TO DISASTER.
I GOT THAT FEELING TOO. BUT SHE'S FREAKISHLY INTENSE ABOUT IT.
IT'S LIKE SHE THINKS I HAVE SOME FATAL DISEASE.

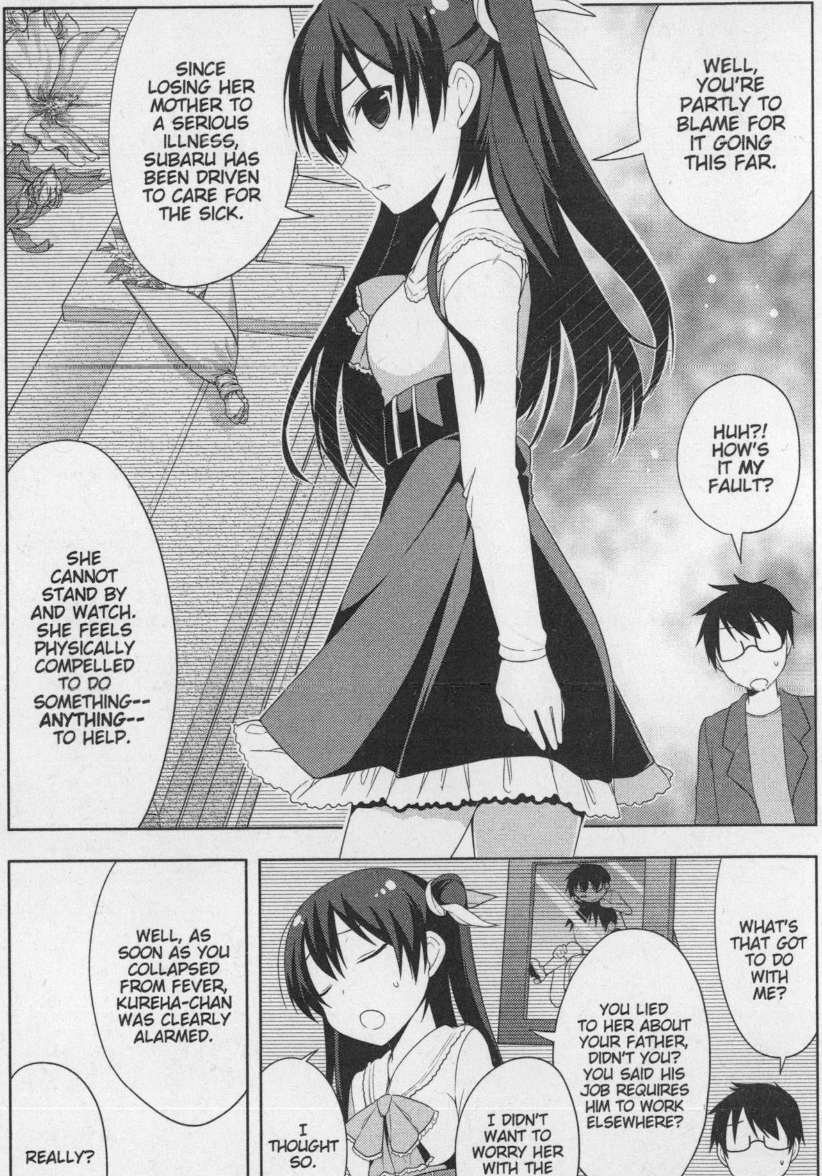
WELL, YOU'RE PARTLY TO BLAME FOR IT GOING THIS FAR.
SINCE LOSING HER MOTHER TO A SERIOUS ILLNESS, SUBARU HAS BEEN DRIVEN TO CARE FOR THE SICK.
HUH?! HOW'S IT MY FAULT?
SHE CANNOT STAND BY AND WATCH. SHE FEELS PHYSICALLY COMPELLED TO DO SOMETHING-- ANYTHING-- TO HELP.
WHAT'S THAT GOT TO DO WITH ME?
YOU LIED TO HER ABOUT YOUR FATHER, DIDN'T YOU? YOU SAID HIS JOB REQUIRES HIM TO WORK ELSEWHERE?
I DIDN'T WANT TO WORRY HER WITH THE TRUTH.
I THOUGHT SO.
WELL, AS SOON AS YOU COLLAPSED FROM FEVER, KUREHA-CHAN WAS CLEARLY ALARMED.
REALLY?

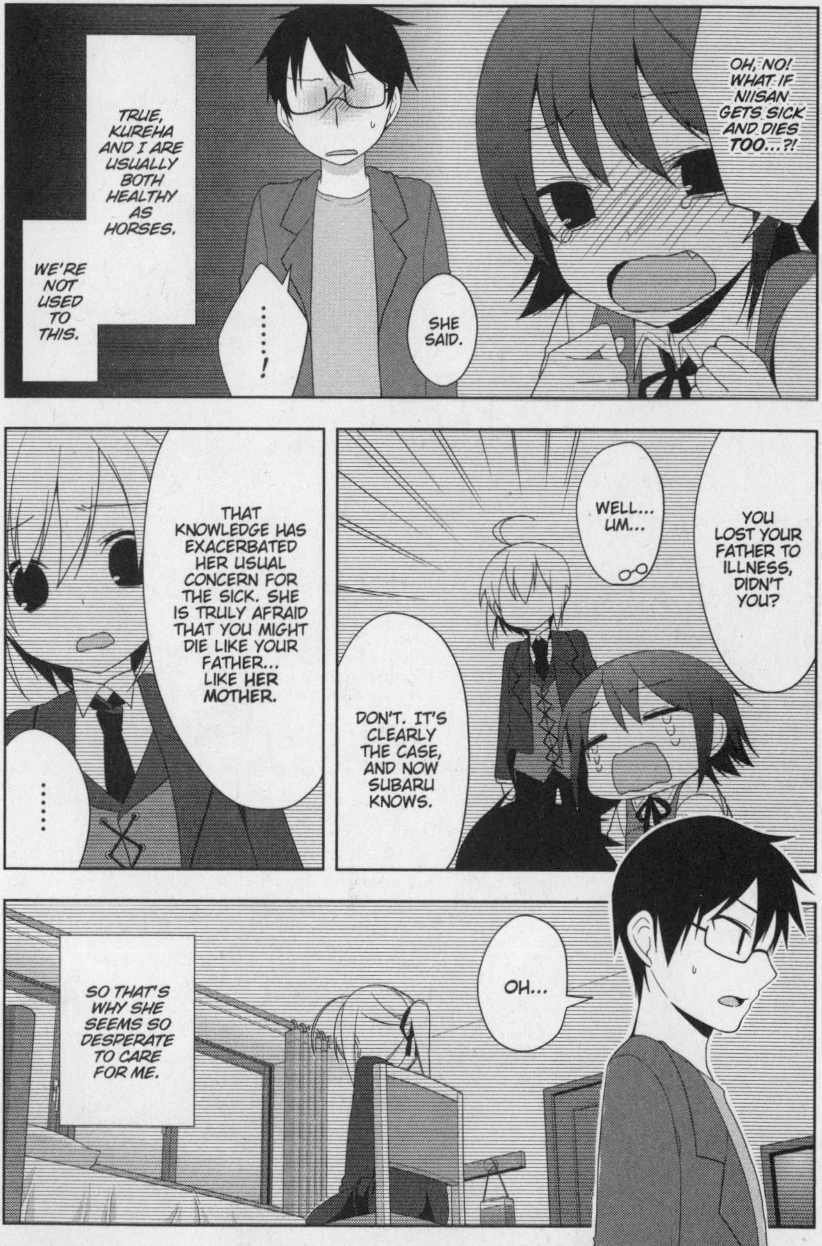
OH, NO! WHAT IF NIISAN GETS SICK AND DIES TOO...?!
SHE SAID.
......!
TRUE, KUREHA AND I ARE USUALLY BOTH HEALTHY AS HORSES.
WE'RE NOT USED TO THIS.
YOU LOST YOUR FATHER TO ILLNESS, DIDN'T YOU?
WELL... UM...
DON'T. IT'S CLEARLY THE CASE, AND NOW SUBARU KNOWS.
THAT KNOWLEDGE HAS EXACERBATED HER USUAL CONCERN FOR THE SICK. SHE IS TRULY AFRAID THAT YOU MIGHT DIE LIKE YOUR FATHER... LIKE HER MOTHER.
......
OH...
SO THAT'S WHY SHE SEEMS SO DESPERATE TO CARE FOR ME.

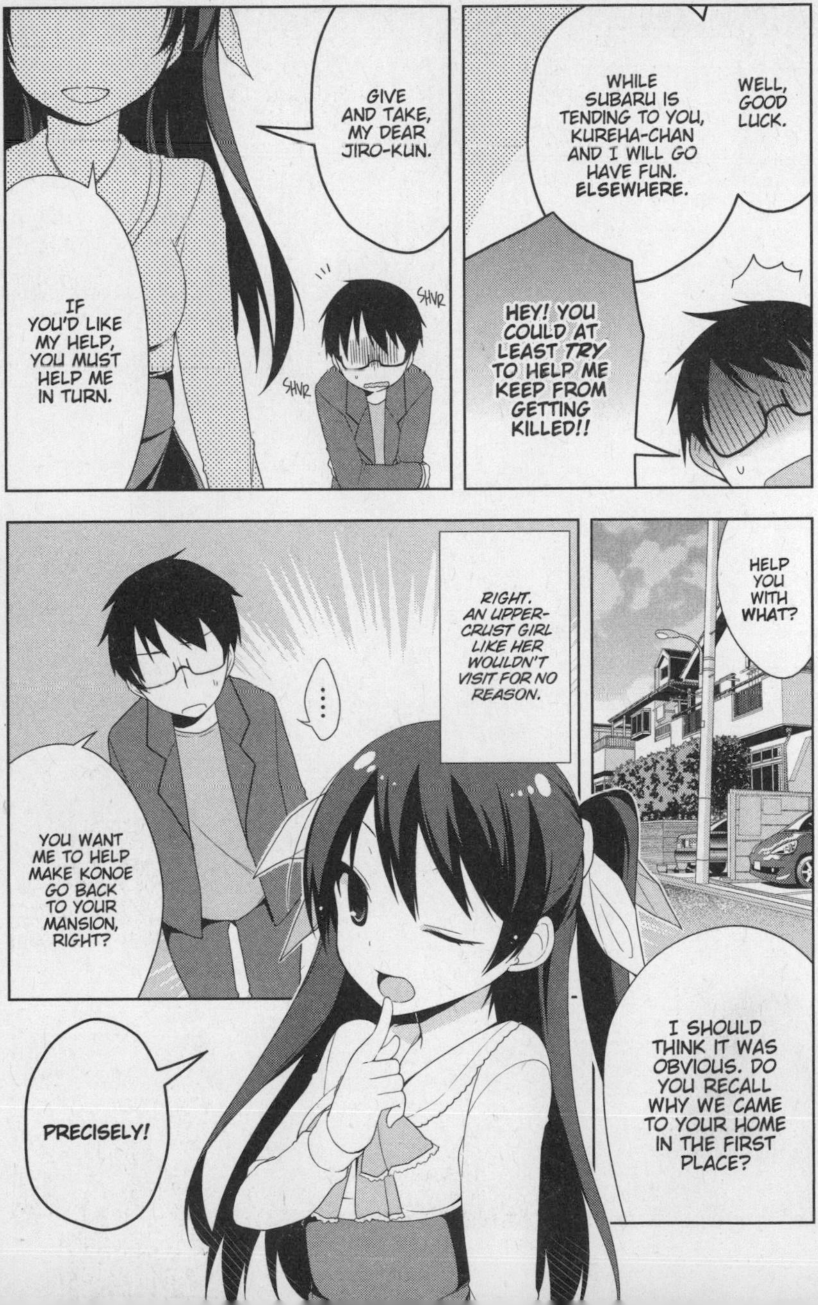
WELL, GOOD LUCK.
WHILE SUBARU IS TENDING TO YOU, KUREHA-CHAN AND I WILL GO HAVE FUN. ELSEWHERE.
HEY! YOU COULD AT LEAST *TRY* TO HELP ME KEEP FROM GETTING KILLED!!
GIVE AND TAKE, MY DEAR JIRO-KUN.
SHVR
SHVR
IF YOU'D LIKE MY HELP, YOU MUST HELP ME IN TURN.
HELP YOU WITH WHAT?
I SHOULD THINK IT WAS OBVIOUS. DO YOU RECALL WHY WE CAME TO YOUR HOME IN THE FIRST PLACE?
RIGHT. AN UPPER-CRUST GIRL LIKE HER WOULDN'T VISIT FOR NO REASON.
....
YOU WANT ME TO HELP MAKE KONOE GO BACK TO YOUR MANSION, RIGHT?
PRECISELY!

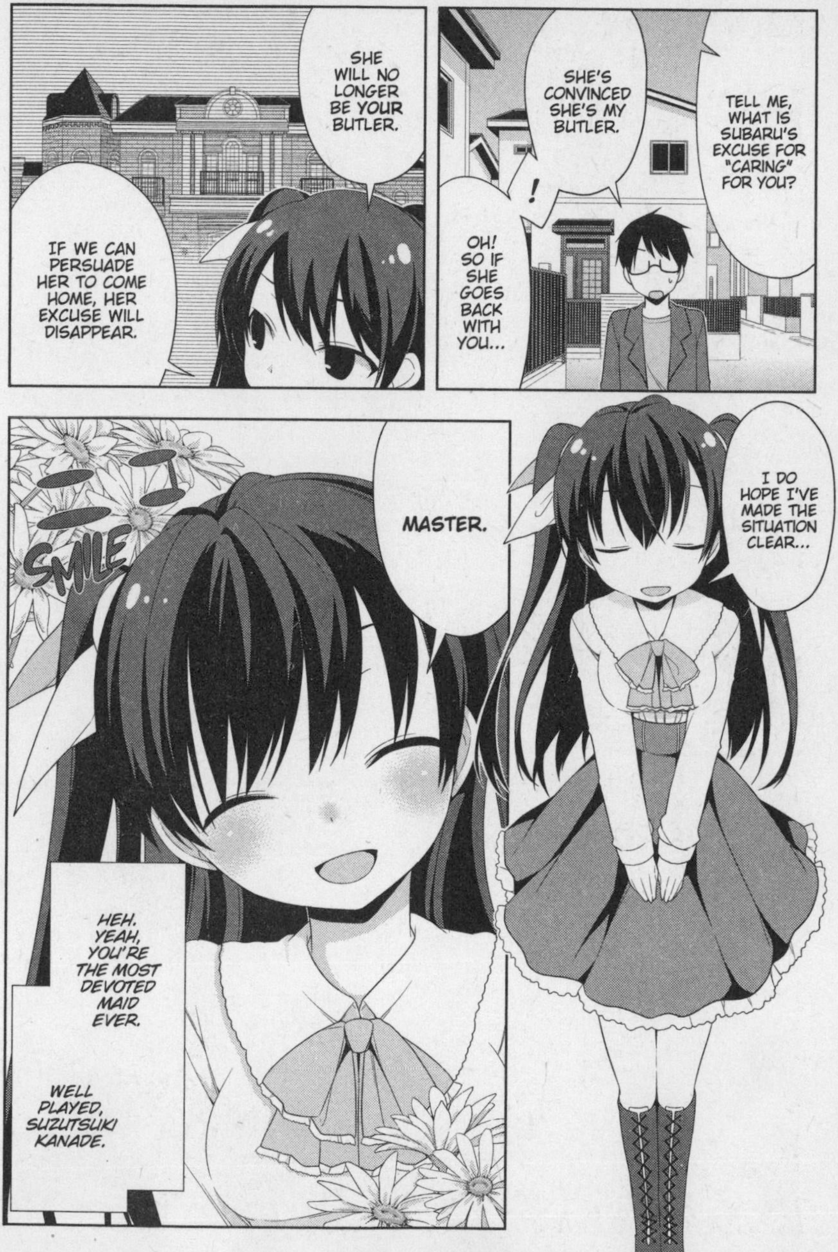
TELL ME, WHAT IS SUBARU'S EXCUSE FOR "CARING" FOR YOU?
SHE'S CONVINCED SHE'S MY BUTLER.
!
OH! SO IF SHE GOES BACK WITH YOU...
SHE WILL NO LONGER BE YOUR BUTLER.
IF WE CAN PERSUADE HER TO COME HOME, HER EXCUSE WILL DISAPPEAR.
I DO HOPE I'VE MADE THE SITUATION CLEAR...
MASTER.
SMILE
HEH. YEAH, YOU'RE THE MOST DEVOTED MAID EVER.
WELL PLAYED, SUZUTSUKI KANADE.

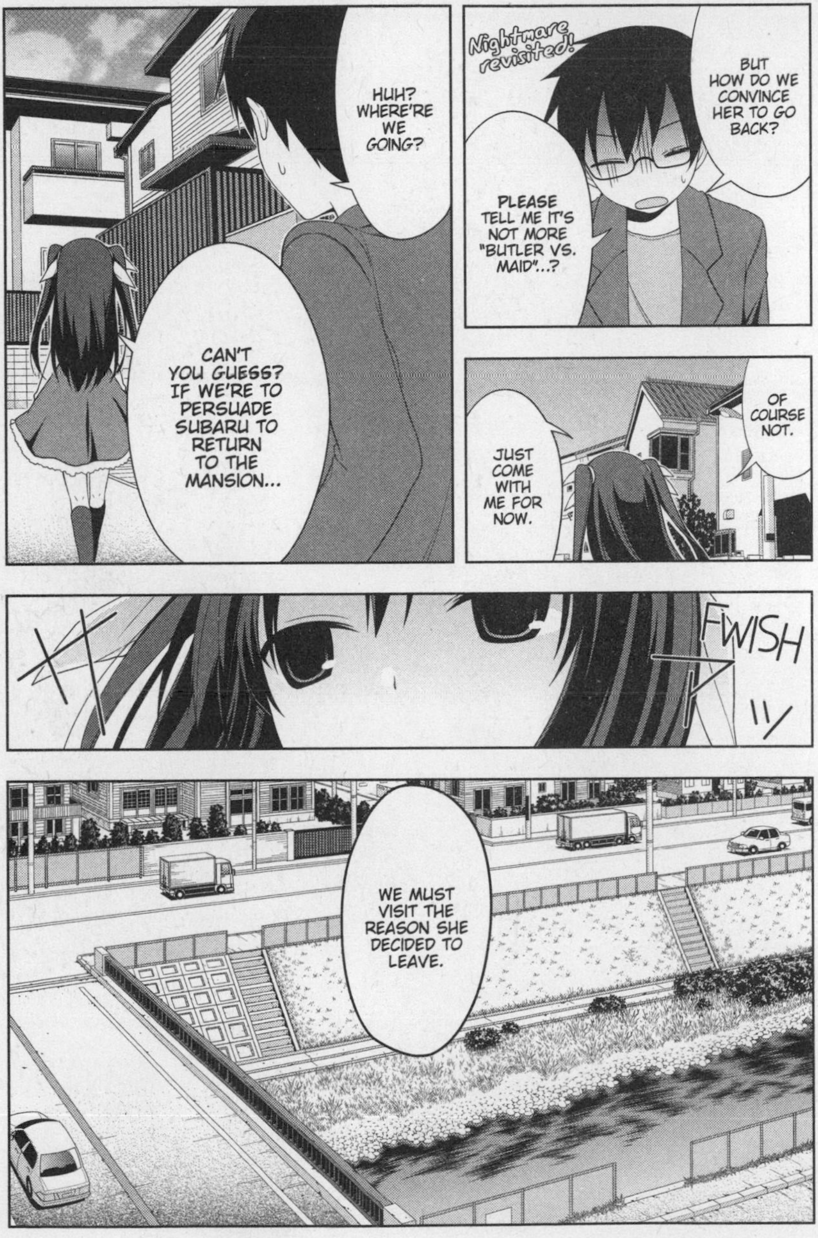
Nightmare revisited!
BUT HOW DO WE CONVINCE HER TO GO BACK?
PLEASE TELL ME IT'S NOT MORE "BUTLER VS. MAID"...?
OF COURSE NOT.
JUST COME WITH ME FOR NOW.
HUH? WHERE'RE WE GOING?
CAN'T YOU GUESS? IF WE'RE TO PERSUADE SUBARU TO RETURN TO THE MANSION...
FWISH
WE MUST VISIT THE REASON SHE DECIDED TO LEAVE.

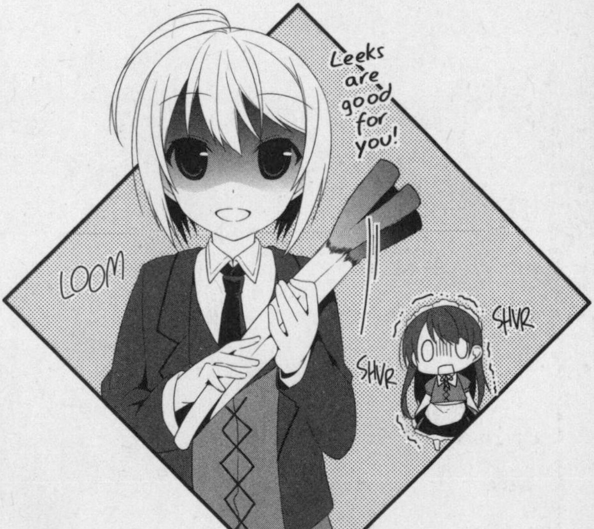
Leeks are good for you!
LOOM
SHVR
SHVR

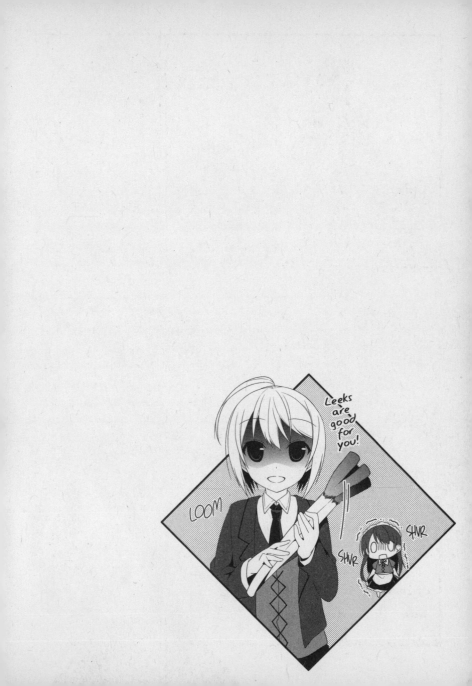

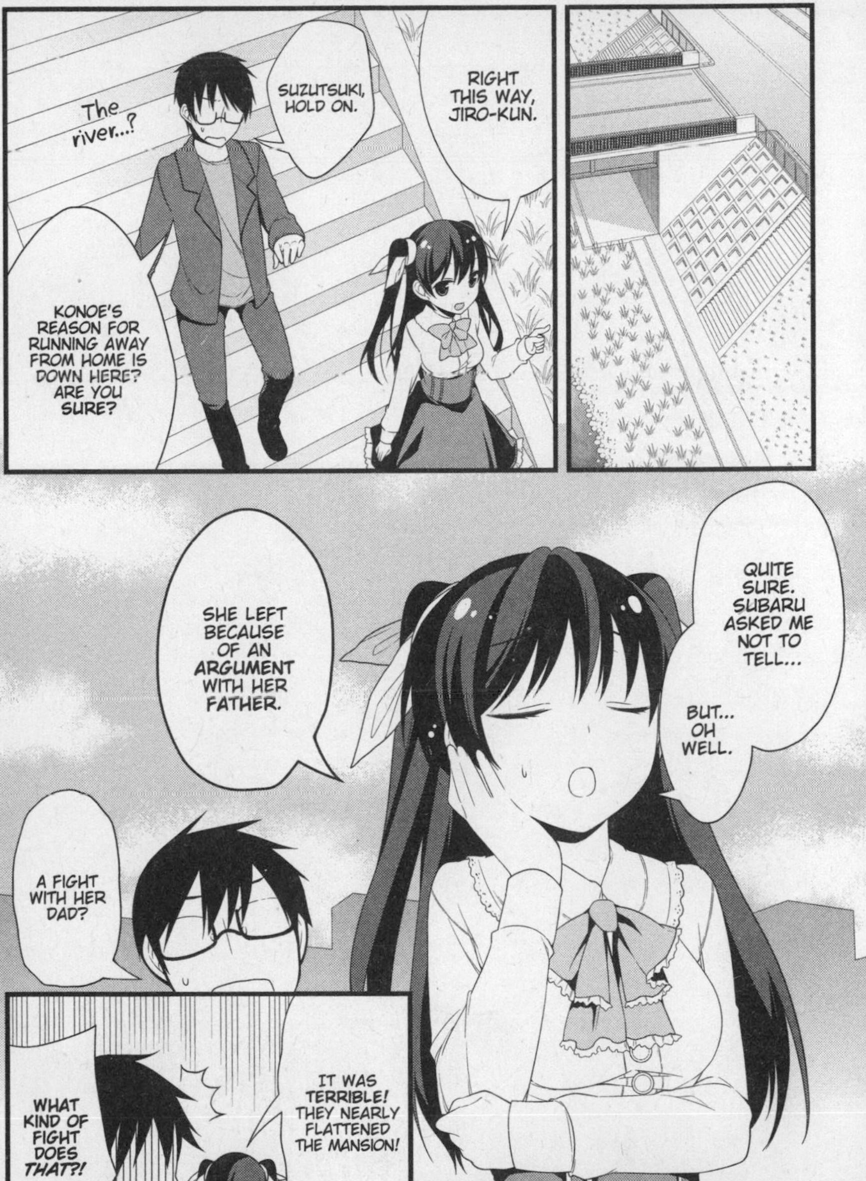
RIGHT THIS WAY, JIRO-KUN.
SUZUTSUKI, HOLD ON.
The river...?
KONOE'S REASON FOR RUNNING AWAY FROM HOME IS DOWN HERE? ARE YOU SURE?
QUITE SURE. SUBARU ASKED ME NOT TO TELL...
BUT... OH WELL.
SHE LEFT BECAUSE OF AN ARGUMENT WITH HER FATHER.
A FIGHT WITH HER DAD?
IT WAS TERRIBLE! THEY NEARLY FLATTENED THE MANSION!
WHAT KIND OF FIGHT DOES *THAT*?!

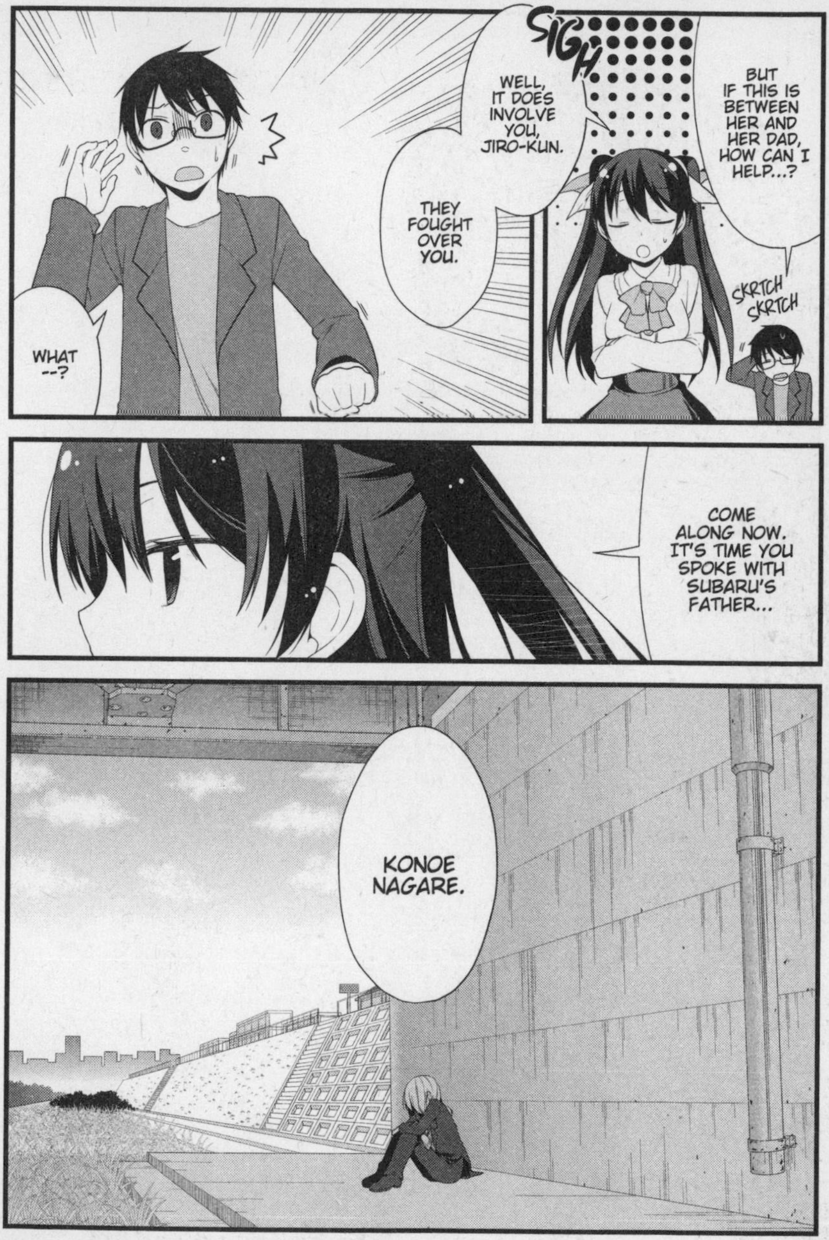
BUT IF THIS IS BETWEEN HER AND HER DAD, HOW CAN I HELP...?
SKRTCH SKRTCH
SIGH
WELL, IT DOES INVOLVE YOU, JIRO-KUN.
THEY FOUGHT OVER YOU.
WHAT --?
COME ALONG NOW. IT'S TIME YOU SPOKE WITH SUBARU'S FATHER...
KONOE NAGARE.

chapter 8 baby, please go home

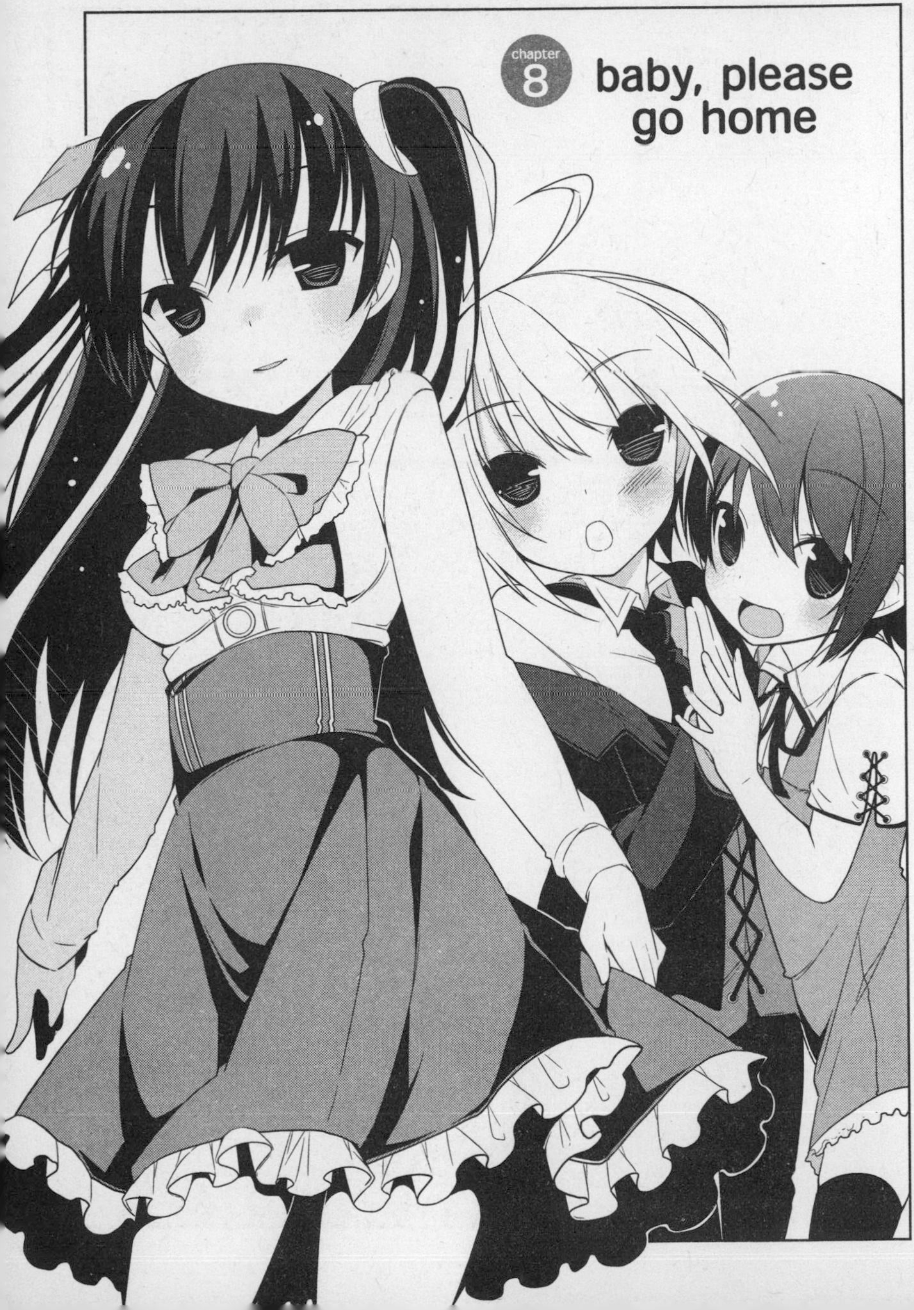

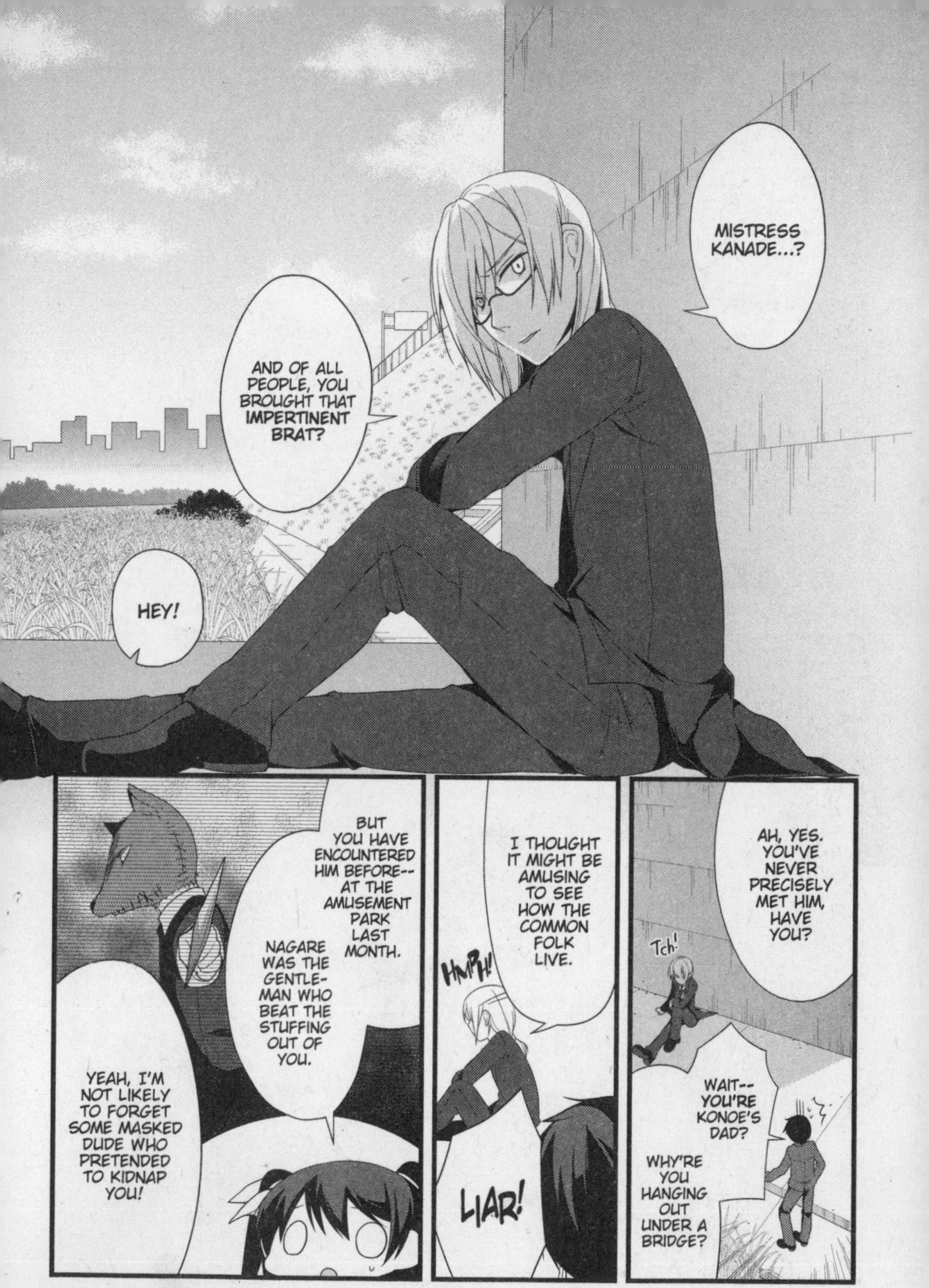
MISTRESS KANADE...?
AND OF ALL PEOPLE, YOU BROUGHT THAT IMPERTINENT BRAT?
HEY!
AH, YES. YOU'VE NEVER PRECISELY MET HIM, HAVE YOU?
Tch!
WAIT-- YOU'RE KONOE'S DAD?
WHY'RE YOU HANGING OUT UNDER A BRIDGE?
I THOUGHT IT MIGHT BE AMUSING TO SEE HOW THE COMMON FOLK LIVE.
HMPH!
LIAR!
BUT YOU HAVE ENCOUNTERED HIM BEFORE-- AT THE AMUSEMENT PARK LAST MONTH.
NAGARE WAS THE GENTLE-MAN WHO BEAT THE STUFFING OUT OF YOU.
YEAH, I'M NOT LIKELY TO FORGET SOME MASKED DUDE WHO PRETENDED TO KIDNAP YOU!

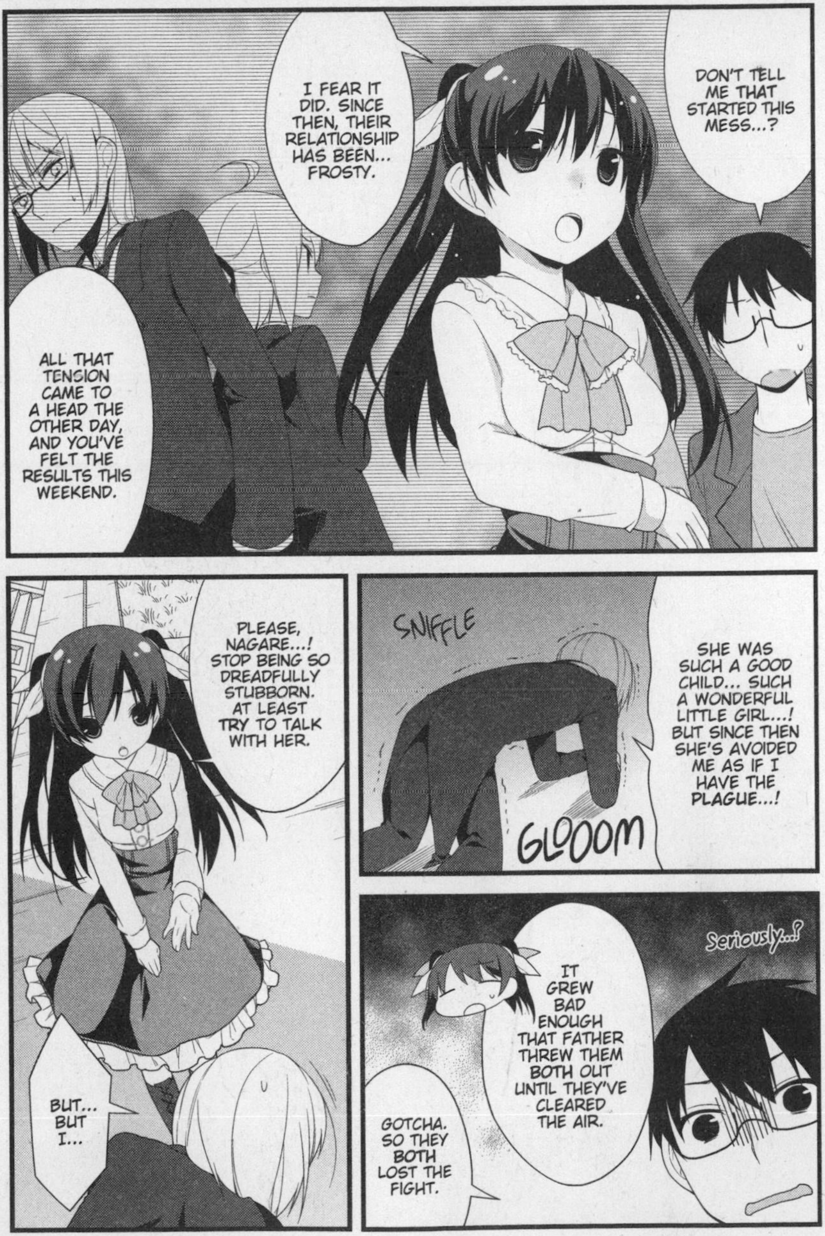
DON'T TELL ME THAT STARTED THIS MESS...?
I FEAR IT DID. SINCE THEN, THEIR RELATIONSHIP HAS BEEN... FROSTY.
ALL THAT TENSION CAME TO A HEAD THE OTHER DAY, AND YOU'VE FELT THE RESULTS THIS WEEKEND.
SNIFFLE
SHE WAS SUCH A GOOD CHILD... SUCH A WONDERFUL LITTLE GIRL...! BUT SINCE THEN SHE'S AVOIDED ME AS IF I HAVE THE PLAGUE...!
GLOOOM
Seriously...?
IT GREW BAD ENOUGH THAT FATHER THREW THEM BOTH OUT UNTIL THEY'VE CLEARED THE AIR.
GOTCHA. SO THEY BOTH LOST THE FIGHT.
PLEASE, NAGARE...! STOP BEING SO DREADFULLY STUBBORN. AT LEAST TRY TO TALK WITH HER.
BUT... BUT I...

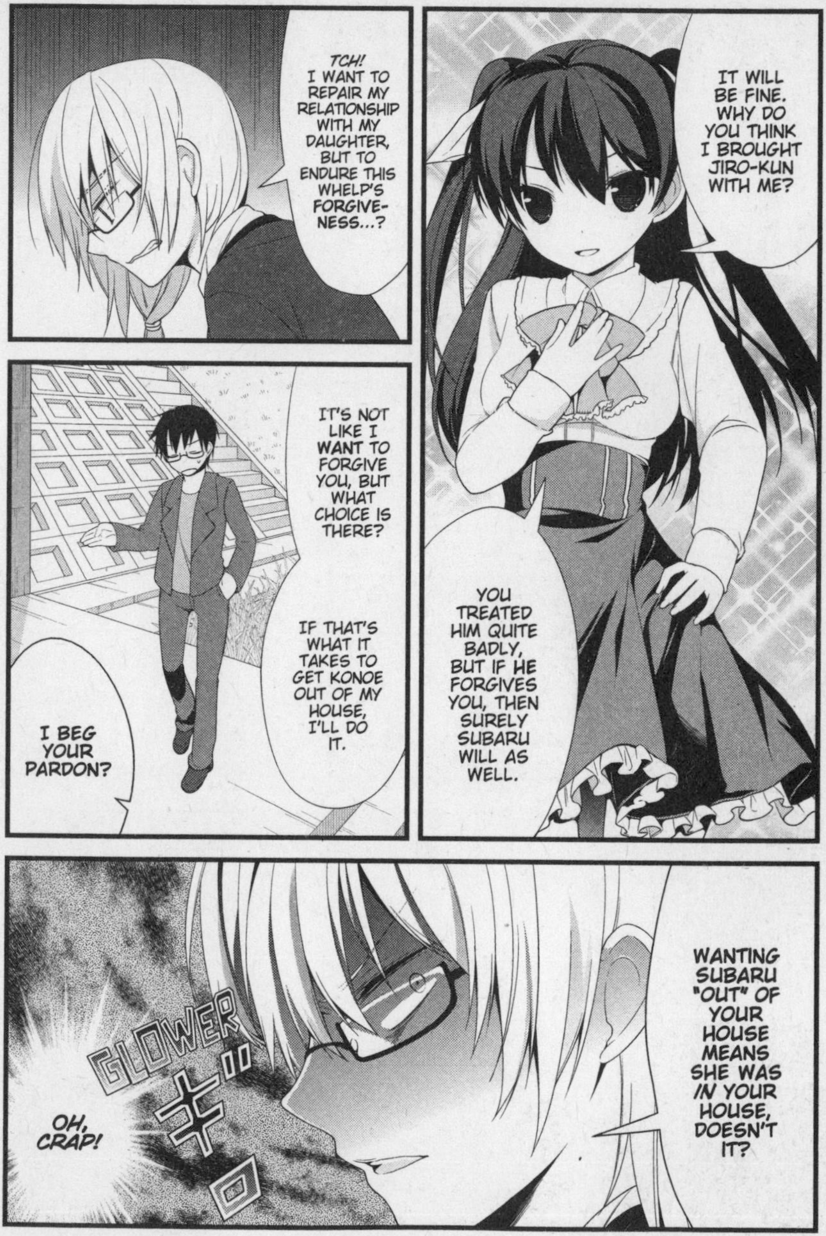
IT WILL BE FINE. WHY DO YOU THINK I BROUGHT JIRO-KUN WITH ME?
YOU TREATED HIM QUITE BADLY, BUT IF HE FORGIVES YOU, THEN SURELY SUBARU WILL AS WELL.
TCH! I WANT TO REPAIR MY RELATIONSHIP WITH MY DAUGHTER, BUT TO ENDURE THIS WHELP'S FORGIVE-NESS...?
IT'S NOT LIKE I WANT TO FORGIVE YOU, BUT WHAT CHOICE IS THERE?
IF THAT'S WHAT IT TAKES TO GET KONOE OUT OF MY HOUSE, I'LL DO IT.
I BEG YOUR PARDON?
WANTING SUBARU "OUT" OF YOUR HOUSE MEANS SHE WAS *IN* YOUR HOUSE, DOESN'T IT?
GLOWER
OH, CRAP!

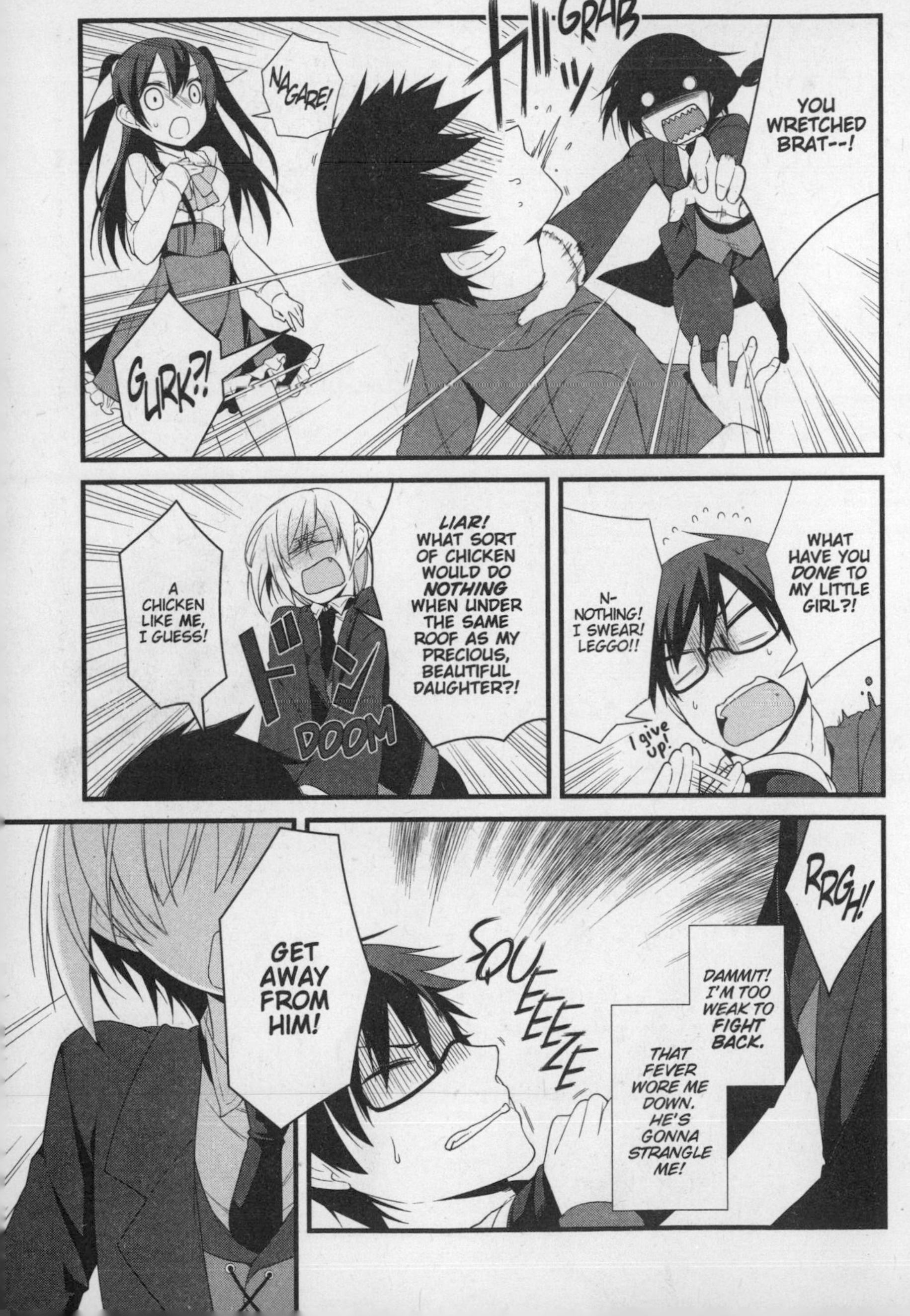
GRAB
YOU WRETCHED BRAT--!
NAGARE!
GURK?!
WHAT HAVE YOU DONE TO MY LITTLE GIRL?!
N-NOTHING! I SWEAR! LEGGO!!
I give up!
LIAR! WHAT SORT OF CHICKEN WOULD DO NOTHING WHEN UNDER THE SAME ROOF AS MY PRECIOUS, BEAUTIFUL DAUGHTER?!
A CHICKEN LIKE ME, I GUESS!
DOOM
RRGH!
DAMMIT! I'M TOO WEAK TO FIGHT BACK.
THAT FEVER WORE ME DOWN. HE'S GONNA STRANGLE ME!
SQUEEEEZE
GET AWAY FROM HIM!

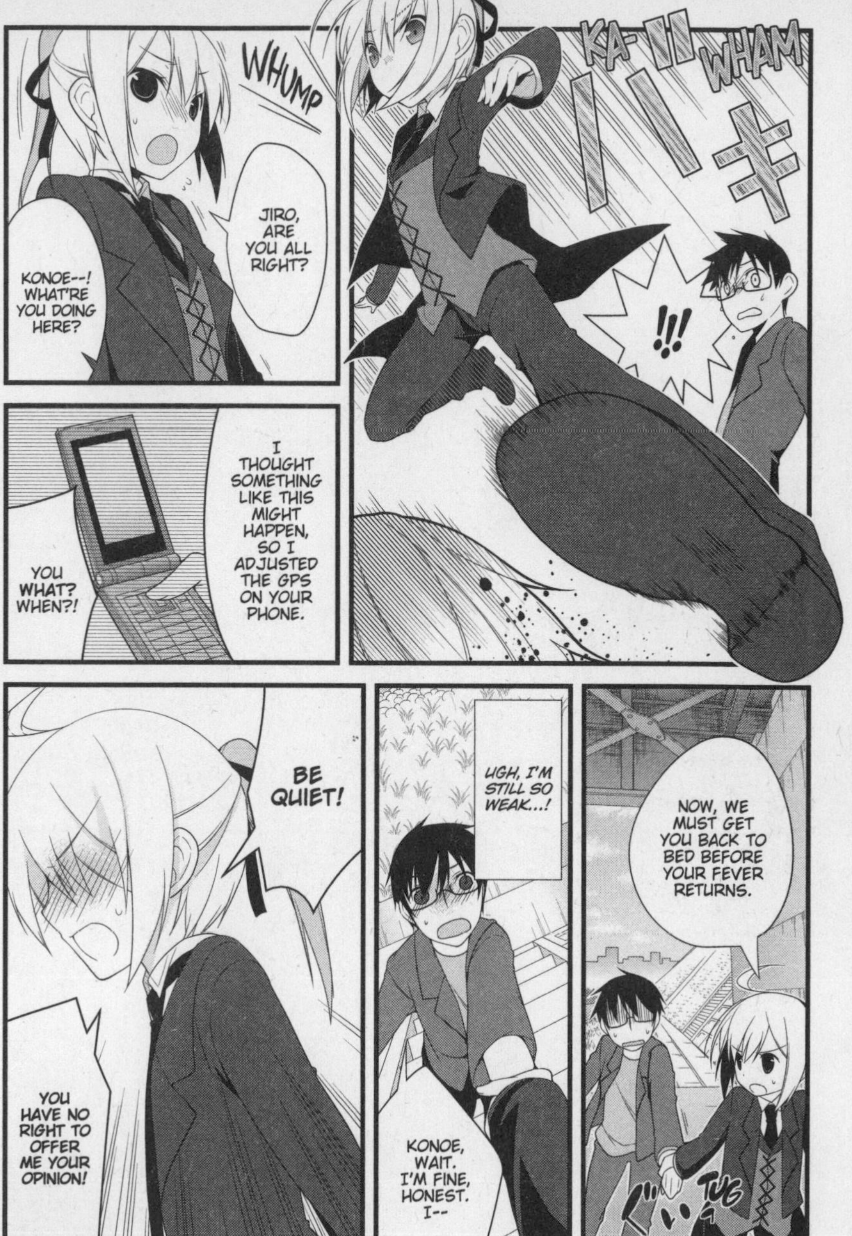
KA-!!
WHAM
!!!
WHUMP
JIRO, ARE YOU ALL RIGHT?
KONOE--! WHAT'RE YOU DOING HERE?
I THOUGHT SOMETHING LIKE THIS MIGHT HAPPEN, SO I ADJUSTED THE GPS ON YOUR PHONE.
YOU WHAT? WHEN?!
NOW, WE MUST GET YOU BACK TO BED BEFORE YOUR FEVER RETURNS.
TUG
UGH, I'M STILL SO WEAK...!
KONOE, WAIT. I'M FINE, HONEST. I--
BE QUIET!
YOU HAVE NO RIGHT TO OFFER ME YOUR OPINION!

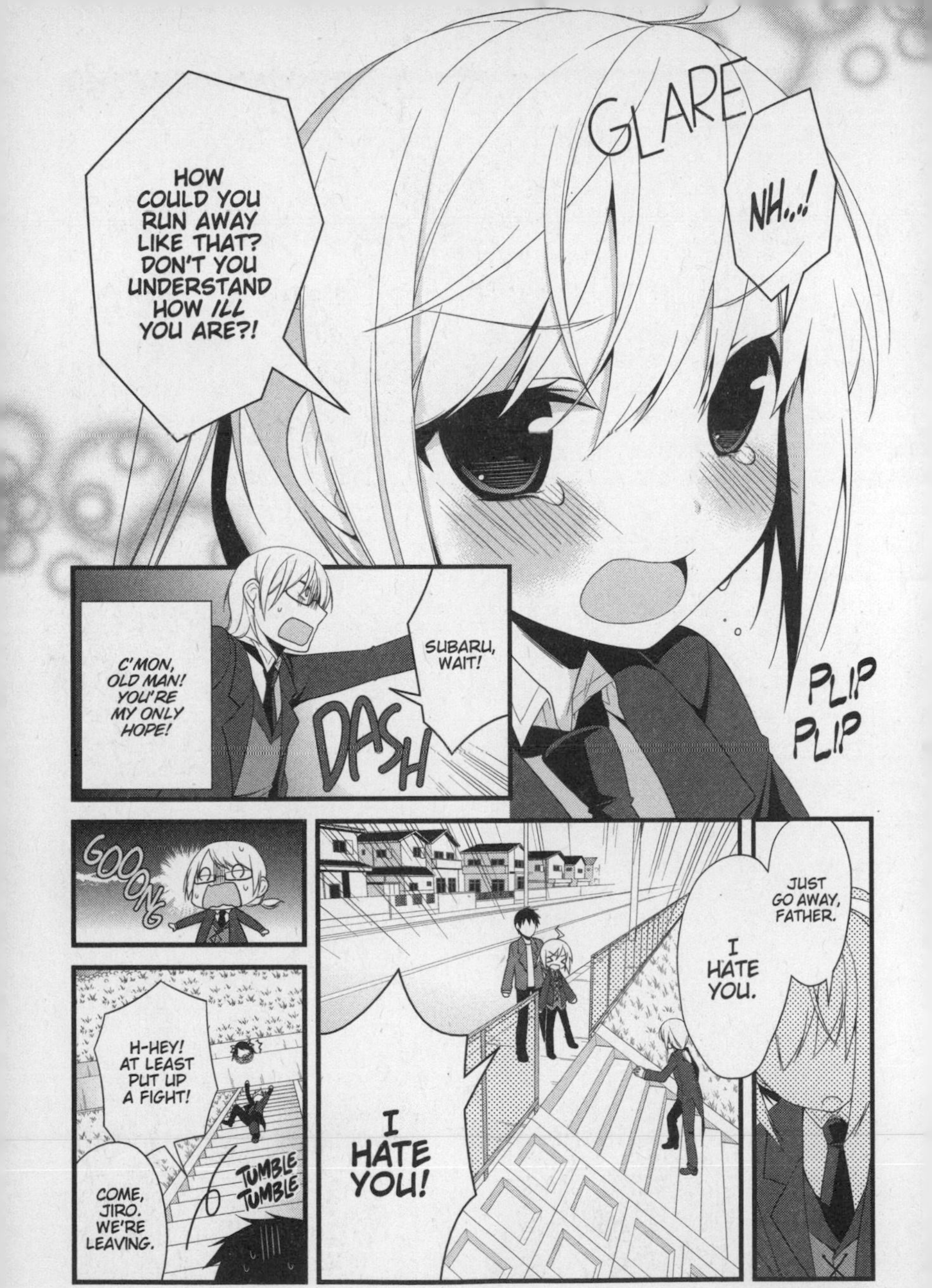
GLARE
NH..!
HOW COULD YOU RUN AWAY LIKE THAT? DON'T YOU UNDERSTAND HOW *ILL* YOU ARE?!
PLIP PLIP
SUBARU, WAIT!
DASH
C'MON, OLD MAN! YOU'RE MY ONLY HOPE!
JUST GO AWAY, FATHER.
I HATE YOU.
I HATE YOU!
GOOONG
H-HEY! AT LEAST PUT UP A FIGHT!
TUMBLE TUMBLE
COME, JIRO. WE'RE LEAVING.

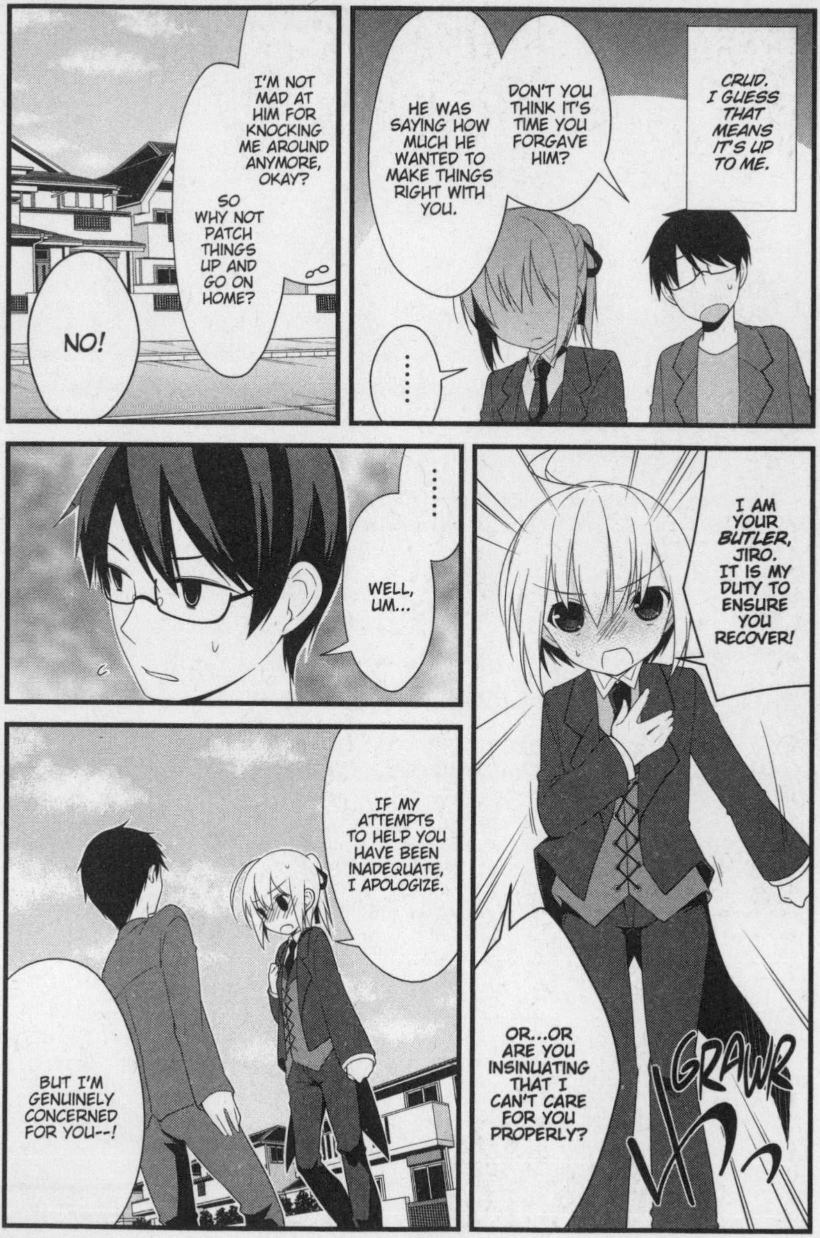
CRUD. I GUESS THAT MEANS IT'S UP TO ME.
DON'T YOU THINK IT'S TIME YOU FORGAVE HIM?
HE WAS SAYING HOW MUCH HE WANTED TO MAKE THINGS RIGHT WITH YOU.
......
I'M NOT MAD AT HIM FOR KNOCKING ME AROUND ANYMORE, OKAY?
SO WHY NOT PATCH THINGS UP AND GO ON HOME?
NO!
I AM YOUR BUTLER, JIRO. IT IS MY DUTY TO ENSURE YOU RECOVER!
OR...OR ARE YOU INSINUATING THAT I CAN'T CARE FOR YOU PROPERLY?
GRAWR
......
WELL, UM...
IF MY ATTEMPTS TO HELP YOU HAVE BEEN INADEQUATE, I APOLOGIZE.
BUT I'M GENUINELY CONCERNED FOR YOU--!

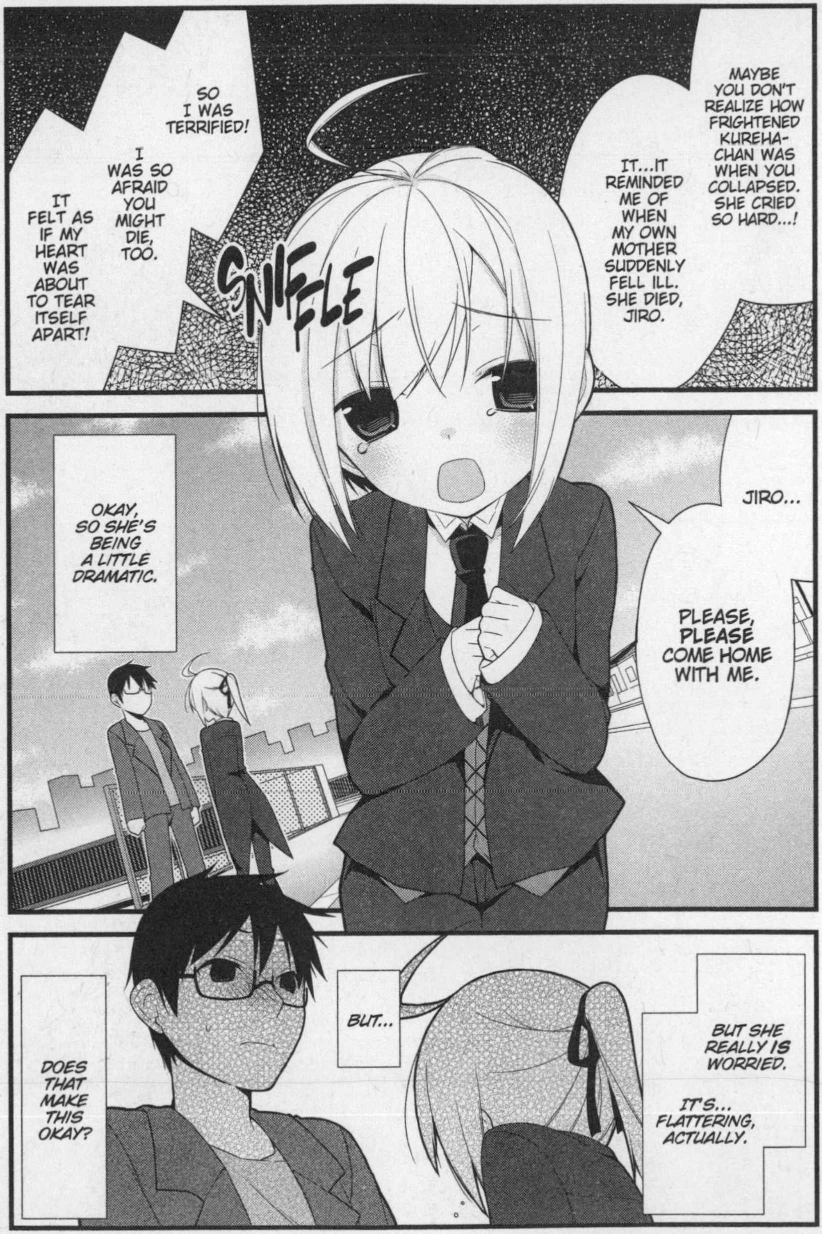
MAYBE YOU DON'T REALIZE HOW FRIGHTENED KUREHA-CHAN WAS WHEN YOU COLLAPSED. SHE CRIED SO HARD...!
IT...IT REMINDED ME OF WHEN MY OWN MOTHER SUDDENLY FELL ILL. SHE DIED, JIRO.
SNIFFLE
SO I WAS TERRIFIED!
I WAS SO AFRAID YOU MIGHT DIE, TOO.
IT FELT AS IF MY HEART WAS ABOUT TO TEAR ITSELF APART!
JIRO...
PLEASE, PLEASE COME HOME WITH ME.
OKAY, SO SHE'S BEING A LITTLE DRAMATIC.
BUT SHE REALLY IS WORRIED.
IT'S... FLATTERING, ACTUALLY.
BUT...
DOES THAT MAKE THIS OKAY?

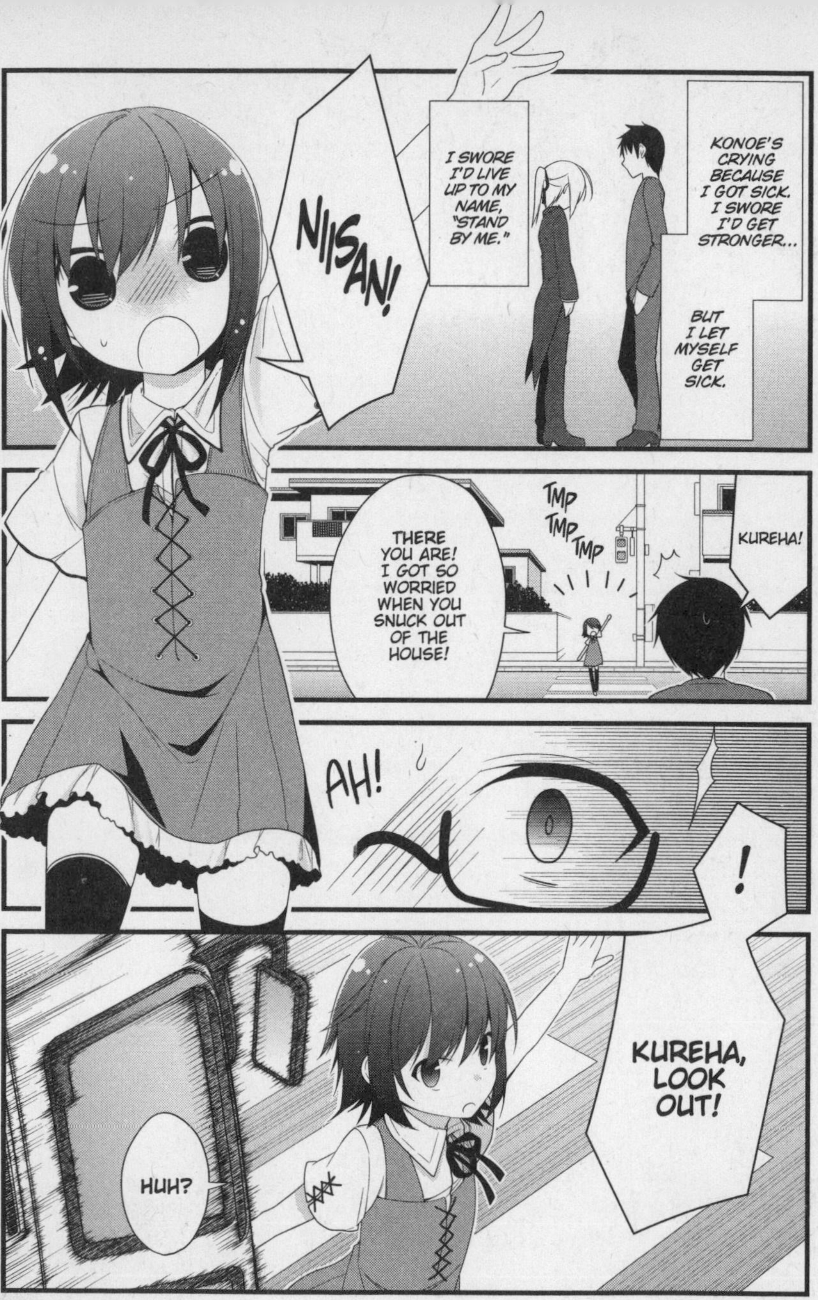
KONOE'S CRYING BECAUSE I GOT SICK. I SWORE I'D GET STRONGER...
BUT I LET MYSELF GET SICK.
I SWORE I'D LIVE UP TO MY NAME, "STAND BY ME."
NIISAN!
KUREHA!
TMP TMP TMP
THERE YOU ARE! I GOT SO WORRIED WHEN YOU SNUCK OUT OF THE HOUSE!
!
AH!
KUREHA, LOOK OUT!
HUH?

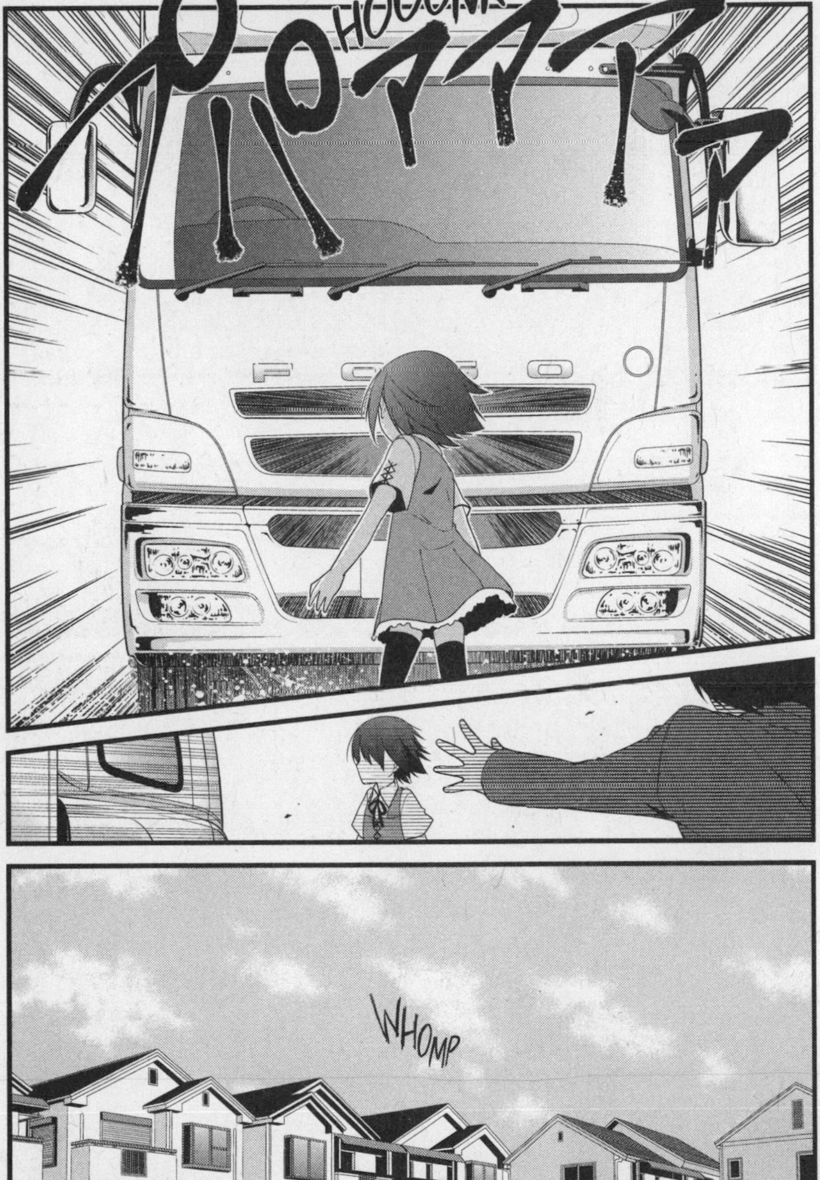
HOOONK
WHOMP

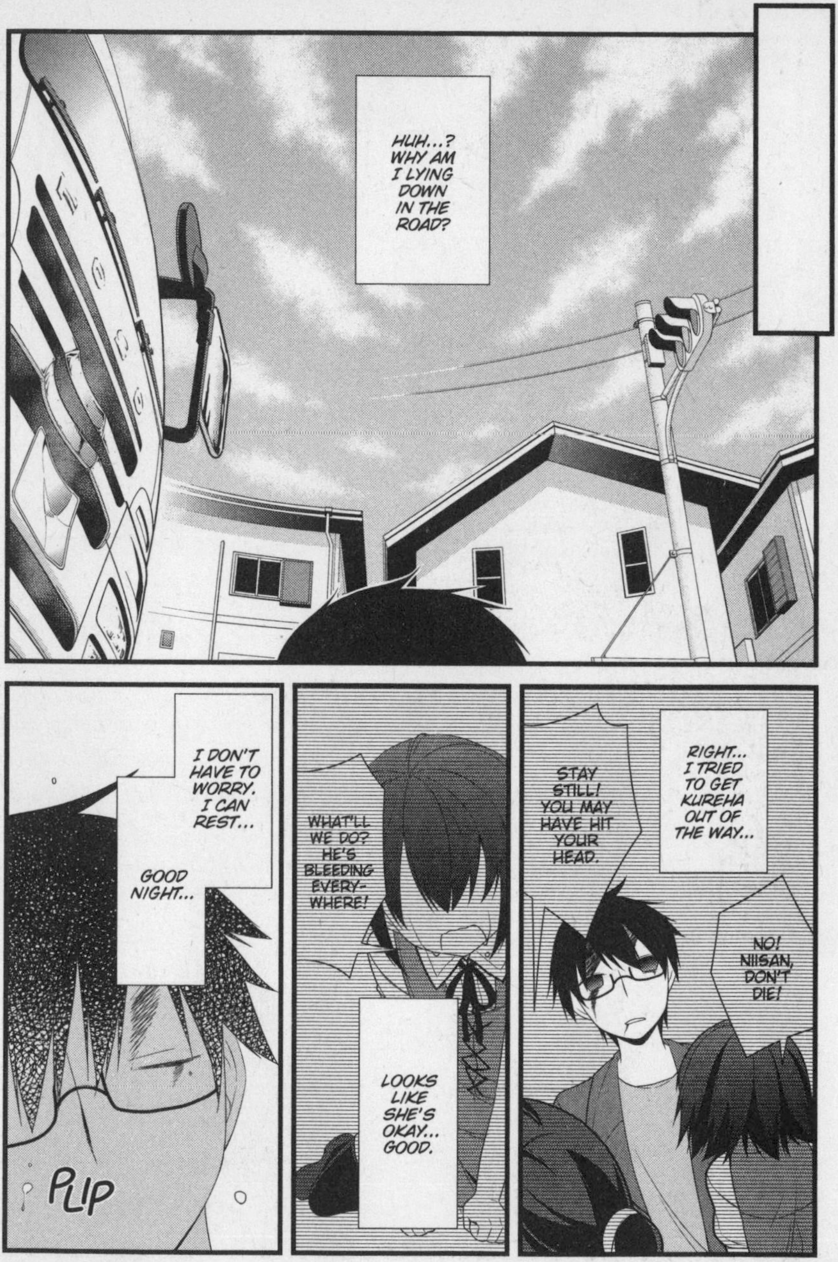
HUH...? WHY AM I LYING DOWN IN THE ROAD?
RIGHT... I TRIED TO GET KUREHA OUT OF THE WAY...
STAY STILL! YOU MAY HAVE HIT YOUR HEAD.
NO! NIISAN, DON'T DIE!
WHAT'LL WE DO? HE'S BLEEDING EVERY-WHERE!
LOOKS LIKE SHE'S OKAY... GOOD.
I DON'T HAVE TO WORRY. I CAN REST...
GOOD NIGHT...
PLIP

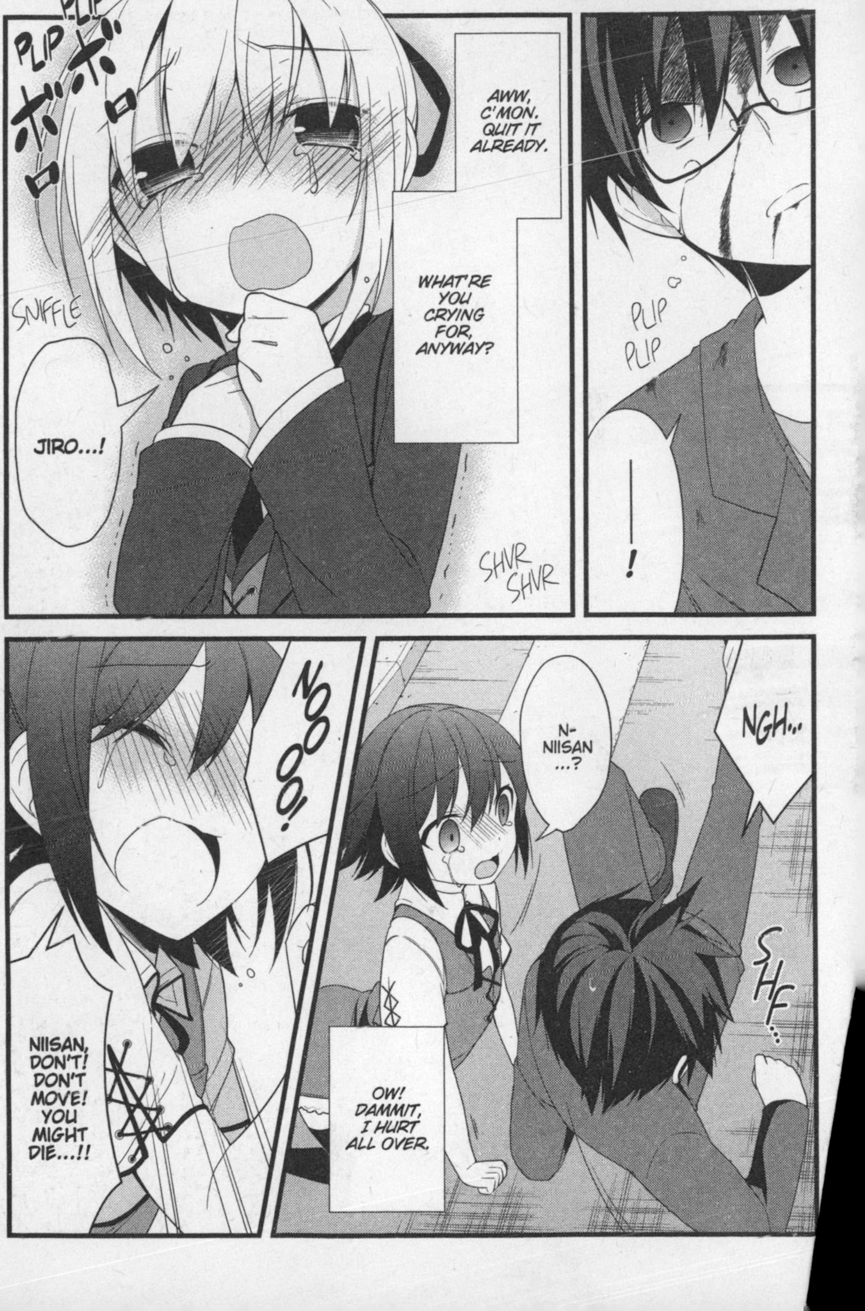
PLIP PLIP
—!
PLIP PLIP PLIP
ボロボロ
AWW, C'MON. QUIT IT ALREADY.
WHAT'RE YOU CRYING FOR, ANYWAY?
SNIFFLE
JIRO...!
SHVR SHVR
NGH...
N-NIISAN...?
SHF...
OW! DAMMIT, I HURT ALL OVER.
NOOOO!
NIISAN, DON'T! DON'T MOVE! YOU MIGHT DIE...!!

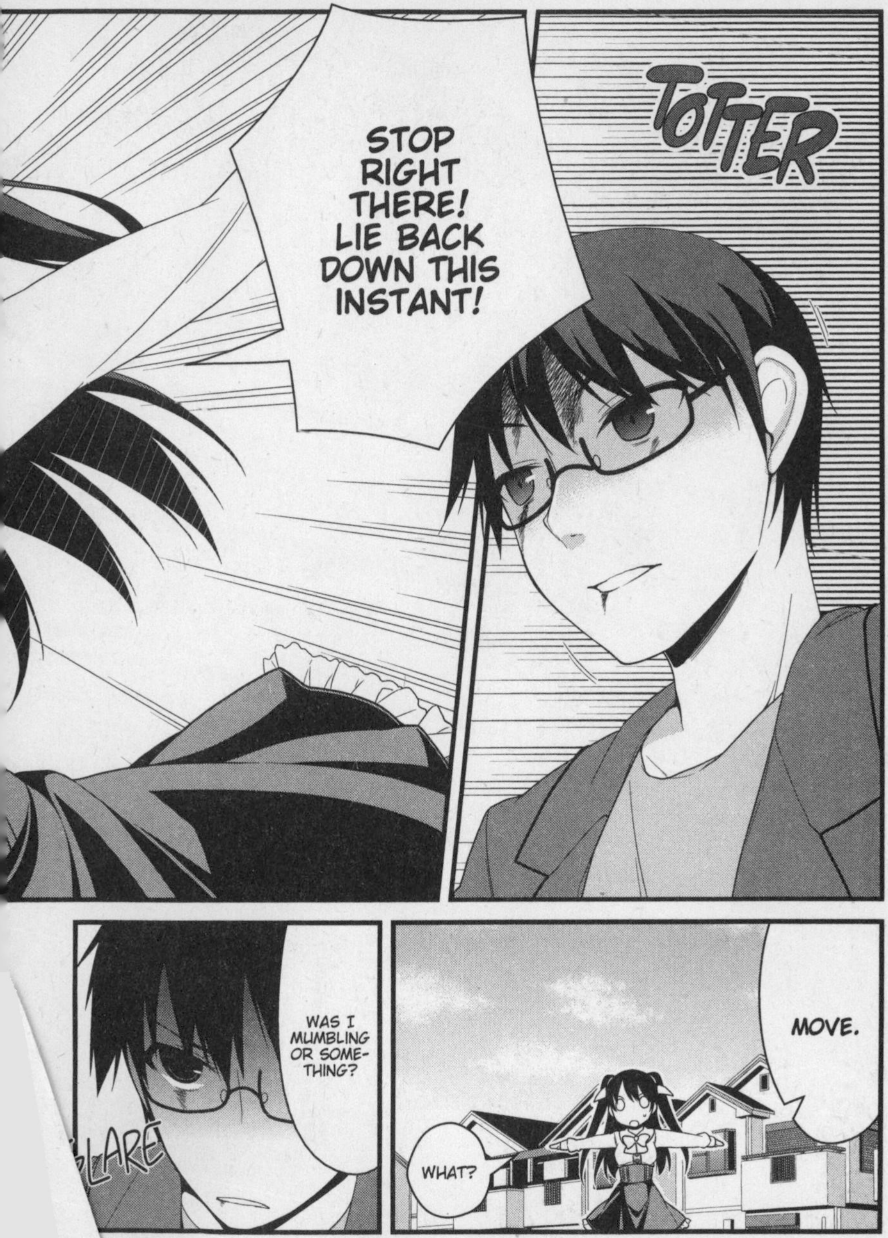
TOTTER
STOP RIGHT THERE! LIE BACK DOWN THIS INSTANT!
MOVE.
WHAT?
WAS I MUMBLING OR SOME-THING?
GLARE

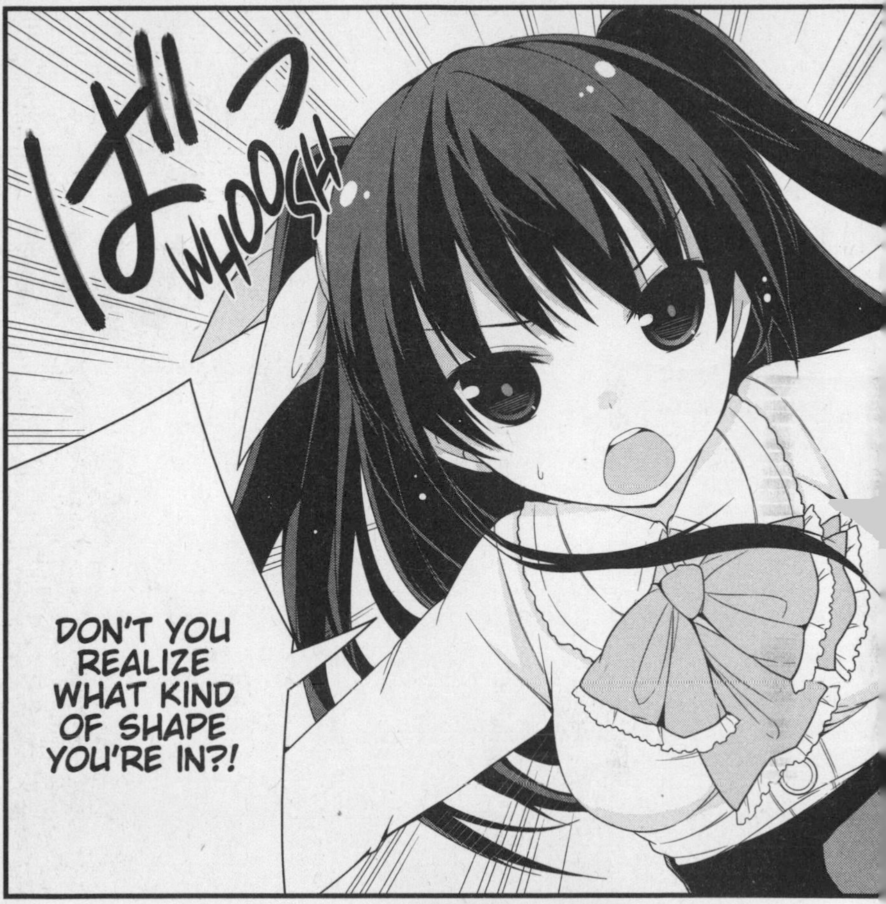
はっ
WHOOSH
DON'T YOU REALIZE WHAT KIND OF SHAPE YOU'RE IN?!
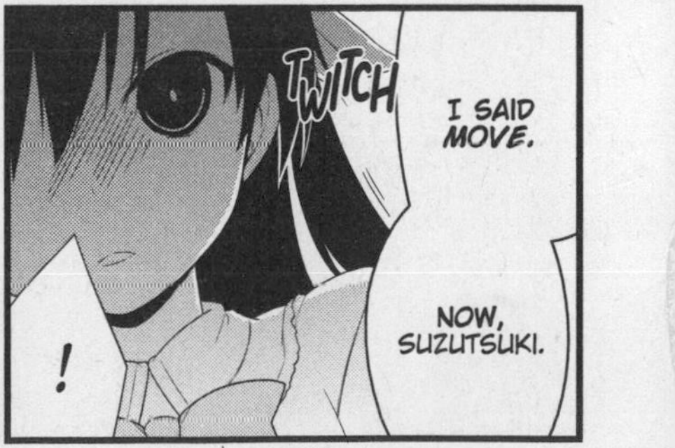
I SAID MOVE.
TWITCH
NOW, SUZUTSUKI.
!
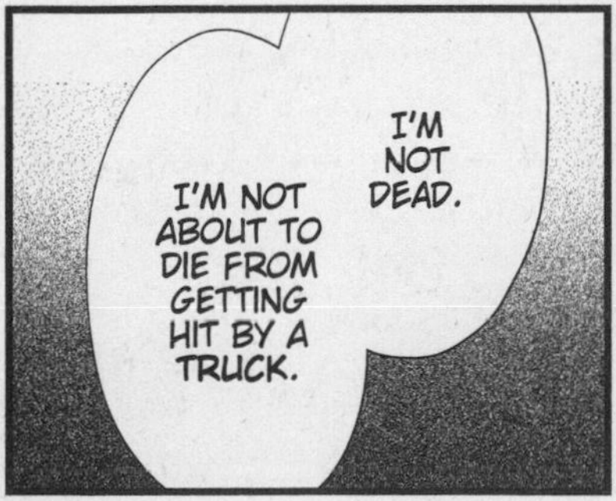
I'M NOT DEAD.
I'M NOT ABOUT TO DIE FROM GETTING HIT BY A TRUCK.

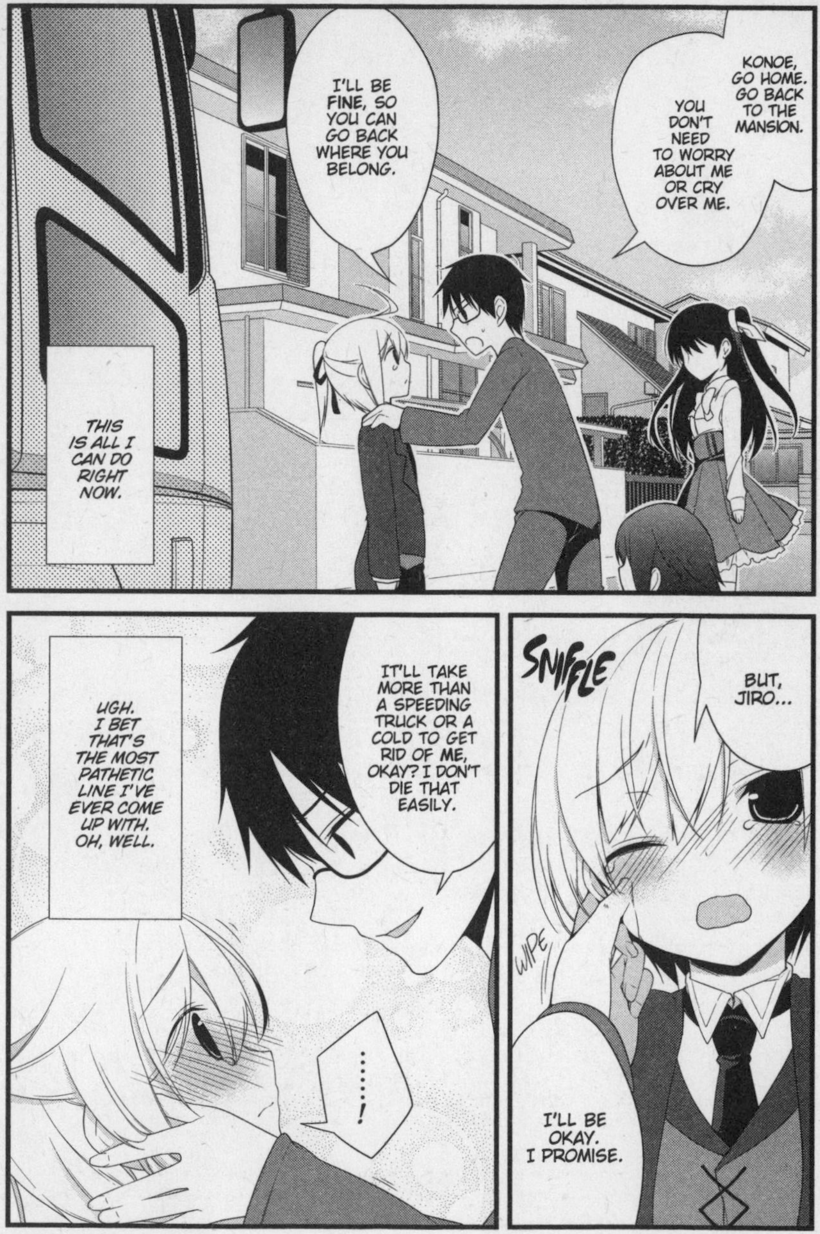
KONOE, GO HOME. GO BACK TO THE MANSION.
YOU DON'T NEED TO WORRY ABOUT ME OR CRY OVER ME.
I'LL BE FINE, SO YOU CAN GO BACK WHERE YOU BELONG.
THIS IS ALL I CAN DO RIGHT NOW.
SNIFFLE
BUT, JIRO...
WIPE
I'LL BE OKAY. I PROMISE.
IT'LL TAKE MORE THAN A SPEEDING TRUCK OR A COLD TO GET RID OF ME, OKAY? I DON'T DIE THAT EASILY.
UGH. I BET THAT'S THE MOST PATHETIC LINE I'VE EVER COME UP WITH. OH, WELL.
......!

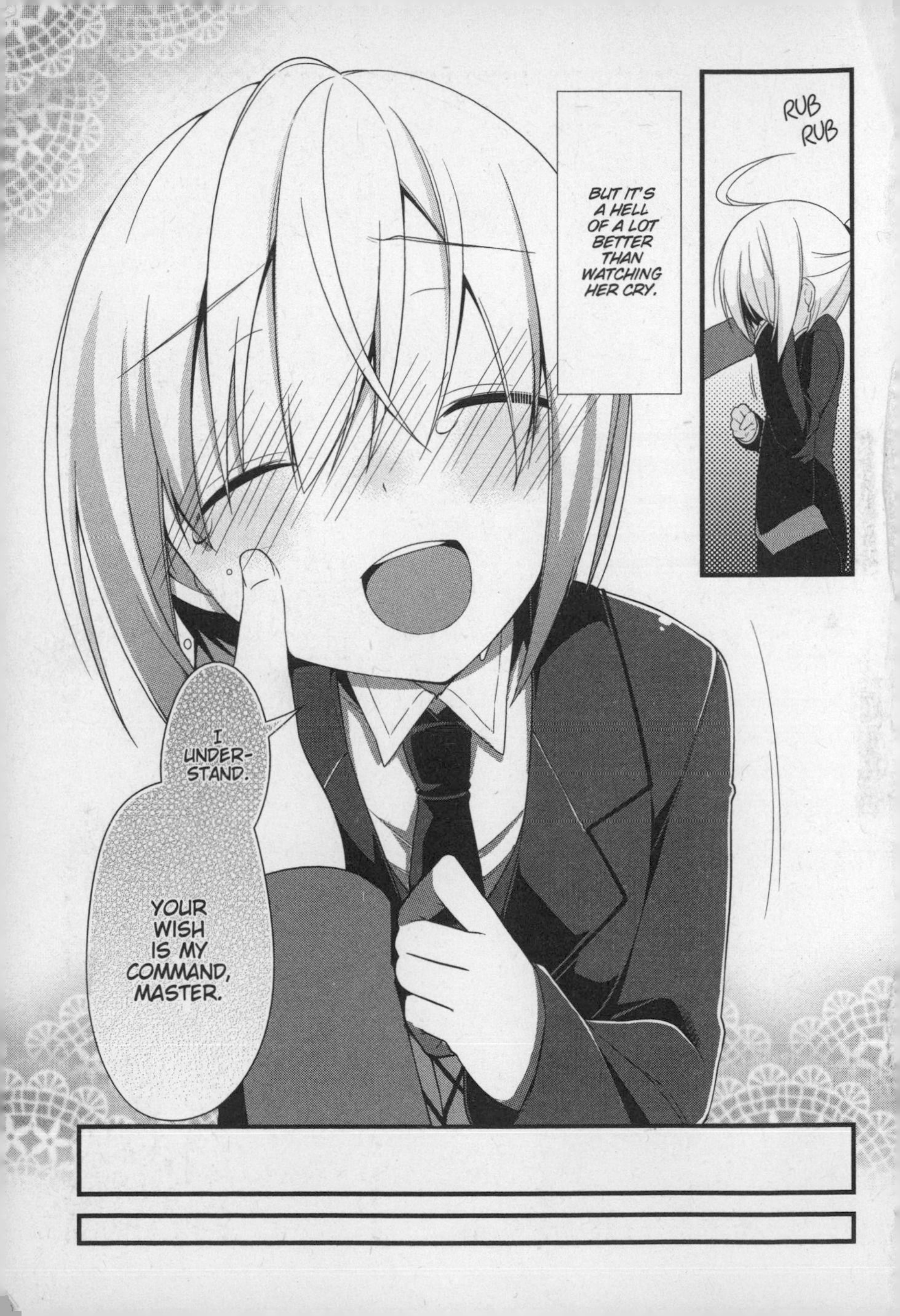
RUB RUB
BUT IT'S A HELL OF A LOT BETTER THAN WATCHING HER CRY.
I UNDER-STAND.
YOUR WISH IS MY COMMAND, MASTER.

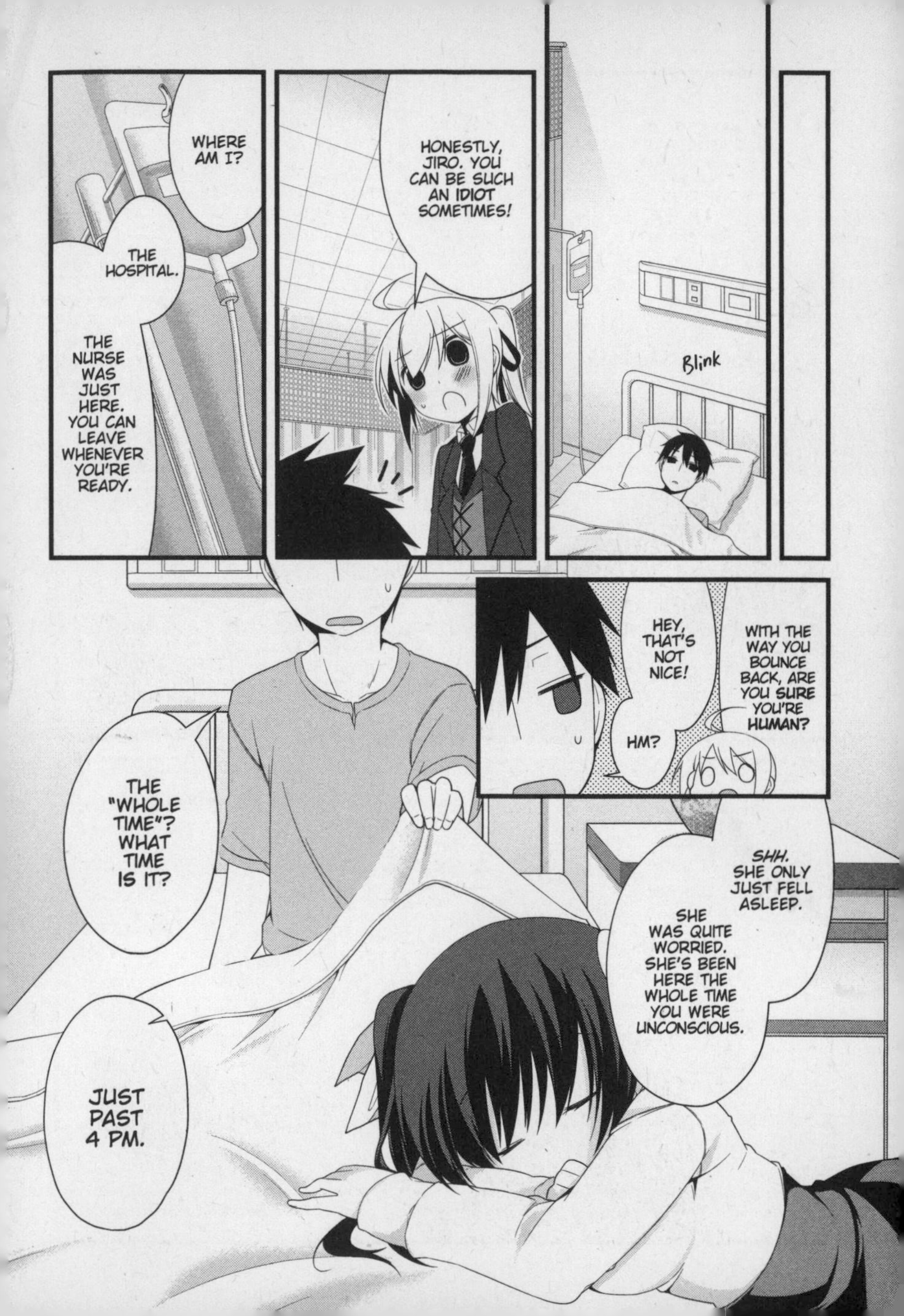
Blink
HONESTLY, JIRO. YOU CAN BE SUCH AN IDIOT SOMETIMES!
WHERE AM I?
THE HOSPITAL.
THE NURSE WAS JUST HERE. YOU CAN LEAVE WHENEVER YOU'RE READY.
WITH THE WAY YOU BOUNCE BACK, ARE YOU SURE YOU'RE HUMAN?
HEY, THAT'S NOT NICE!
HM?
SHH. SHE ONLY JUST FELL ASLEEP.
SHE WAS QUITE WORRIED. SHE'S BEEN HERE THE WHOLE TIME YOU WERE UNCONSCIOUS.
THE "WHOLE TIME"? WHAT TIME IS IT?
JUST PAST 4 PM.

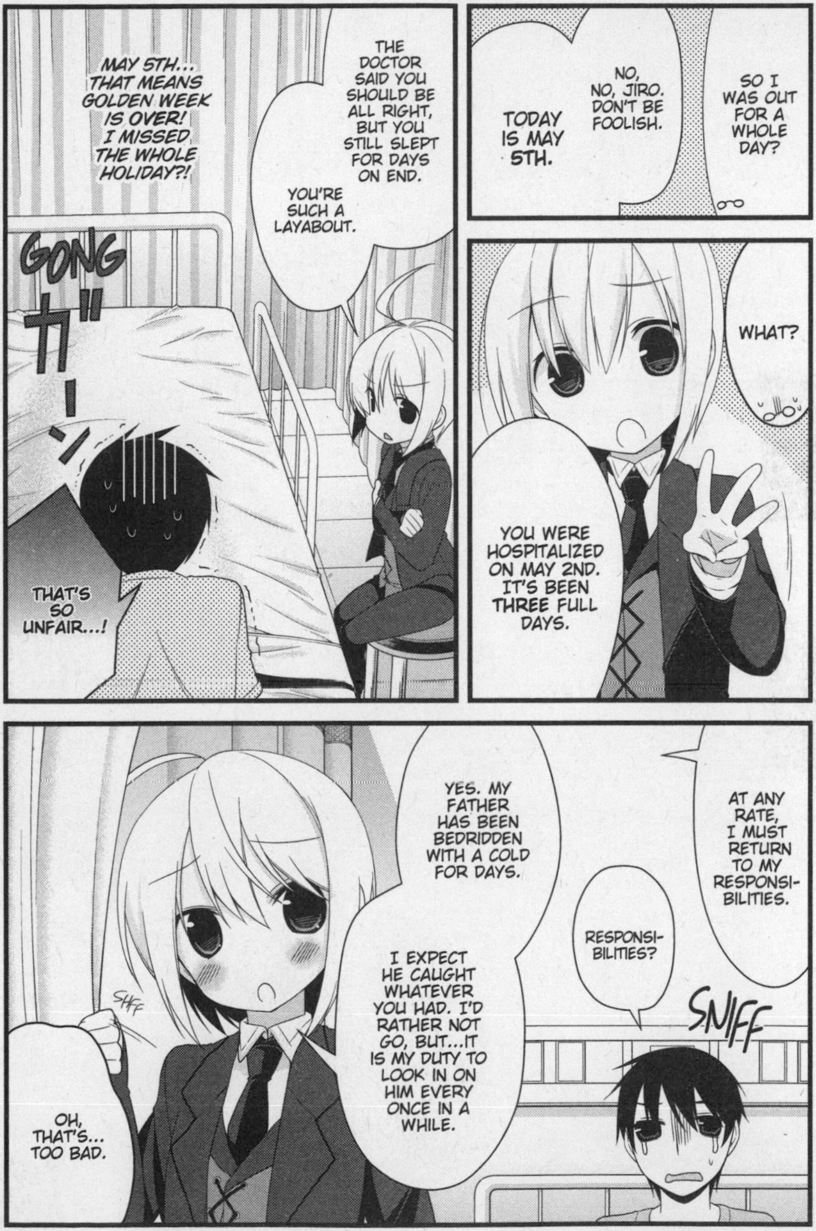
SO I WAS OUT FOR A WHOLE DAY?
NO, NO, JIRO. DON'T BE FOOLISH.
TODAY IS MAY 5TH.
WHAT?
YOU WERE HOSPITALIZED ON MAY 2ND. IT'S BEEN THREE FULL DAYS.
THE DOCTOR SAID YOU SHOULD BE ALL RIGHT, BUT YOU STILL SLEPT FOR DAYS ON END.
YOU'RE SUCH A LAYABOUT.
MAY 5TH... THAT MEANS GOLDEN WEEK IS OVER! I MISSED THE WHOLE HOLIDAY?!
GONG
ガーン
THAT'S SO UNFAIR...!
AT ANY RATE, I MUST RETURN TO MY RESPONSI-BILITIES.
RESPONSI-BILITIES?
SNIFF
YES. MY FATHER HAS BEEN BEDRIDDEN WITH A COLD FOR DAYS.
I EXPECT HE CAUGHT WHATEVER YOU HAD. I'D RATHER NOT GO, BUT...IT IS MY DUTY TO LOOK IN ON HIM EVERY ONCE IN A WHILE.
SHFF
OH, THAT'S... TOO BAD.

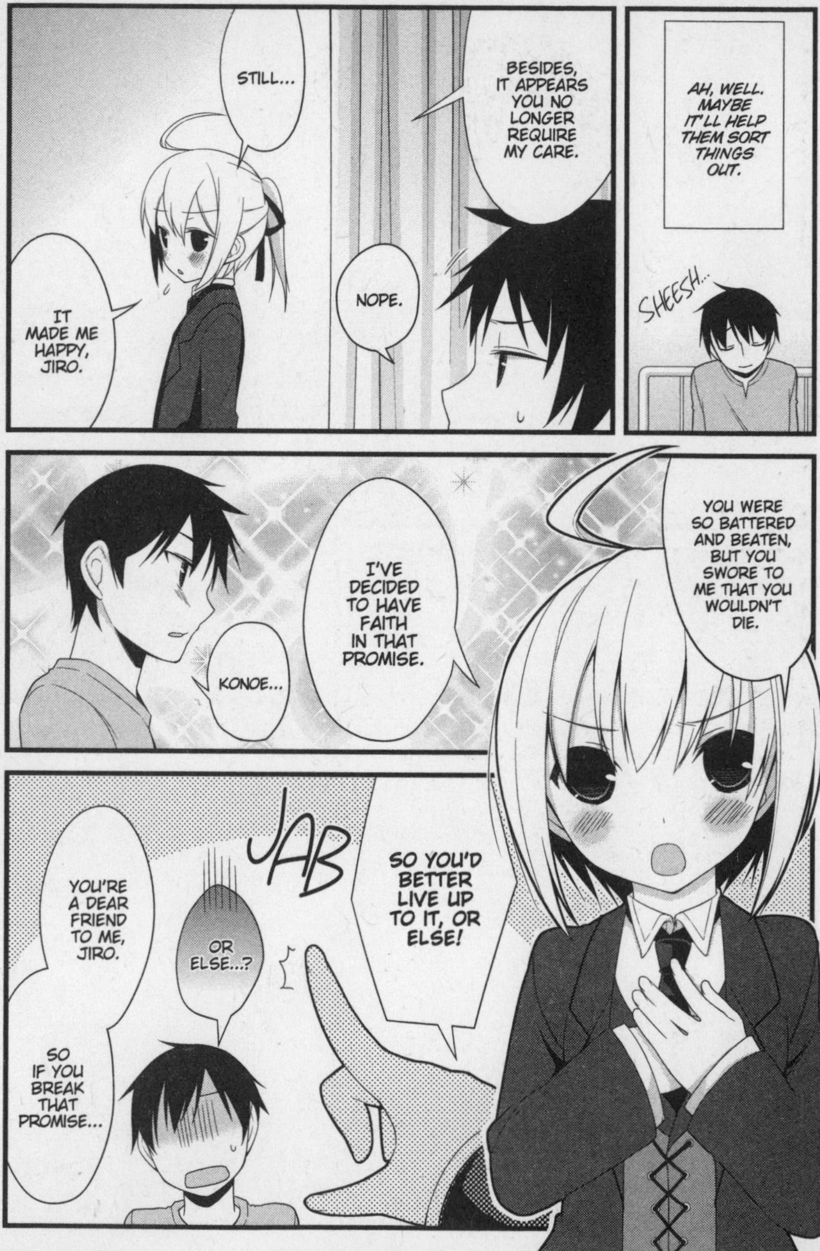
AH, WELL. MAYBE IT'LL HELP THEM SORT THINGS OUT.
SHEESH...
BESIDES, IT APPEARS YOU NO LONGER REQUIRE MY CARE.
NOPE.
STILL...
IT MADE ME HAPPY, JIRO.
YOU WERE SO BATTERED AND BEATEN, BUT YOU SWORE TO ME THAT YOU WOULDN'T DIE.
I'VE DECIDED TO HAVE FAITH IN THAT PROMISE.
KONOE...
SO YOU'D BETTER LIVE UP TO IT, OR ELSE!
JAB
OR ELSE...?
YOU'RE A DEAR FRIEND TO ME, JIRO.
SO IF YOU BREAK THAT PROMISE...

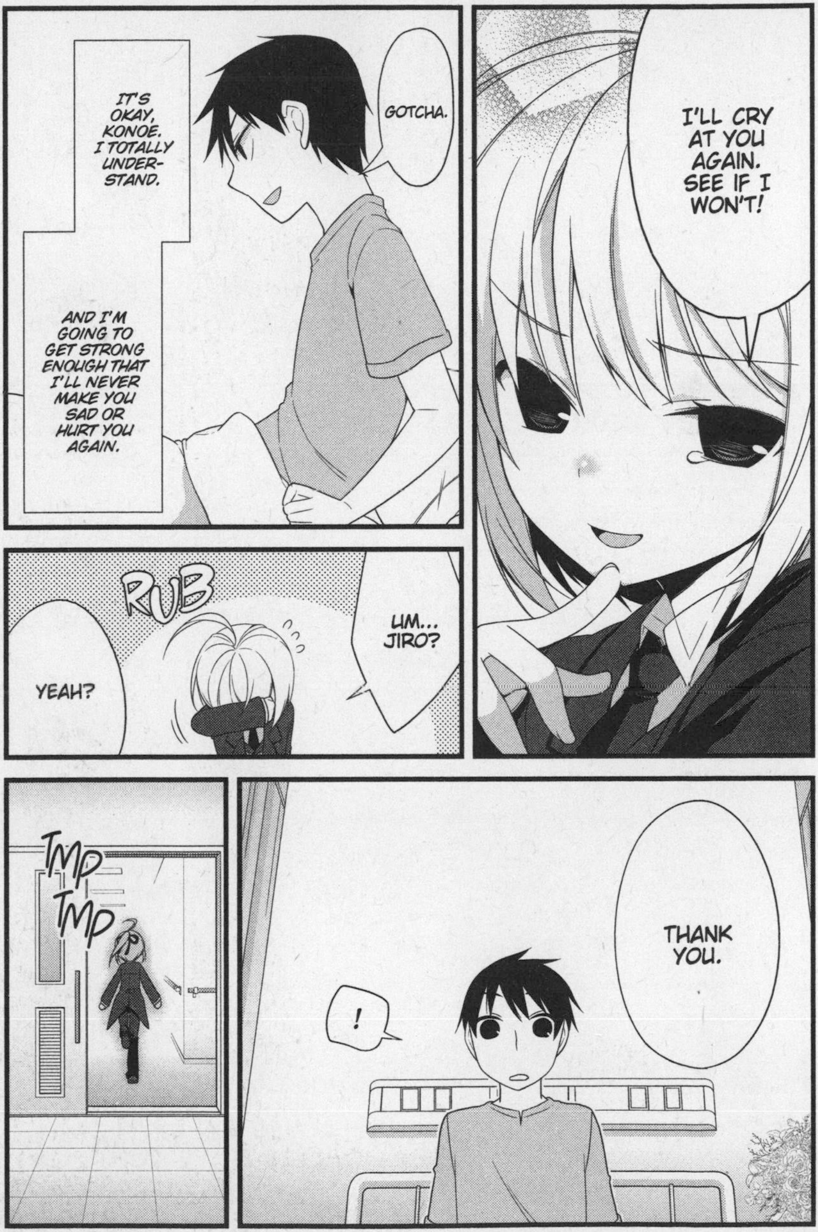
I'LL CRY AT YOU AGAIN. SEE IF I WON'T!
GOTCHA.
IT'S OKAY, KONOE. I TOTALLY UNDER-STAND.
AND I'M GOING TO GET STRONG ENOUGH THAT I'LL NEVER MAKE YOU SAD OR HURT YOU AGAIN.
UM... JIRO?
RUB
YEAH?
THANK YOU.
!
TMP TMP

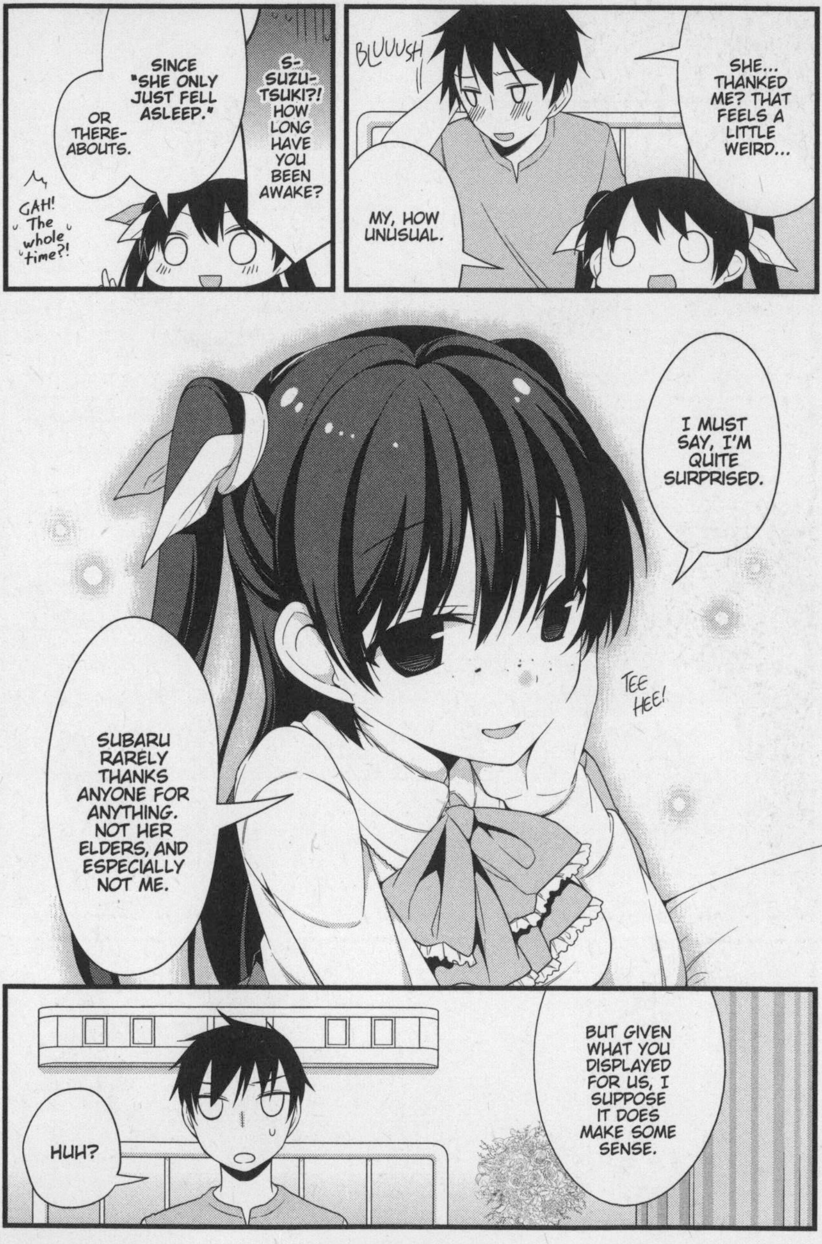
SHE... THANKED ME? THAT FEELS A LITTLE WEIRD...
BLUUUSH
MY, HOW UNUSUAL.
S-SUZUTSUKI?! HOW LONG HAVE YOU BEEN AWAKE?
SINCE "SHE ONLY JUST FELL ASLEEP."
OR THEREABOUTS.
GAH! The whole time?!
I MUST SAY, I'M QUITE SURPRISED.
TEE HEE!
SUBARU RARELY THANKS ANYONE FOR ANYTHING. NOT HER ELDERS, AND ESPECIALLY NOT ME.
BUT GIVEN WHAT YOU DISPLAYED FOR US, I SUPPOSE IT DOES MAKE SOME SENSE.
HUH?

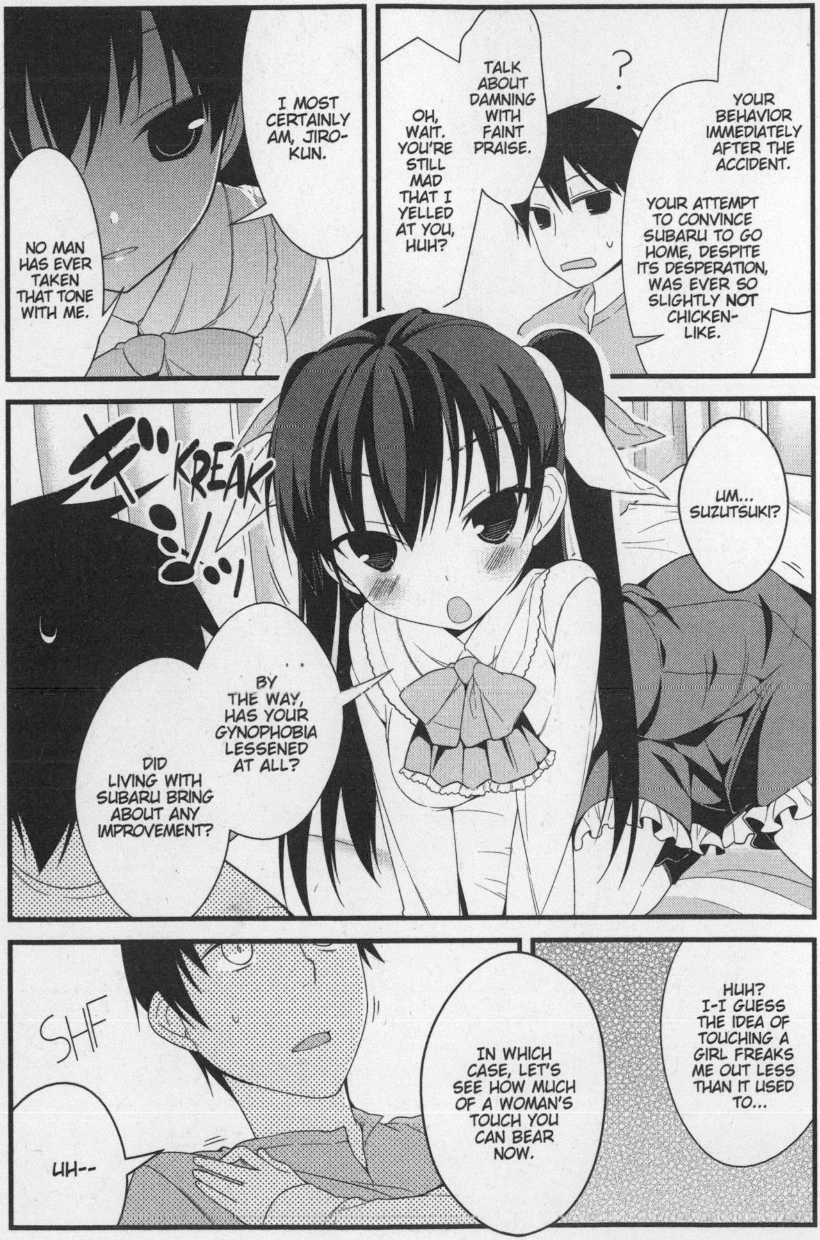
?
YOUR BEHAVIOR IMMEDIATELY AFTER THE ACCIDENT.
YOUR ATTEMPT TO CONVINCE SUBARU TO GO HOME, DESPITE ITS DESPERATION, WAS EVER SO SLIGHTLY NOT CHICKEN-LIKE.
TALK ABOUT DAMNING WITH FAINT PRAISE.
OH, WAIT. YOU'RE STILL MAD THAT I YELLED AT YOU, HUH?
I MOST CERTAINLY AM, JIRO-KUN.
NO MAN HAS EVER TAKEN THAT TONE WITH ME.
UM... SUZUTSUKI?
KREAK
BY THE WAY, HAS YOUR GYNOPHOBIA LESSENED AT ALL?
DID LIVING WITH SUBARU BRING ABOUT ANY IMPROVEMENT?
HUH? I-I GUESS THE IDEA OF TOUCHING A GIRL FREAKS ME OUT LESS THAN IT USED TO...
IN WHICH CASE, LET'S SEE HOW MUCH OF A WOMAN'S TOUCH YOU CAN BEAR NOW.
SHF
UH--

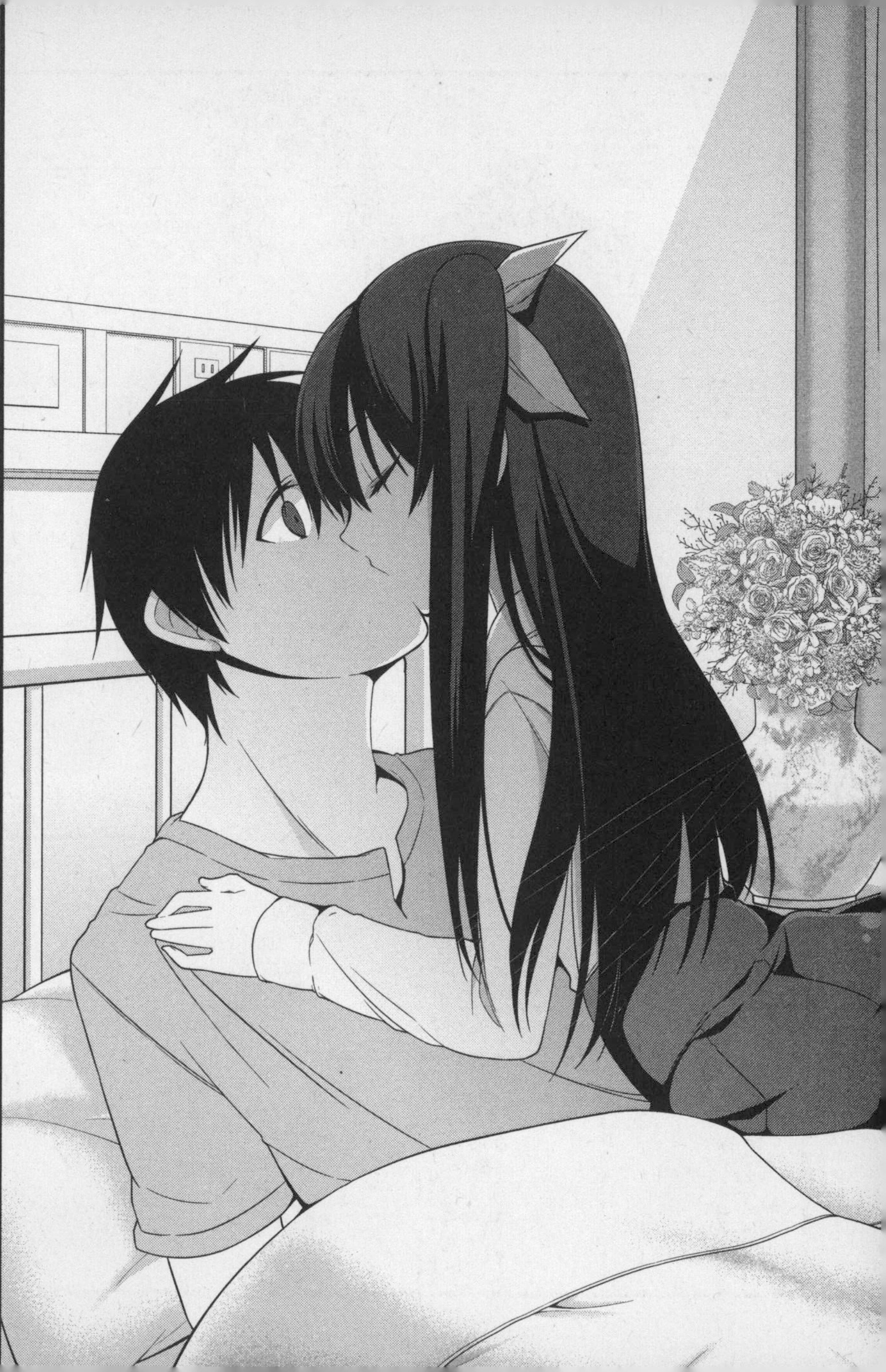

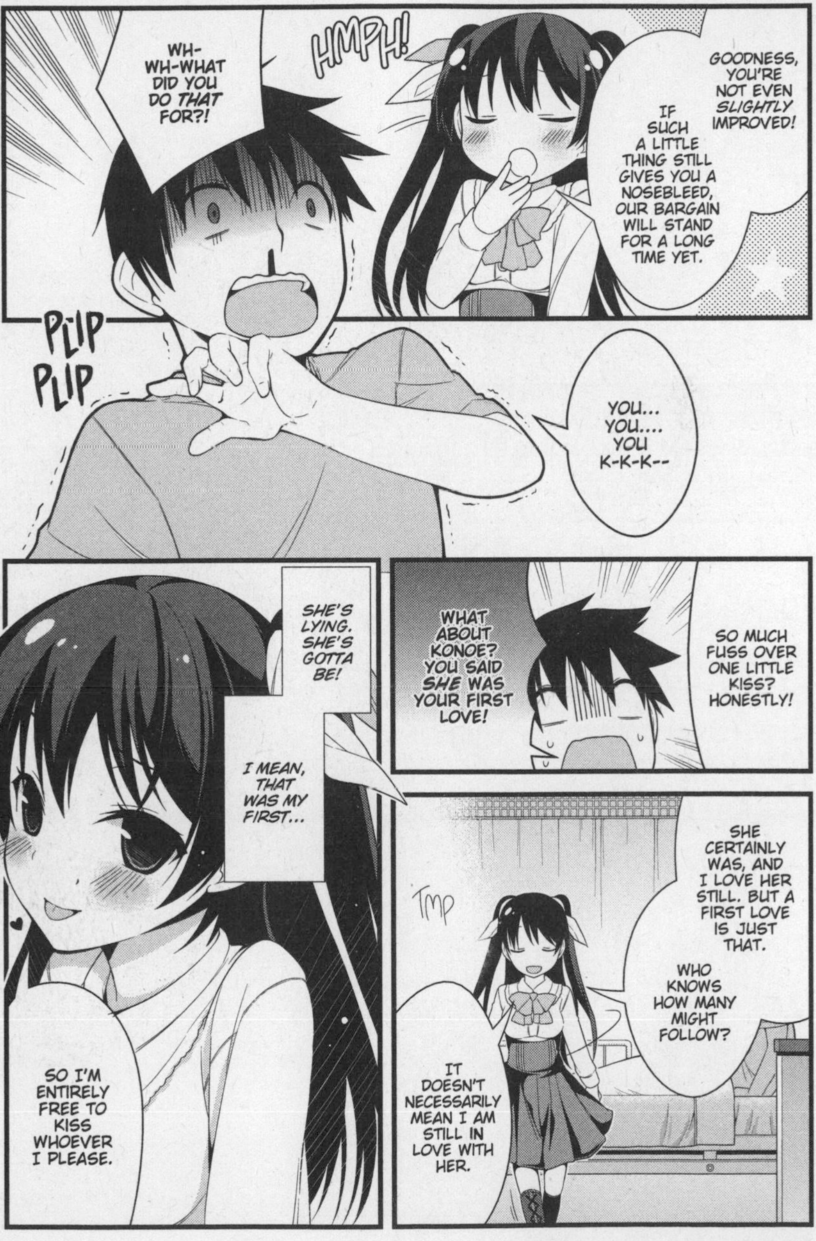
GOODNESS, YOU'RE NOT EVEN *SLIGHTLY* IMPROVED!
IF SUCH A LITTLE THING STILL GIVES YOU A NOSEBLEED, OUR BARGAIN WILL STAND FOR A LONG TIME YET.
HMPH!
WH- WH-WHAT DID YOU DO *THAT* FOR?!
YOU... YOU.... YOU K-K-K--
PLIP PLIP
SO MUCH FUSS OVER ONE LITTLE KISS? HONESTLY!
WHAT ABOUT KONOE? YOU SAID *SHE* WAS YOUR FIRST LOVE!
SHE CERTAINLY WAS, AND I LOVE HER STILL. BUT A FIRST LOVE IS JUST THAT.
WHO KNOWS HOW MANY MIGHT FOLLOW?
IT DOESN'T NECESSARILY MEAN I AM STILL IN LOVE WITH HER.
TMP
SHE'S LYING. SHE'S GOTTA BE!
I MEAN, THAT WAS MY FIRST...
SO I'M ENTIRELY FREE TO KISS WHOEVER I PLEASE.

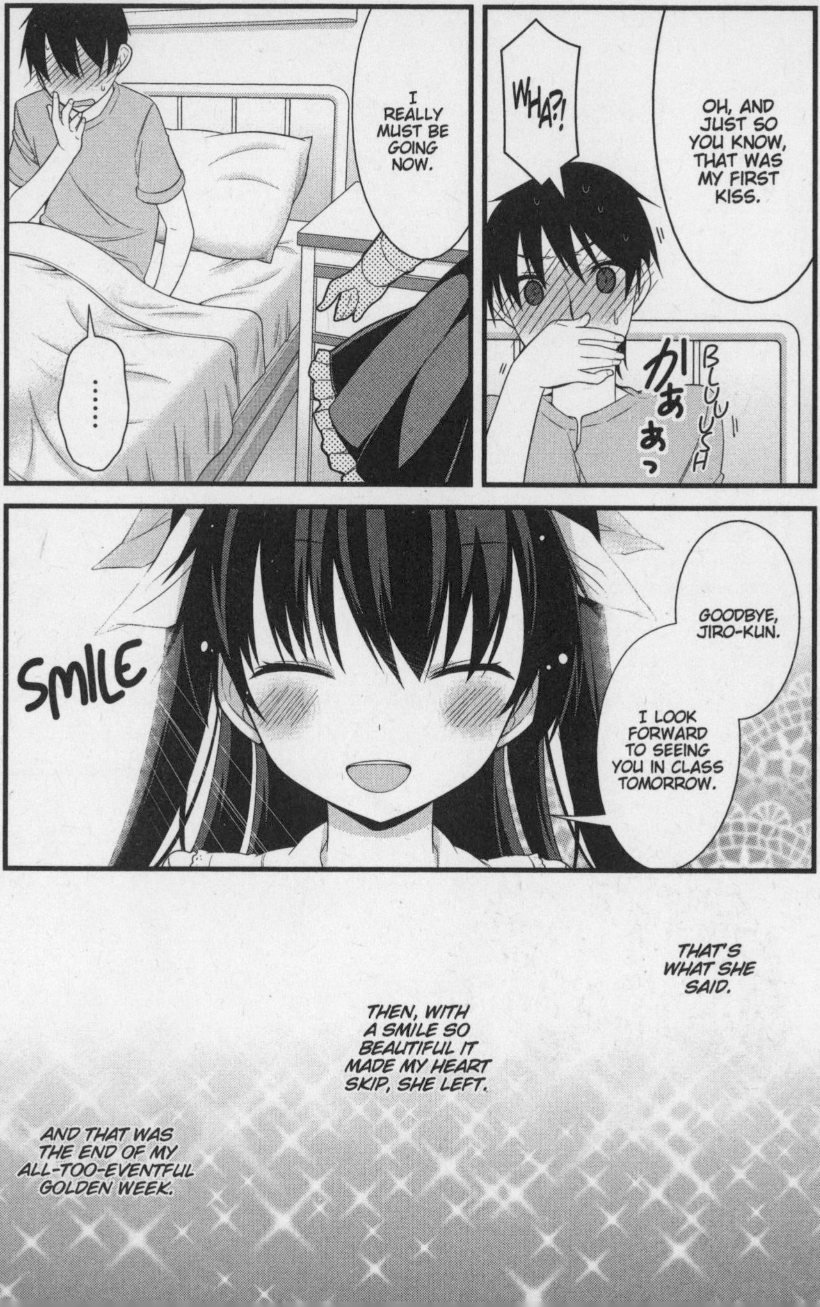
OH, AND JUST SO YOU KNOW, THAT WAS MY FIRST KISS.
WHA?!
BLUUUSH
かぁぁっ
I REALLY MUST BE GOING NOW.
......
GOODBYE, JIRO-KUN.
I LOOK FORWARD TO SEEING YOU IN CLASS TOMORROW.
SMILE
THAT'S WHAT SHE SAID.
THEN, WITH A SMILE SO BEAUTIFUL IT MADE MY HEART SKIP, SHE LEFT.
AND THAT WAS THE END OF MY ALL-TOO-EVENTFUL GOLDEN WEEK.

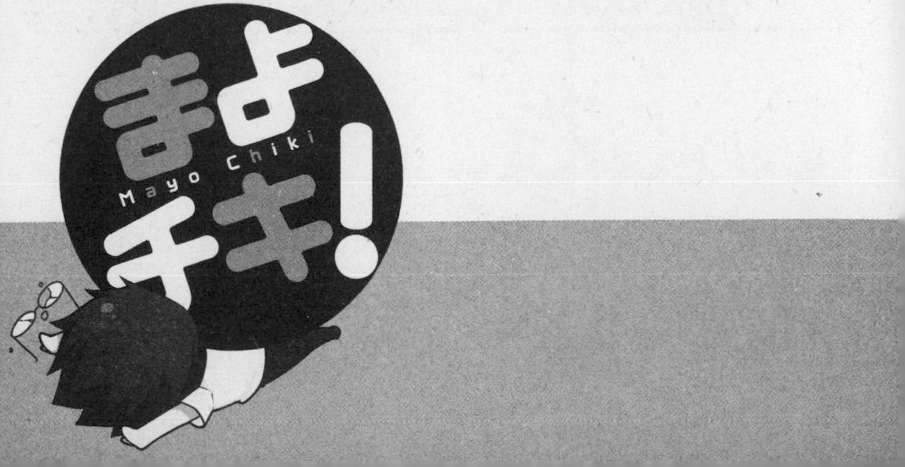
まよチキ!
Mayo Chiki

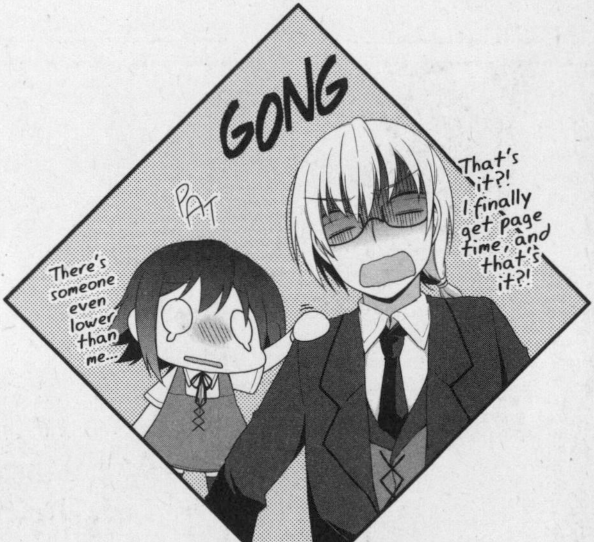
GONG
That's it?! I finally get page time, and that's it?!
PAT
There's someone even lower than me...

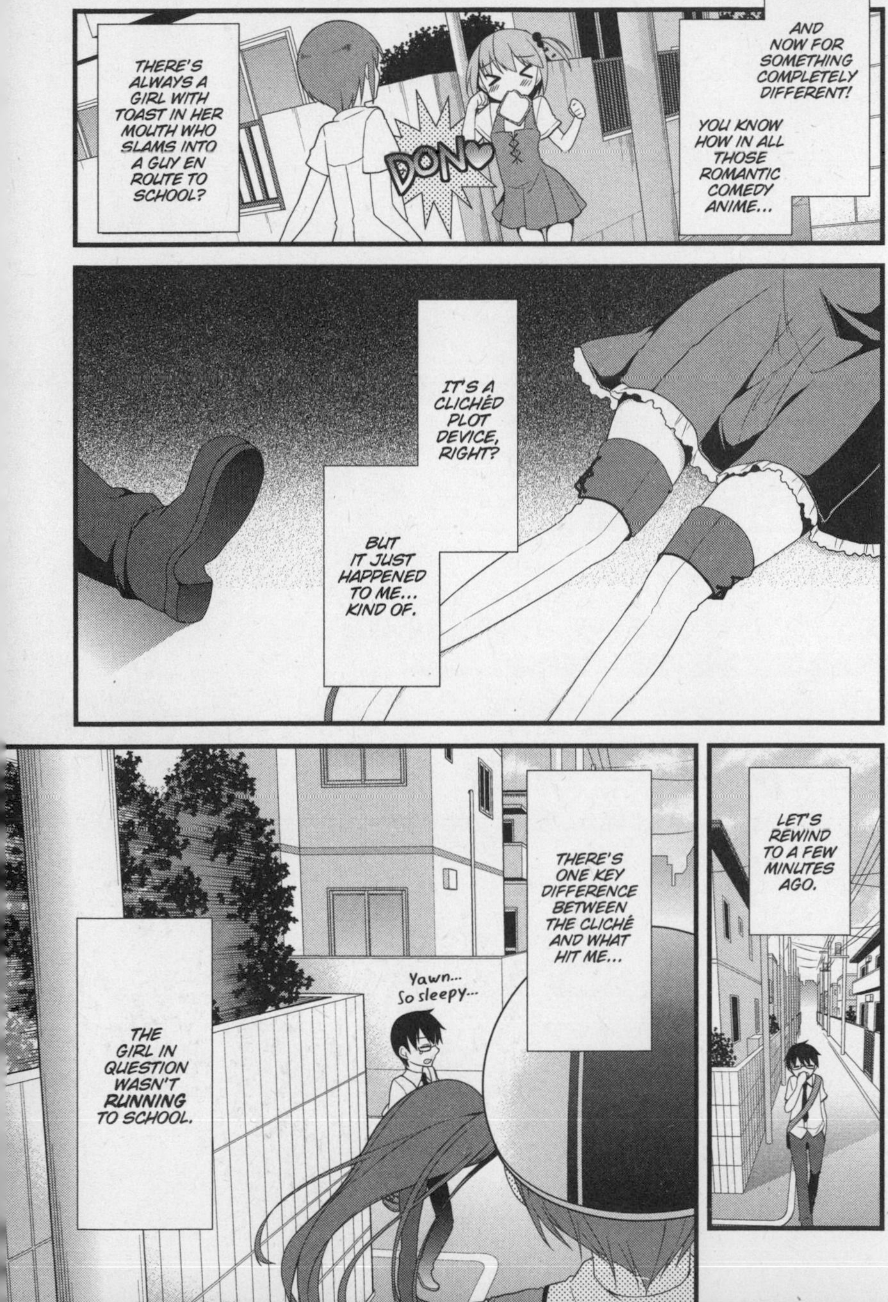

AND NOW FOR SOMETHING COMPLETELY DIFFERENT!
YOU KNOW HOW IN ALL THOSE ROMANTIC COMEDY ANIME...
THERE'S ALWAYS A GIRL WITH TOAST IN HER MOUTH WHO SLAMS INTO A GUY EN ROUTE TO SCHOOL?
DON♥
IT'S A CLICHÉD PLOT DEVICE, RIGHT?
BUT IT JUST HAPPENED TO ME... KIND OF.
LET'S REWIND TO A FEW MINUTES AGO.
THERE'S ONE KEY DIFFERENCE BETWEEN THE CLICHÉ AND WHAT HIT ME...
Yawn... So sleepy...
THE GIRL IN QUESTION WASN'T RUNNING TO SCHOOL.

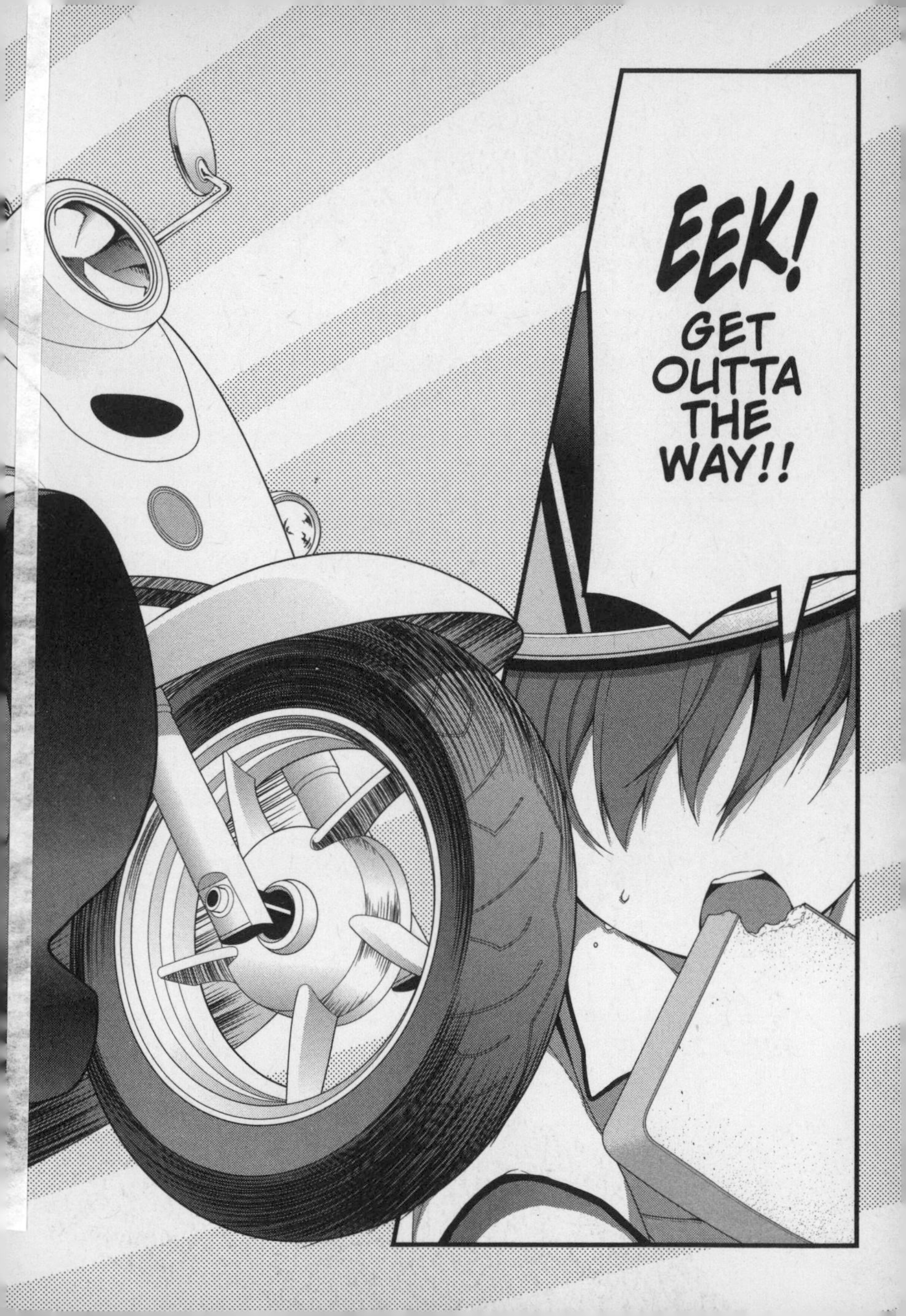
EEK!
GET OUTTA THE WAY!!

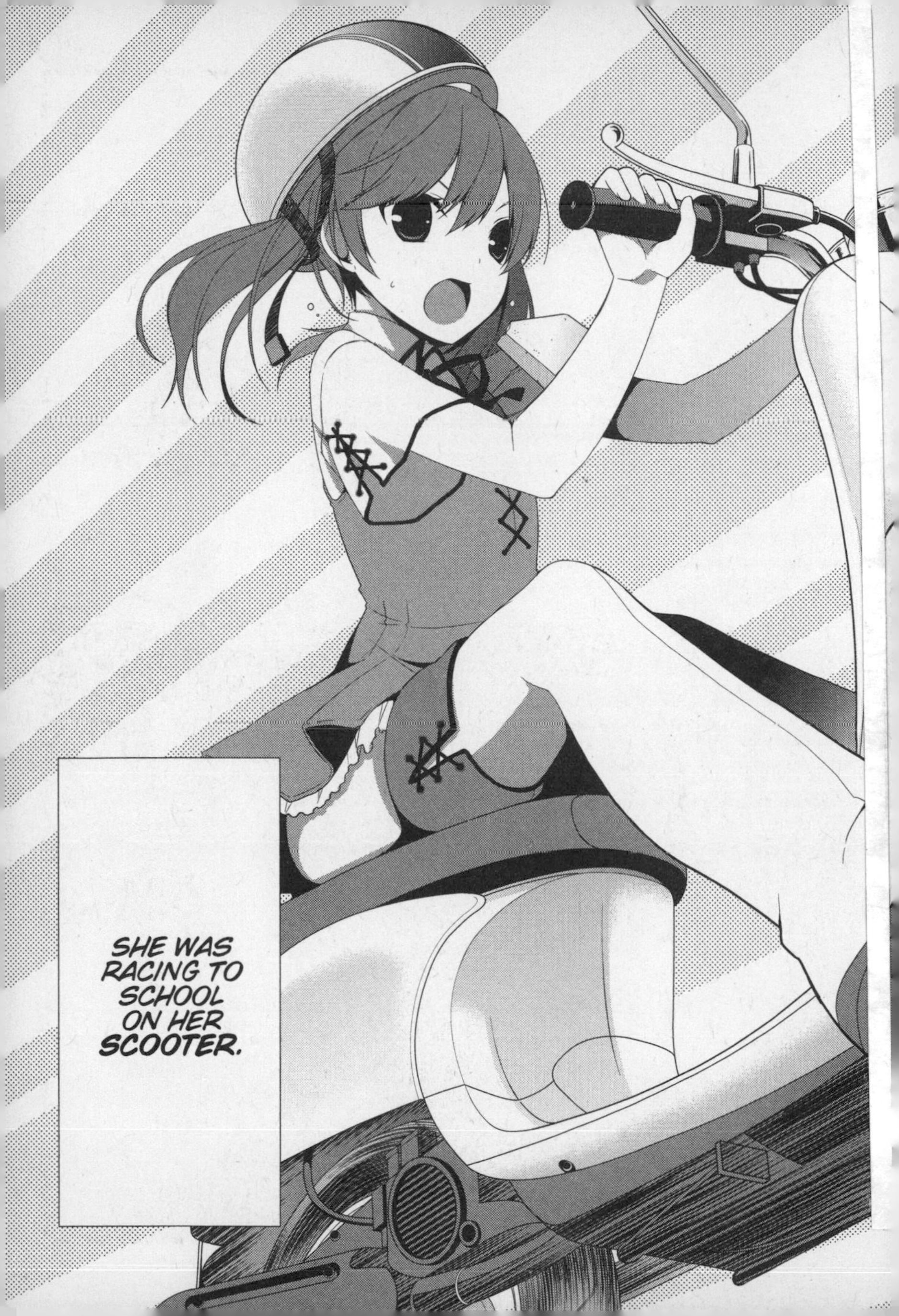
SHE WAS RACING TO SCHOOL ON HER SCOOTER.

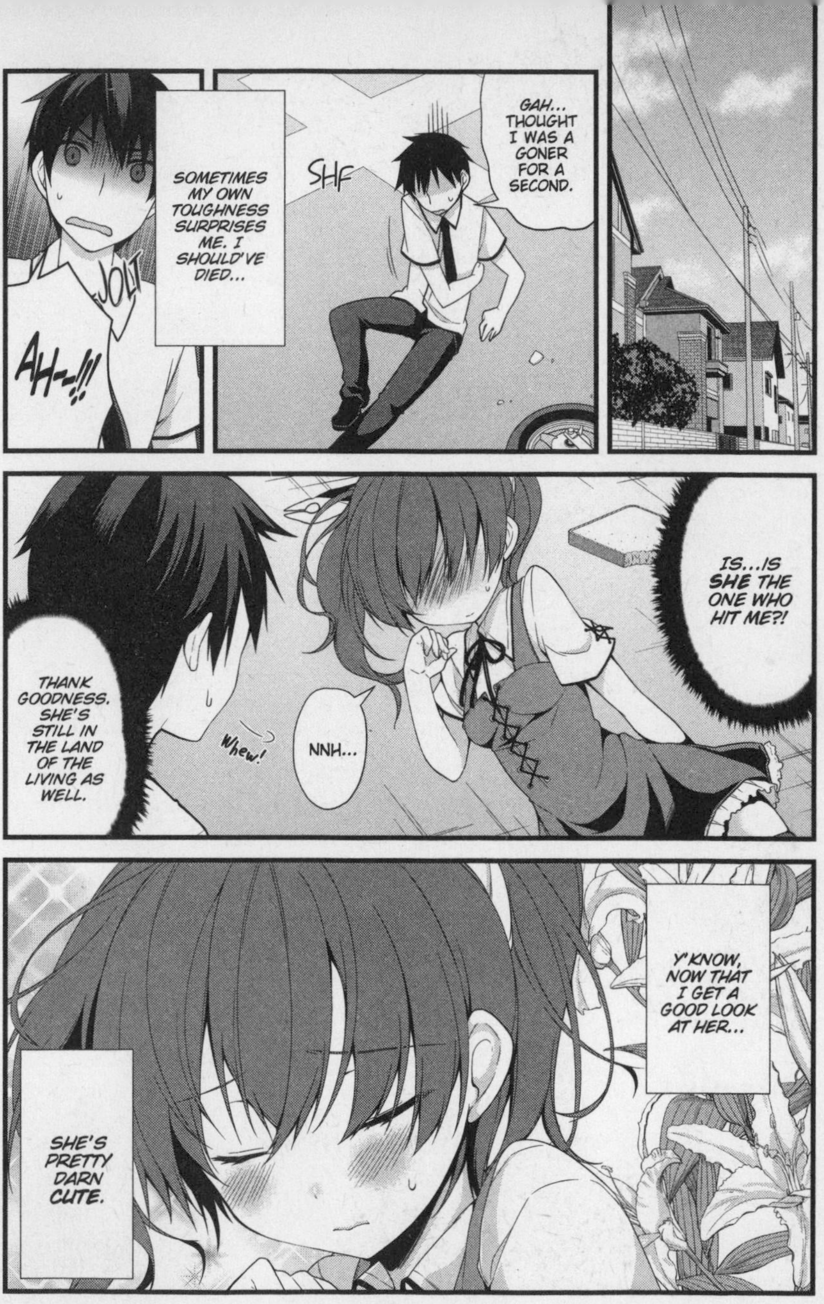
GAH... THOUGHT I WAS A GONER FOR A SECOND.
SHF
SOMETIMES MY OWN TOUGHNESS SURPRISES ME. I SHOULD'VE DIED...
JOLT
AH--!!!
IS...IS SHE THE ONE WHO HIT ME?!
NNH...
Whew!
THANK GOODNESS. SHE'S STILL IN THE LAND OF THE LIVING AS WELL.
Y'KNOW, NOW THAT I GET A GOOD LOOK AT HER...
SHE'S PRETTY DARN CUTE.

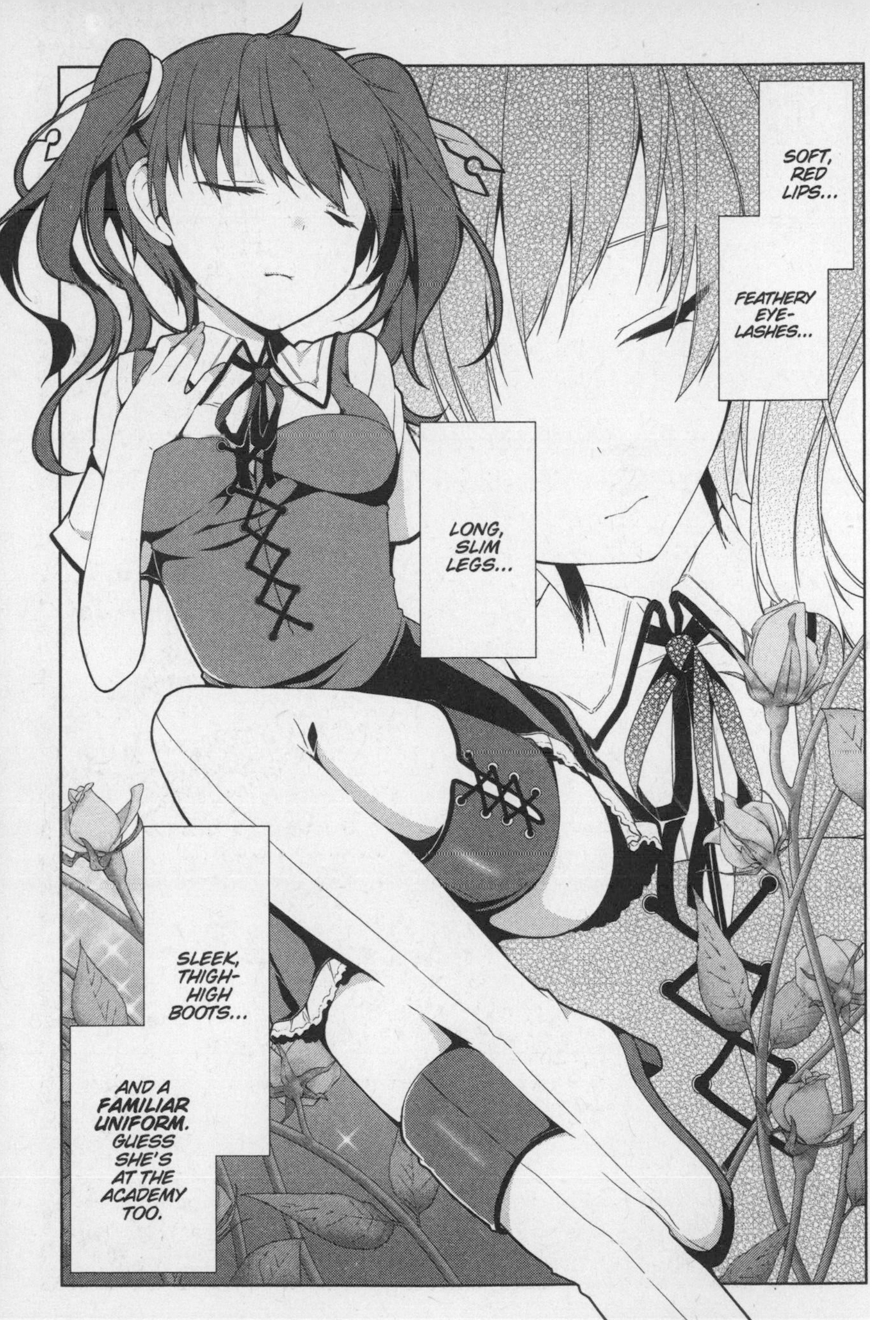
SOFT, RED LIPS...
FEATHERY EYE-LASHES...
LONG, SLIM LEGS...
SLEEK, THIGH-HIGH BOOTS...
AND A FAMILIAR UNIFORM. GUESS SHE'S AT THE ACADEMY TOO.

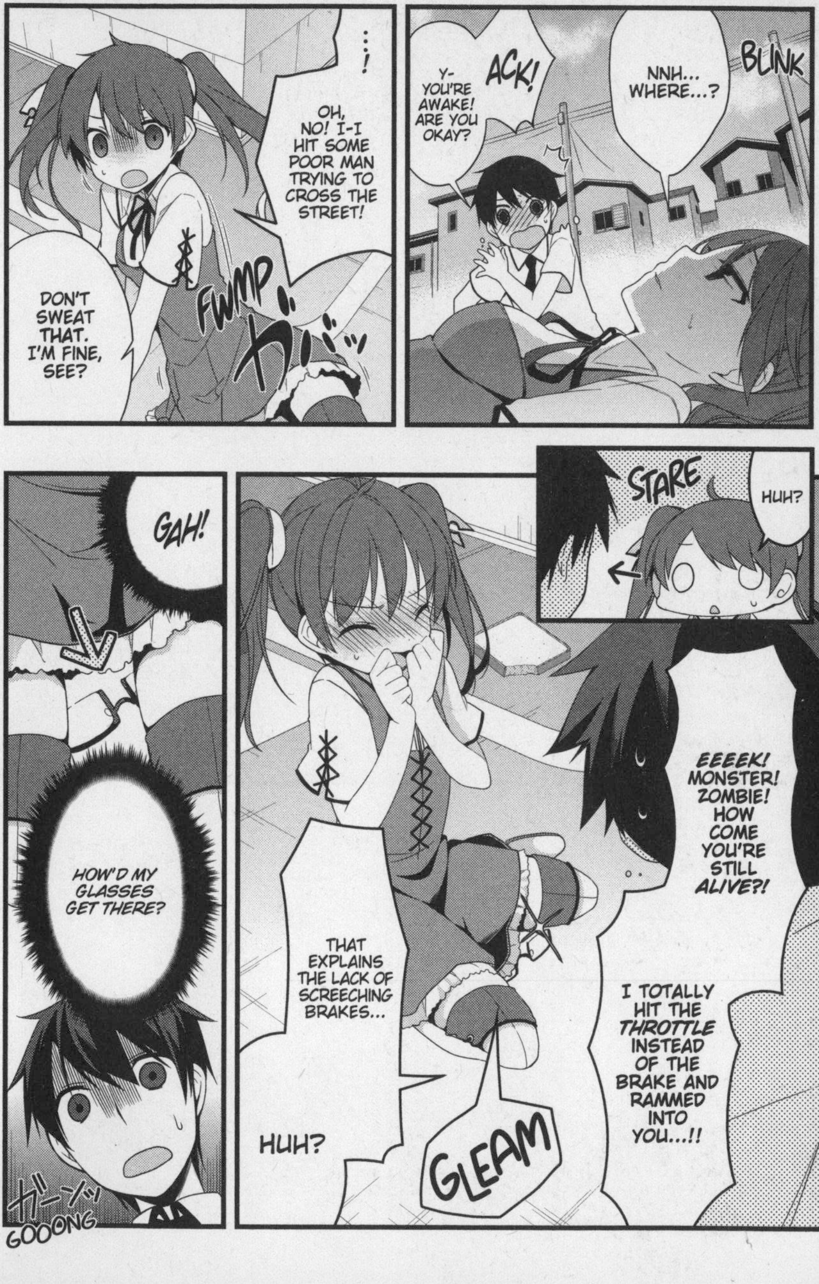
BLINK
NNH... WHERE...?
ACK!
Y- YOU'RE AWAKE! ARE YOU OKAY?
...!
OH, NO! I-I HIT SOME POOR MAN TRYING TO CROSS THE STREET!
FWMP
DON'T SWEAT THAT. I'M FINE, SEE?
STARE
HUH?
EEEEK! MONSTER! ZOMBIE! HOW COME YOU'RE STILL ALIVE?!
I TOTALLY HIT THE THROTTLE INSTEAD OF THE BRAKE AND RAMMED INTO YOU...!!
THAT EXPLAINS THE LACK OF SCREECHING BRAKES...
GLEAM
HUH?
GAH!
HOW'D MY GLASSES GET THERE?
GOOONG

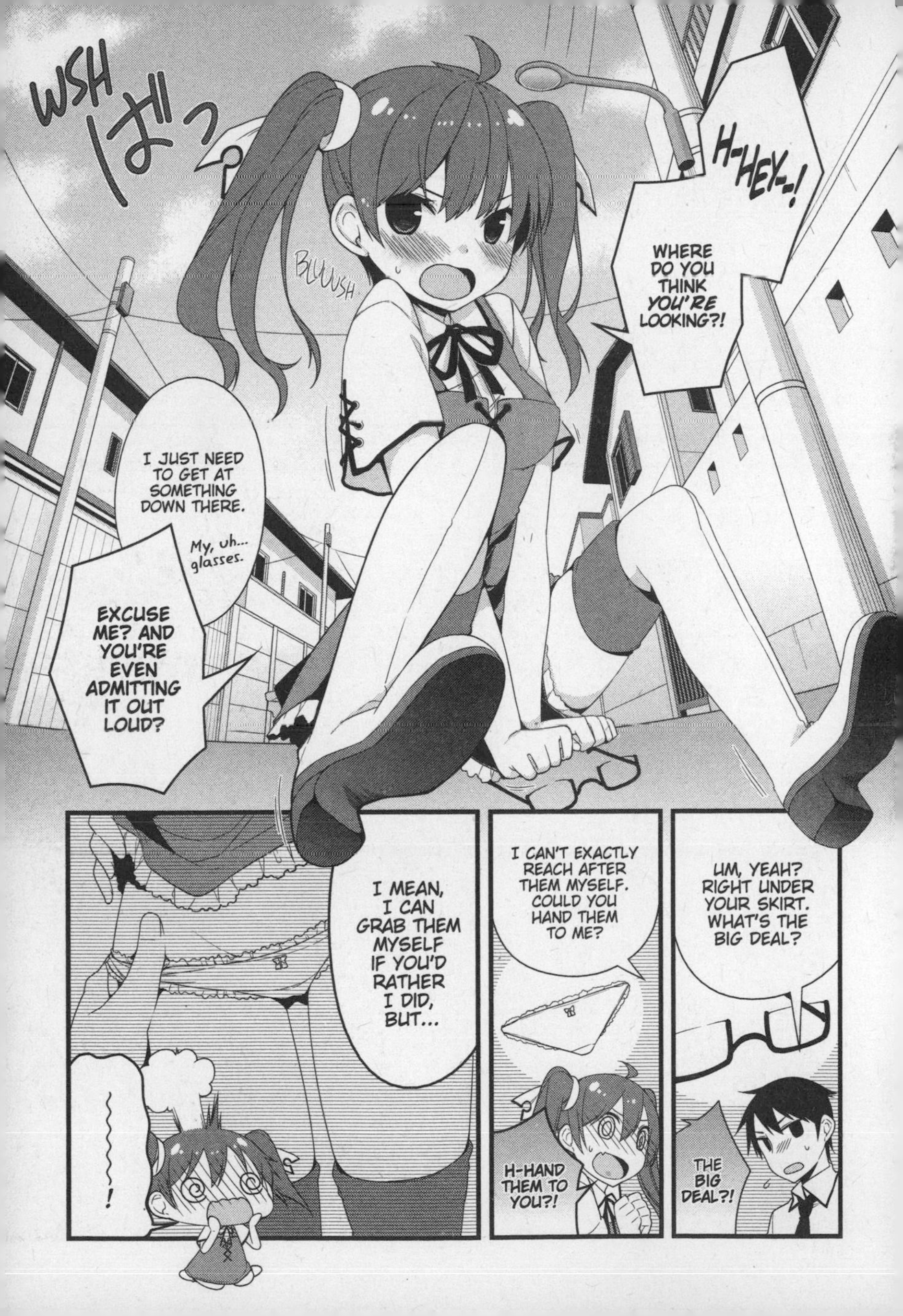
H-HEY--!
WHERE DO YOU THINK YOU'RE LOOKING?!
WSH ばっ
BLUUUSH
I JUST NEED TO GET AT SOMETHING DOWN THERE.
My, uh... glasses.
EXCUSE ME? AND YOU'RE EVEN ADMITTING IT OUT LOUD?
UM, YEAH? RIGHT UNDER YOUR SKIRT. WHAT'S THE BIG DEAL?
THE BIG DEAL?!
I CAN'T EXACTLY REACH AFTER THEM MYSELF. COULD YOU HAND THEM TO ME?
H-HAND THEM TO YOU?!
I MEAN, I CAN GRAB THEM MYSELF IF YOU'D RATHER I DID, BUT...
〜〜〜〜!

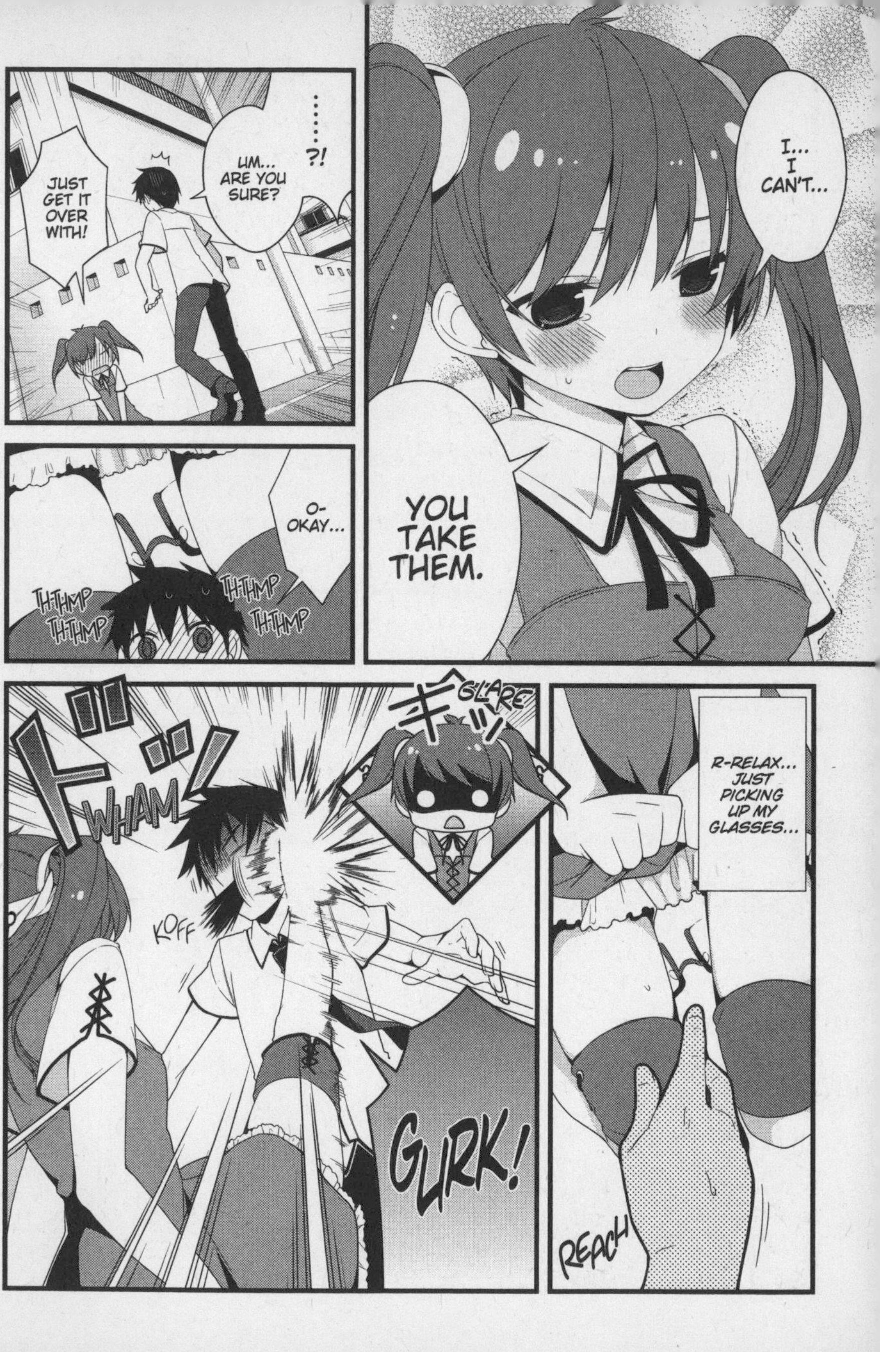
I... I CAN'T...
YOU TAKE THEM.
......?!
UM... ARE YOU SURE?
JUST GET IT OVER WITH!
O-OKAY...
TH-THMP
TH-THMP
TH-THMP
TH-THMP
R-RELAX... JUST PICKING UP MY GLASSES...
REACH
GLARE
WHAM!
KOFF
GURK!

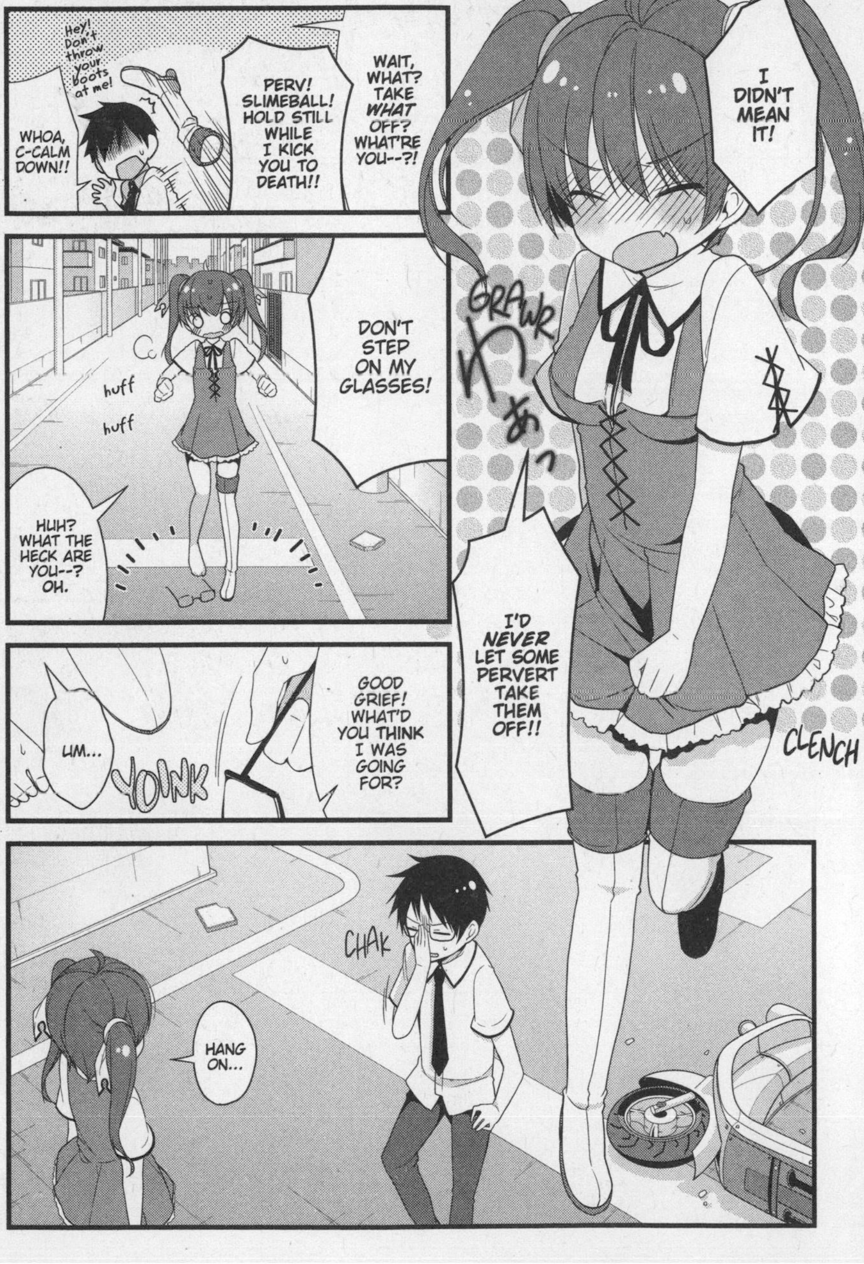
I DIDN'T MEAN IT!
GRAWR
ゆあっ
I'D NEVER LET SOME PERVERT TAKE THEM OFF!!
CLENCH
WAIT, WHAT? TAKE WHAT OFF? WHAT'RE YOU--?!
PERV! SLIMEBALL! HOLD STILL WHILE I KICK YOU TO DEATH!!
Hey! Don't throw your boots at me!
WHOA, C-CALM DOWN!!
DON'T STEP ON MY GLASSES!
huff
huff
HUH? WHAT THE HECK ARE YOU--? OH.
GOOD GRIEF! WHAT'D YOU THINK I WAS GOING FOR?
YOINK
UM...
CHAK
HANG ON...

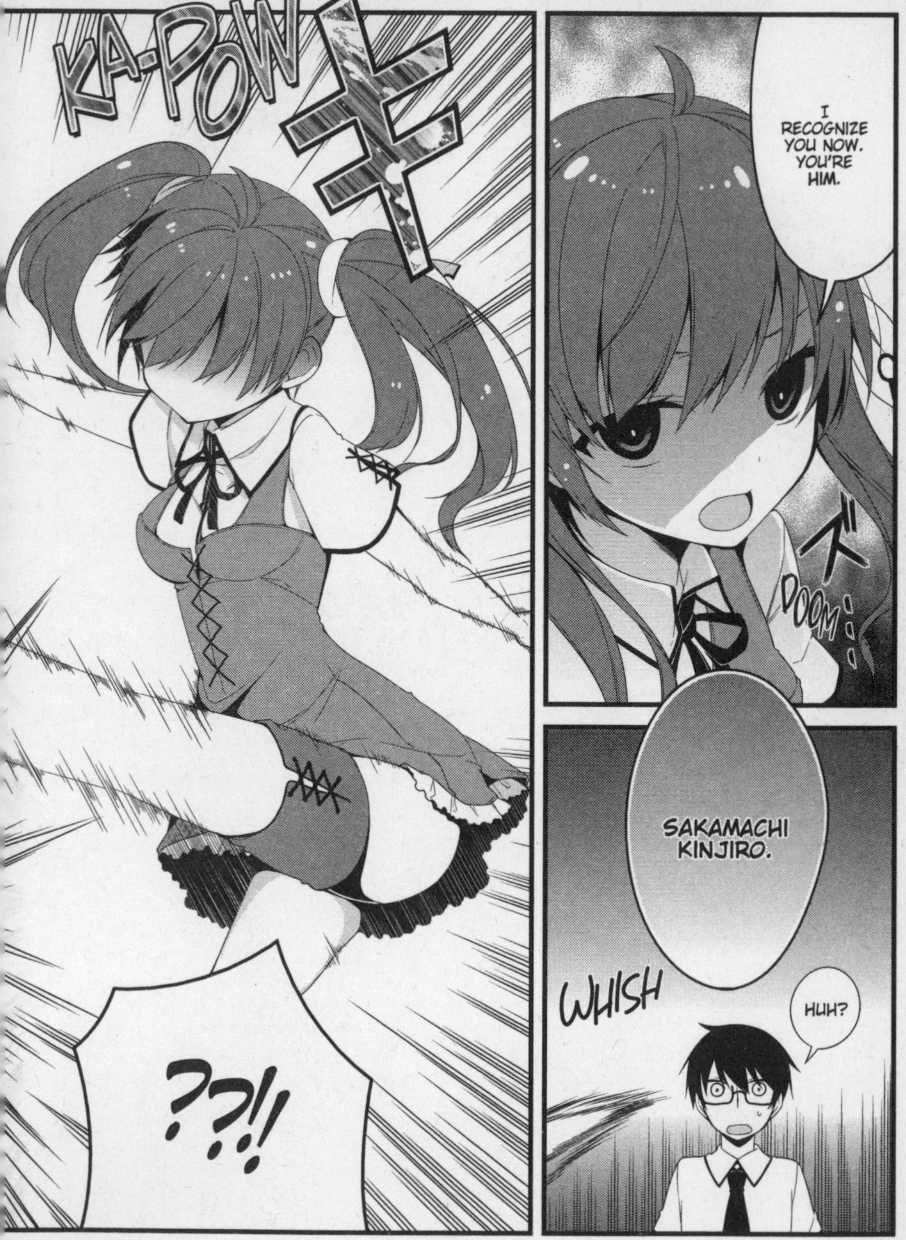
I RECOGNIZE YOU NOW. YOU'RE HIM.
DOOM
SAKAMACHI KINJIRO.
WHISH
HUH?
KA-POW
??!!

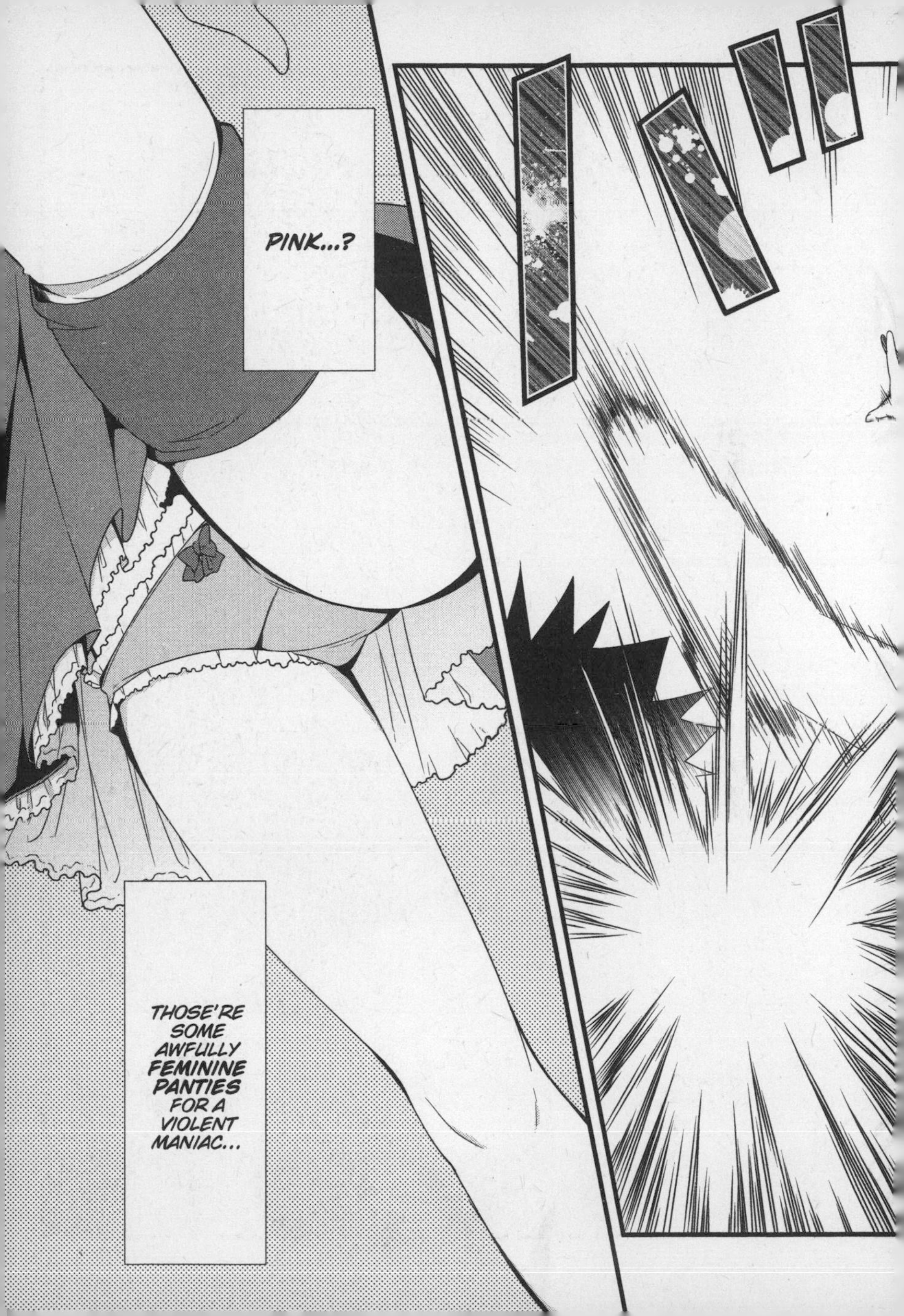
PINK...?
THOSE'RE SOME AWFULLY FEMININE PANTIES FOR A VIOLENT MANIAC...

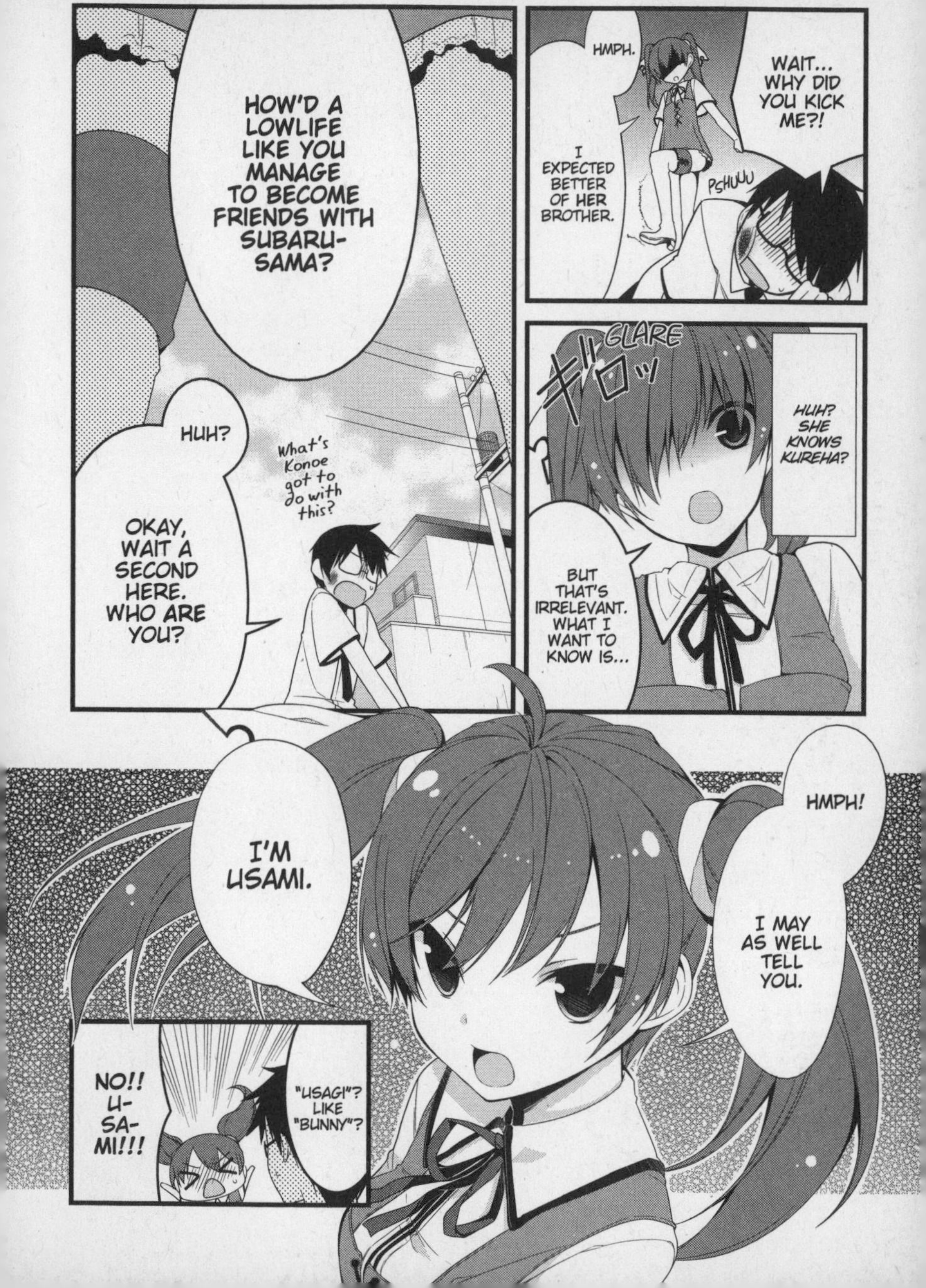
WAIT... WHY DID YOU KICK ME?!
HMPH.
PSHUUU
I EXPECTED BETTER OF HER BROTHER.
GLARE
ギロッ
HUH? SHE KNOWS KUREHA?
BUT THAT'S IRRELEVANT. WHAT I WANT TO KNOW IS...
HOW'D A LOWLIFE LIKE YOU MANAGE TO BECOME FRIENDS WITH SUBARU-SAMA?
HUH?
What's Konoe got to do with this?
OKAY, WAIT A SECOND HERE. WHO ARE YOU?
HMPH!
I MAY AS WELL TELL YOU.
I'M USAMI.
"USAGI"? LIKE "BUNNY"?
NO!! U-SA-MI!!!

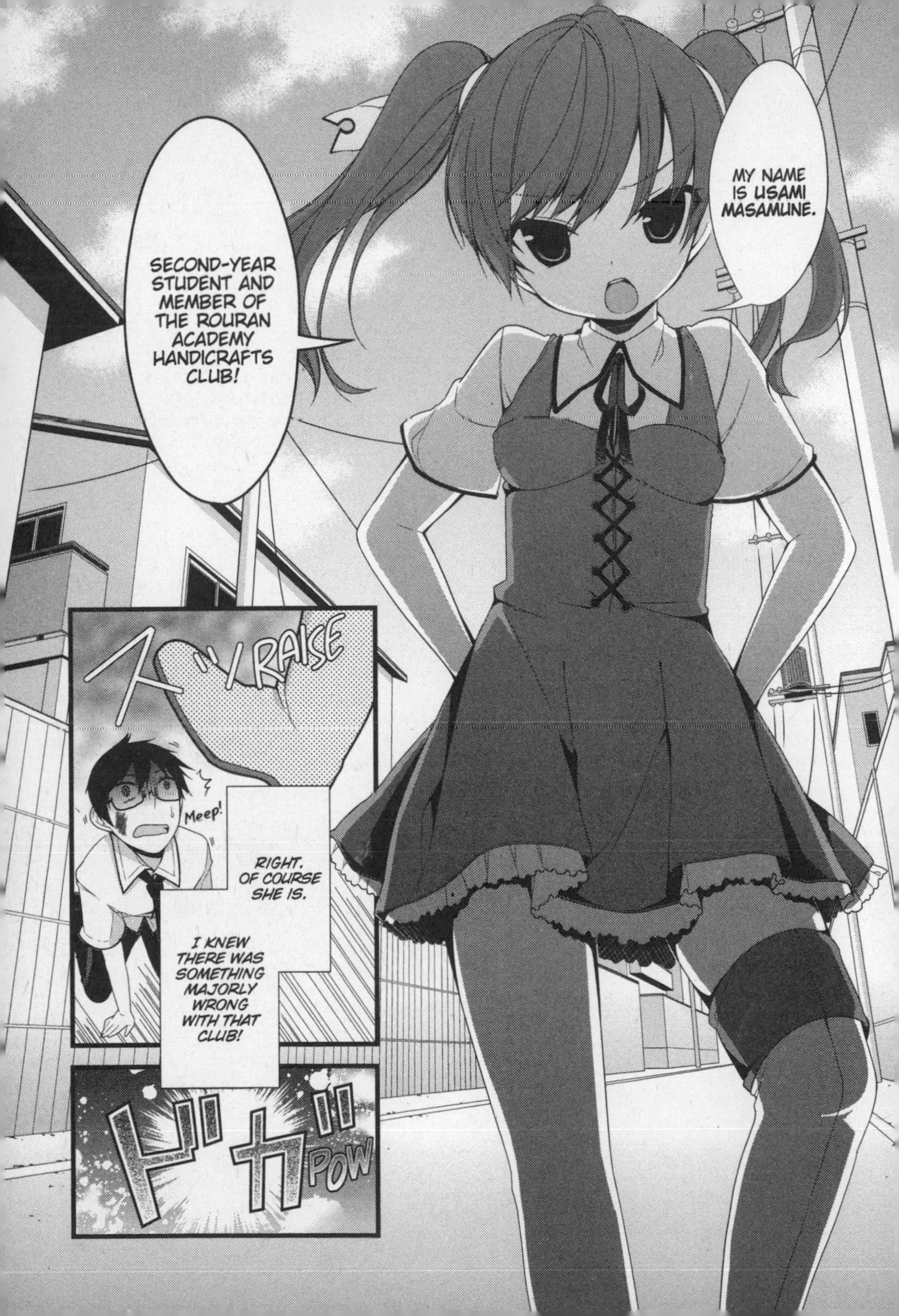
MY NAME IS USAMI MASAMUNE.
SECOND-YEAR STUDENT AND MEMBER OF THE ROURAN ACADEMY HANDICRAFTS CLUB!
RAISE
Meep!
RIGHT. OF COURSE SHE IS.
I KNEW THERE WAS SOMETHING MAJORLY WRONG WITH THAT CLUB!
POW

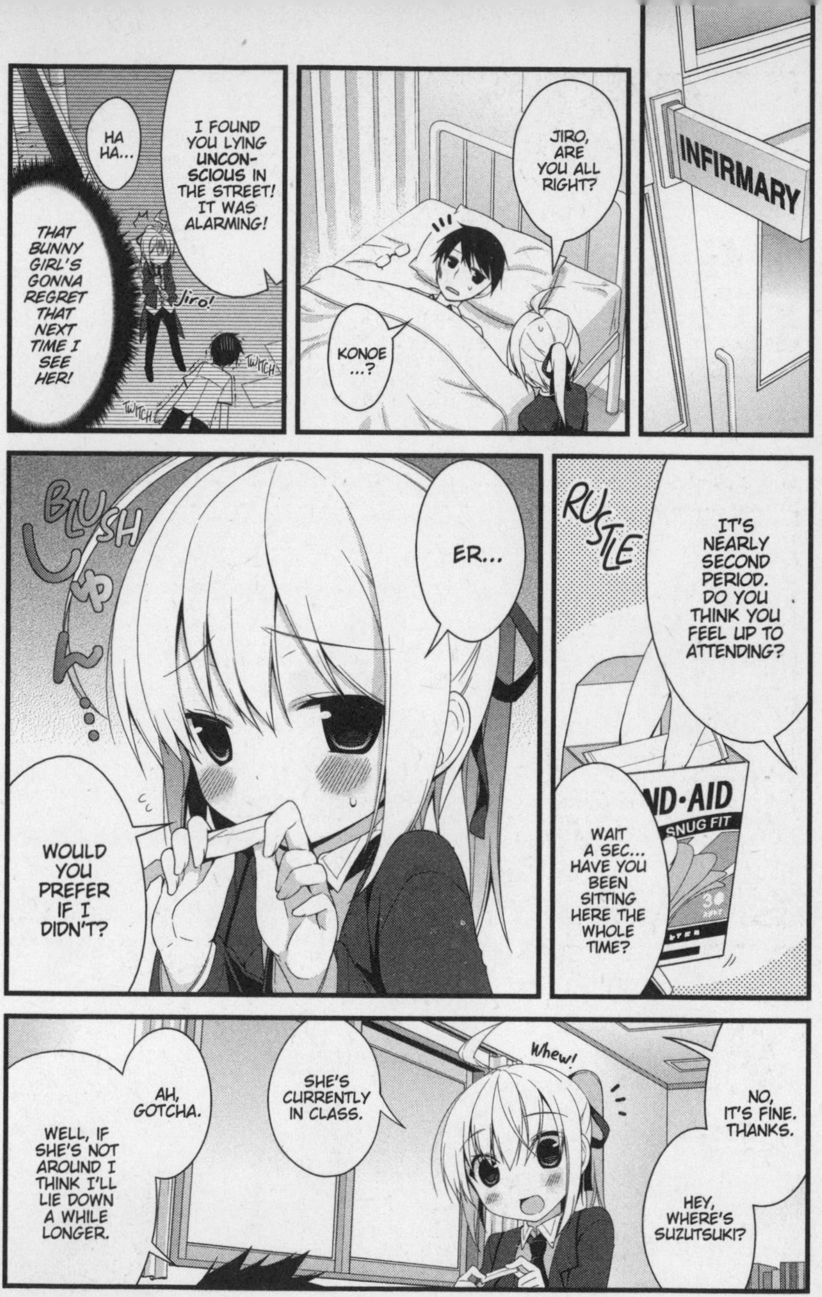
INFIRMARY
JIRO, ARE YOU ALL RIGHT?
KONOE ...?
I FOUND YOU LYING UNCON-SCIOUS IN THE STREET! IT WAS ALARMING!
HA HA...
Jiro!
THAT BUNNY GIRL'S GONNA REGRET THAT NEXT TIME I SEE HER!
TWITCH
TWITCH
RUSTLE
IT'S NEARLY SECOND PERIOD. DO YOU THINK YOU FEEL UP TO ATTENDING?
ND·AID
SNUG FIT
WAIT A SEC... HAVE YOU BEEN SITTING HERE THE WHOLE TIME?
ER...
BLUSH
WOULD YOU PREFER IF I DIDN'T?
NO, IT'S FINE. THANKS.
HEY, WHERE'S SUZUTSUKI?
Whew!
SHE'S CURRENTLY IN CLASS.
AH, GOTCHA.
WELL, IF SHE'S NOT AROUND I THINK I'LL LIE DOWN A WHILE LONGER.

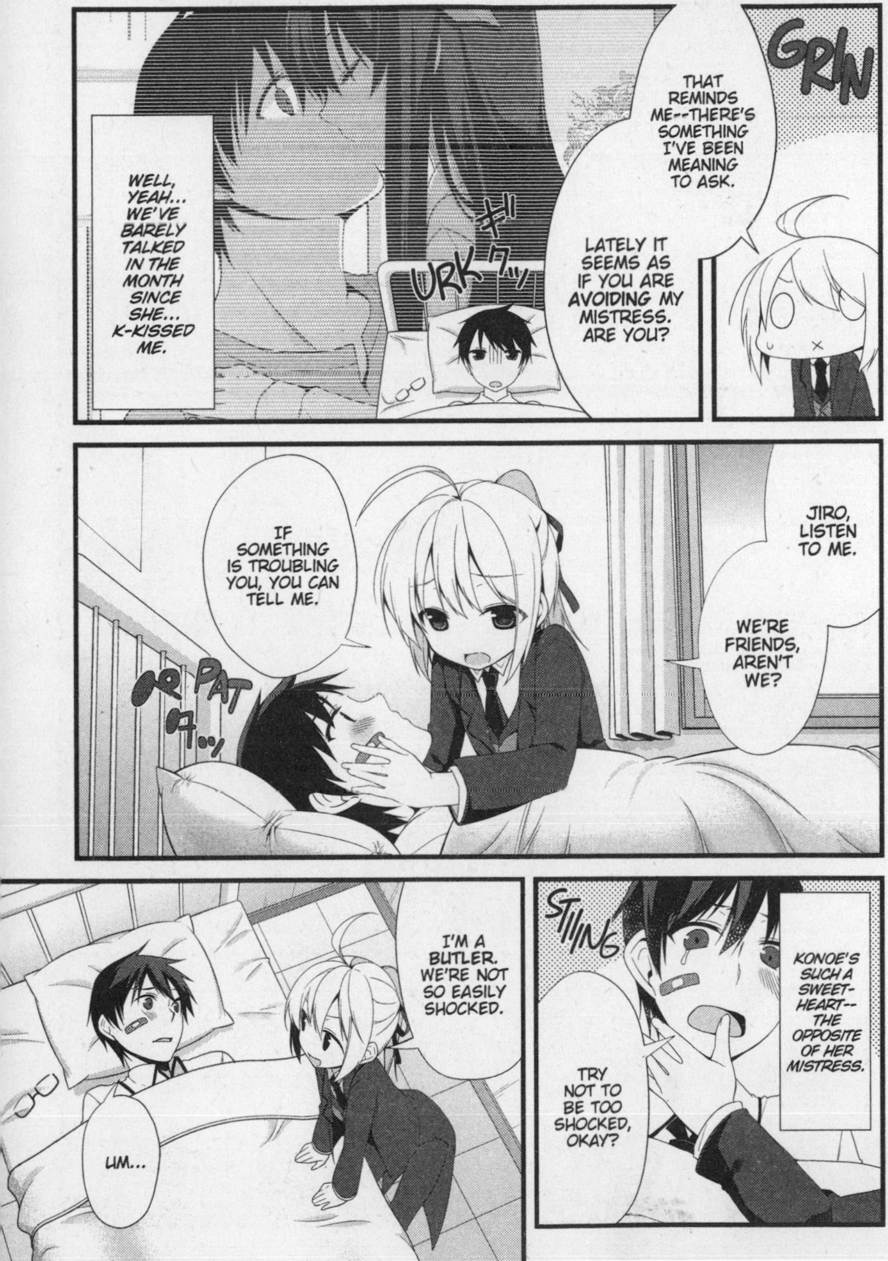
GRIN
THAT REMINDS ME--THERE'S SOMETHING I'VE BEEN MEANING TO ASK.
LATELY IT SEEMS AS IF YOU ARE AVOIDING MY MISTRESS. ARE YOU?
URK
WELL, YEAH... WE'VE BARELY TALKED IN THE MONTH SINCE SHE... K-KISSED ME.
JIRO, LISTEN TO ME.
WE'RE FRIENDS, AREN'T WE?
IF SOMETHING IS TROUBLING YOU, YOU CAN TELL ME.
PAT
STING
KONOE'S SUCH A SWEET-HEART--THE OPPOSITE OF HER MISTRESS.
TRY NOT TO BE TOO SHOCKED, OKAY?
I'M A BUTLER. WE'RE NOT SO EASILY SHOCKED.
UM...

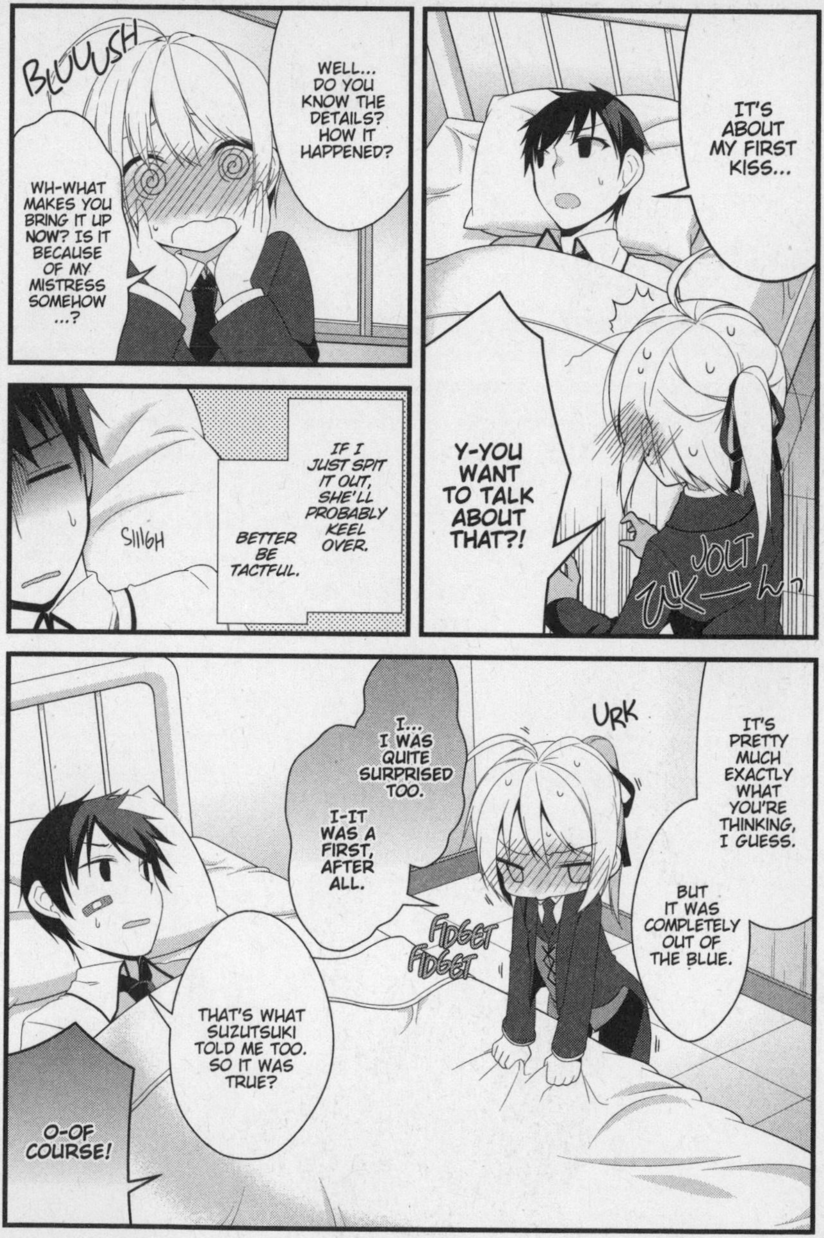
IT'S ABOUT MY FIRST KISS...
Y-YOU WANT TO TALK ABOUT THAT?!
JOLT
びくーんっ
WELL... DO YOU KNOW THE DETAILS? HOW IT HAPPENED?
BLUUUSH
WH-WHAT MAKES YOU BRING IT UP NOW? IS IT BECAUSE OF MY MISTRESS SOMEHOW ...?
IF I JUST SPIT IT OUT, SHE'LL PROBABLY KEEL OVER.
BETTER BE TACTFUL.
SIIIGH
IT'S PRETTY MUCH EXACTLY WHAT YOU'RE THINKING, I GUESS.
BUT IT WAS COMPLETELY OUT OF THE BLUE.
URK
I... I WAS QUITE SURPRISED TOO.
I-IT WAS A FIRST, AFTER ALL.
FIDGET FIDGET
THAT'S WHAT SUZUTSUKI TOLD ME TOO. SO IT WAS TRUE?
O-OF COURSE!

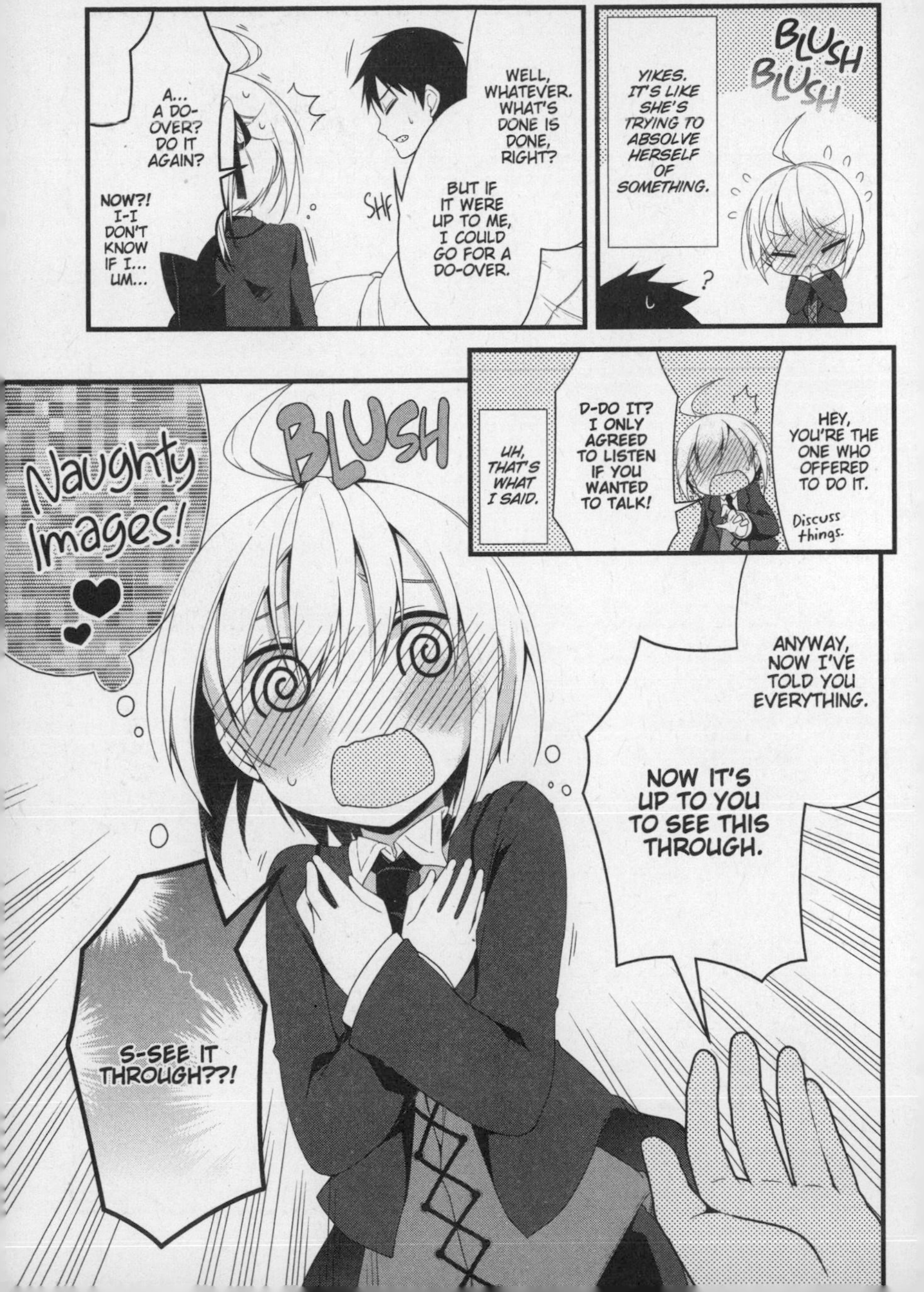
BLUSH BLUSH
YIKES. IT'S LIKE SHE'S TRYING TO ABSOLVE HERSELF OF SOMETHING.
?
WELL, WHATEVER. WHAT'S DONE IS DONE, RIGHT?
BUT IF IT WERE UP TO ME, I COULD GO FOR A DO-OVER.
SHF
A... A DO-OVER? DO IT AGAIN?
NOW?! I-I DON'T KNOW IF I... UM...
HEY, YOU'RE THE ONE WHO OFFERED TO DO IT.
Discuss things.
D-DO IT? I ONLY AGREED TO LISTEN IF YOU WANTED TO TALK!
UH, THAT'S WHAT I SAID.
ANYWAY, NOW I'VE TOLD YOU EVERYTHING.
NOW IT'S UP TO YOU TO SEE THIS THROUGH.
BLUSH
Naughty Images!
S-SEE IT THROUGH??!

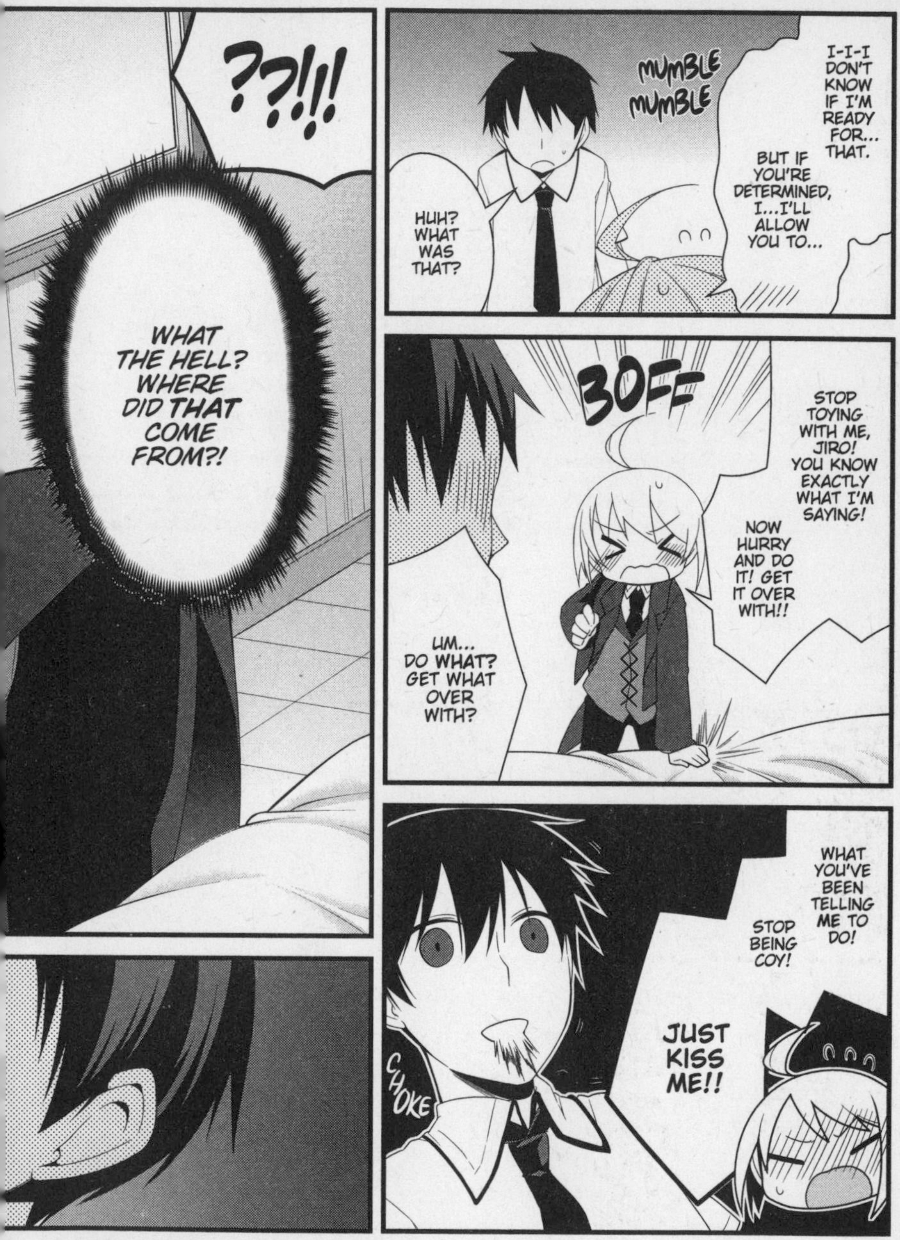
I-I-I DON'T KNOW IF I'M READY FOR... THAT.
BUT IF YOU'RE DETERMINED, I...I'LL ALLOW YOU TO...
MUMBLE MUMBLE
HUH? WHAT WAS THAT?
BOFF
STOP TOYING WITH ME, JIRO! YOU KNOW EXACTLY WHAT I'M SAYING!
NOW HURRY AND DO IT! GET IT OVER WITH!!
UM... DO WHAT? GET WHAT OVER WITH?
WHAT YOU'VE BEEN TELLING ME TO DO!
STOP BEING COY!
JUST KISS ME!!
CHOKE
??!!!
WHAT THE HELL? WHERE DID THAT COME FROM?!

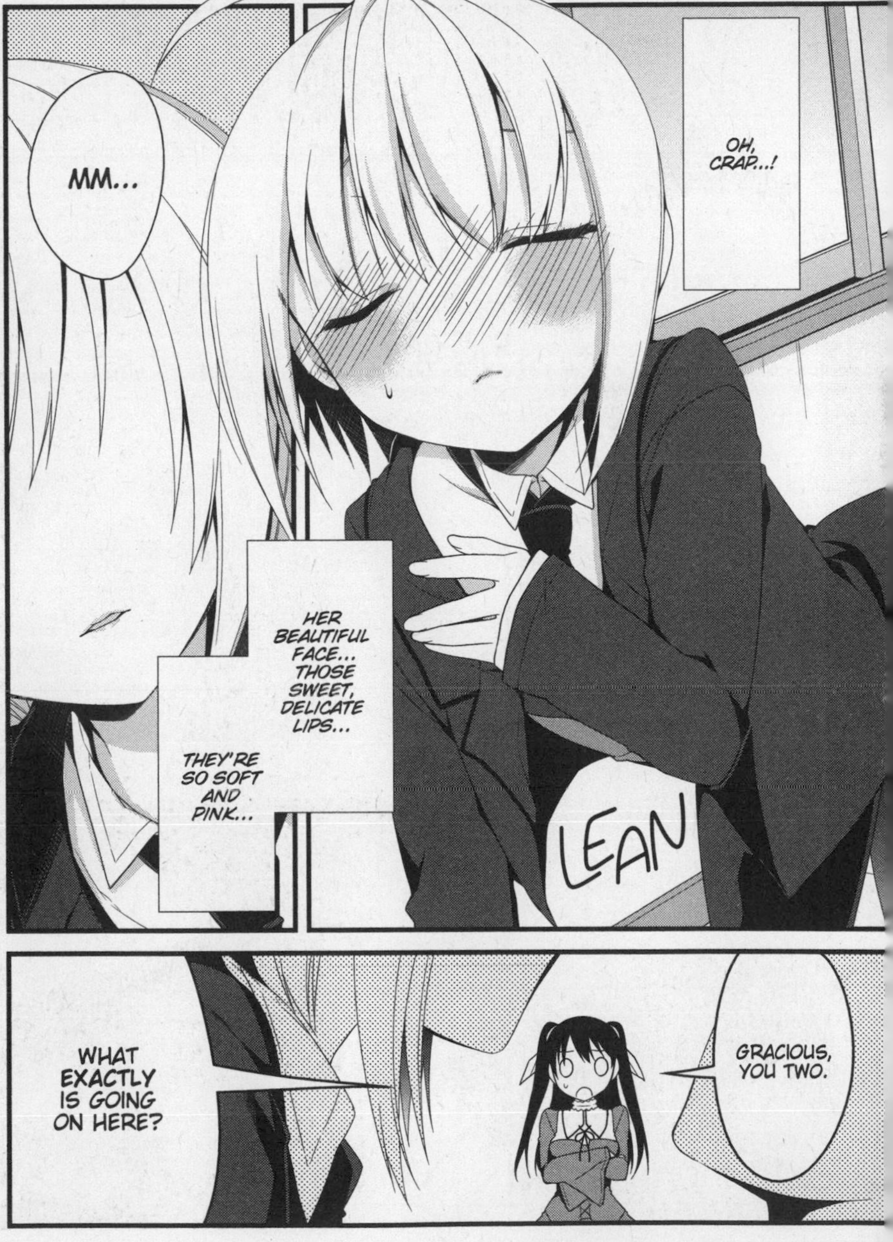

OH, CRAP...!
HER BEAUTIFUL FACE... THOSE SWEET, DELICATE LIPS...
THEY'RE SO SOFT AND PINK...
LEAN
MM...
GRACIOUS, YOU TWO.
WHAT EXACTLY IS GOING ON HERE?

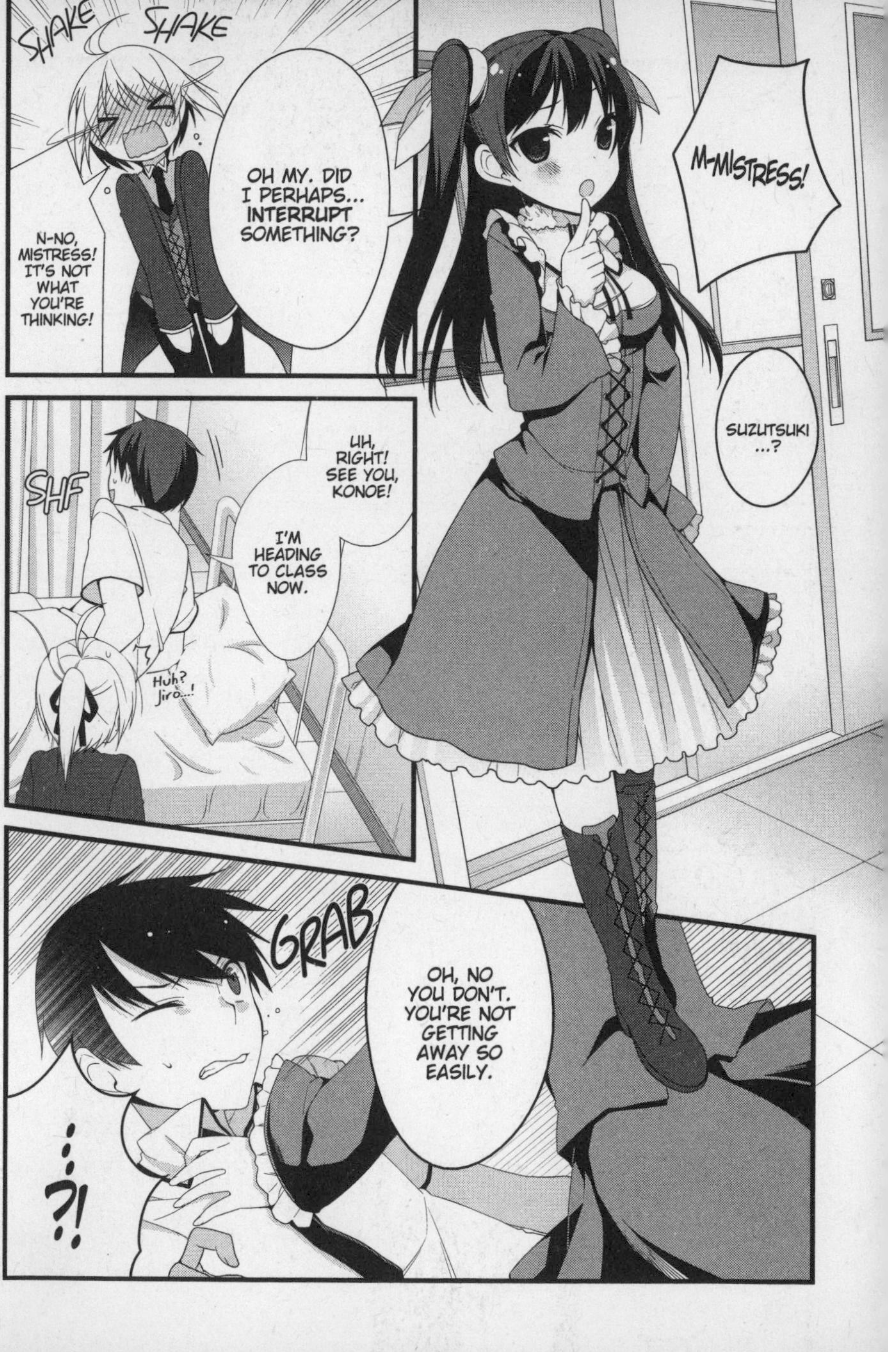
M-MISTRESS!
SUZUTSUKI ...?
OH MY. DID I PERHAPS... INTERRUPT SOMETHING?
SHAKE SHAKE
N-NO, MISTRESS! IT'S NOT WHAT YOU'RE THINKING!
SHF
UH, RIGHT! SEE YOU, KONOE!
I'M HEADING TO CLASS NOW.
Huh? Jiro...!
GRAB
OH, NO YOU DON'T. YOU'RE NOT GETTING AWAY SO EASILY.
...?!

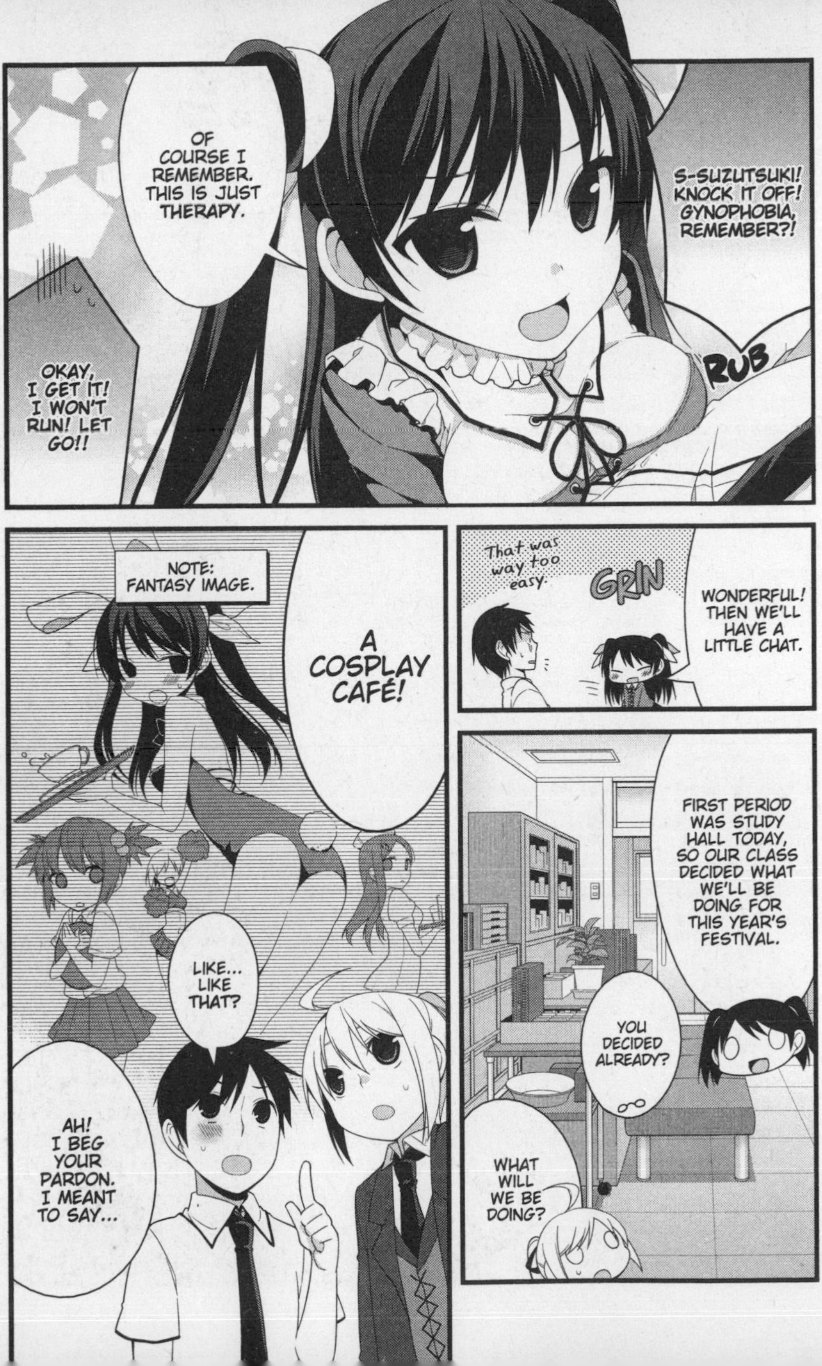
S-SUZUTSUKI! KNOCK IT OFF! GYNOPHOBIA, REMEMBER?!
OF COURSE I REMEMBER. THIS IS JUST THERAPY.
RUB
OKAY, I GET IT! I WON'T RUN! LET GO!!
WONDERFUL! THEN WE'LL HAVE A LITTLE CHAT.
GRIN
That was way too easy.
FIRST PERIOD WAS STUDY HALL TODAY, SO OUR CLASS DECIDED WHAT WE'LL BE DOING FOR THIS YEAR'S FESTIVAL.
YOU DECIDED ALREADY?
WHAT WILL WE BE DOING?
A COSPLAY CAFÉ!
NOTE: FANTASY IMAGE.
LIKE... LIKE THAT?
AH! I BEG YOUR PARDON. I MEANT TO SAY...

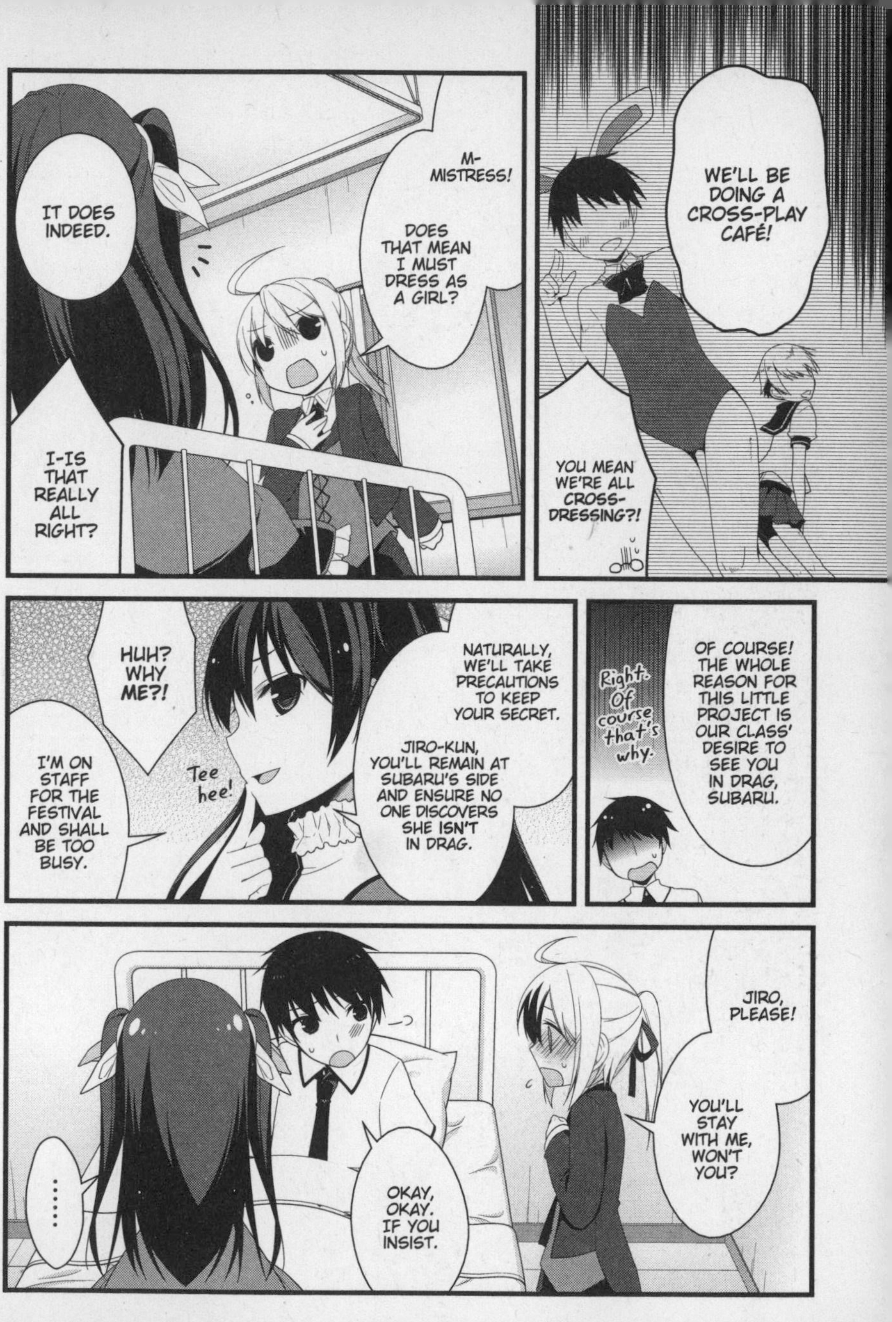
WE'LL BE DOING A CROSS-PLAY CAFÉ!
YOU MEAN WE'RE ALL CROSS-DRESSING?!
M-MISTRESS!
DOES THAT MEAN I MUST DRESS AS A GIRL?
IT DOES INDEED.
I-IS THAT REALLY ALL RIGHT?
OF COURSE! THE WHOLE REASON FOR THIS LITTLE PROJECT IS OUR CLASS' DESIRE TO SEE YOU IN DRAG, SUBARU.
Right. Of course that's why.
NATURALLY, WE'LL TAKE PRECAUTIONS TO KEEP YOUR SECRET.
JIRO-KUN, YOU'LL REMAIN AT SUBARU'S SIDE AND ENSURE NO ONE DISCOVERS SHE ISN'T IN DRAG.
HUH? WHY ME?!
Tee hee!
I'M ON STAFF FOR THE FESTIVAL AND SHALL BE TOO BUSY.
JIRO, PLEASE!
YOU'LL STAY WITH ME, WON'T YOU?
OKAY, OKAY. IF YOU INSIST.
......

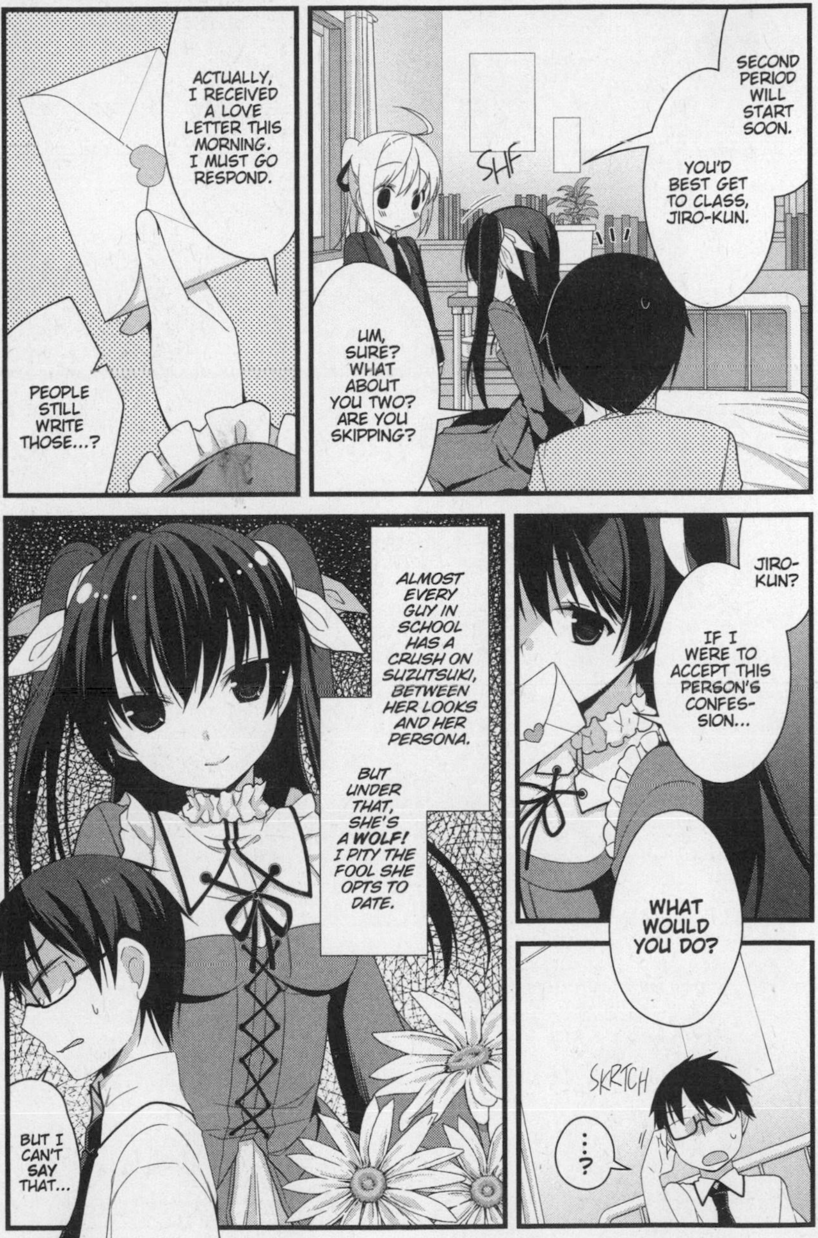
SECOND PERIOD WILL START SOON.
YOU'D BEST GET TO CLASS, JIRO-KUN.
SHF
UM, SURE? WHAT ABOUT YOU TWO? ARE YOU SKIPPING?
ACTUALLY, I RECEIVED A LOVE LETTER THIS MORNING. I MUST GO RESPOND.
PEOPLE STILL WRITE THOSE...?
JIRO-KUN?
IF I WERE TO ACCEPT THIS PERSON'S CONFESSION...
WHAT WOULD YOU DO?
SKRTCH
...?
ALMOST EVERY GUY IN SCHOOL HAS A CRUSH ON SUZUTSUKI, BETWEEN HER LOOKS AND HER PERSONA.
BUT UNDER THAT, SHE'S A WOLF! I PITY THE FOOL SHE OPTS TO DATE.
BUT I CAN'T SAY THAT...

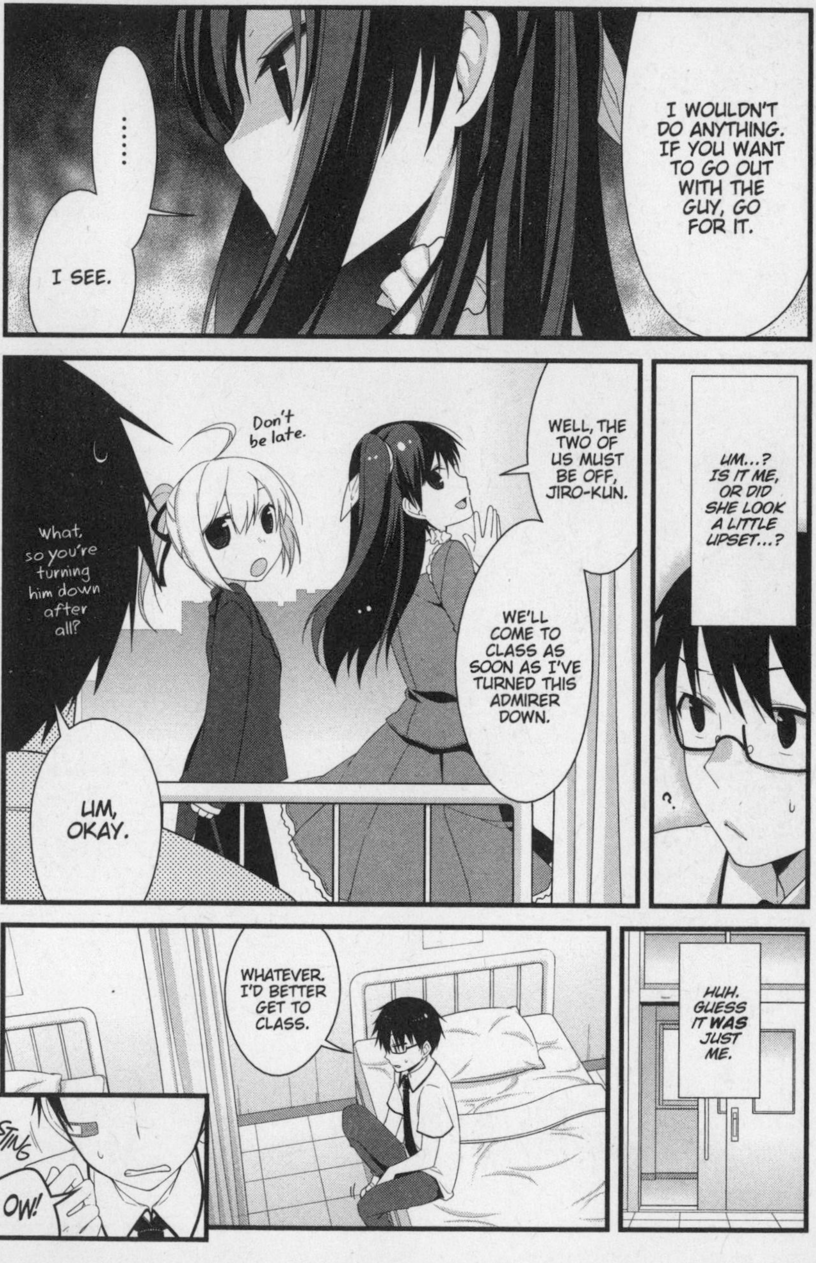
I WOULDN'T DO ANYTHING. IF YOU WANT TO GO OUT WITH THE GUY, GO FOR IT.
......
I SEE.
UM...? IS IT ME, OR DID SHE LOOK A LITTLE UPSET...?
WELL, THE TWO OF US MUST BE OFF, JIRO-KUN.
WE'LL COME TO CLASS AS SOON AS I'VE TURNED THIS ADMIRER DOWN.
Don't be late.
What, so you're turning him down after all?
UM, OKAY.
HUH. GUESS IT WAS JUST ME.
WHATEVER. I'D BETTER GET TO CLASS.
STING
OW!

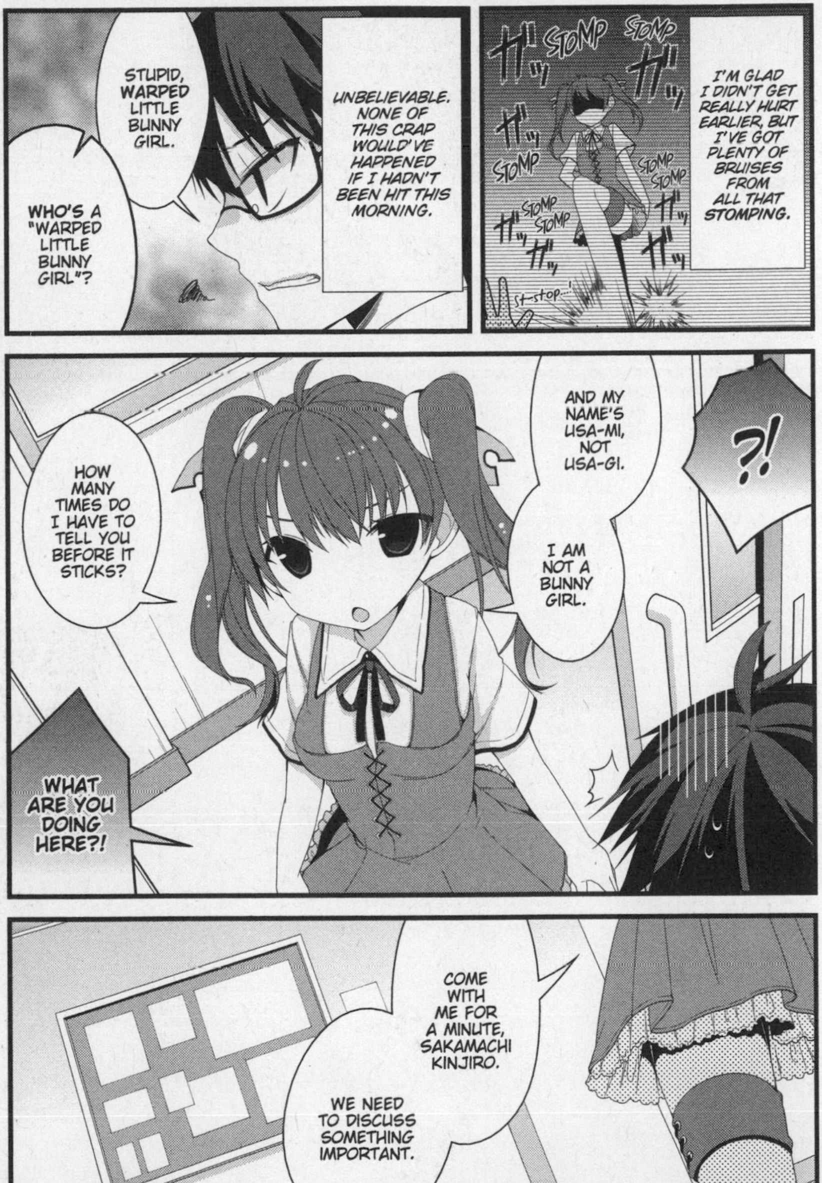
STOMP STOMP
I'M GLAD I DIDN'T GET REALLY HURT EARLIER, BUT I'VE GOT PLENTY OF BRUISES FROM ALL THAT STOMPING.
STOMP STOMP STOMP
STOMP STOMP
st-stop...!
UNBELIEVABLE. NONE OF THIS CRAP WOULD'VE HAPPENED IF I HADN'T BEEN HIT THIS MORNING.
STUPID, WARPED LITTLE BUNNY GIRL.
WHO'S A "WARPED LITTLE BUNNY GIRL"?
?!
AND MY NAME'S USA-MI, NOT USA-GI.
I AM NOT A BUNNY GIRL.
HOW MANY TIMES DO I HAVE TO TELL YOU BEFORE IT STICKS?
WHAT ARE YOU DOING HERE?!
COME WITH ME FOR A MINUTE, SAKAMACHI KINJIRO.
WE NEED TO DISCUSS SOMETHING IMPORTANT.

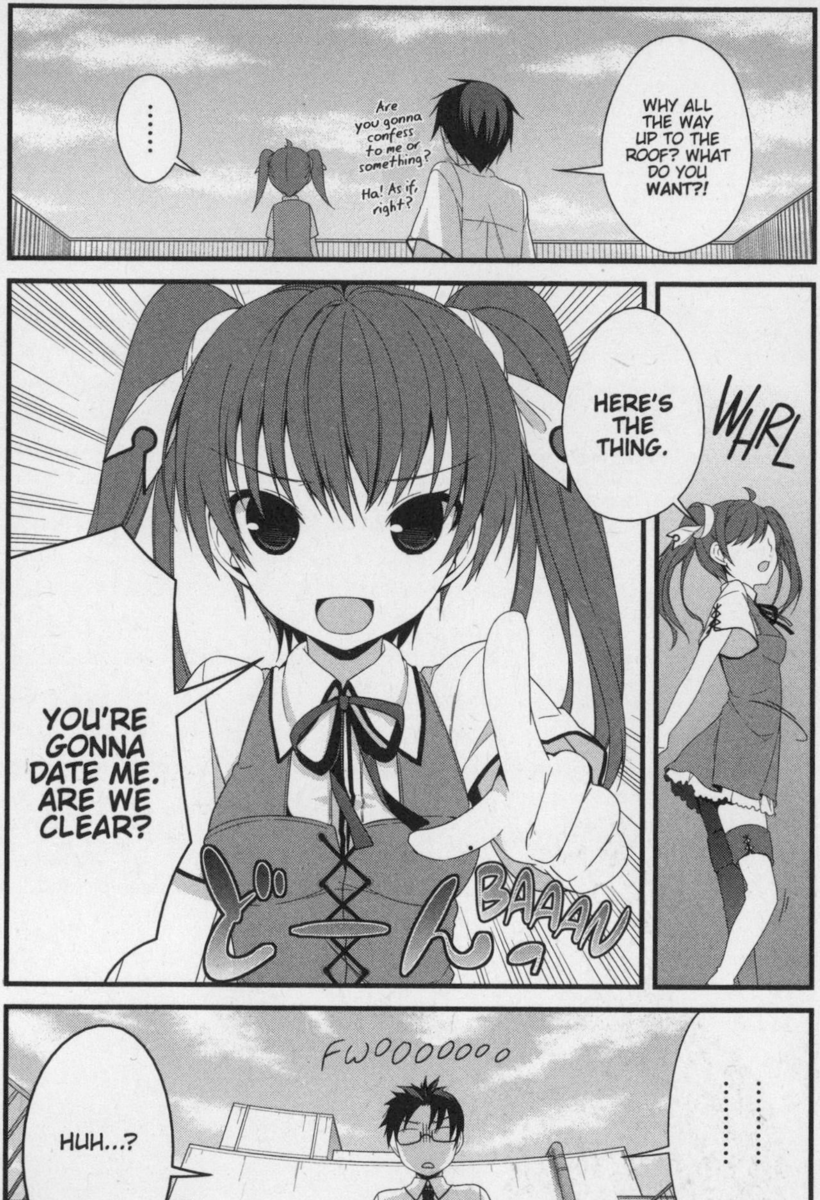
WHY ALL THE WAY UP TO THE ROOF? WHAT DO YOU WANT?!
Are you gonna confess to me or something?
Ha! As if, right?
......
WHRL
HERE'S THE THING.
YOU'RE GONNA DATE ME. ARE WE CLEAR?
BAAAAN
......
FWOOOOOOO
HUH...?

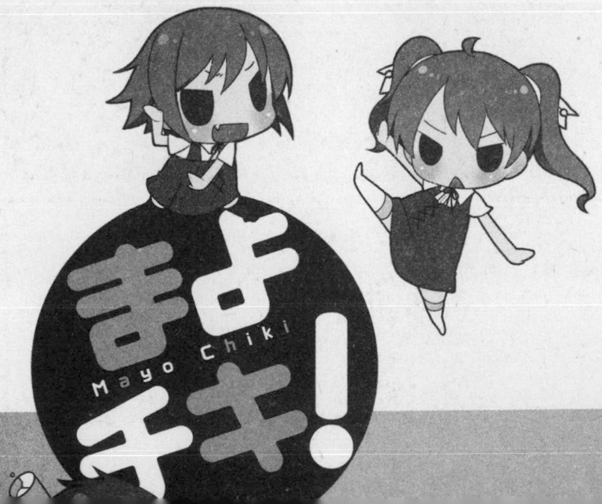
まよチキ!
Mayo Chiki

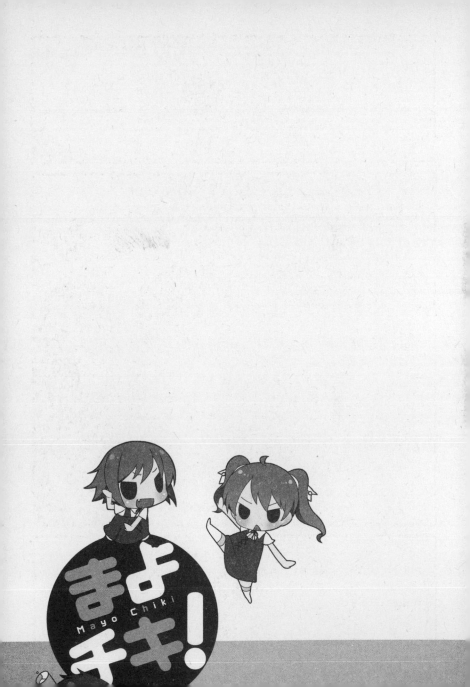

Do you
WANT
to get
stomped?

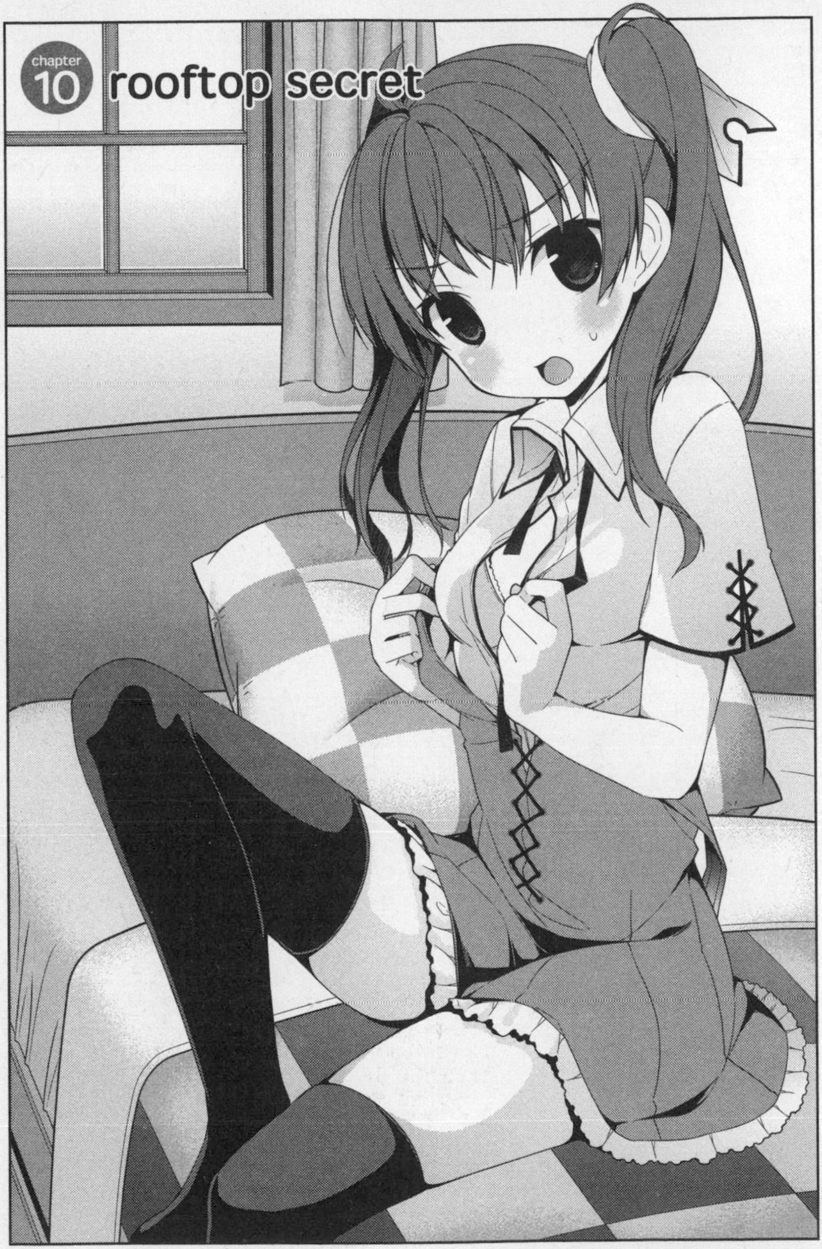
chapter 10 rooftop secret

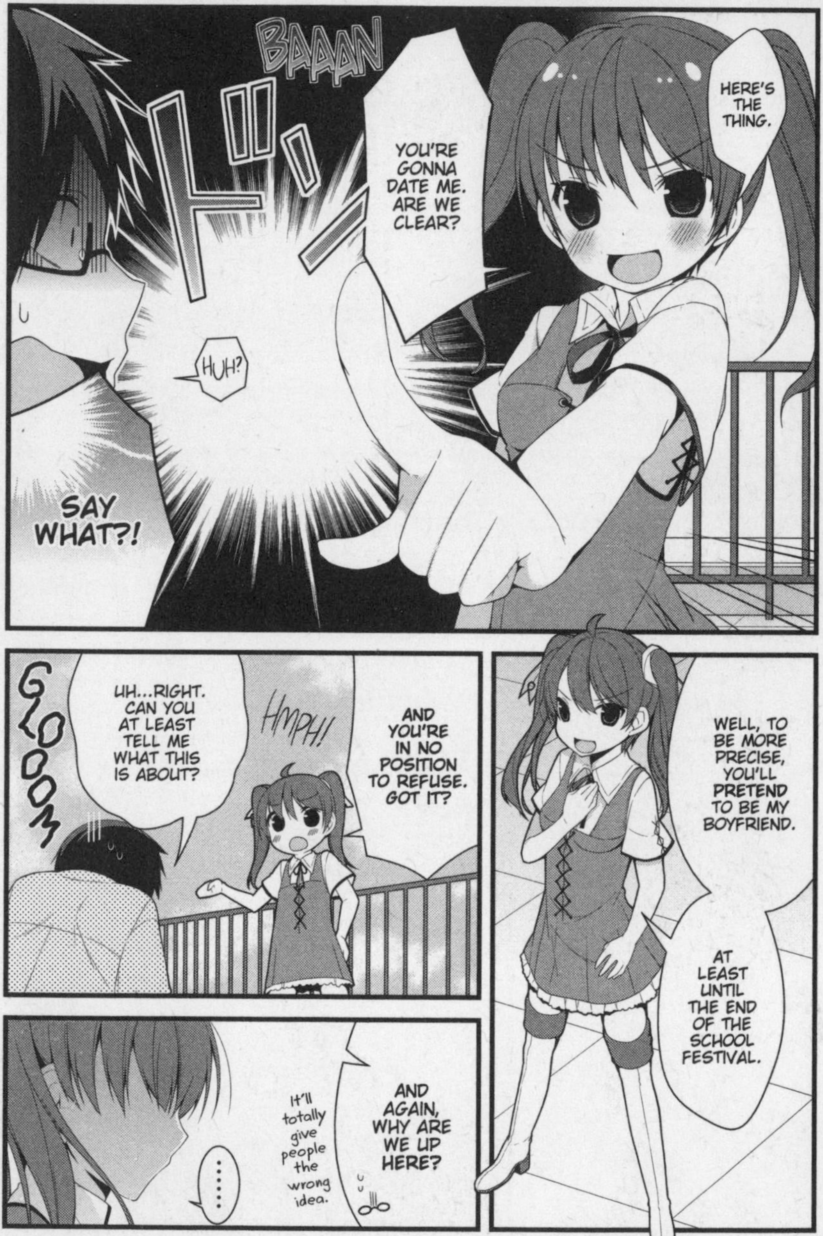
HERE'S THE THING.
YOU'RE GONNA DATE ME. ARE WE CLEAR?
BAAAN
HUH?
SAY WHAT?!
WELL, TO BE MORE PRECISE, YOU'LL PRETEND TO BE MY BOYFRIEND.
AT LEAST UNTIL THE END OF THE SCHOOL FESTIVAL.
AND YOU'RE IN NO POSITION TO REFUSE. GOT IT?
HMPH!
UH...RIGHT. CAN YOU AT LEAST TELL ME WHAT THIS IS ABOUT?
GLOOOOM
AND AGAIN, WHY ARE WE UP HERE?
It'll totally give people the wrong idea.
......

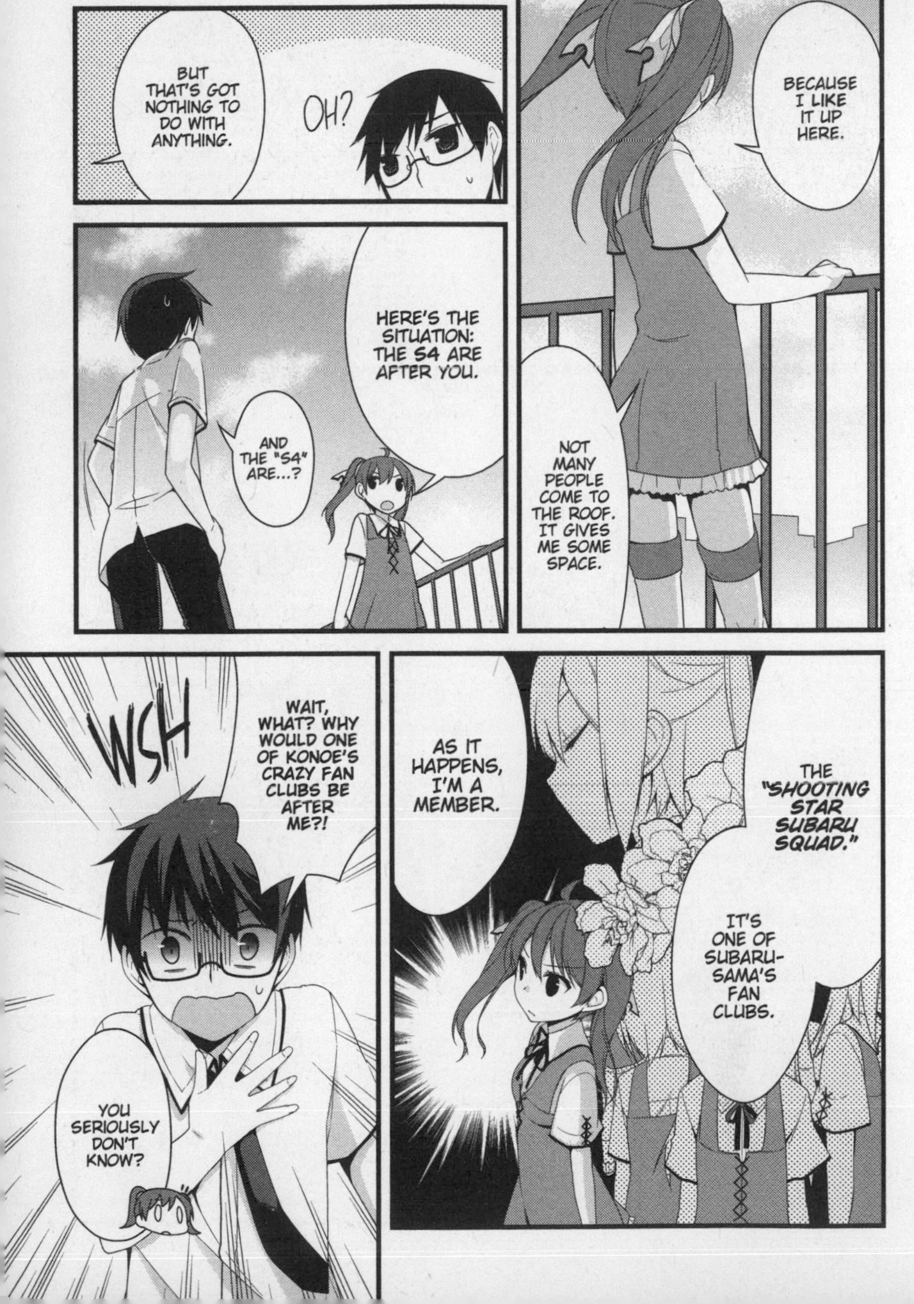
BECAUSE I LIKE IT UP HERE.
NOT MANY PEOPLE COME TO THE ROOF. IT GIVES ME SOME SPACE.
BUT THAT'S GOT NOTHING TO DO WITH ANYTHING.
OH?
HERE'S THE SITUATION: THE S4 ARE AFTER YOU.
AND THE "S4" ARE...?
THE "SHOOTING STAR SUBARU SQUAD."
IT'S ONE OF SUBARU-SAMA'S FAN CLUBS.
AS IT HAPPENS, I'M A MEMBER.
WSH
WAIT, WHAT? WHY WOULD ONE OF KONOE'S CRAZY FAN CLUBS BE AFTER ME?!
YOU SERIOUSLY DON'T KNOW?

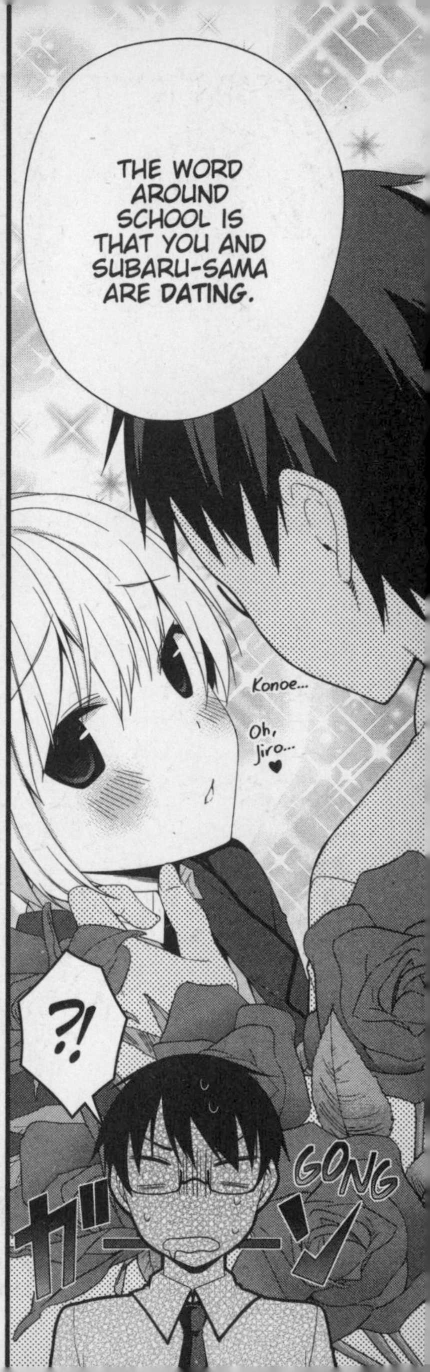
THE WORD AROUND SCHOOL IS THAT YOU AND SUBARU-SAMA ARE DATING.
Konoe...
Oh, Jiro...♥
?!
GONG

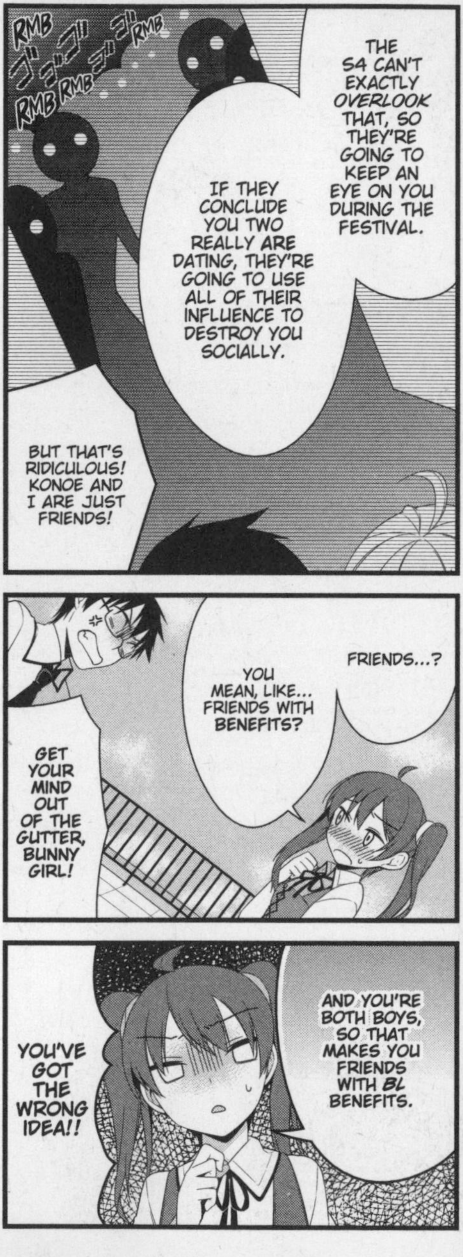
THE S4 CAN'T EXACTLY *OVERLOOK* THAT, SO THEY'RE GOING TO KEEP AN EYE ON YOU DURING THE FESTIVAL.
IF THEY CONCLUDE YOU TWO REALLY *ARE* DATING, THEY'RE GOING TO USE ALL OF THEIR INFLUENCE TO DESTROY YOU SOCIALLY.
RMB RMB RMB RMB
BUT THAT'S RIDICULOUS! KONOE AND I ARE JUST FRIENDS!
FRIENDS...?
YOU MEAN, LIKE... FRIENDS WITH BENEFITS?
GET YOUR MIND OUT OF THE GUTTER, BUNNY GIRL!
AND YOU'RE BOTH BOYS, SO THAT MAKES YOU FRIENDS WITH *BL* BENEFITS.
YOU'VE GOT THE WRONG IDEA!!

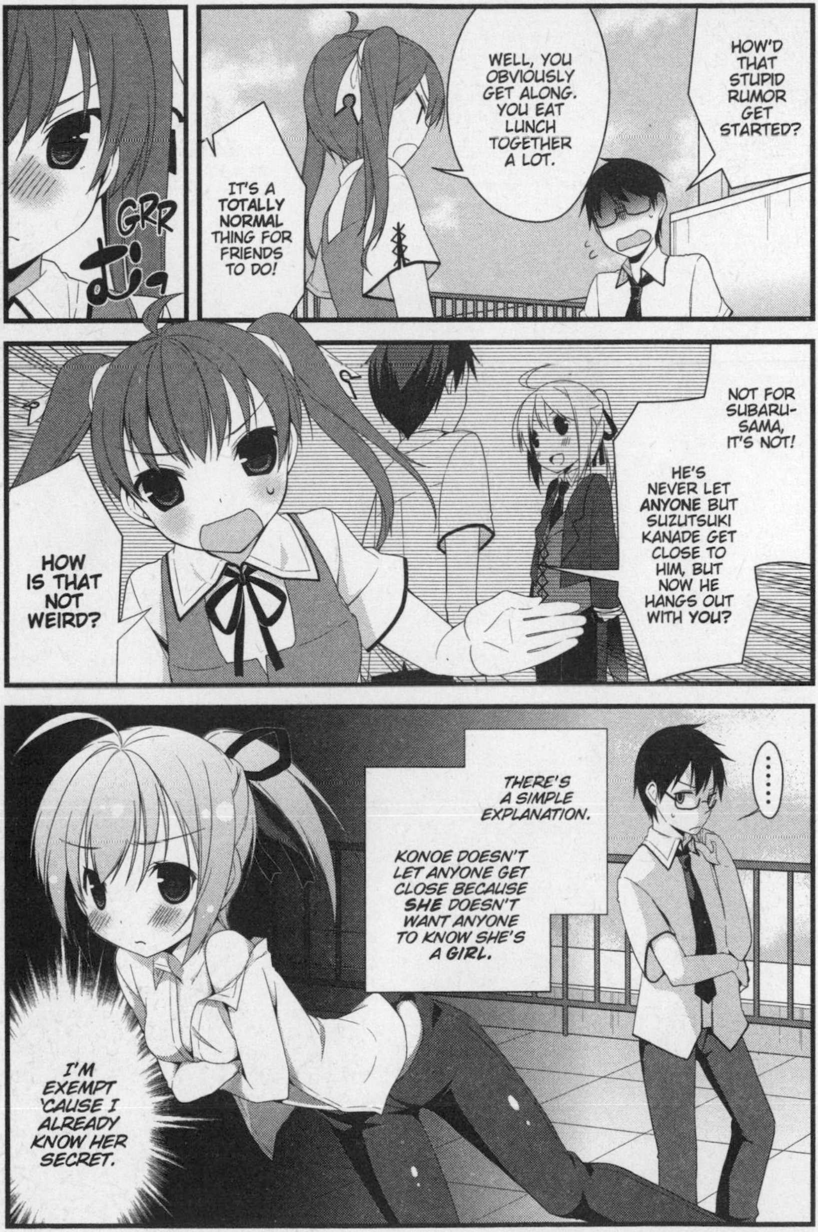
HOW'D THAT STUPID RUMOR GET STARTED?
WELL, YOU OBVIOUSLY GET ALONG. YOU EAT LUNCH TOGETHER A LOT.
IT'S A TOTALLY NORMAL THING FOR FRIENDS TO DO!
GRR
NOT FOR SUBARU-SAMA, IT'S NOT!
HE'S NEVER LET ANYONE BUT SUZUTSUKI KANADE GET CLOSE TO HIM, BUT NOW HE HANGS OUT WITH YOU?
HOW IS THAT NOT WEIRD?
......
THERE'S A SIMPLE EXPLANATION.
KONOE DOESN'T LET ANYONE GET CLOSE BECAUSE **SHE** DOESN'T WANT ANYONE TO KNOW SHE'S A **GIRL**.
I'M EXEMPT 'CAUSE I ALREADY KNOW HER SECRET.

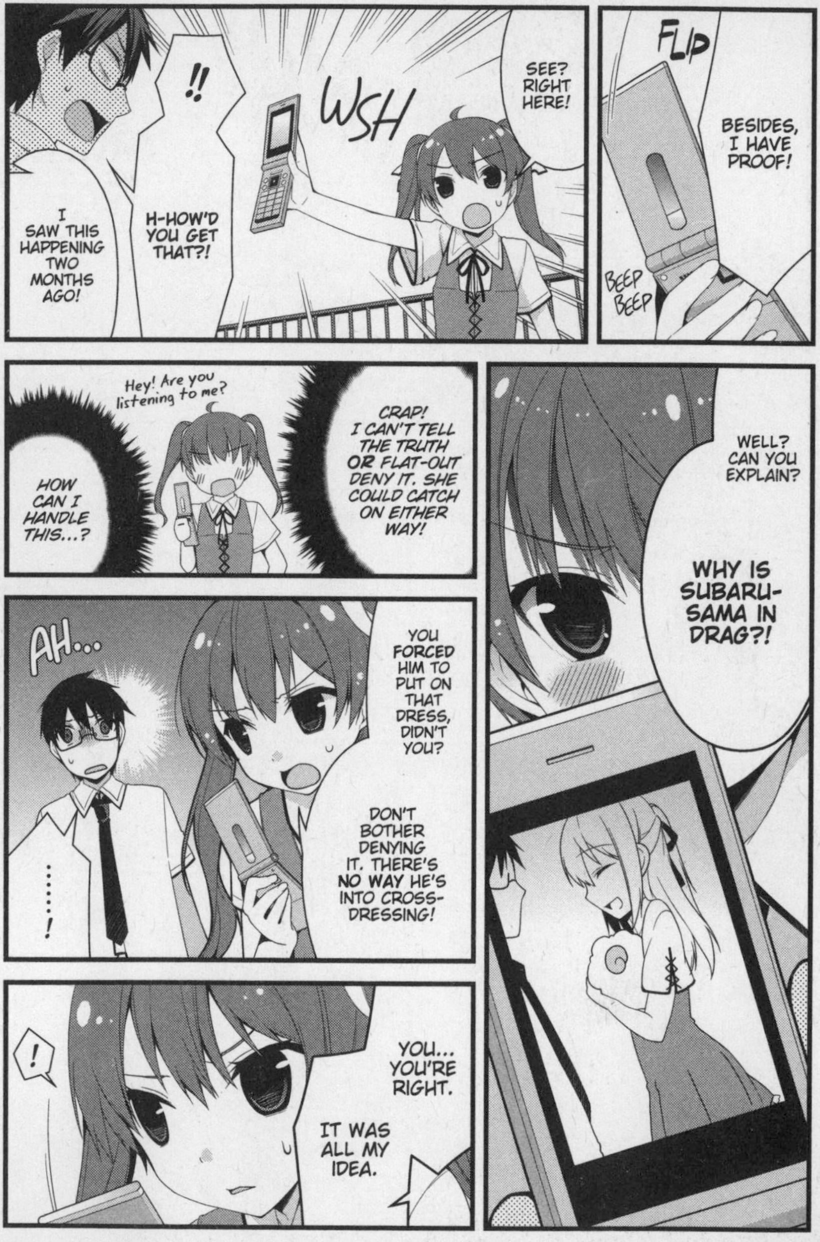
FLIP
BESIDES, I HAVE PROOF!
BEEP BEEP
SEE? RIGHT HERE!
WSH
!!
H-HOW'D YOU GET THAT?!
I SAW THIS HAPPENING TWO MONTHS AGO!
WELL? CAN YOU EXPLAIN?
WHY IS SUBARU-SAMA IN DRAG?!
CRAP! I CAN'T TELL THE TRUTH OR FLAT-OUT DENY IT. SHE COULD CATCH ON EITHER WAY!
Hey! Are you listening to me?
HOW CAN I HANDLE THIS...?
YOU FORCED HIM TO PUT ON THAT DRESS, DIDN'T YOU?
DON'T BOTHER DENYING IT. THERE'S NO WAY HE'S INTO CROSS-DRESSING!
AH...
......!
YOU... YOU'RE RIGHT.
IT WAS ALL MY IDEA.
!

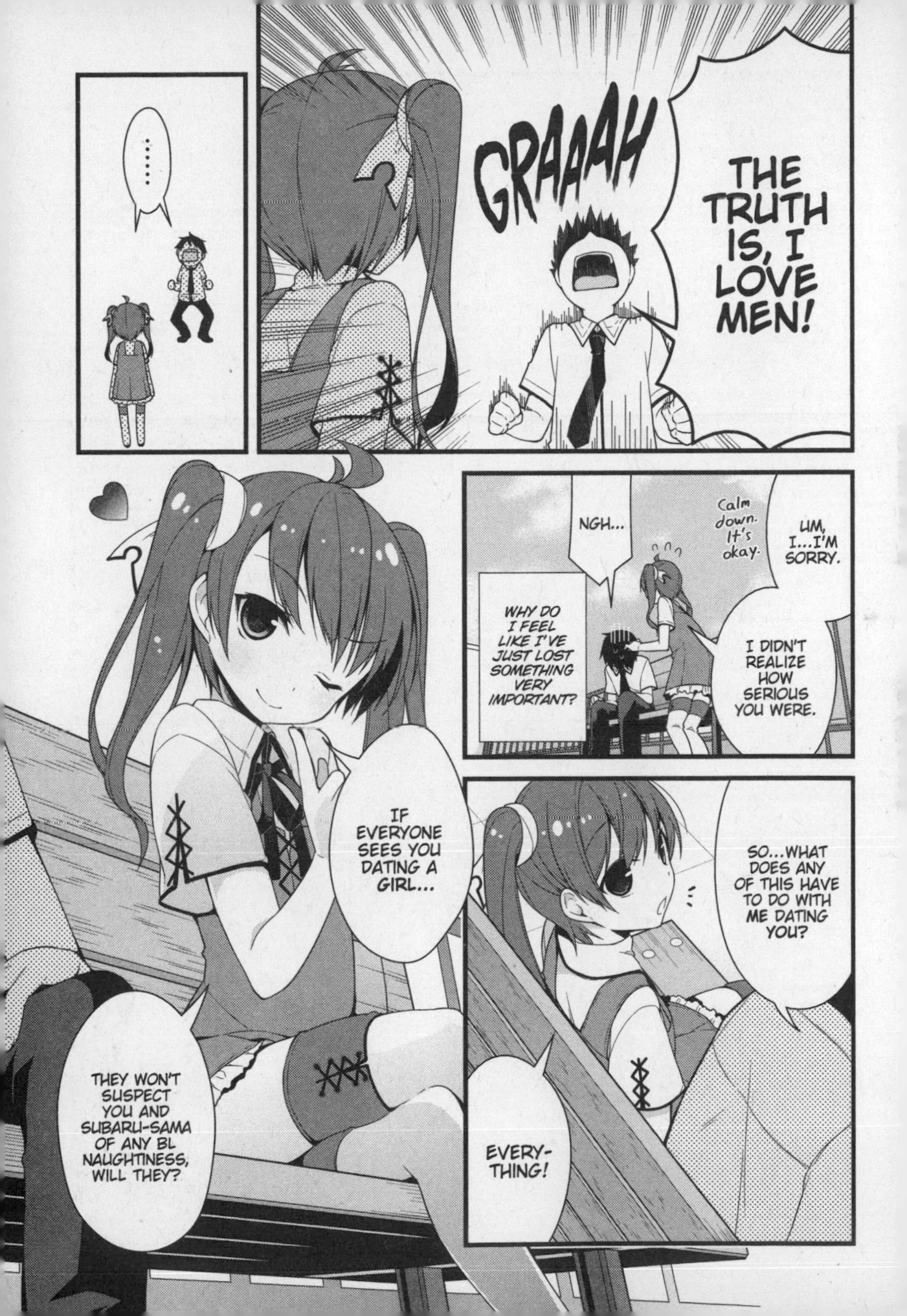
THE TRUTH IS, I LOVE MEN!
GRAAAH
……
UM, I…I'M SORRY.
I DIDN'T REALIZE HOW SERIOUS YOU WERE.
Calm down. It's okay.
NGH…
WHY DO I FEEL LIKE I'VE JUST LOST SOMETHING VERY IMPORTANT?
SO…WHAT DOES ANY OF THIS HAVE TO DO WITH ME DATING YOU?
EVERY-THING!
IF EVERYONE SEES YOU DATING A GIRL…
THEY WON'T SUSPECT YOU AND SUBARU-SAMA OF ANY BL NAUGHTINESS, WILL THEY?

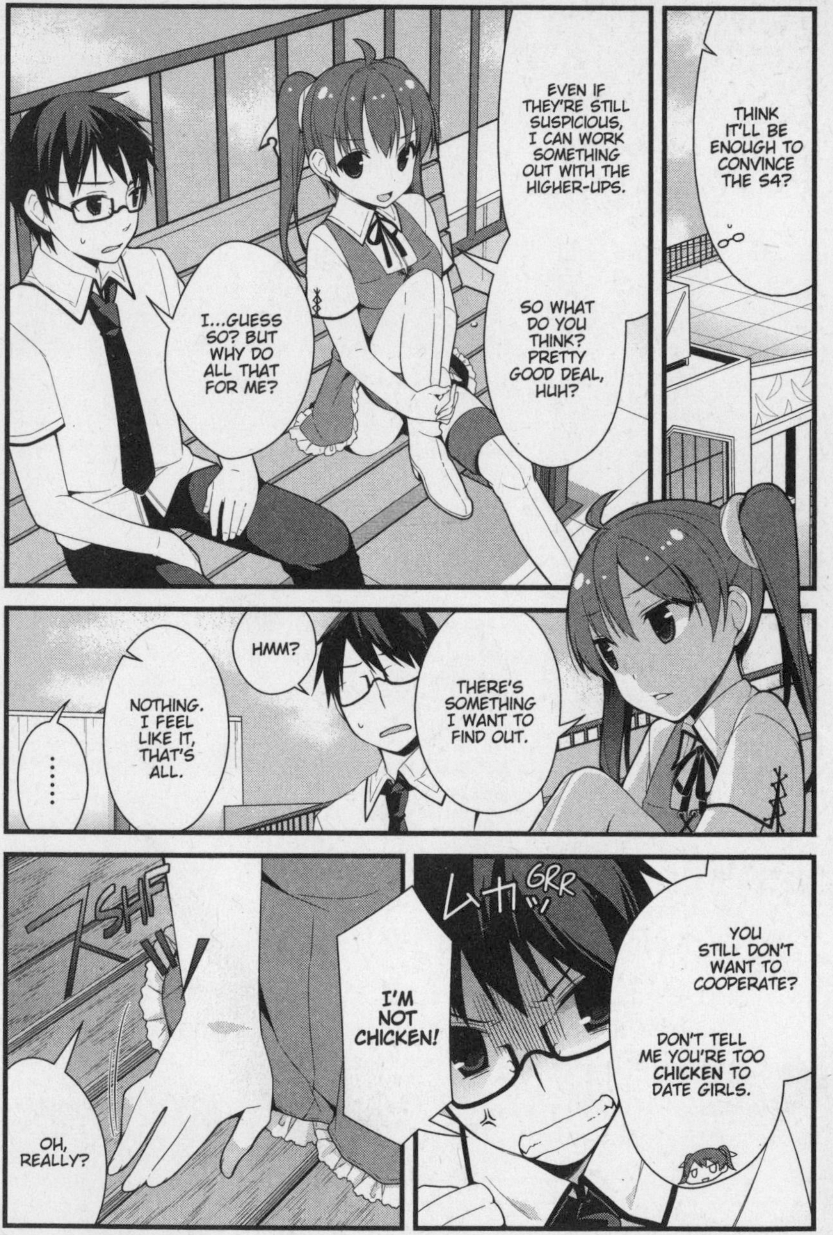
THINK IT'LL BE ENOUGH TO CONVINCE THE S4?
EVEN IF THEY'RE STILL SUSPICIOUS, I CAN WORK SOMETHING OUT WITH THE HIGHER-UPS.
SO WHAT DO YOU THINK? PRETTY GOOD DEAL, HUH?
I...GUESS SO? BUT WHY DO ALL THAT FOR ME?
THERE'S SOMETHING I WANT TO FIND OUT.
HMM?
NOTHING. I FEEL LIKE IT, THAT'S ALL.
......
GRR
YOU STILL DON'T WANT TO COOPERATE?
DON'T TELL ME YOU'RE TOO CHICKEN TO DATE GIRLS.
I'M NOT CHICKEN!
SHF
OH, REALLY?

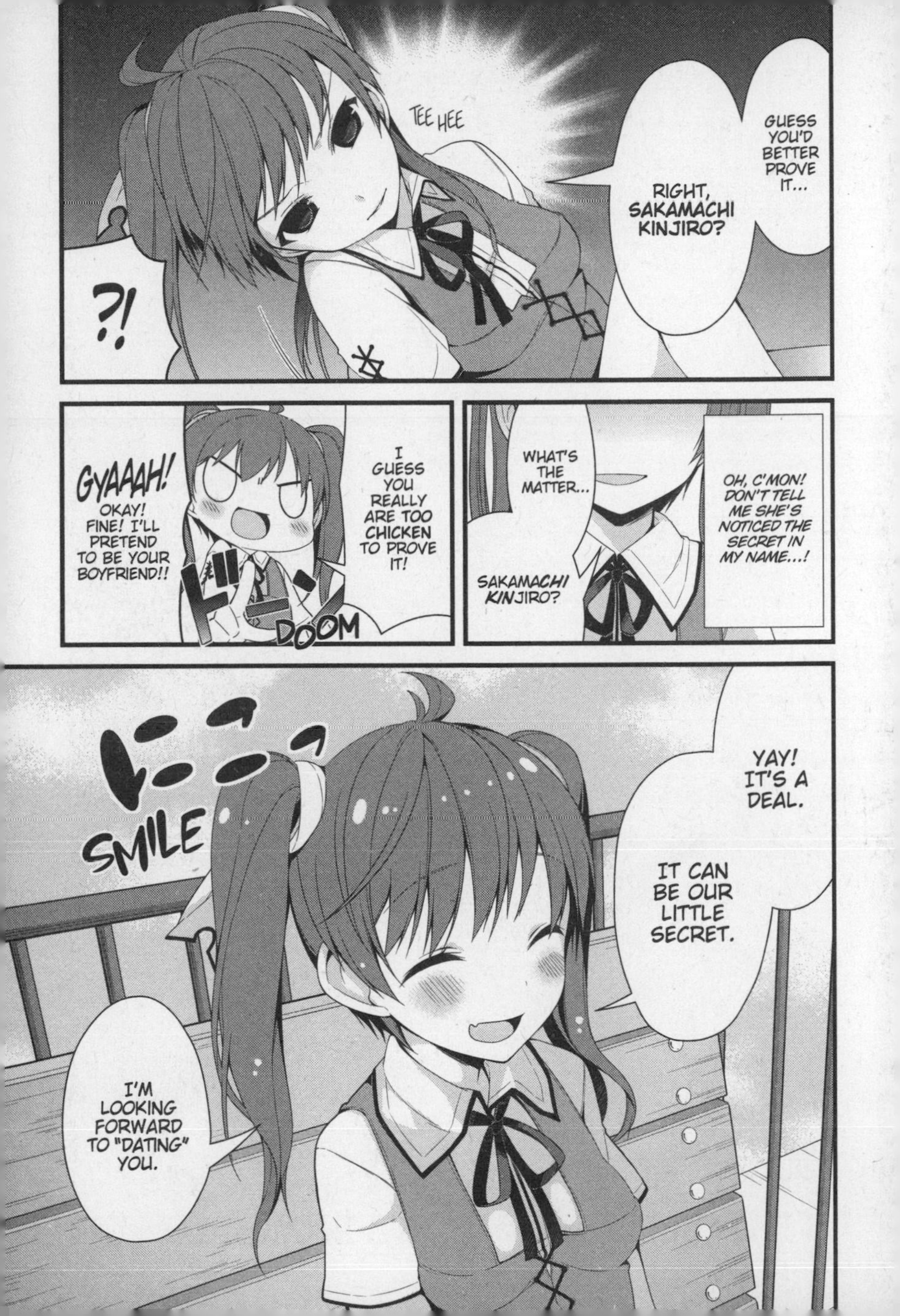
GUESS YOU'D BETTER PROVE IT...
RIGHT, SAKAMACHI KINJIRO?
TEE HEE
?!
OH, C'MON! DON'T TELL ME SHE'S NOTICED THE SECRET IN MY NAME...!
WHAT'S THE MATTER...
SAKAMACHI KINJIRO?
I GUESS YOU REALLY ARE TOO CHICKEN TO PROVE IT!
GYAAAH!
OKAY! FINE! I'LL PRETEND TO BE YOUR BOYFRIEND!!
DOOM
YAY! IT'S A DEAL.
IT CAN BE OUR LITTLE SECRET.
SMILE
I'M LOOKING FORWARD TO "DATING" YOU.

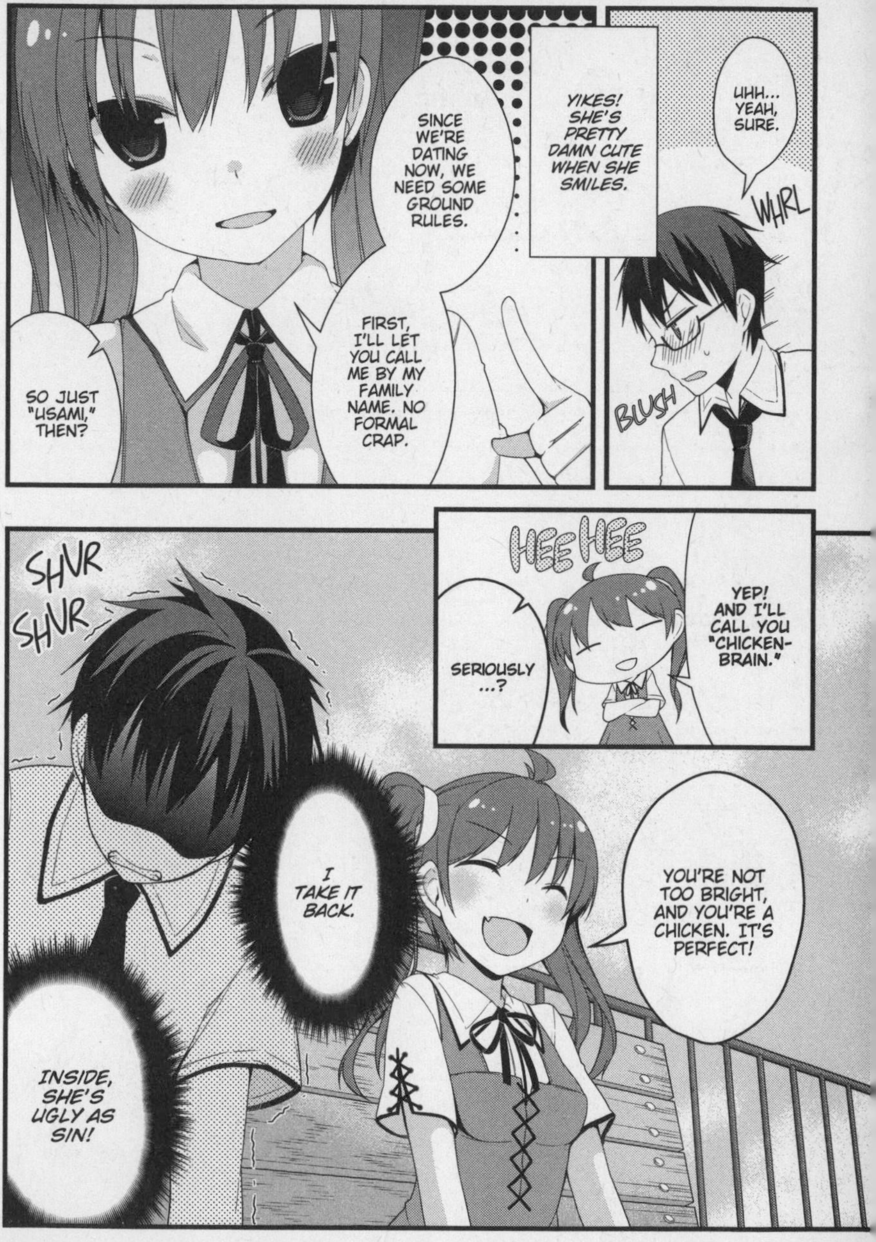
UHH... YEAH, SURE.
WHRL
BLUSH
YIKES! SHE'S PRETTY DAMN CUTE WHEN SHE SMILES.
SINCE WE'RE DATING NOW, WE NEED SOME GROUND RULES.
FIRST, I'LL LET YOU CALL ME BY MY FAMILY NAME. NO FORMAL CRAP.
SO JUST "USAMI," THEN?
YEP! AND I'LL CALL YOU "CHICKEN-BRAIN."
HEE HEE
SERIOUSLY ...?
YOU'RE NOT TOO BRIGHT, AND YOU'RE A CHICKEN. IT'S PERFECT!
SHVR
SHVR
I TAKE IT BACK.
INSIDE, SHE'S UGLY AS SIN!

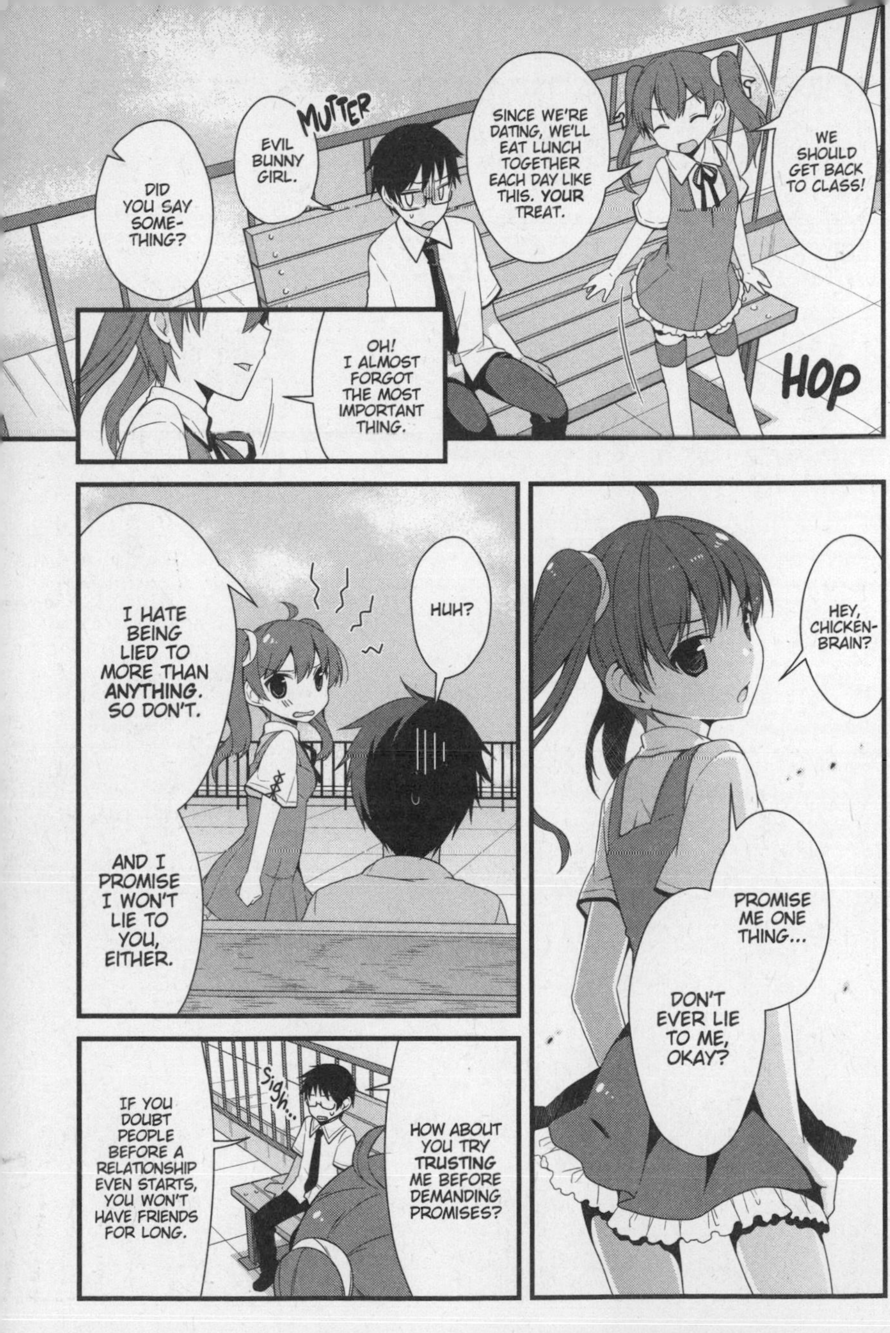
WE SHOULD GET BACK TO CLASS!
HOP
SINCE WE'RE DATING, WE'LL EAT LUNCH TOGETHER EACH DAY LIKE THIS. YOUR TREAT.
MUTTER
EVIL BUNNY GIRL.
DID YOU SAY SOME-THING?
OH! I ALMOST FORGOT THE MOST IMPORTANT THING.
HEY, CHICKEN-BRAIN?
PROMISE ME ONE THING...
DON'T EVER LIE TO ME, OKAY?
HUH?
I HATE BEING LIED TO MORE THAN ANYTHING. SO DON'T.
AND I PROMISE I WON'T LIE TO YOU, EITHER.
Sigh...
HOW ABOUT YOU TRY TRUSTING ME BEFORE DEMANDING PROMISES?
IF YOU DOUBT PEOPLE BEFORE A RELATIONSHIP EVEN STARTS, YOU WON'T HAVE FRIENDS FOR LONG.

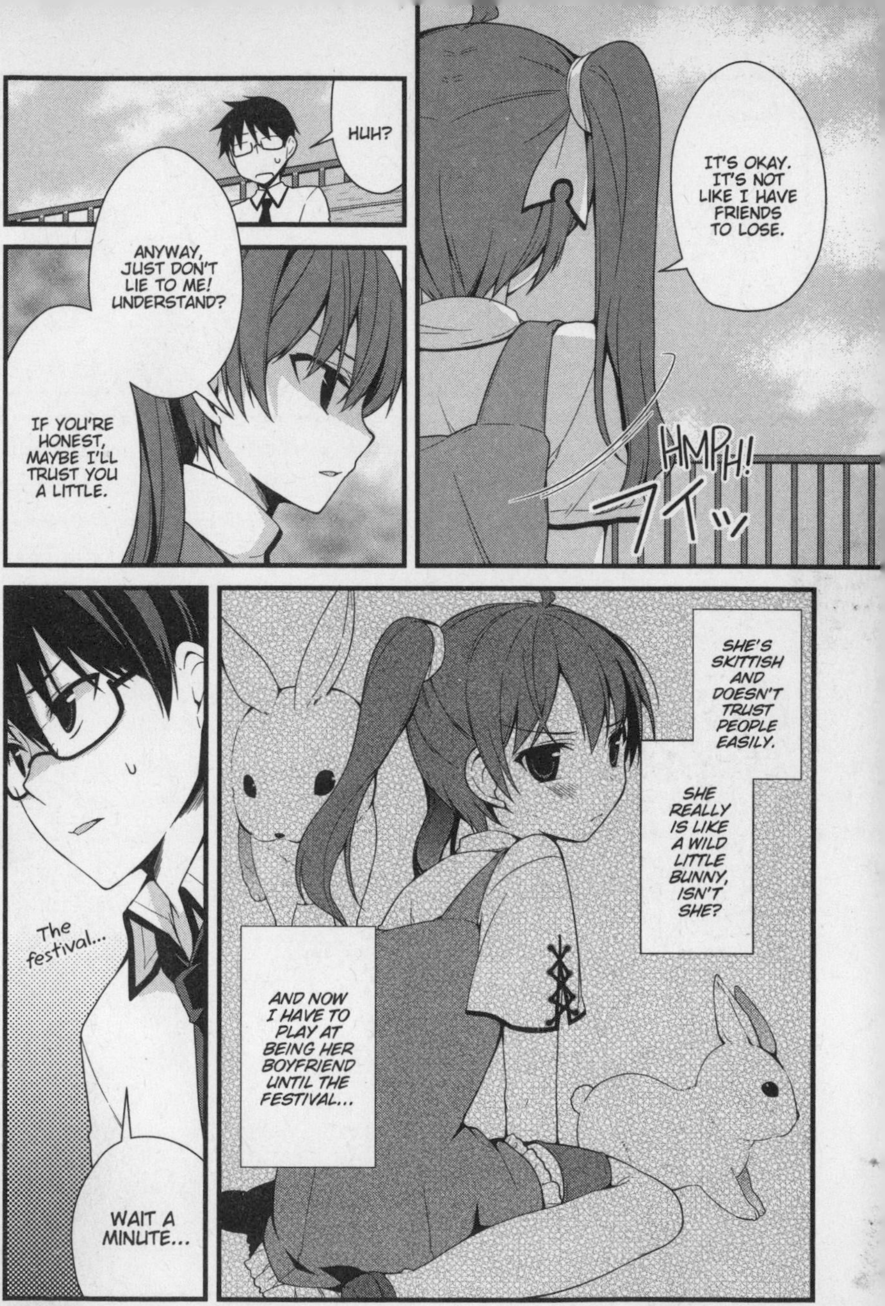
IT'S OKAY. IT'S NOT LIKE I HAVE FRIENDS TO LOSE.
HMPH!
フイッ
HUH?
ANYWAY, JUST DON'T LIE TO ME! UNDERSTAND?
IF YOU'RE HONEST, MAYBE I'LL TRUST YOU A LITTLE.
SHE'S SKITTISH AND DOESN'T TRUST PEOPLE EASILY.
SHE REALLY IS LIKE A WILD LITTLE BUNNY, ISN'T SHE?
AND NOW I HAVE TO PLAY AT BEING HER BOYFRIEND UNTIL THE FESTIVAL...
The festival...
WAIT A MINUTE...

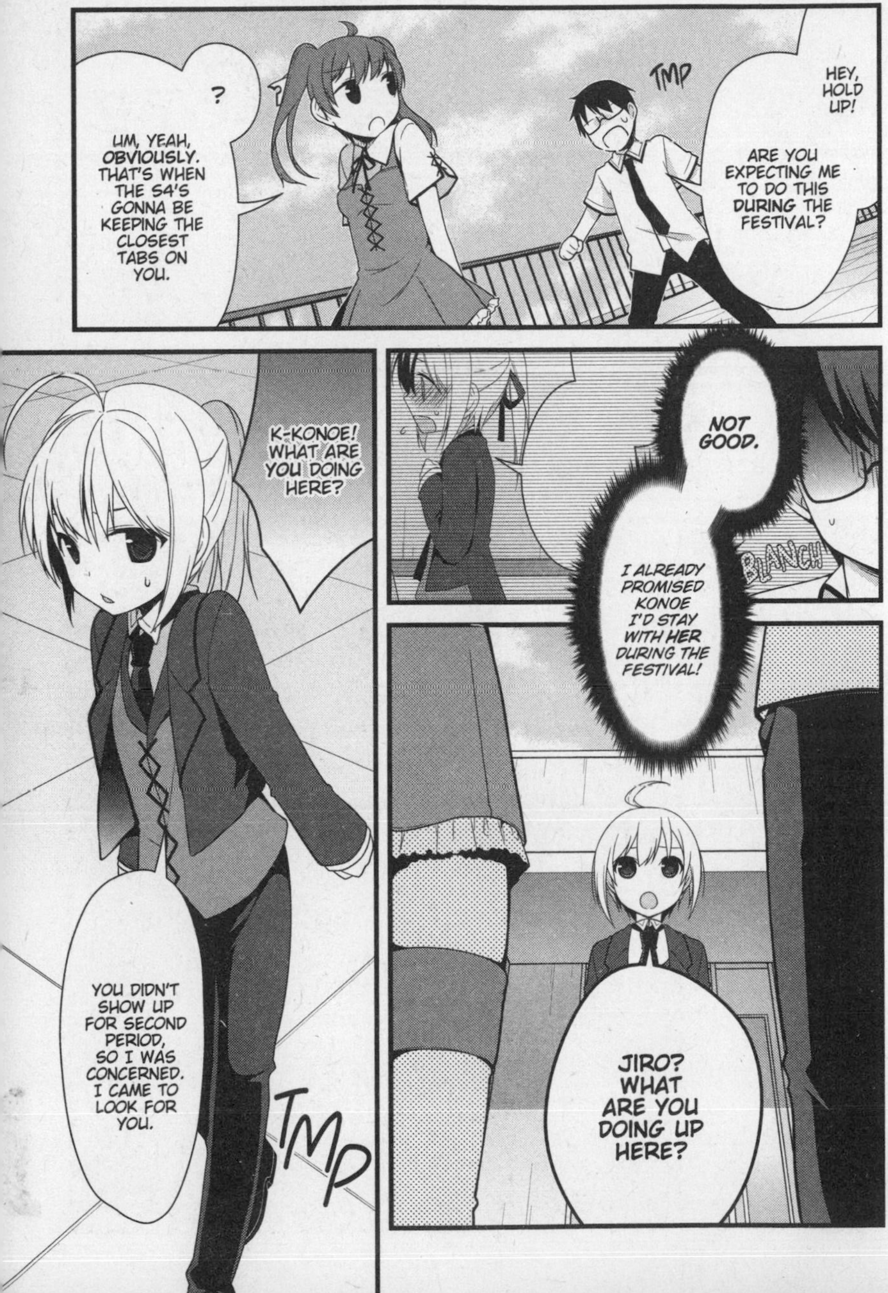
HEY, HOLD UP!
ARE YOU EXPECTING ME TO DO THIS DURING THE FESTIVAL?
TMP
?
UM, YEAH, OBVIOUSLY. THAT'S WHEN THE S4'S GONNA BE KEEPING THE CLOSEST TABS ON YOU.
NOT GOOD.
I ALREADY PROMISED KONOE I'D STAY WITH HER DURING THE FESTIVAL!
BLANCH
JIRO? WHAT ARE YOU DOING UP HERE?
K-KONOE! WHAT ARE YOU DOING HERE?
YOU DIDN'T SHOW UP FOR SECOND PERIOD, SO I WAS CONCERNED. I CAME TO LOOK FOR YOU.
TMP

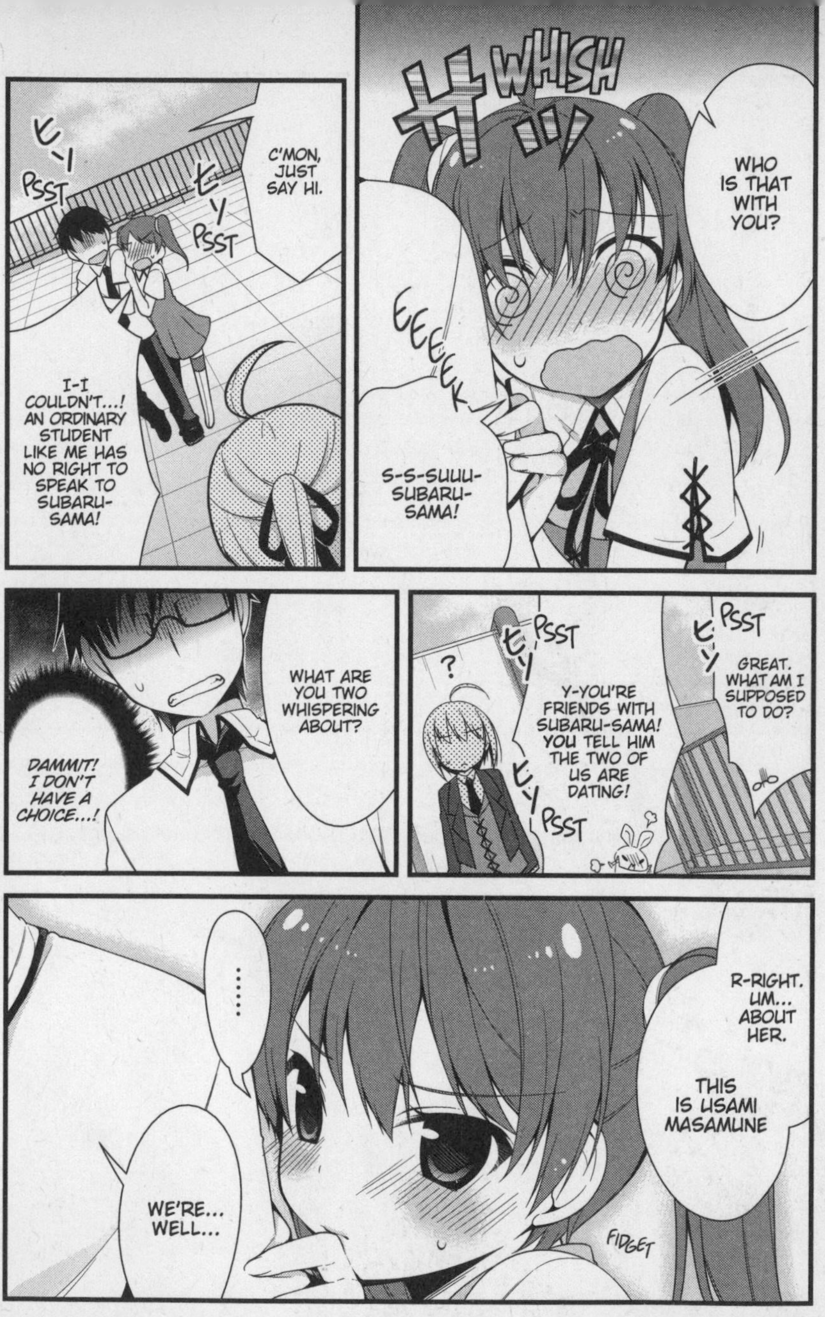
WHISH
WHO IS THAT WITH YOU?
EEEEEK
S-S-SUUU-SUBARU-SAMA!
C'MON, JUST SAY HI.
PSST
PSST
I-I COULDN'T...! AN ORDINARY STUDENT LIKE ME HAS NO RIGHT TO SPEAK TO SUBARU-SAMA!
PSST
GREAT. WHAT AM I SUPPOSED TO DO?
PSST
?
Y-YOU'RE FRIENDS WITH SUBARU-SAMA! YOU TELL HIM THE TWO OF US ARE DATING!
PSST
WHAT ARE YOU TWO WHISPERING ABOUT?
DAMMIT! I DON'T HAVE A CHOICE...!
R-RIGHT. UM... ABOUT HER.
THIS IS USAMI MASAMUNE
......
FIDGET
WE'RE... WELL...

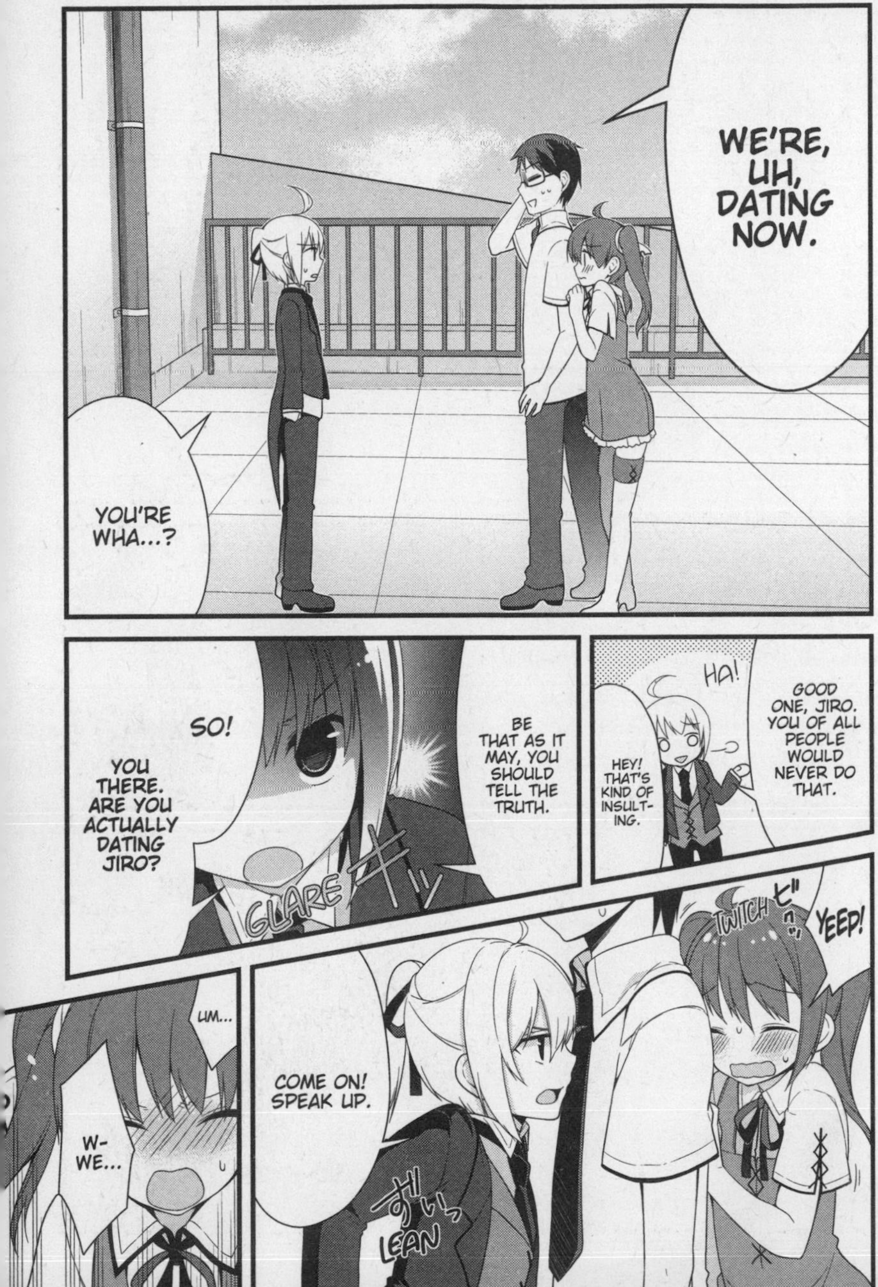
WE'RE, UH, DATING NOW.
YOU'RE WHA...?
HA!
GOOD ONE, JIRO. YOU OF ALL PEOPLE WOULD NEVER DO THAT.
HEY! THAT'S KIND OF INSULTING.
BE THAT AS IT MAY, YOU SHOULD TELL THE TRUTH.
SO!
YOU THERE. ARE YOU ACTUALLY DATING JIRO?
GLARE
TWITCH
YEEP!
COME ON! SPEAK UP.
LEAN
UM...
W-WE...

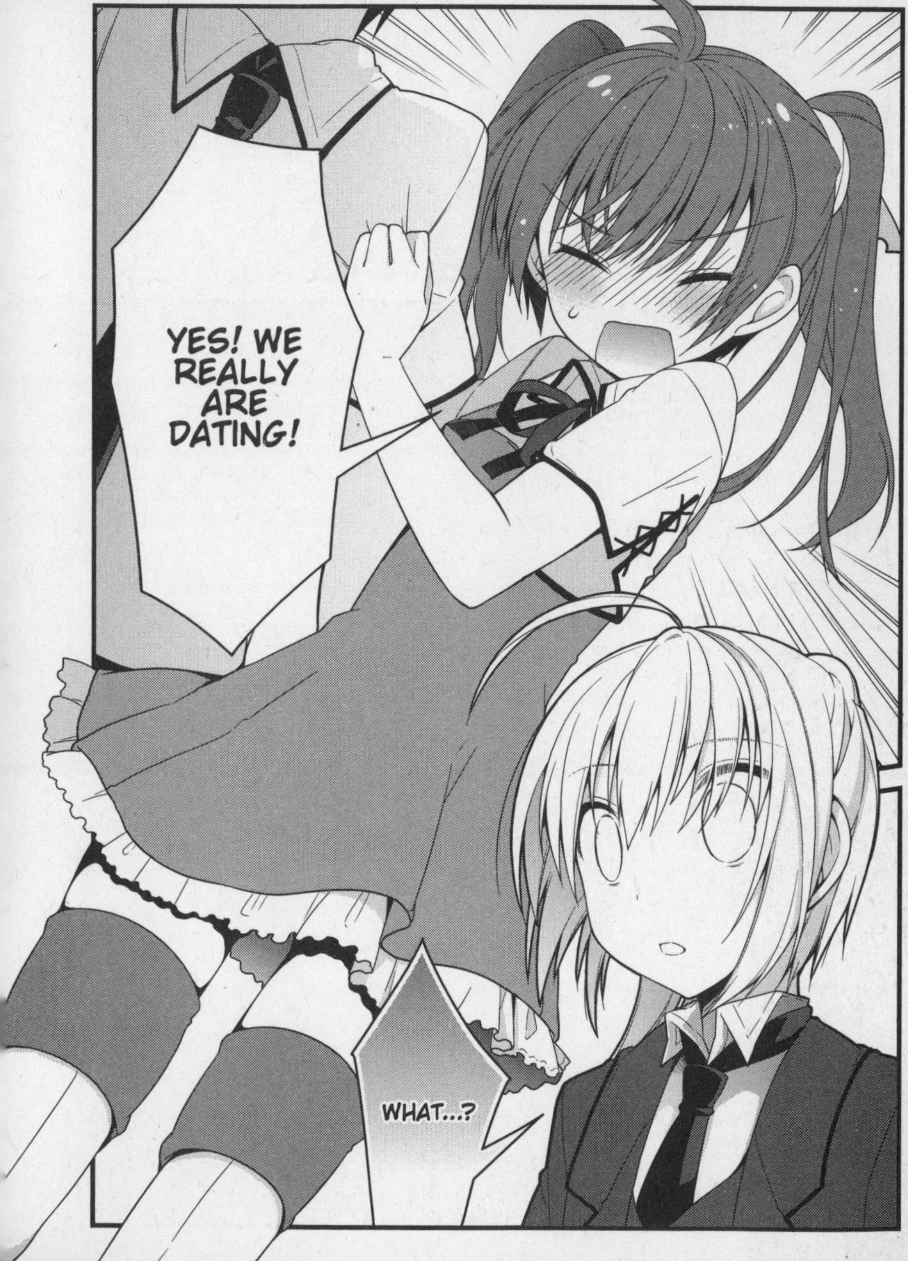
YES! WE REALLY ARE DATING!
WHAT...?

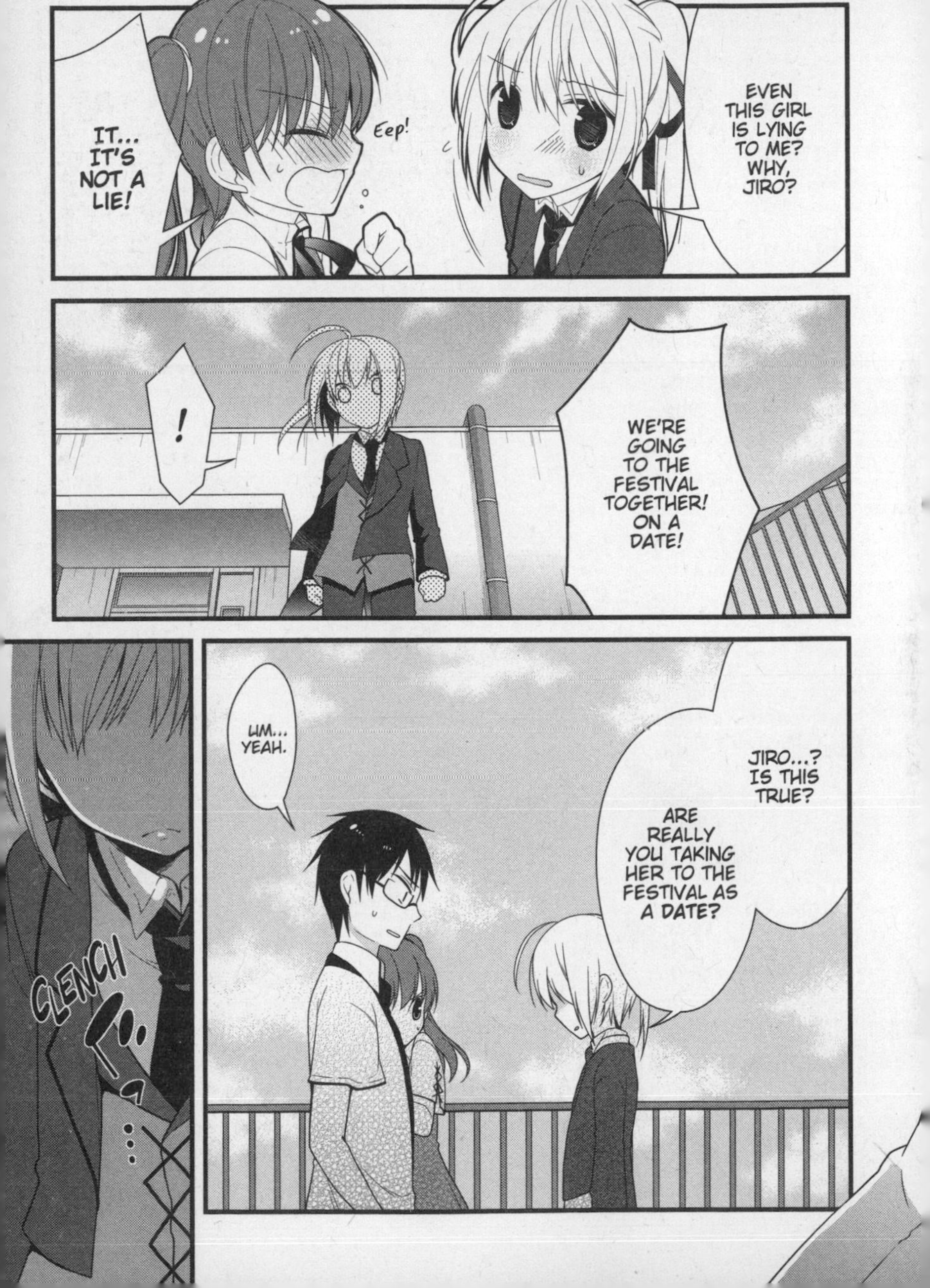
EVEN THIS GIRL IS LYING TO ME? WHY, JIRO?
Eep!
IT... IT'S NOT A LIE!
WE'RE GOING TO THE FESTIVAL TOGETHER! ON A DATE!
!
JIRO...? IS THIS TRUE?
ARE REALLY YOU TAKING HER TO THE FESTIVAL AS A DATE?
UM... YEAH.
CLENCH
...

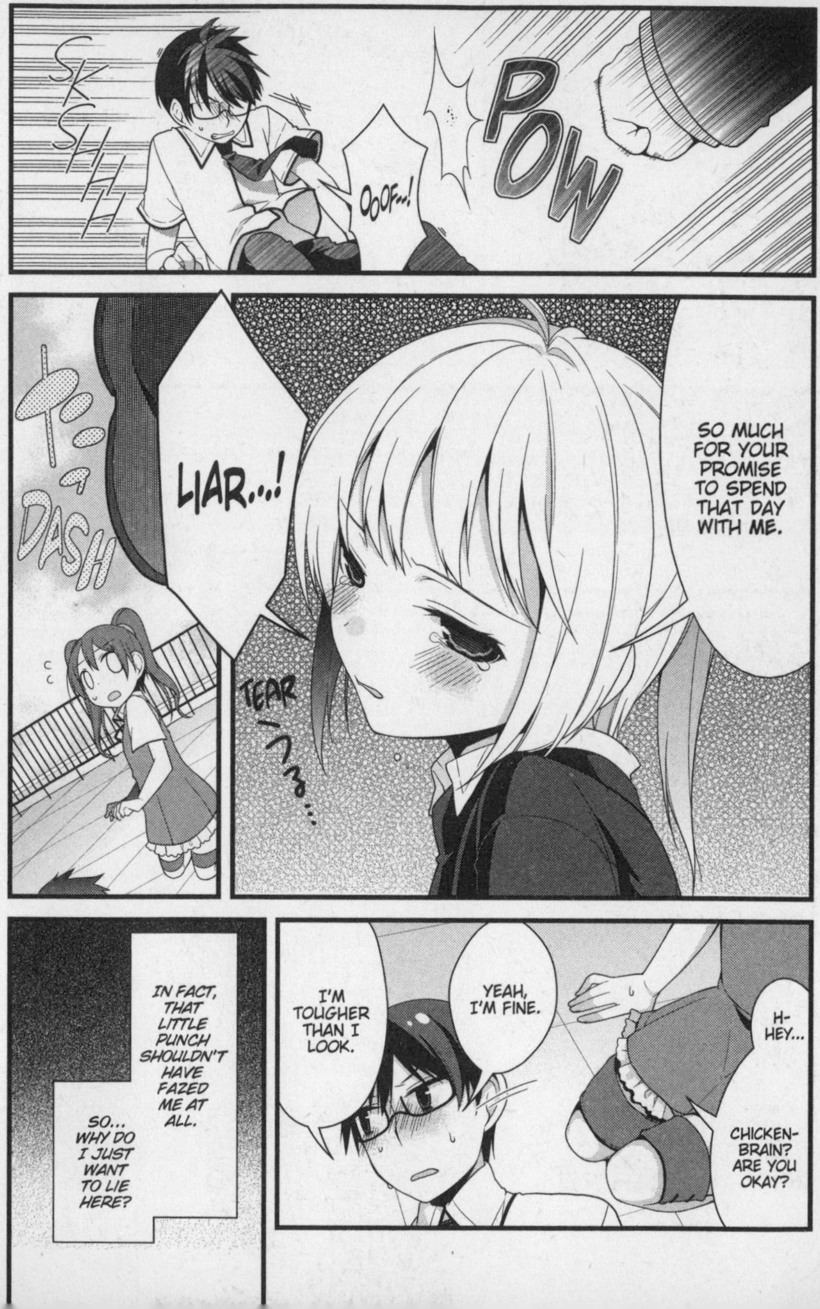
POW
OOOF...!
SK SHHH
SO MUCH FOR YOUR PROMISE TO SPEND THAT DAY WITH ME.
LIAR...!
TEAR
DASH
H- HEY...
CHICKEN-BRAIN? ARE YOU OKAY?
YEAH, I'M FINE.
I'M TOUGHER THAN I LOOK.
IN FACT, THAT LITTLE PUNCH SHOULDN'T HAVE FAZED ME AT ALL.
SO... WHY DO I JUST WANT TO LIE HERE?

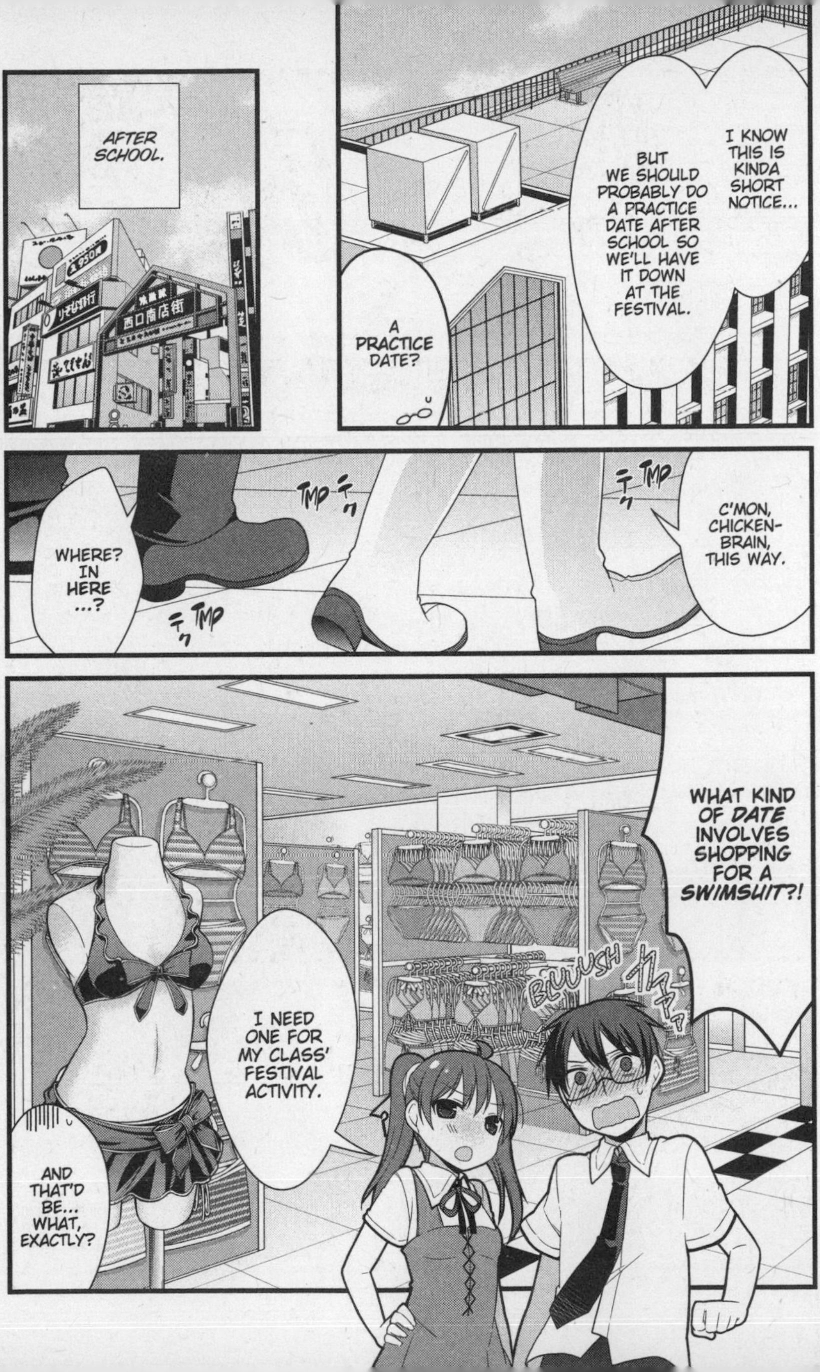
I KNOW THIS IS KINDA SHORT NOTICE...
BUT WE SHOULD PROBABLY DO A PRACTICE DATE AFTER SCHOOL SO WE'LL HAVE IT DOWN AT THE FESTIVAL.
A PRACTICE DATE?
AFTER SCHOOL.
TMP
C'MON, CHICKEN-BRAIN, THIS WAY.
TMP
WHERE? IN HERE ...?
TMP
WHAT KIND OF DATE INVOLVES SHOPPING FOR A SWIMSUIT?!
BLUUSH
I NEED ONE FOR MY CLASS' FESTIVAL ACTIVITY.
AND THAT'D BE... WHAT, EXACTLY?

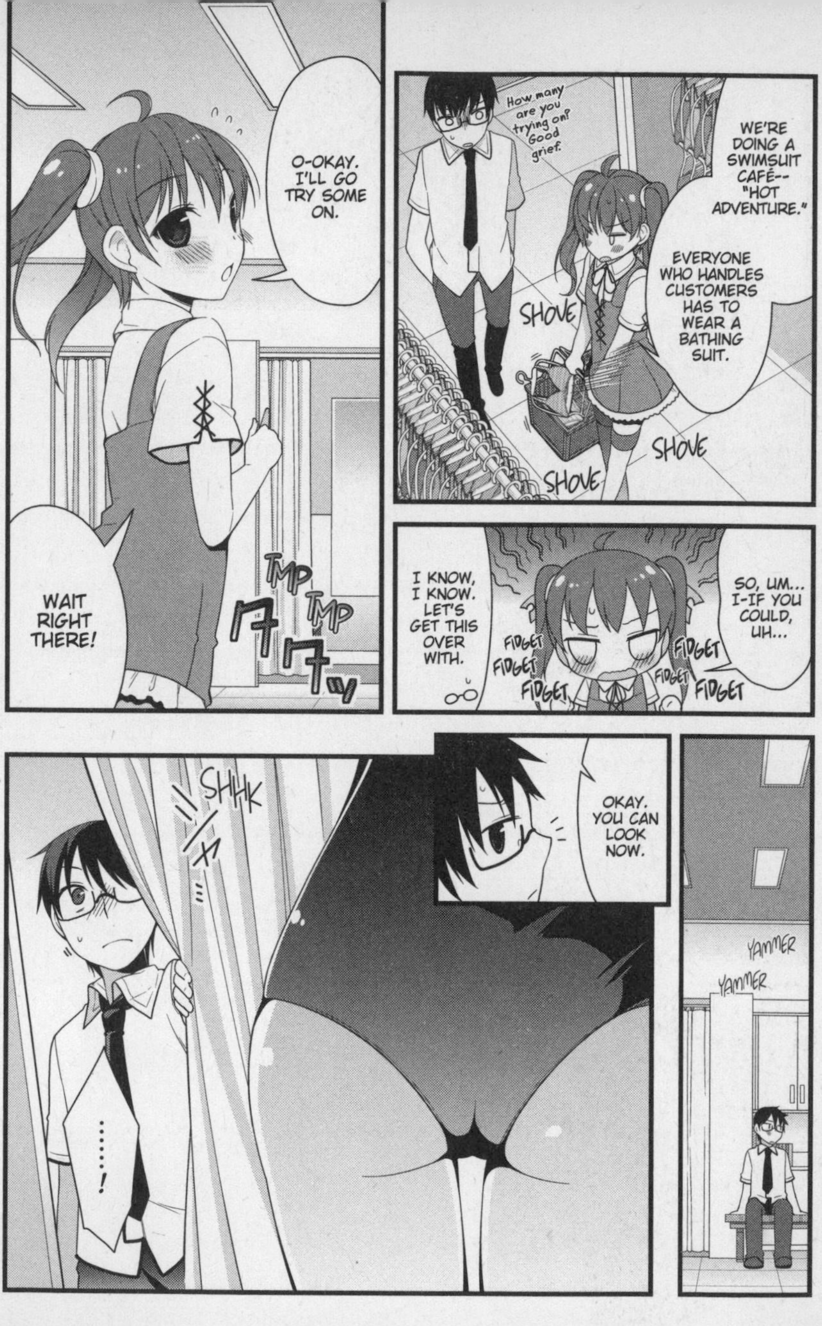
WE'RE DOING A SWIMSUIT CAFÉ-- "HOT ADVENTURE."
EVERYONE WHO HANDLES CUSTOMERS HAS TO WEAR A BATHING SUIT.
How many are you trying on? Good grief.
SHOVE
SHOVE
SHOVE
SO, UM... I-IF YOU COULD, UH...
FIDGET FIDGET FIDGET
FIDGET FIDGET FIDGET
I KNOW, I KNOW. LET'S GET THIS OVER WITH.
O-OKAY. I'LL GO TRY SOME ON.
WAIT RIGHT THERE!
TMP TMP
YAMMER
YAMMER
OKAY. YOU CAN LOOK NOW.
SHHK
......!

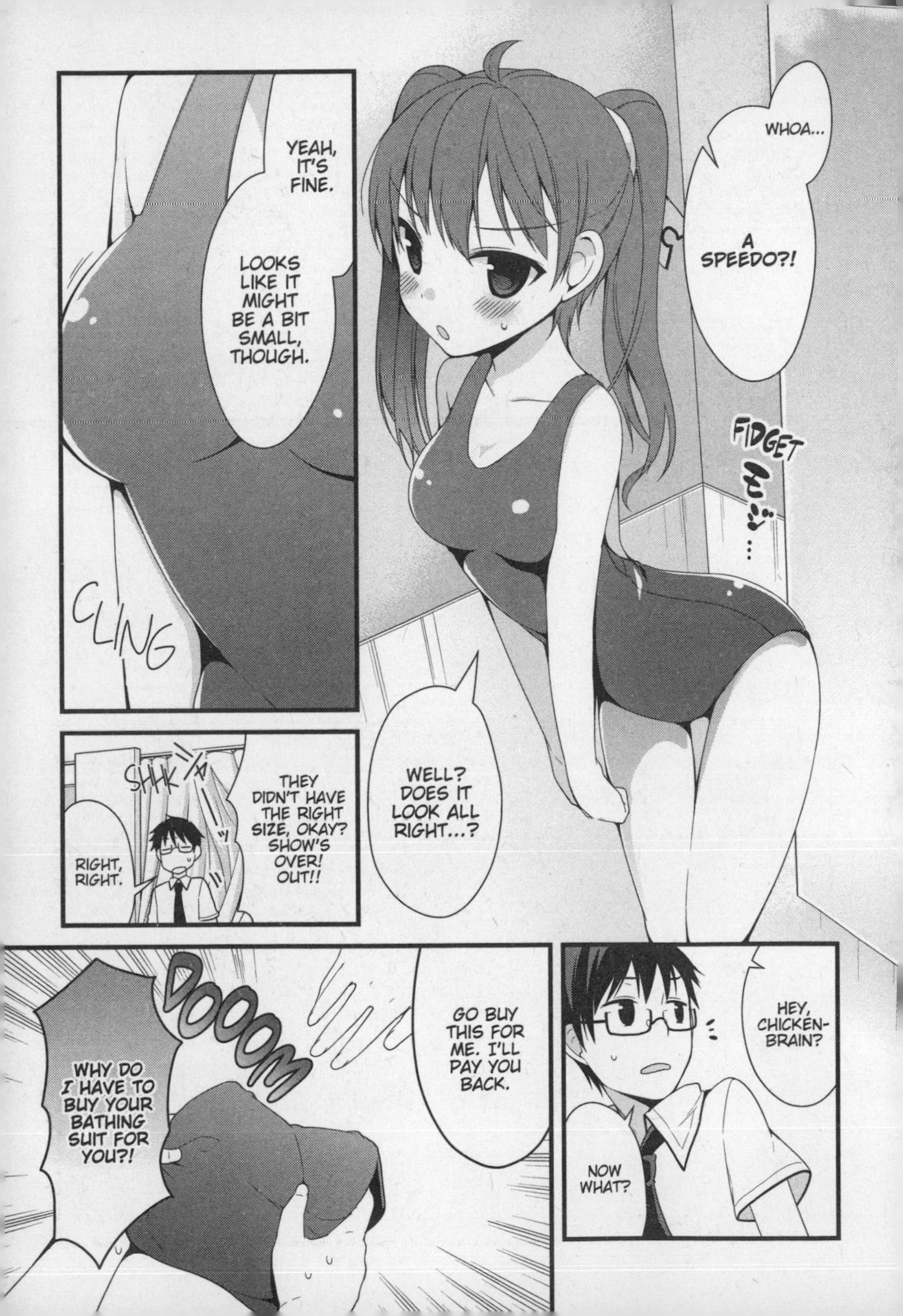
WHOA...
A SPEEDO?!
FIDGET
WELL? DOES IT LOOK ALL RIGHT...?
YEAH, IT'S FINE.
LOOKS LIKE IT MIGHT BE A BIT SMALL, THOUGH.
CLING
THEY DIDN'T HAVE THE RIGHT SIZE, OKAY? SHOW'S OVER! OUT!!
SHHK
RIGHT, RIGHT.
HEY, CHICKEN-BRAIN?
NOW WHAT?
GO BUY THIS FOR ME. I'LL PAY YOU BACK.
DOOOM
WHY DO I HAVE TO BUY YOUR BATHING SUIT FOR YOU?!

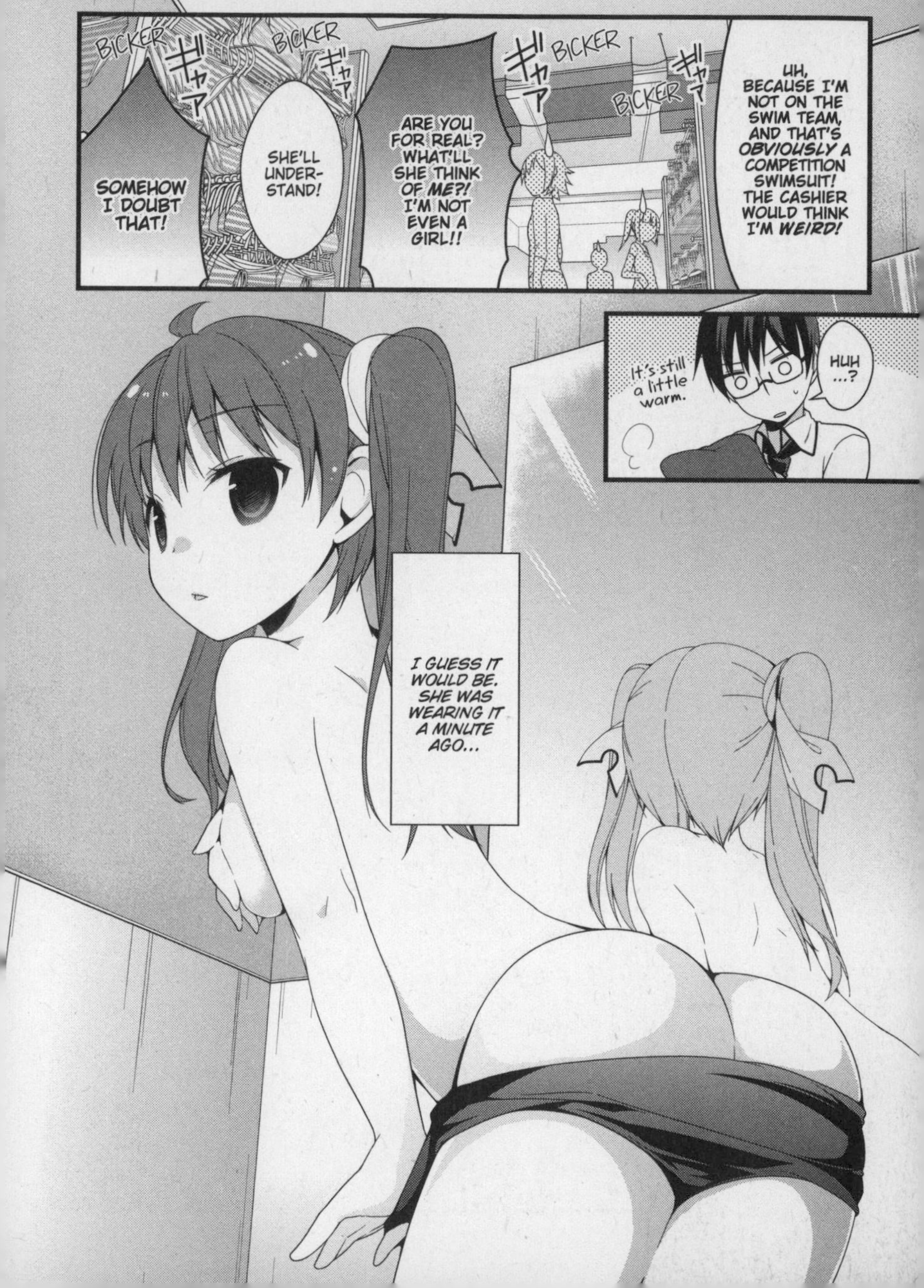
BICKER
ギャア
BICKER
ギャア
UH, BECAUSE I'M NOT ON THE SWIM TEAM, AND THAT'S *OBVIOUSLY* A COMPETITION SWIMSUIT! THE CASHIER WOULD THINK I'M *WEIRD*!
BICKER
ギャア
ARE YOU FOR REAL? WHAT'LL SHE THINK OF *ME*?! I'M NOT EVEN A GIRL!!
BICKER
ギャア
SHE'LL UNDER-STAND!
BICKER
ギャア
SOMEHOW I DOUBT THAT!
HUH ...?
It's still a little warm.
I GUESS IT WOULD BE. SHE WAS WEARING IT A MINUTE AGO...

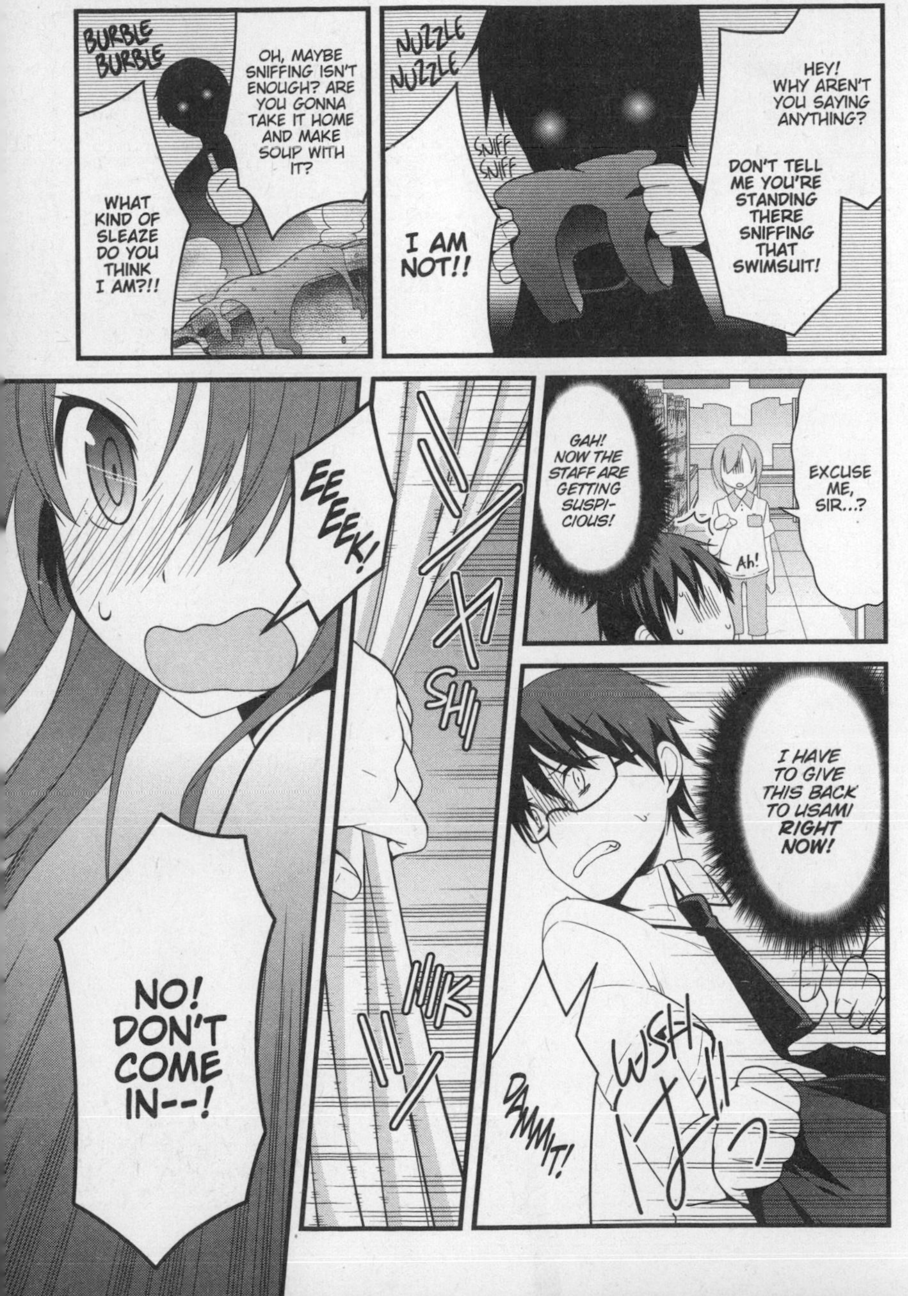
HEY! WHY AREN'T YOU SAYING ANYTHING?
DON'T TELL ME YOU'RE STANDING THERE SNIFFING THAT SWIMSUIT!
NUZZLE NUZZLE
SNIFF SNIFF
I AM NOT!!
OH, MAYBE SNIFFING ISN'T ENOUGH? ARE YOU GONNA TAKE IT HOME AND MAKE SOUP WITH IT?
BURBLE BURBLE
WHAT KIND OF SLEAZE DO YOU THINK I AM?!!
EXCUSE ME, SIR...?
Ah!
GAH! NOW THE STAFF ARE GETTING SUSPI-CIOUS!
I HAVE TO GIVE THIS BACK TO USAMI RIGHT NOW!
WSH
DAMMIT!
SHI
HIK
EEEEK!
NO! DON'T COME IN--!

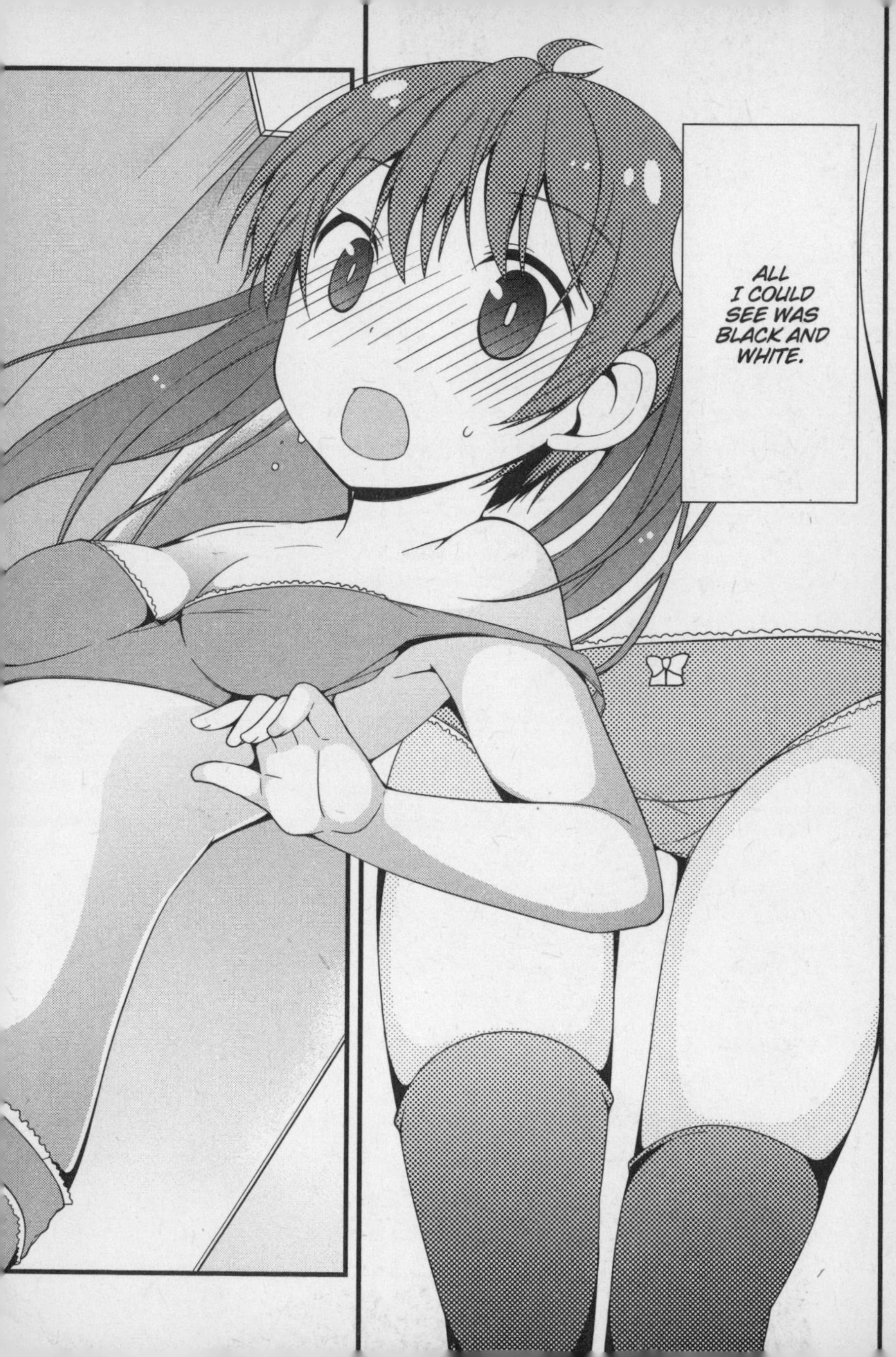
ALL I COULD SEE WAS BLACK AND WHITE.

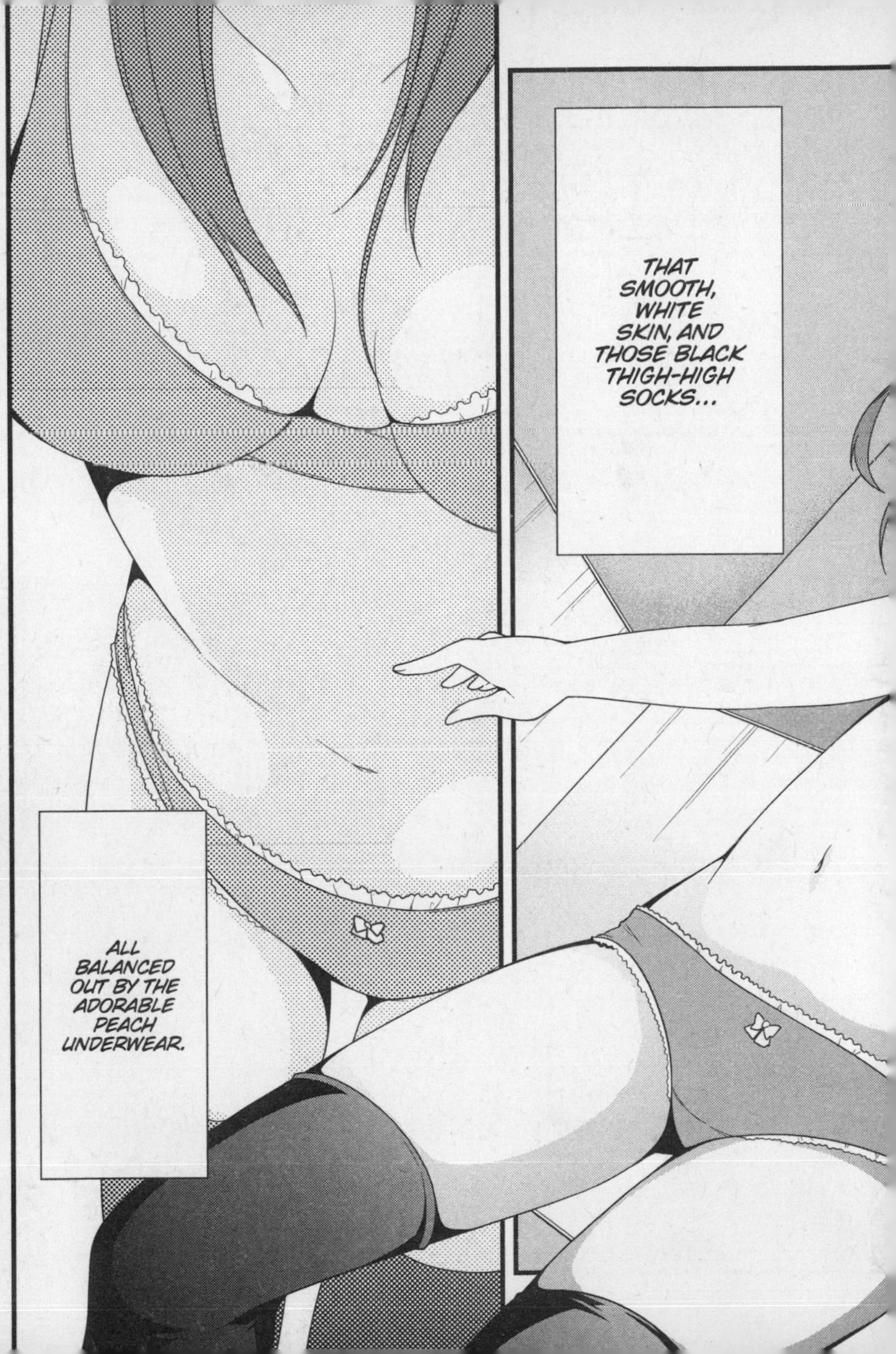
THAT SMOOTH, WHITE SKIN, AND THOSE BLACK THIGH-HIGH SOCKS...
ALL BALANCED OUT BY THE ADORABLE PEACH UNDERWEAR.

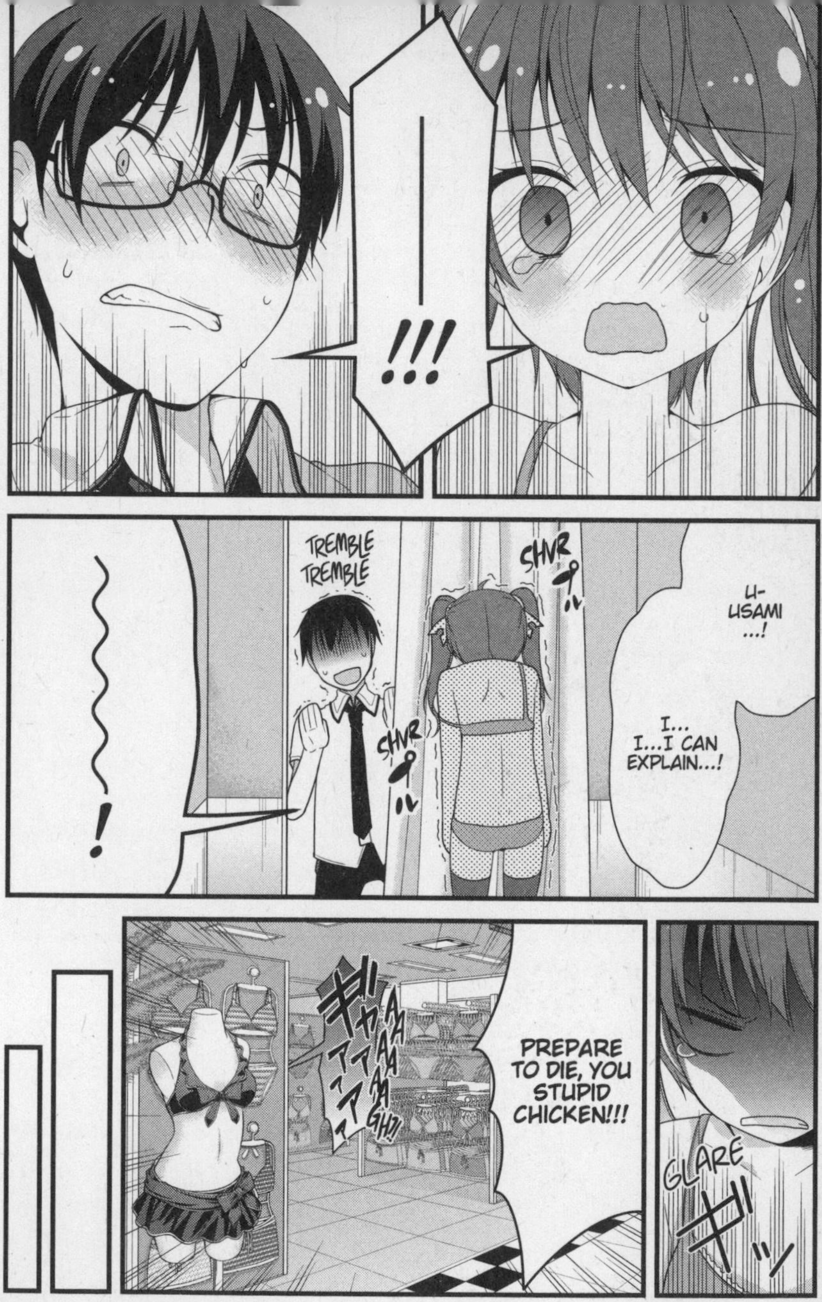
!!!
U-USAMI...!
I... I...I CAN EXPLAIN...!
SHVR
TREMBLE TREMBLE
SHVR
!
GLARE
PREPARE TO DIE, YOU STUPID CHICKEN!!!
AAAAAAGH?!

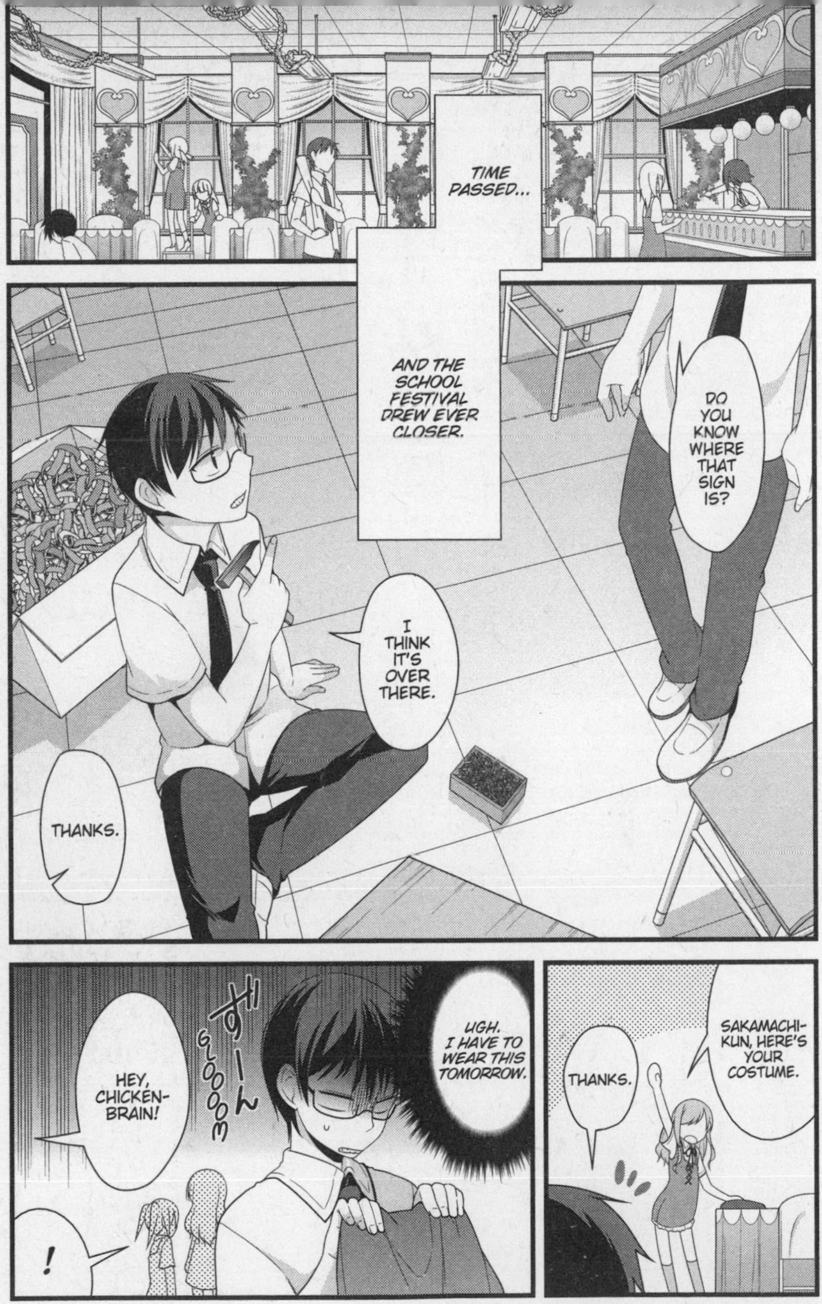
TIME PASSED...
AND THE SCHOOL FESTIVAL DREW EVER CLOSER.
DO YOU KNOW WHERE THAT SIGN IS?
I THINK IT'S OVER THERE.
THANKS.
SAKAMACHI-KUN, HERE'S YOUR COSTUME.
THANKS.
UGH. I HAVE TO WEAR THIS TOMORROW.
ずーん
GLOOOOM
HEY, CHICKEN-BRAIN!
!

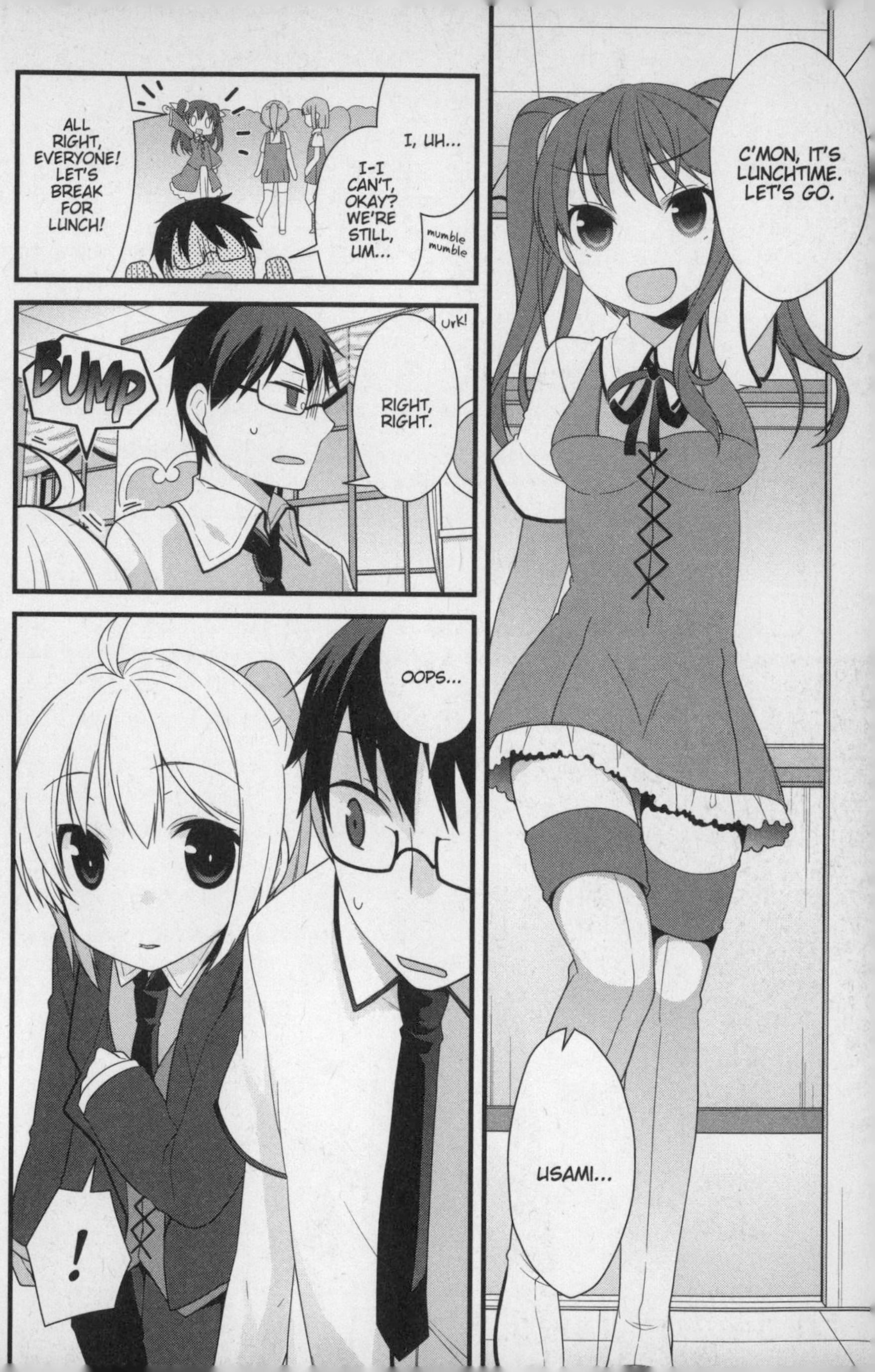
C'MON, IT'S LUNCHTIME. LET'S GO.
USAMI...
I, UH...
I-I CAN'T, OKAY? WE'RE STILL, UM...
mumble mumble
ALL RIGHT, EVERYONE! LET'S BREAK FOR LUNCH!
Urk!
RIGHT, RIGHT.
BUMP
OOPS...
!

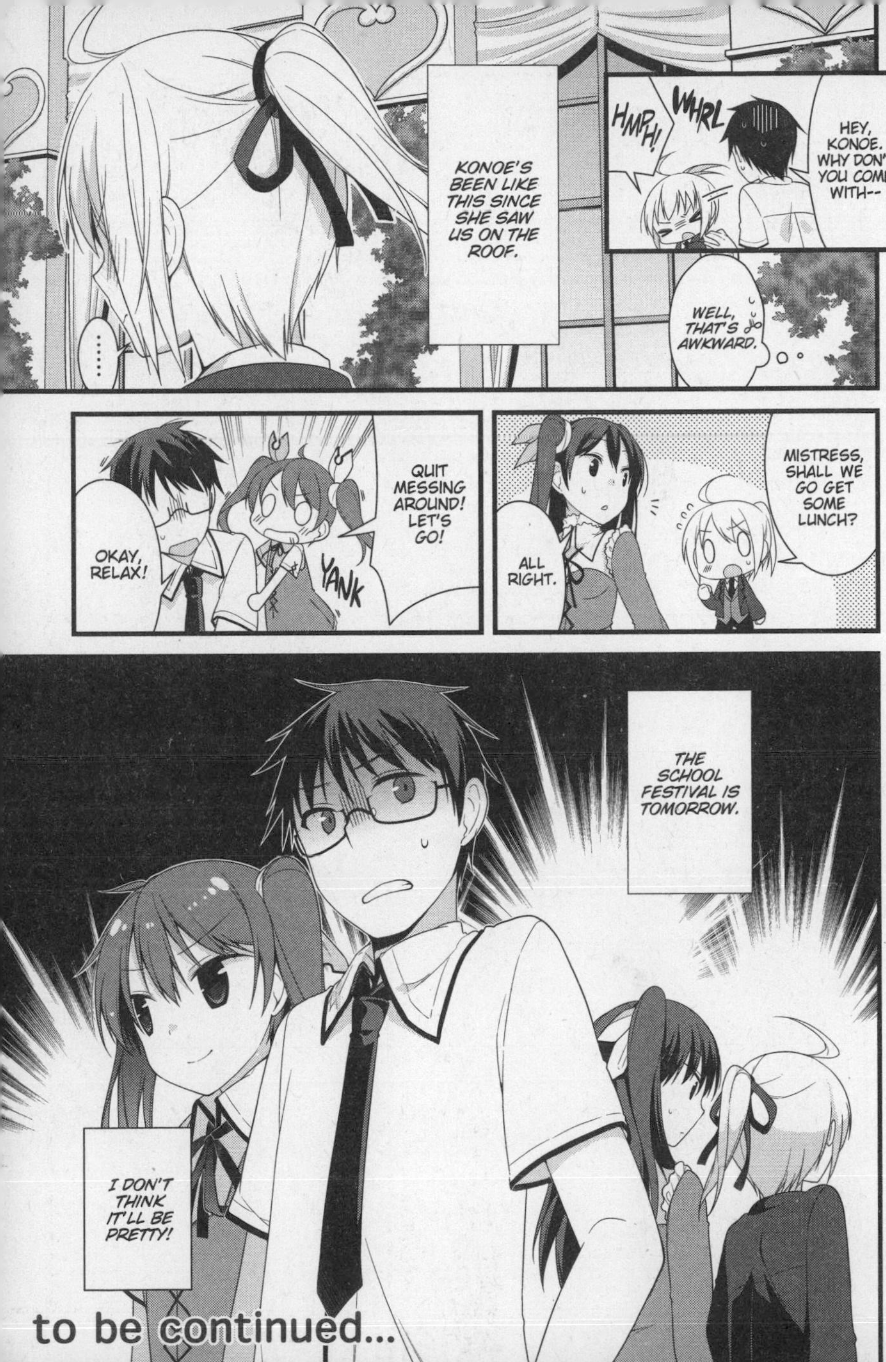
HEY, KONOE. WHY DON'T YOU COME WITH--
WHRL
HMPH!
KONOE'S BEEN LIKE THIS SINCE SHE SAW US ON THE ROOF.
WELL, THAT'S AWKWARD.
......
MISTRESS, SHALL WE GO GET SOME LUNCH?
ALL RIGHT.
QUIT MESSING AROUND! LET'S GO!
YANK
OKAY, RELAX!
THE SCHOOL FESTIVAL IS TOMORROW.
I DON'T THINK IT'LL BE PRETTY!
to be continued...

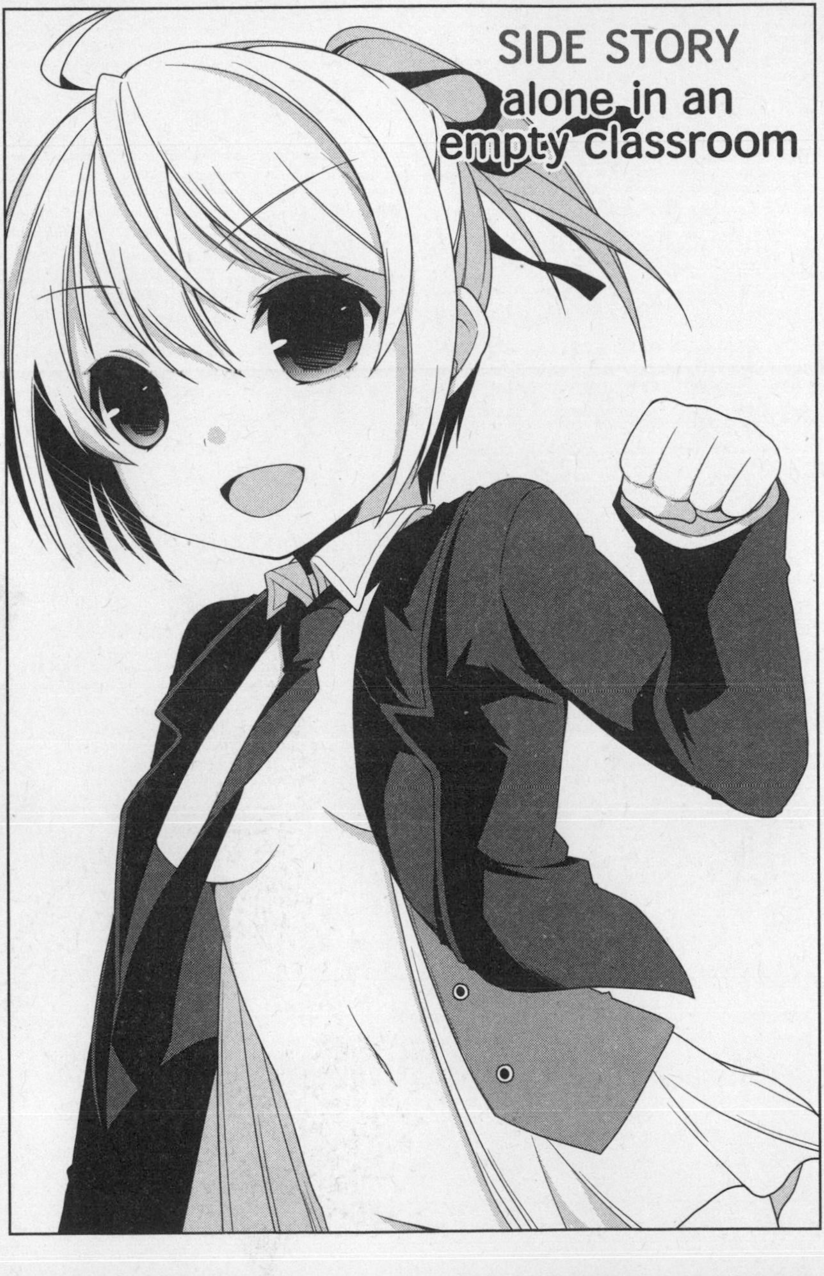
SIDE STORY
alone in an
empty classroom

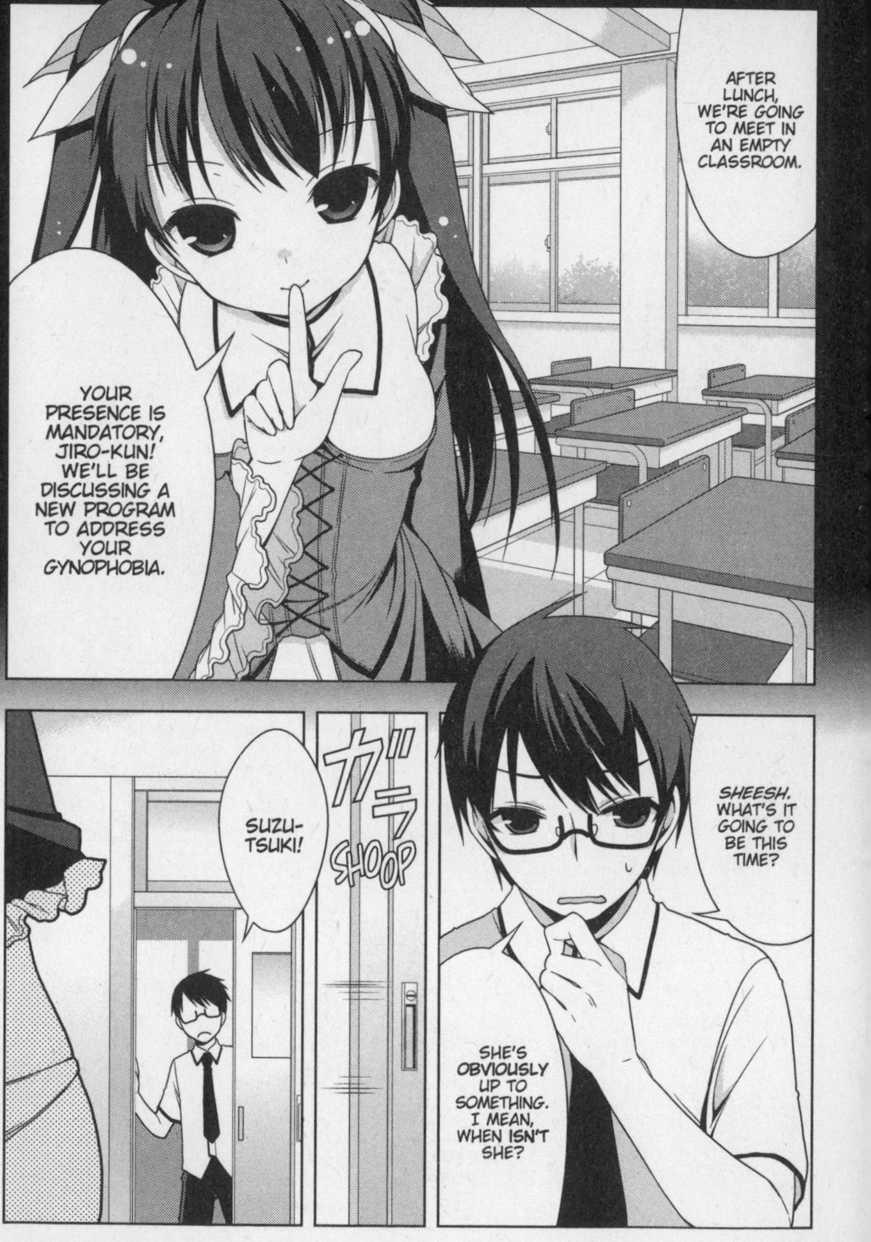
AFTER LUNCH, WE'RE GOING TO MEET IN AN EMPTY CLASSROOM.
YOUR PRESENCE IS MANDATORY, JIRO-KUN! WE'LL BE DISCUSSING A NEW PROGRAM TO ADDRESS YOUR GYNOPHOBIA.
SHEESH. WHAT'S IT GOING TO BE THIS TIME?
SHE'S OBVIOUSLY UP TO SOMETHING. I MEAN, WHEN ISN'T SHE?
ガラ
SHOOP
SUZU-TSUKI!

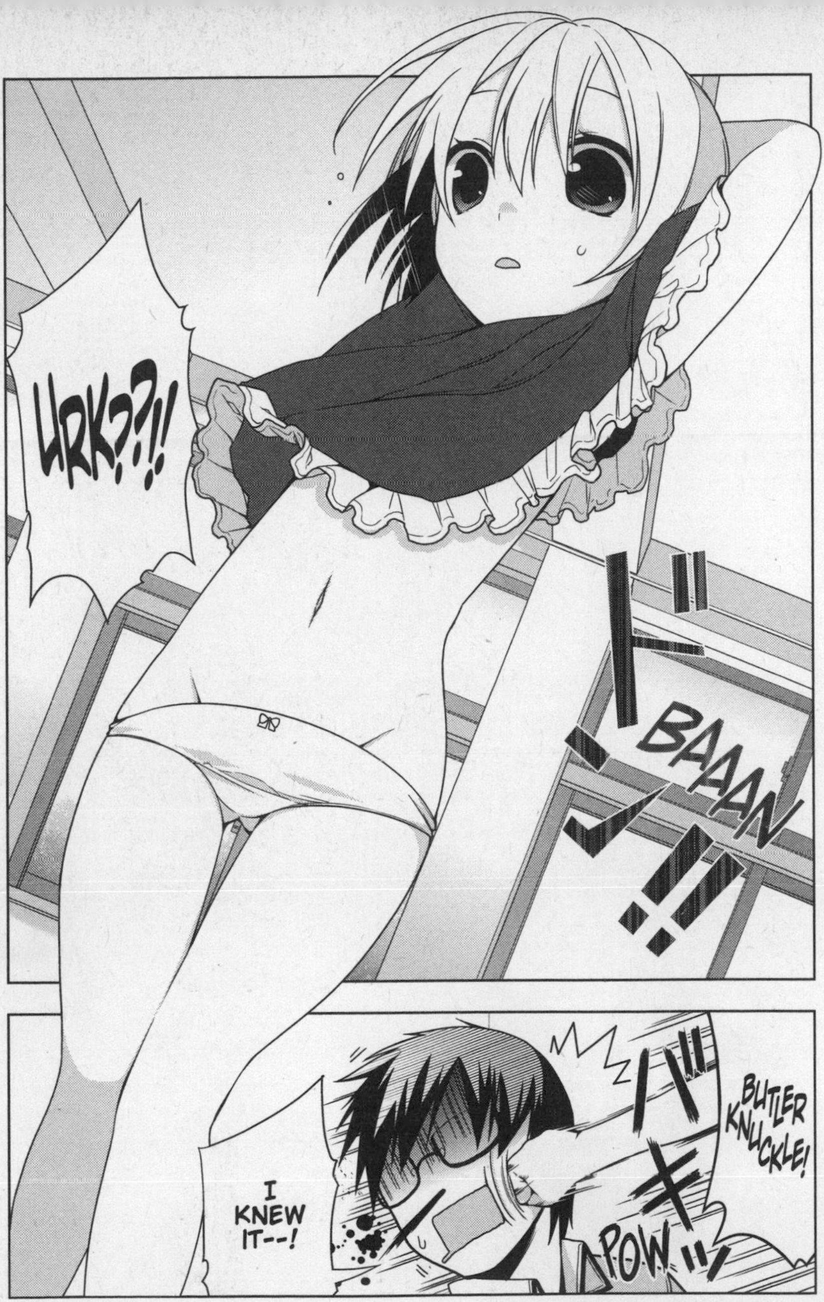
URK??!!
BAAAN!!
BUTLER KNUCKLE!
POW!!
I KNEW IT--!

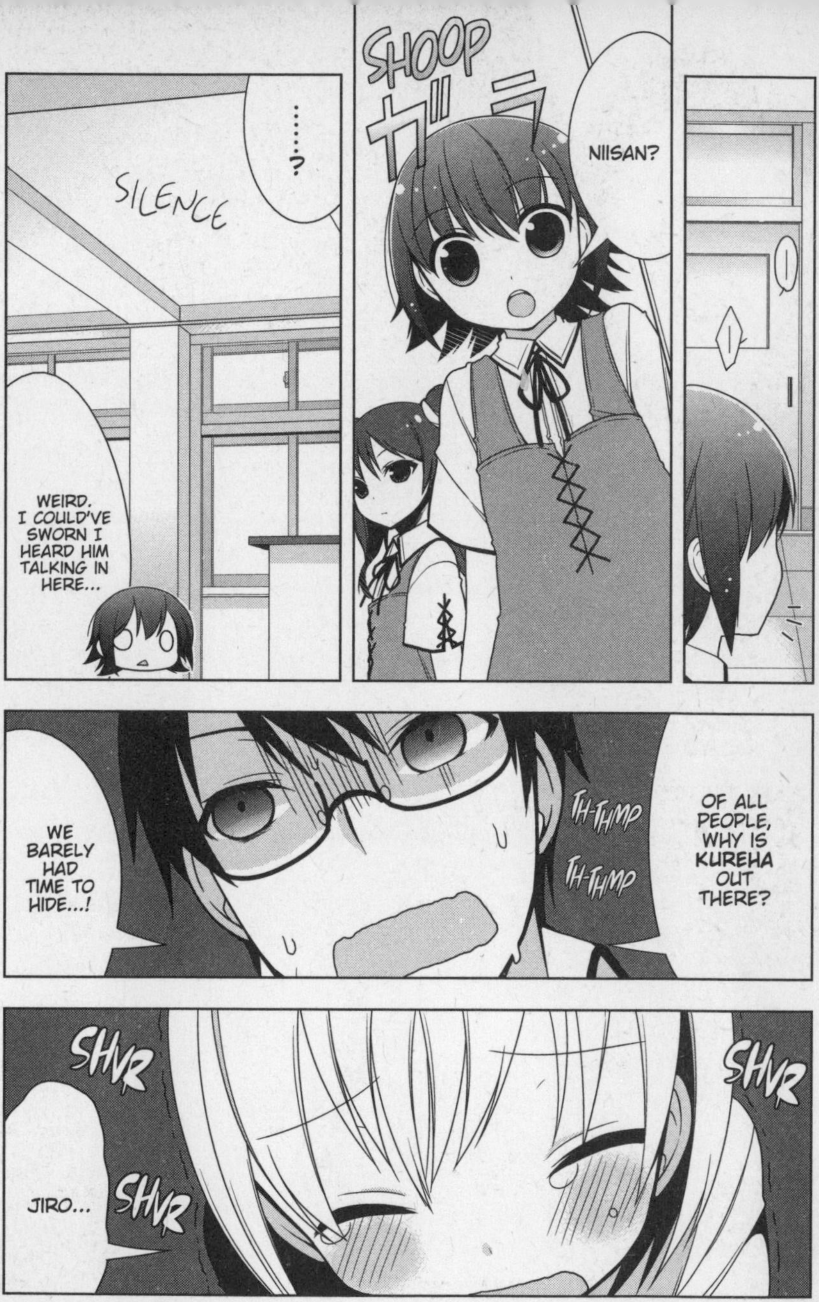
!
!
SHOOP
ガラ
NIISAN?
......?
SILENCE
WEIRD. I COULD'VE SWORN I HEARD HIM TALKING IN HERE...
OF ALL PEOPLE, WHY IS KUREHA OUT THERE?
TH-THMP
TH-THMP
WE BARELY HAD TIME TO HIDE...!
SHVR
SHVR
SHVR
JIRO...

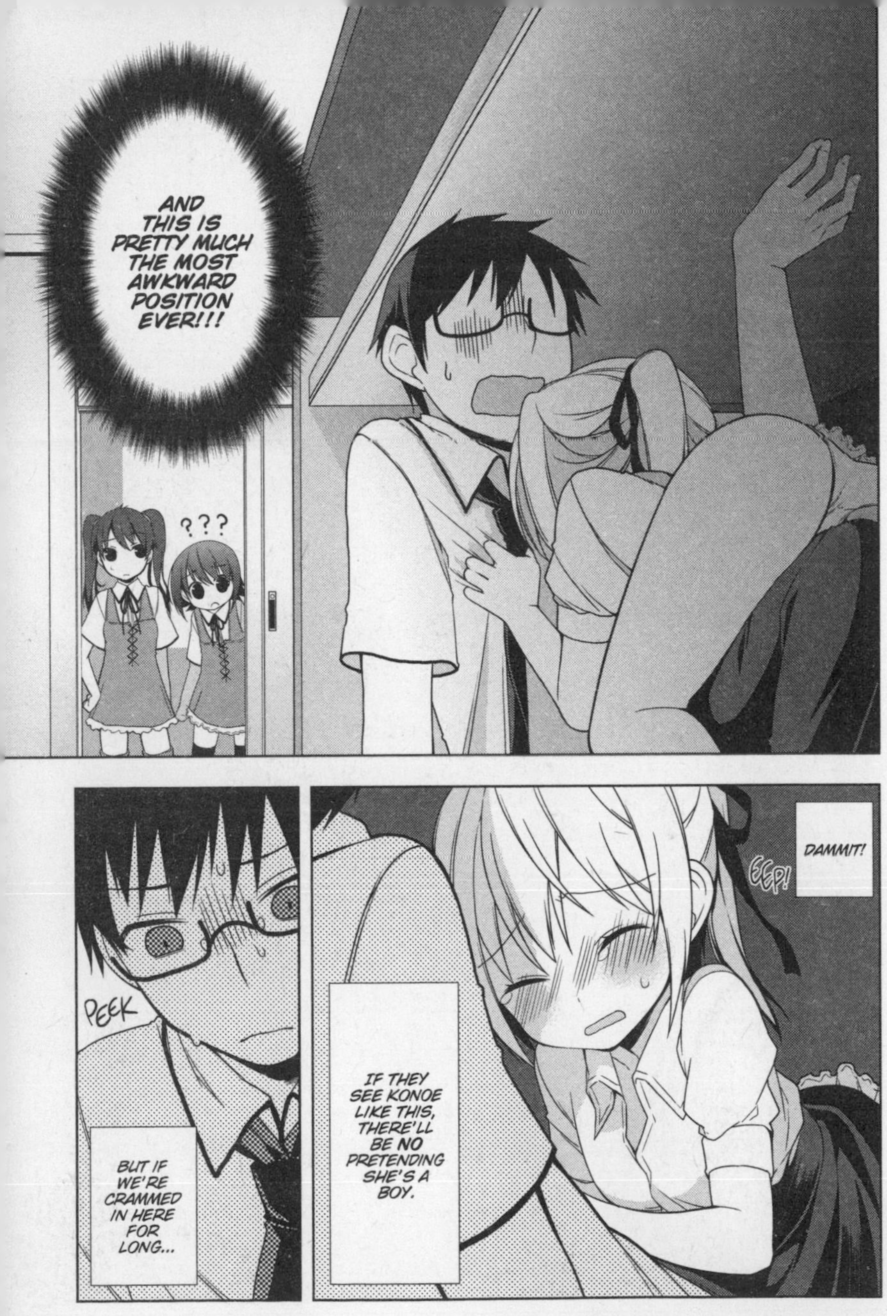
AND THIS IS PRETTY MUCH THE MOST AWKWARD POSITION EVER!!!
???
EEP!
DAMMIT!
IF THEY SEE KONOE LIKE THIS, THERE'LL BE NO PRETENDING SHE'S A BOY.
PEEK
BUT IF WE'RE CRAMMED IN HERE FOR LONG...

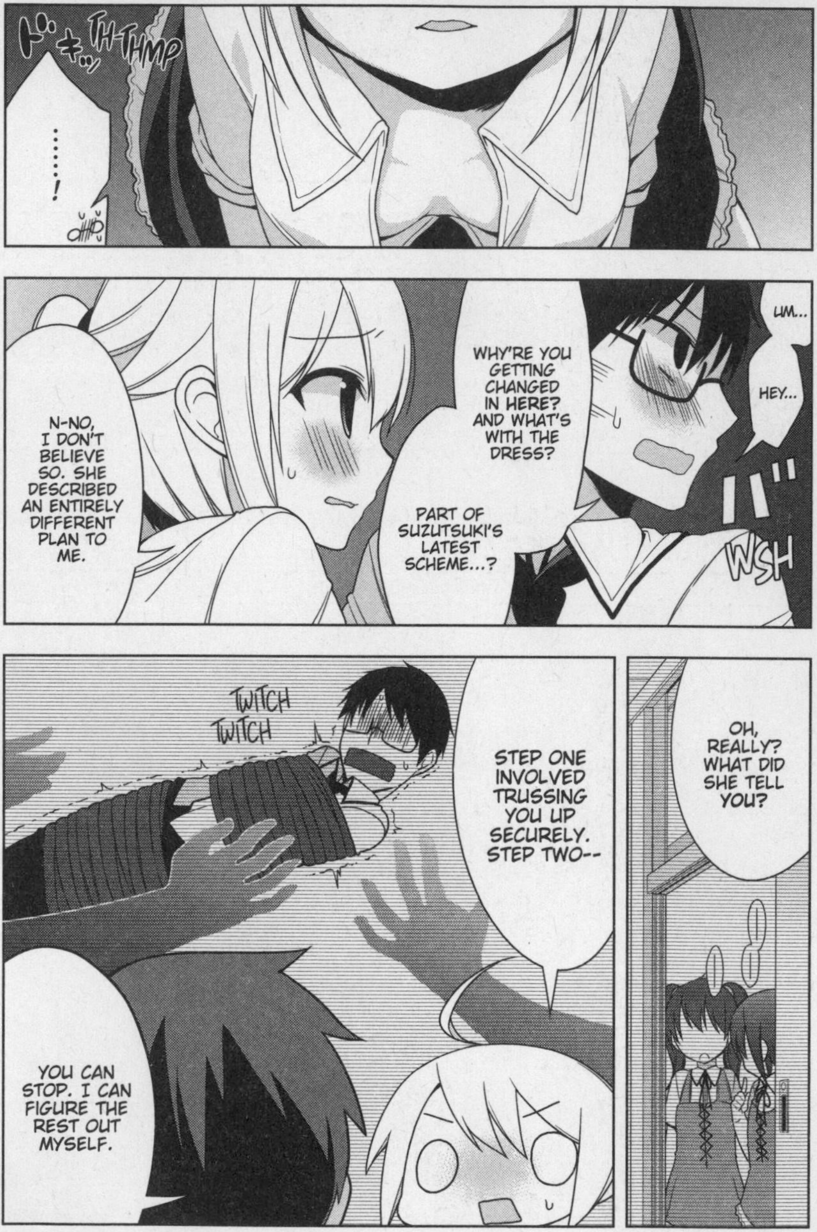
ドキッ TH-THMP
......!
UM...
HEY...
WHY'RE YOU GETTING CHANGED IN HERE? AND WHAT'S WITH THE DRESS?
バ WSH
PART OF SUZUTSUKI'S LATEST SCHEME...?
N-NO, I DON'T BELIEVE SO. SHE DESCRIBED AN ENTIRELY DIFFERENT PLAN TO ME.
OH, REALLY? WHAT DID SHE TELL YOU?
STEP ONE INVOLVED TRUSSING YOU UP SECURELY. STEP TWO--
TWITCH TWITCH
YOU CAN STOP. I CAN FIGURE THE REST OUT MYSELF.

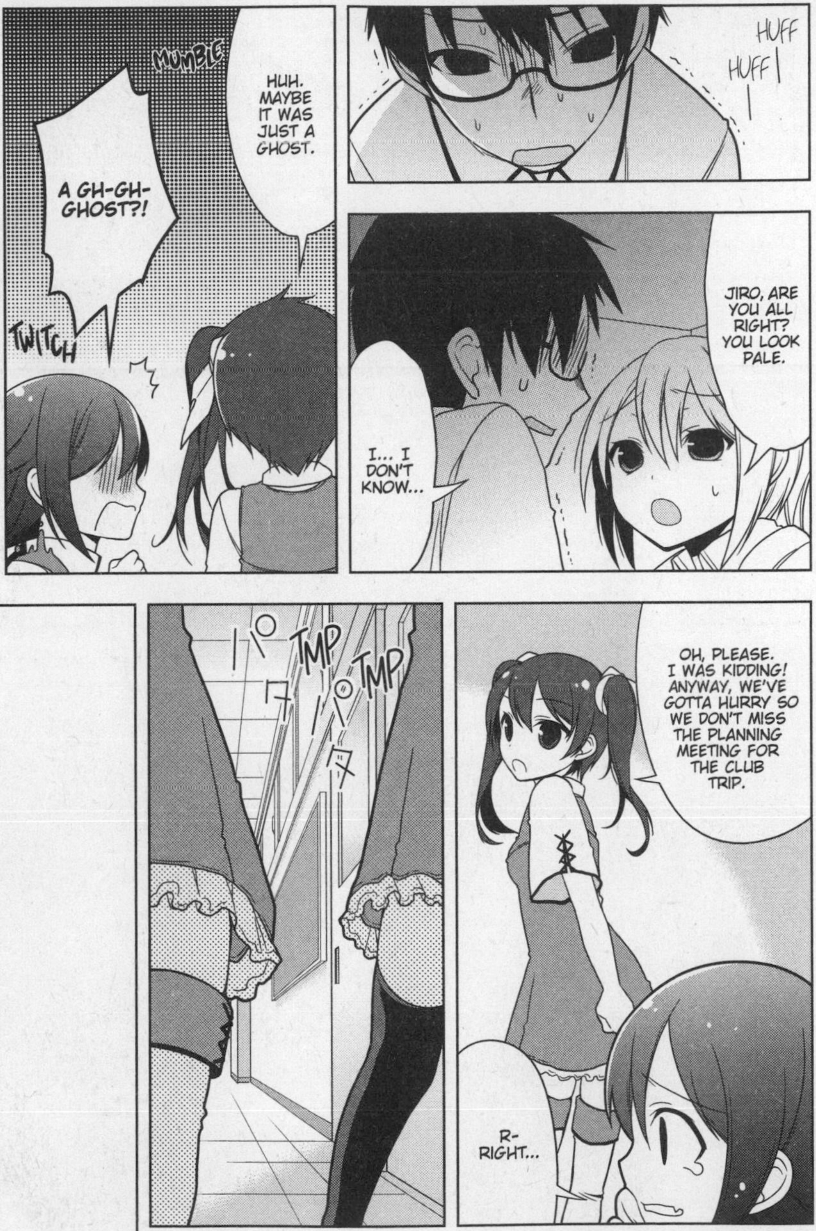
HUFF
HUFF
JIRO, ARE YOU ALL RIGHT? YOU LOOK PALE.
I... I DON'T KNOW...
HUH. MAYBE IT WAS JUST A GHOST.
MUMBLE
A GH-GH-GHOST?!
TWITCH
OH, PLEASE. I WAS KIDDING! ANYWAY, WE'VE GOTTA HURRY SO WE DON'T MISS THE PLANNING MEETING FOR THE CLUB TRIP.
R-RIGHT...
パタ
TMP
パタ
TMP

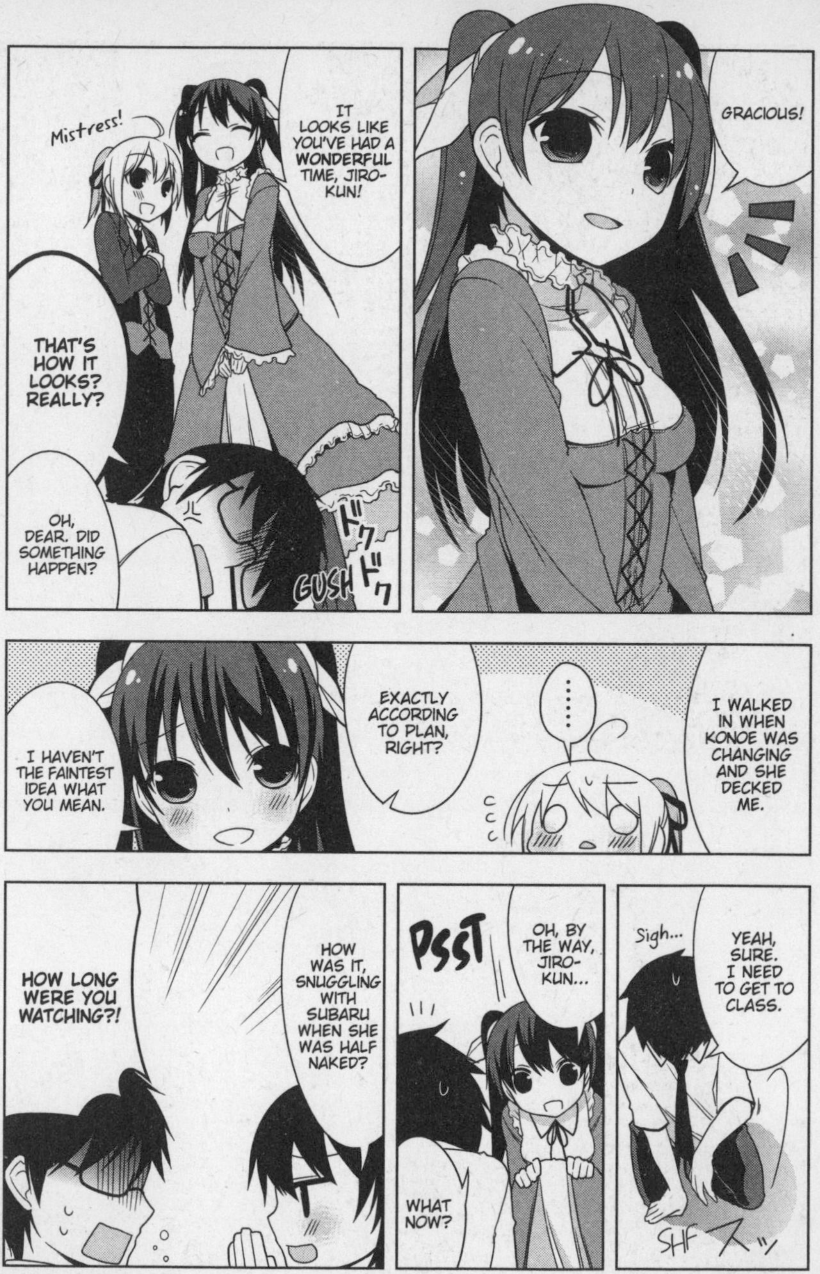
GRACIOUS!
IT LOOKS LIKE YOU'VE HAD A WONDERFUL TIME, JIRO-KUN!
Mistress!
THAT'S HOW IT LOOKS? REALLY?
OH, DEAR. DID SOMETHING HAPPEN?
ドクドク
GUSH
I WALKED IN WHEN KONOE WAS CHANGING AND SHE DECKED ME.
......
EXACTLY ACCORDING TO PLAN, RIGHT?
I HAVEN'T THE FAINTEST IDEA WHAT YOU MEAN.
YEAH, SURE. I NEED TO GET TO CLASS.
Sigh...
SHF
OH, BY THE WAY, JIRO-KUN...
PSST
WHAT NOW?
HOW WAS IT, SNUGGLING WITH SUBARU WHEN SHE WAS HALF NAKED?
HOW LONG WERE YOU WATCHING?!

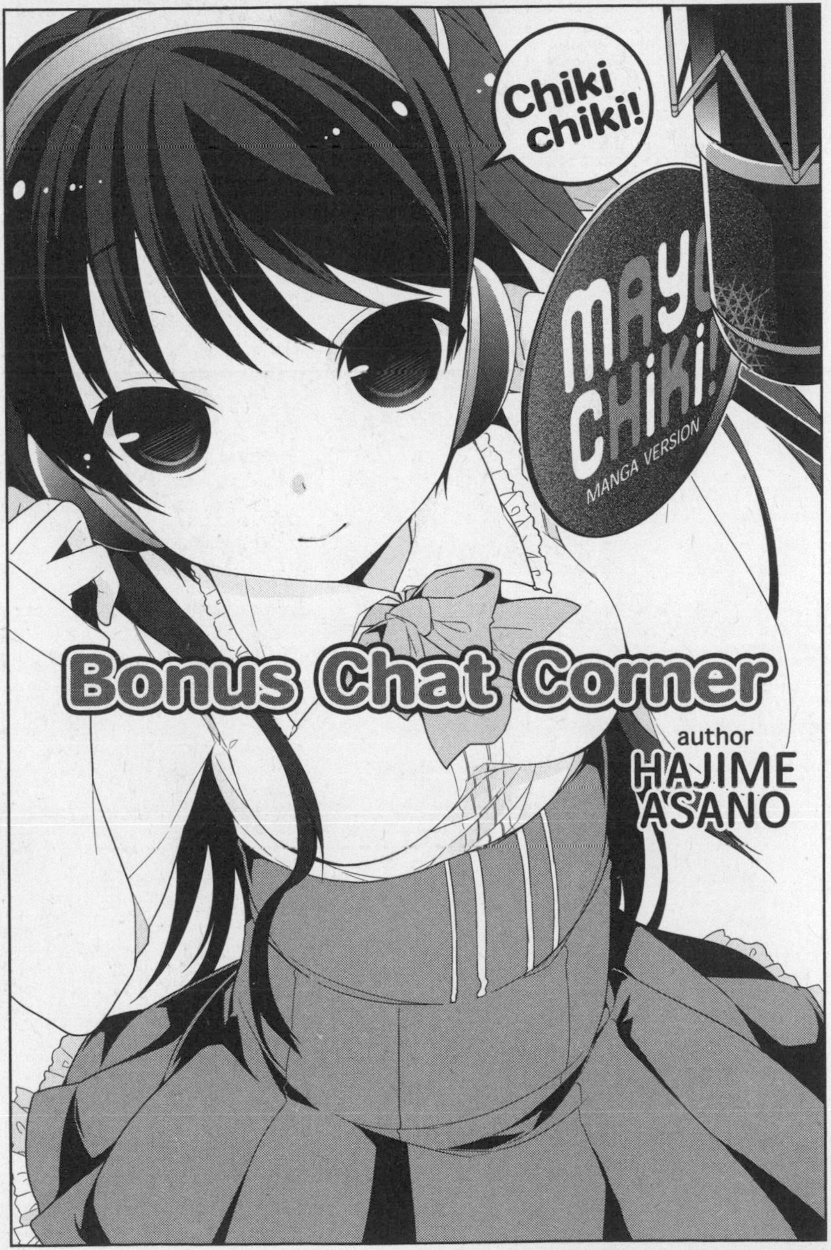

Chiki chiki!
MAYO CHIKI!
MANGA VERSION
Bonus Chat Corner
author
HAJIME ASANO

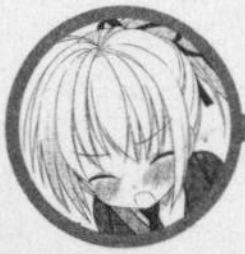

Uh... Er... W-welcome to the second *Chiki Chiki Mayo Chiki!* manga version Chat Corner!

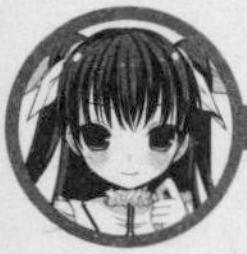

Hello, everyone! I'm Suzutsuki Kanade, a second-year student at Rouran Academy! My butler, Konoe Subaru, and I will be your hosts for today's Chat Corner!

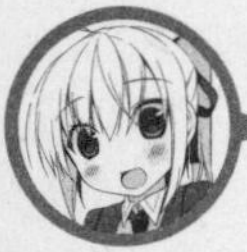

I-I'm delighted to be here!

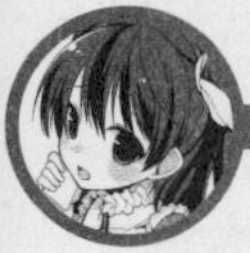

You know, Subaru, you stuttered a little on the introduction. Are you nervous?

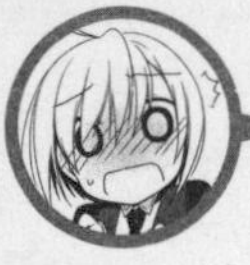

Oh...! My apologies, Mistress. I'm not terribly comfortable in the spotlight...

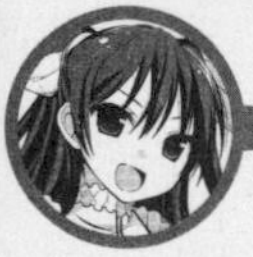

Ah, well. This is only our second Chat Corner, so I guess that's to be expected.

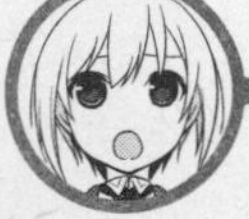

「Hmm? Mistress, is Kureha-chan coming? Kureha-chan, Jiro, and I did the first Chat Corner together.

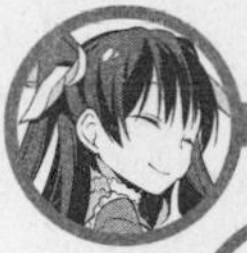

「.........

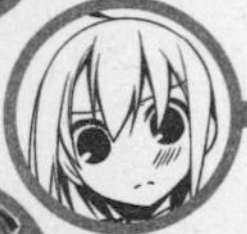

「Mistress? Why the sour face?

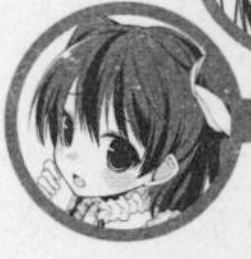

「The truth is that Kureha-chan hasn't been feeling terribly well. I assume you recall how earnestly she pleaded for votes in the novel popularity polls?

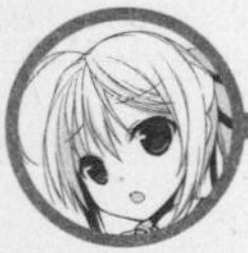

「Of course I do! She ranked rather poorly and was trying her best to improve her position. Oh dear, don't tell me...

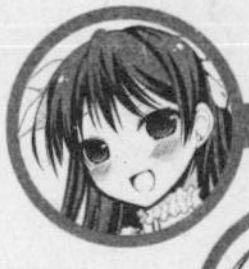

「Indeed. I fear her efforts were all for naught. Her rank didn't improve in the slightest.

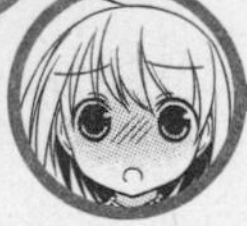

「.........

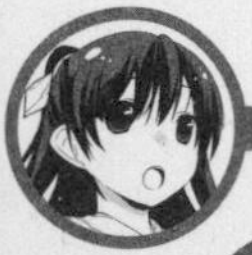

「Therefore, she will not be joining us today. I hear the poor thing is bedridden from the shock.

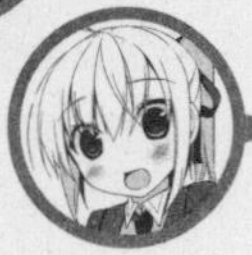

「I-I'm sure she'll be all right, Mistress! If anyone can overcome this setback, it's Kureha-chan. She'll never give up! And one day, she'll have a novel cover all to herself!

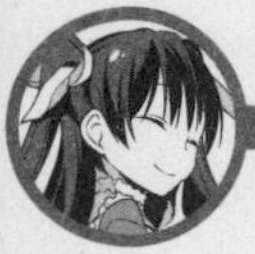

「I fear that might sound less than comforting when coming from someone so securely seated in the #1 spot, Subaru.

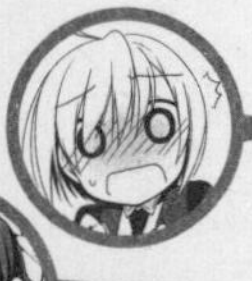

「.........?!

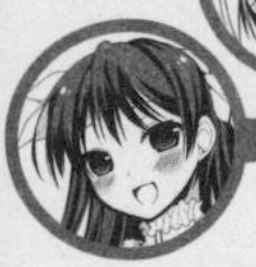

「If you were wondering, these are the current rankings: #1, Subaru; #2, me; #3, Usami; and #4, Jiro-kun. You've trounced us all again.

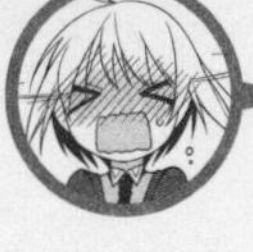

「.........

 Goodness, Subaru! Why are you shivering like that? Are you cold?

Sh-shivering? I-I'm not shivering, Mistress. Honest!

Of course you're not. Good. Anyway, ladies and gentlemen, it's time now for a commercial break. I would be ever so pleased if you'd buy the *Mayo Chiki!* novels and participate in the character popularity polls. It's so much fun!

I-I agree! I'm very happy that some people deign to vote for me, but I would be so much happier if you voted for my mistress! Oh, and don't forget Kureha-chan!

 My, my. You're being quite **earnest** yourself, Subaru.

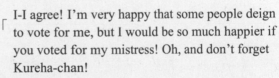 It's just that I... I...!

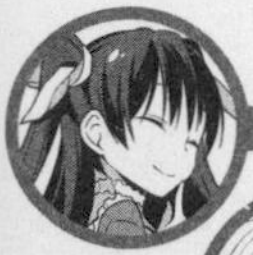

「You what...?

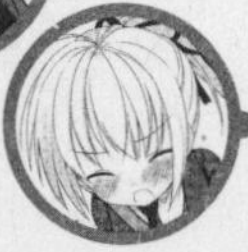

「N-no, it's nothing. Moving right along! Yes, ladies and gentlemen, please do buy the *Mayo Chiki!* novels and participate in the polls. You can vote via cell phone simply by scanning the barcode on the back of the book!

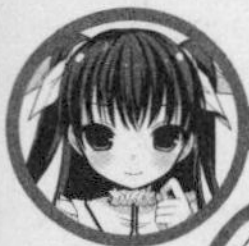

「We'll all be anxiously awaiting your votes!

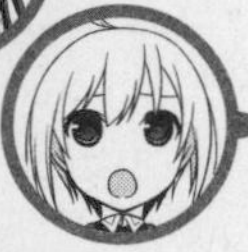

「Oh! I asked about Kureha-chan, but I entirely forgot about Jiro. Mistress, why couldn't Jiro join us today? His rank has held steady.

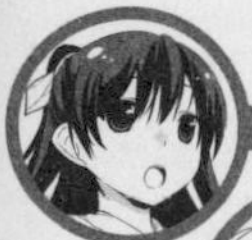

「He's bedridden at home as well.

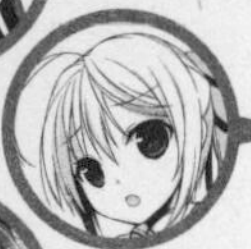

「He...he's what?

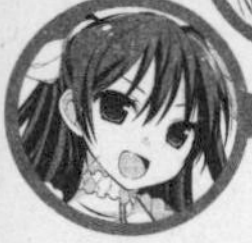

「You see, when he saw how dreadfully shocked poor Kureha-chan was, he offered to help her relax.

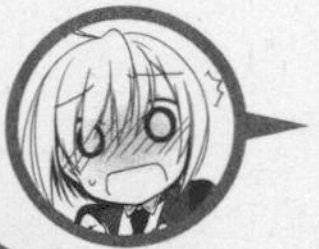

「By which you mean she took out all her frustrations on him...?

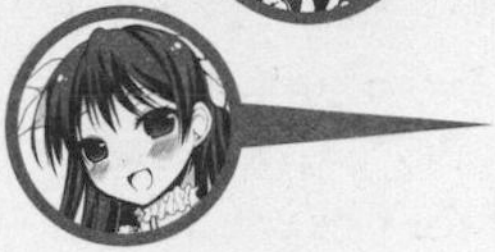

「That is another way of phrasing it, yes. At any rate, gentle readers, this concludes our commercial break. I look forward to seeing you all again! Bye bye! ♪

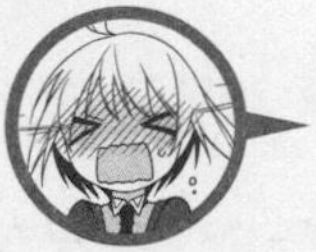

「Ack! Mistress, please wait for me! A-am I supposed to wrap up the Chat Corner all by myself? Er... Uh... L-ladies and gentlemen, thank you for supporting the manga version of *Mayo Chiki!* Bye bye...!

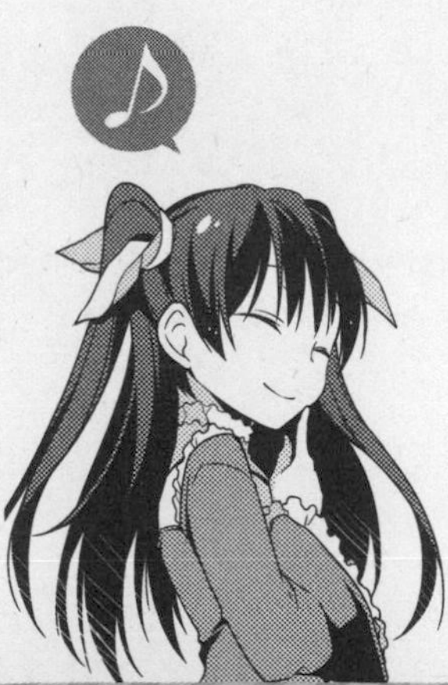

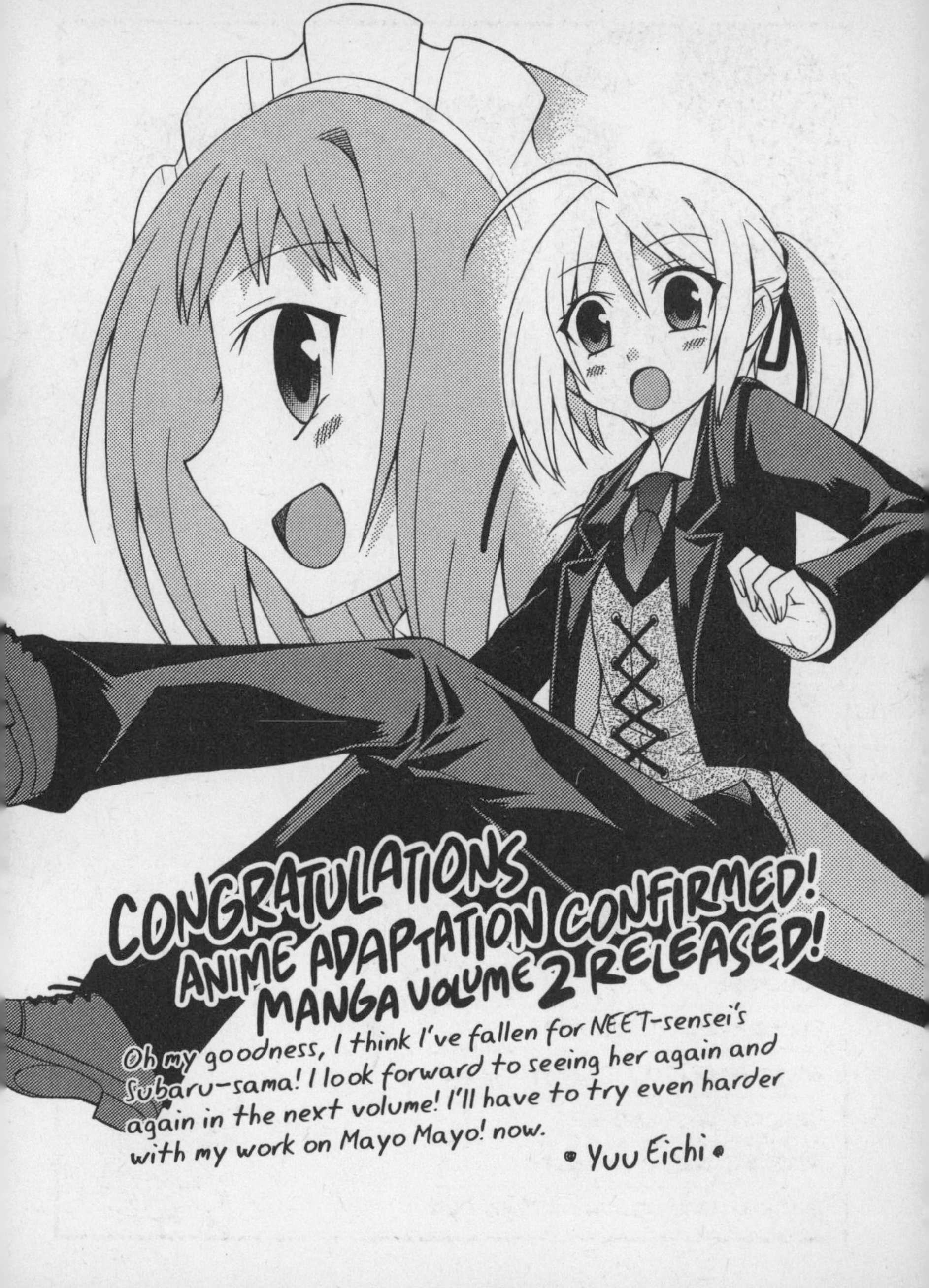
CONGRATULATIONS
ANIME ADAPTATION CONFIRMED!
MANGA VOLUME 2 RELEASED!
Oh my goodness, I think I've fallen for NEET-sensei's Subaru-sama! I look forward to seeing her again and again in the next volume! I'll have to try even harder with my work on Mayo Mayo! now.
• Yuu Eichi •

まよチキ!

Mayo Chiki

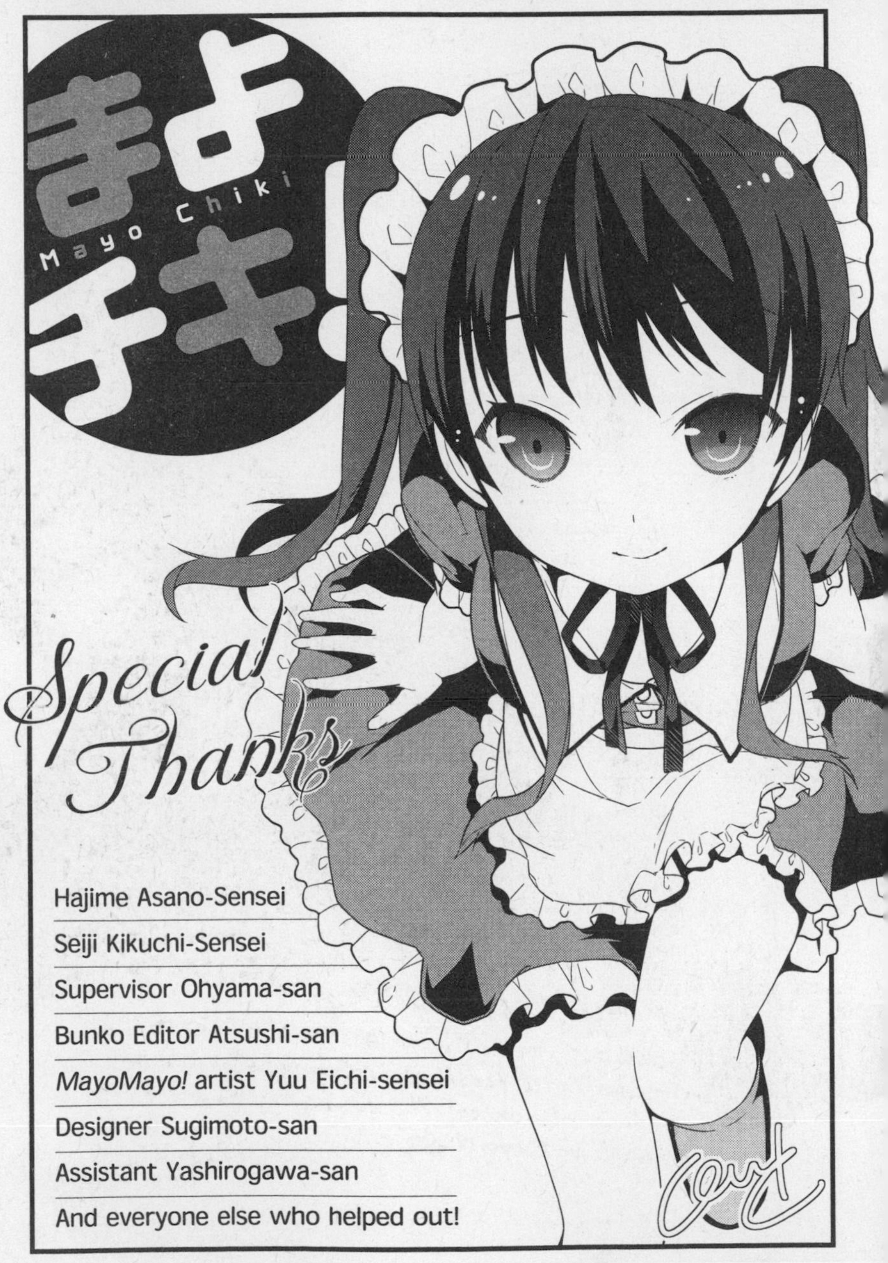

Special Thanks

Hajime Asano-Sensei

Seiji Kikuchi-Sensei

Supervisor Ohyama-san

Bunko Editor Atsushi-san

MayoMayo! artist Yuu Eichi-sensei

Designer Sugimoto-san

Assistant Yashirogawa-san

And everyone else who helped out!

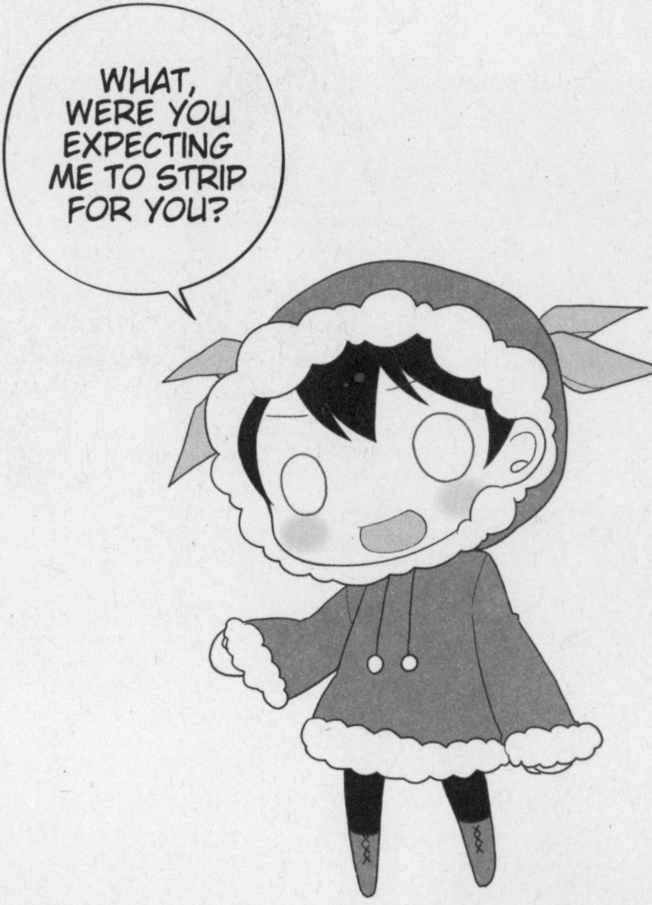
WHAT, WERE YOU EXPECTING ME TO STRIP FOR YOU?

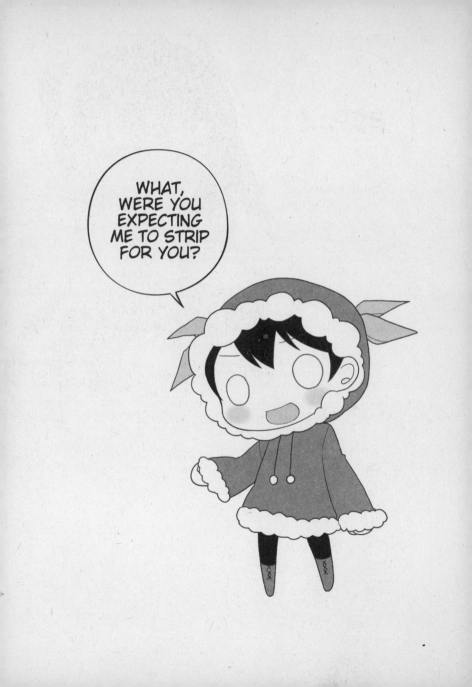

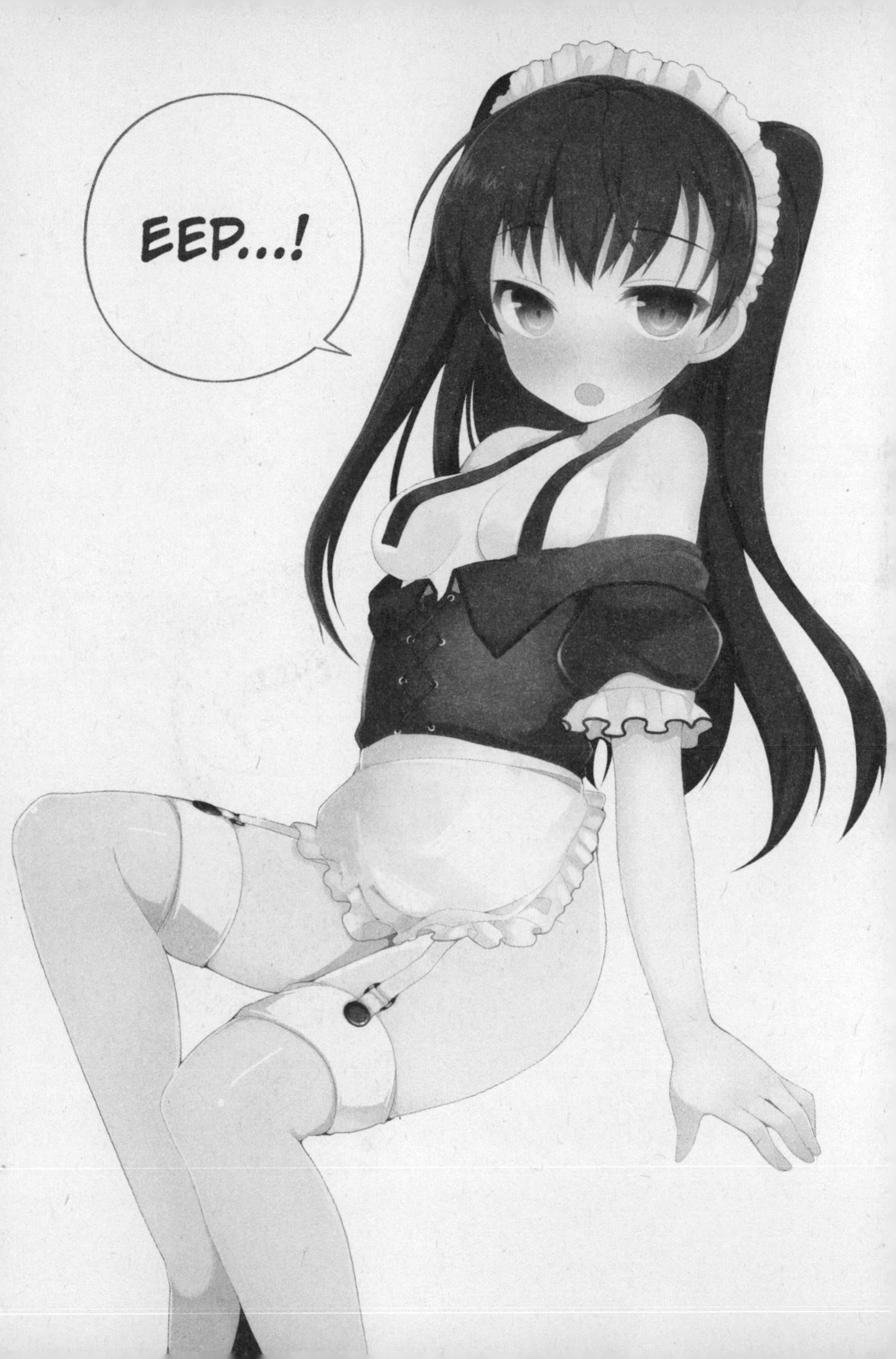
EEP...!

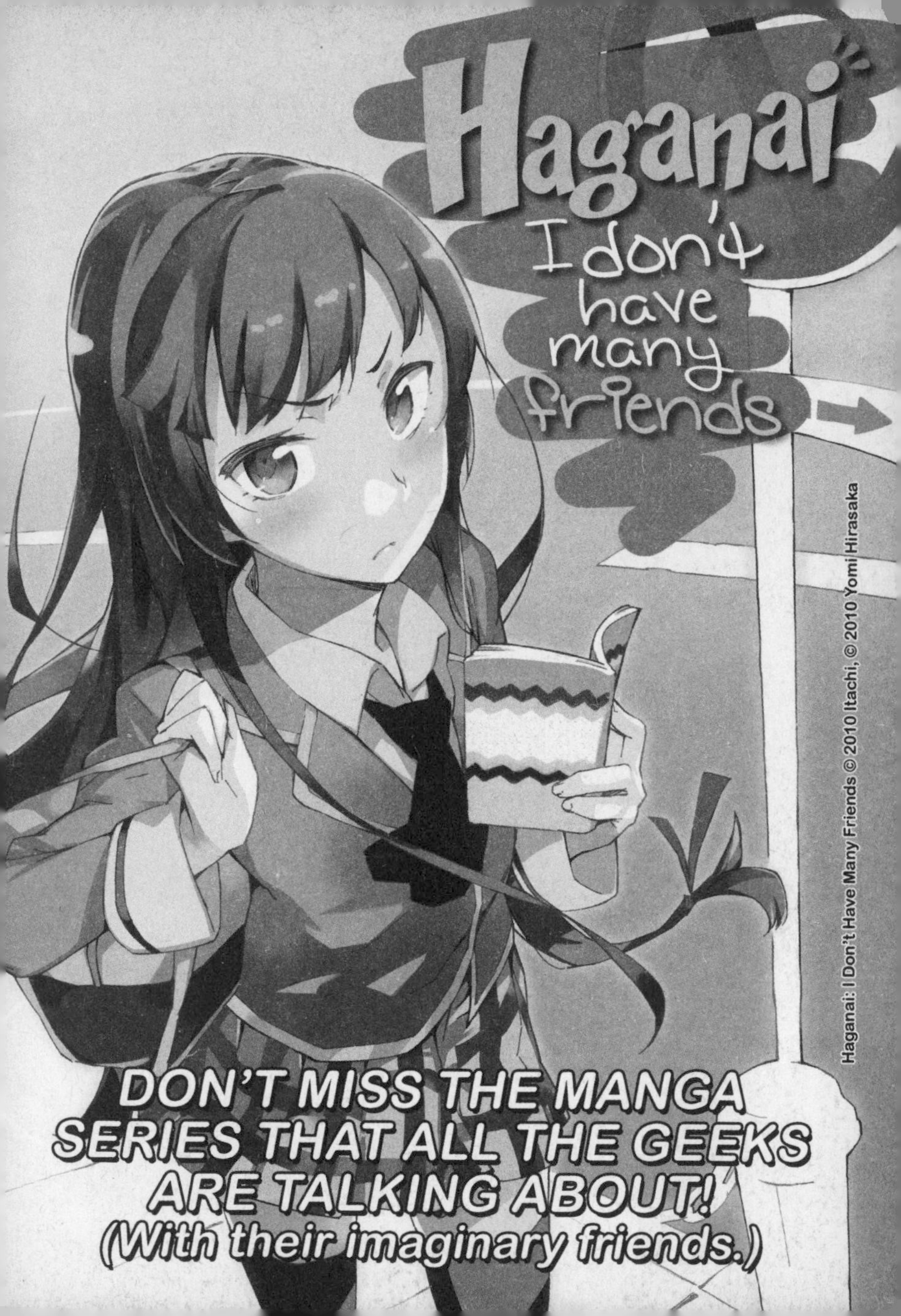
Haganai
I don't have many friends
DON'T MISS THE MANGA SERIES THAT ALL THE GEEKS ARE TALKING ABOUT!
(With their imaginary friends.)
Haganai: I Don't Have Many Friends © 2010 Itachi, © 2010 Yomi Hirasaka

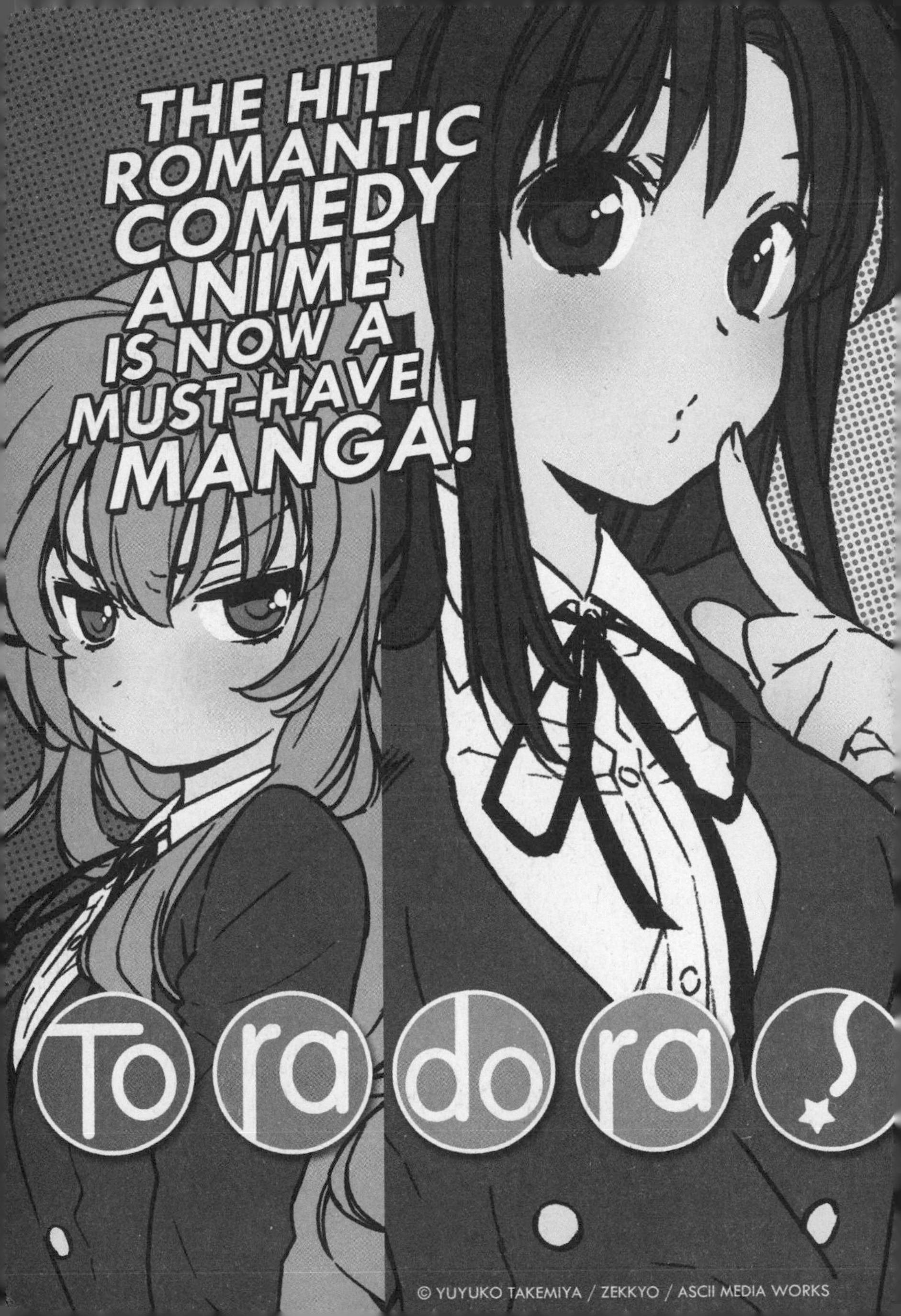
THE HIT ROMANTIC COMEDY ANIME IS NOW A MUST-HAVE MANGA!
Toradora!
© YUYUKO TAKEMIYA / ZEKKYO / ASCII MEDIA WORKS

♡GIRL FRIENDS

DON'T FEAR   THE RAZOR.

JACK THE RIPPER
Hell Blade

AN ALL-NEW ULTRAVIOLENT SERIES
WRITTEN AND ILLUSTRATED BY JE-TAE YOO.

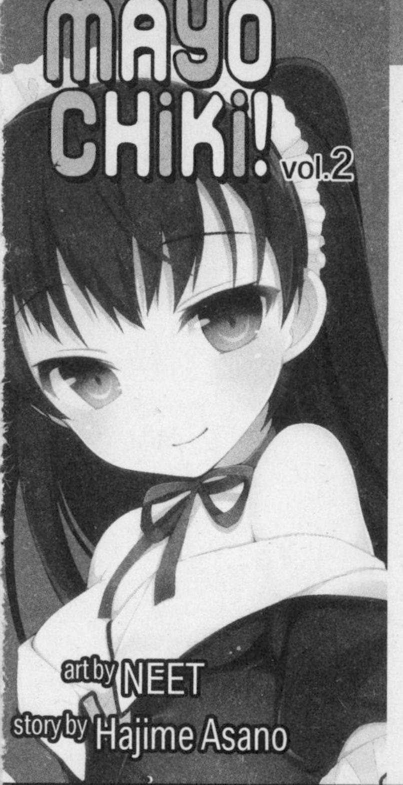
MAYO CHIKI! vol.2
art by NEET
story by Hajime Asano

STAFF CREDITS

translation Adrienne Beck
adaptation Ysabet Reinhardt MacFarlane
lettering & design Nicky Lim
proofreader Rebecca Scoble
editor Adam Arnold

publisher Jason DeAngelis
Seven Seas Entertainment

MAYO CHIKI! VOL. 2

ISBN: 978-1-937867-18-8

Printed in Canada

First Printing: March 2013

10 9 8 7 6 5 4 3 2 1

Seven Seas

FOLLOW US ONLINE: ***www.gomanga.com***

READING DIRECTIONS

This book reads from ***right to left***, Japanese style. If this is your first time reading manga, you start reading from the top right panel on each page and take it from there. If you get lost, just follow the numbered diagram here. It may seem backwards at first, but you'll get the hang of it! Have fun!!

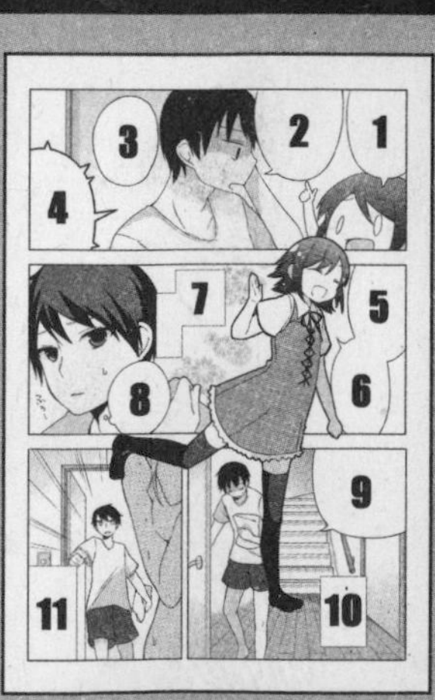
1
2
3
4
5
6
7
8
9
10
11